悠

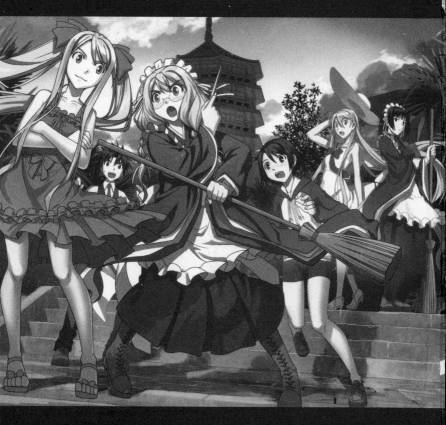

KEN AKAMATSU

vol.10

# CHARACTERS

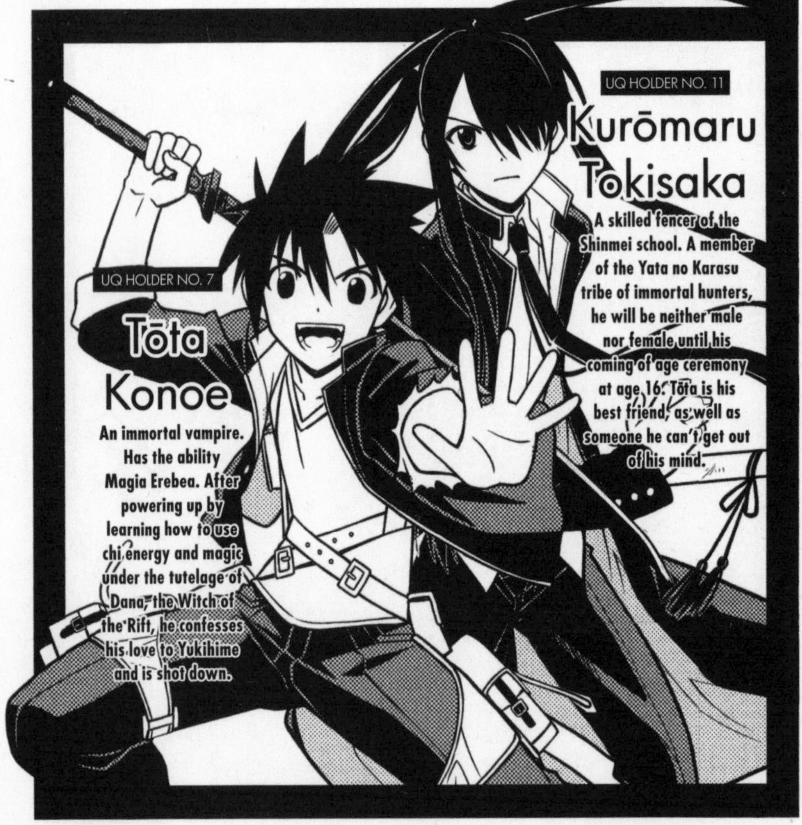

UQ HOLDER NO. 11
Kurōmaru Tokisaka
A skilled fencer of the Shinmei school. A member of the Yata no Karasu tribe of immortal hunters, he will be neither male nor female until his coming of age ceremony at age 16. Tōta is his best friend, as well as someone he can't get out of his mind.
UQ HOLDER NO. 7
Tōta Konoe
An immortal vampire. Has the ability Magia Erebea. After powering up by learning how to use chi energy and magic under the tutelage of Dana, the Witch of the Rift, he confesses his love to Yukihime and is shot down.


## UQ HOLDER NUMBERS

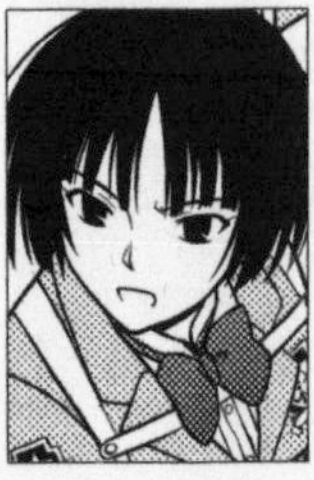

UQ HOLDER NO. 4

**KARIN**

Cool-headed and ruthless. Her immortality is S-class. Also known as the Saintess of Steel. Loves Eva.

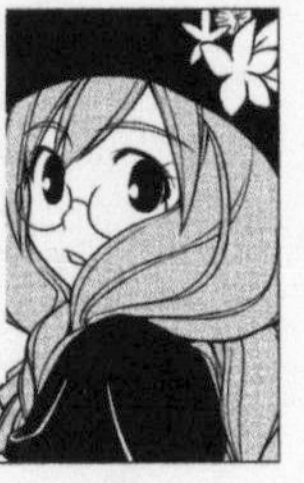

UQ HOLDER NO. 9

**KIRIË SAKURAME**

The greatest financial contributor to UQ Holder, and constantly calls Tōta incompetent. Her ability is called Reset & Restart.

# UQ HOLDER!

Ken Akamatsu Presents

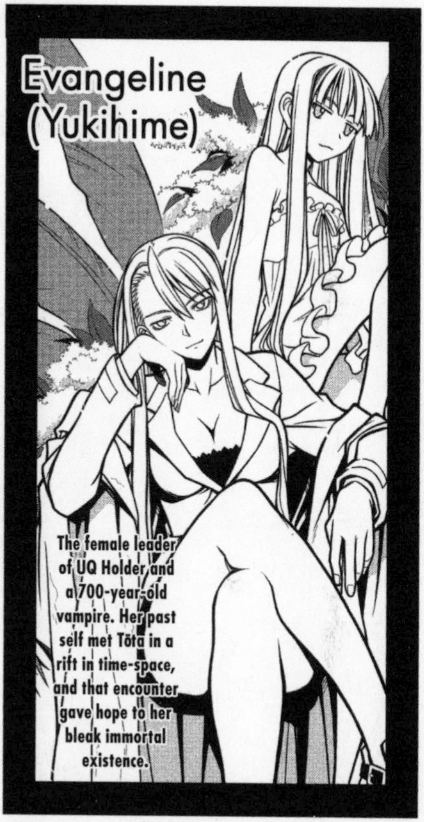
Evangeline (Yukihime)
The female leader of UQ Holder and a 700-year-old vampire. Her past self met Tōta in a rift in time-space, and that encounter gave hope to her bleak immortal existence.

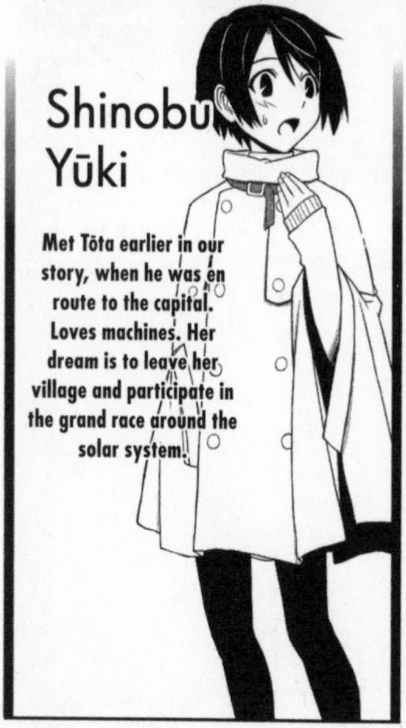
Shinobu Yūki
Met Tōta earlier in our story, when he was en route to the capital. Loves machines. Her dream is to leave her village and participate in the grand race around the solar system.

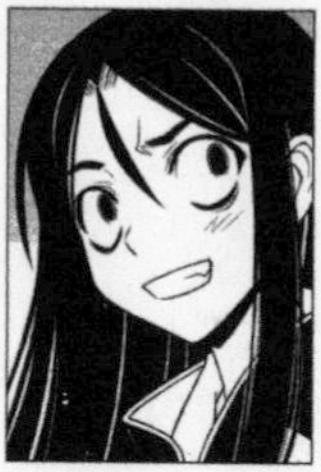

UQ HOLDER NO. 12

**SANTA SASAKI**

**After a tormented past as a victim of bullying, he became a shut-in. He thought he was alive, but is actually a ghost. Because of that, he can use multiple abilities.**

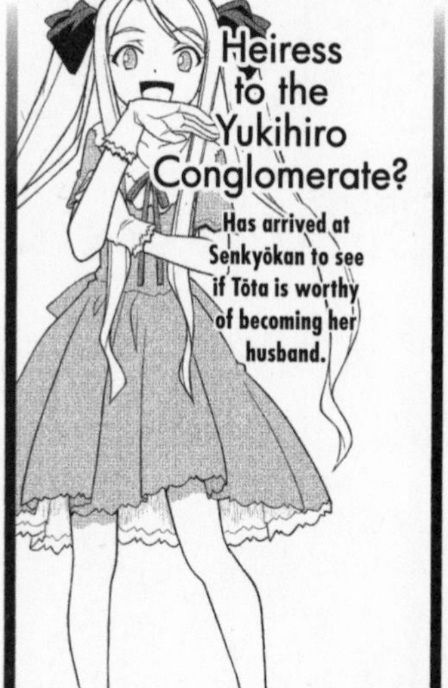
Heiress to the Yukihiro Conglomerate?
Has arrived at Senkyōkan to see if Tōta is worthy of becoming her husband.

# THE STORY SO FAR

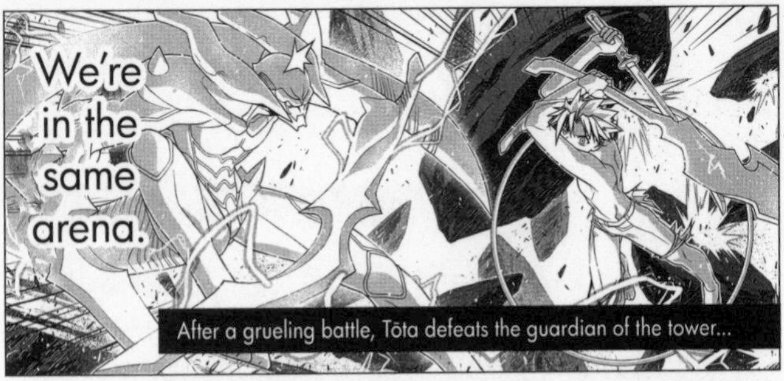
We're in the same arena.
After a grueling battle, Tōta defeats the guardian of the tower...

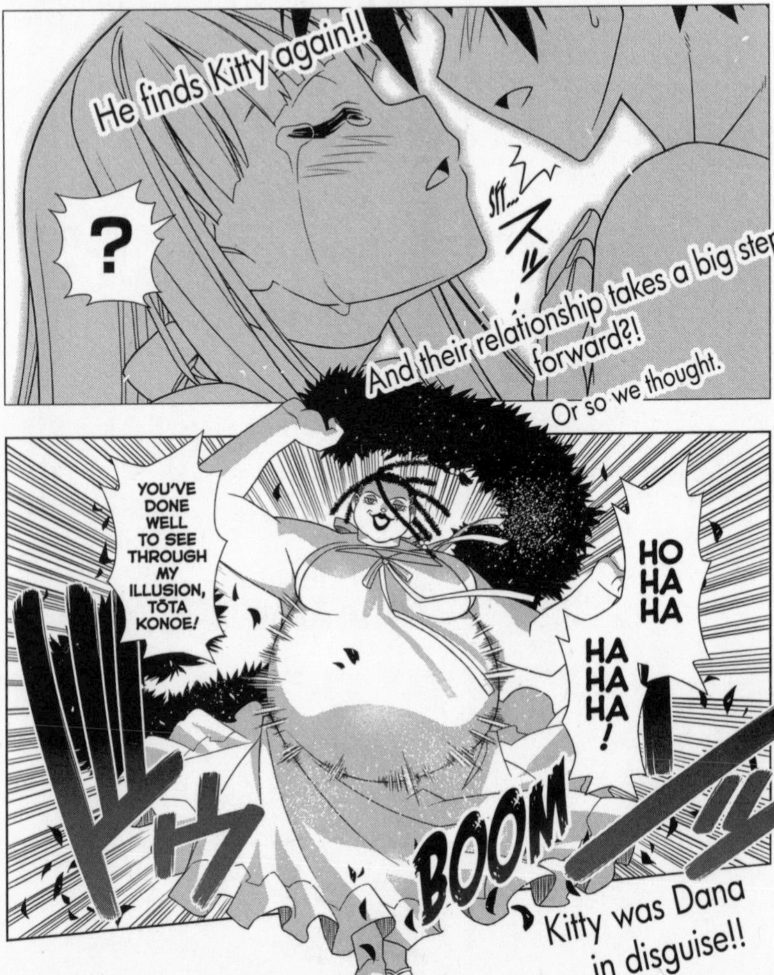
He finds Kitty again!!
?
SFF...
And their relationship takes a big step forward?!
Or so we thought.
HO HA HA
HA HA HA!
YOU'VE DONE WELL TO SEE THROUGH MY ILLUSION, TŌTA KONOE!
BOOM
Kitty was Dana in disguise!!

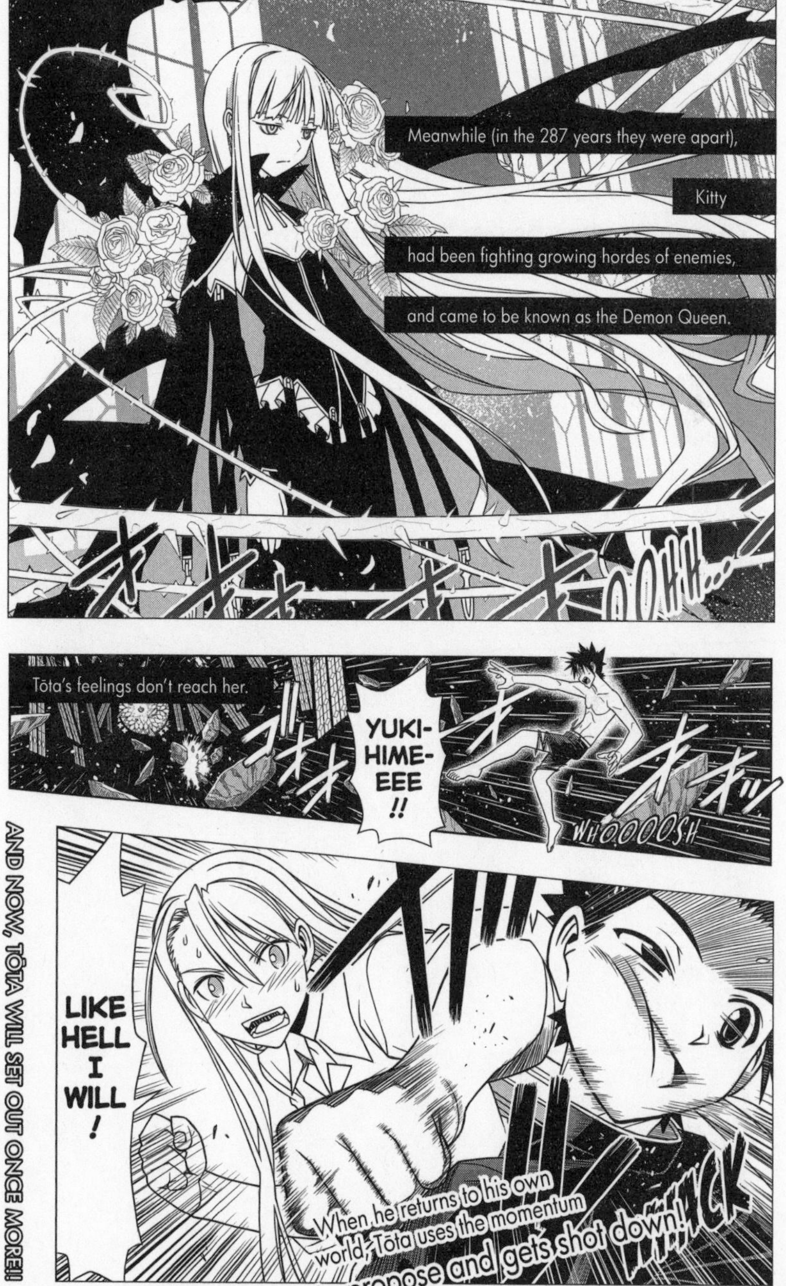
Meanwhile (in the 287 years they were apart),
Kitty
had been fighting growing hordes of enemies,
and came to be known as the Demon Queen.
OOHH...
Tōta's feelings don't reach her.
YUKI-HIME-EEE!!
WHOOOOOSH
LIKE HELL I WILL!
When he returns to his own world, Tōta uses the momentum to propose and gets shot down!

AND NOW, TŌTA WILL SET OUT ONCE MORE!!

# CONTENTS

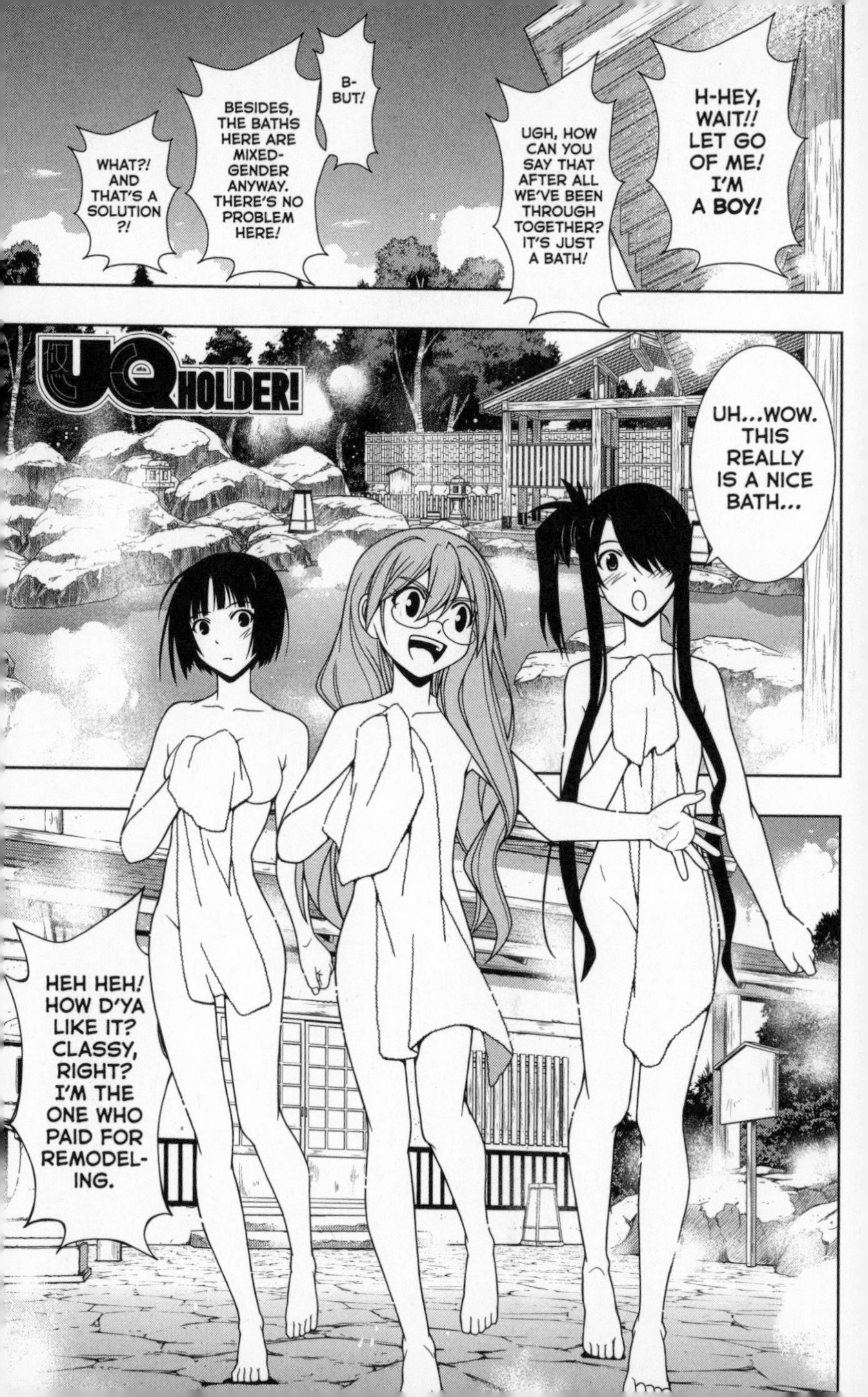
H-HEY, WAIT!! LET GO OF ME! I'M A BOY!
UGH, HOW CAN YOU SAY THAT AFTER ALL WE'VE BEEN THROUGH TOGETHER? IT'S JUST A BATH!
B-BUT!
BESIDES, THE BATHS HERE ARE MIXED-GENDER ANYWAY. THERE'S NO PROBLEM HERE!
WHAT?! AND THAT'S A SOLUTION?!
UQ HOLDER!
UH...WOW. THIS REALLY IS A NICE BATH...
HEH HEH! HOW D'YA LIKE IT? CLASSY, RIGHT? I'M THE ONE WHO PAID FOR REMODEL-ING.

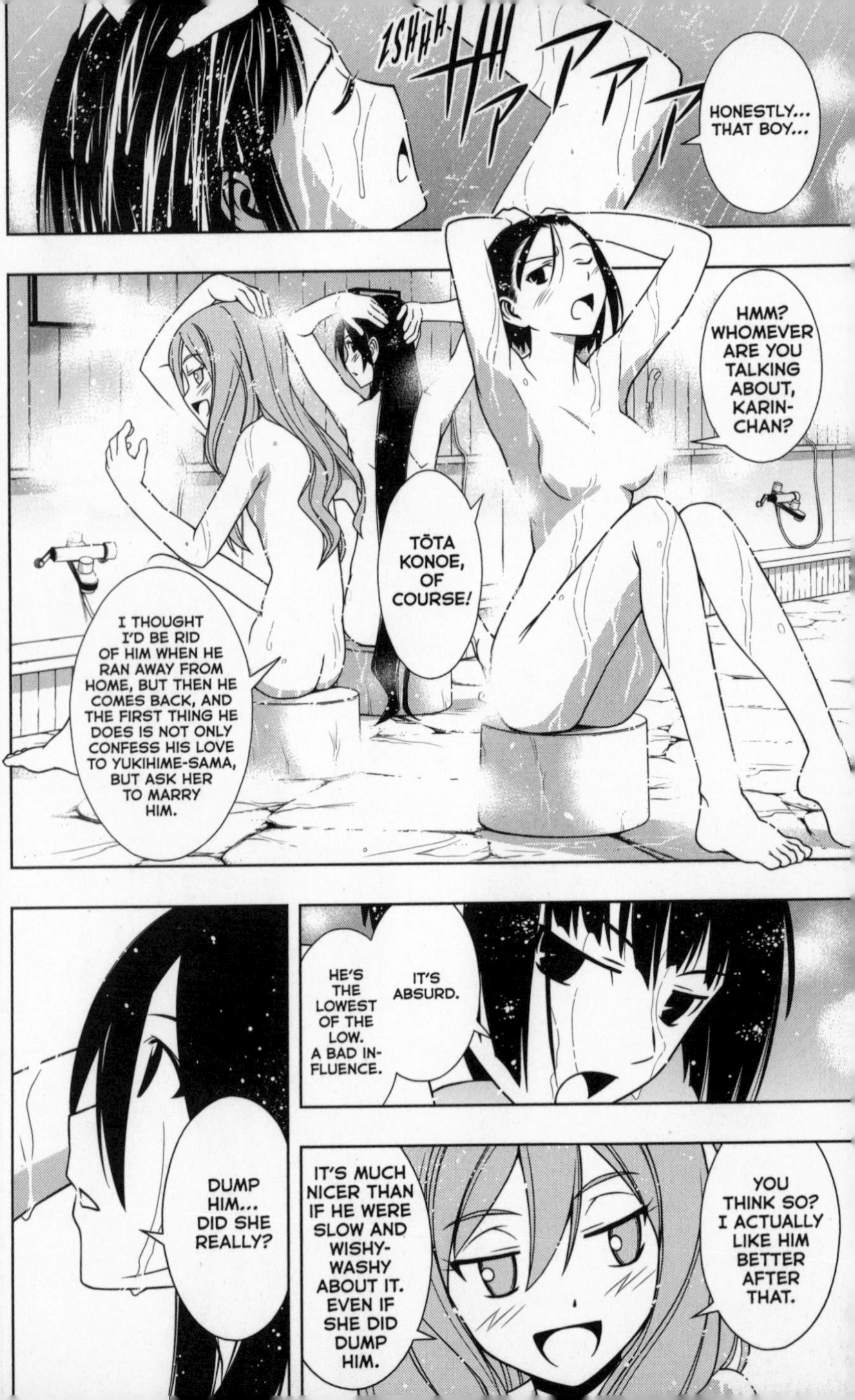
ZSHHH-HH
HONESTLY... THAT BOY...
HMM? WHOMEVER ARE YOU TALKING ABOUT, KARIN-CHAN?
TŌTA KONOE, OF COURSE!
I THOUGHT I'D BE RID OF HIM WHEN HE RAN AWAY FROM HOME, BUT THEN HE COMES BACK, AND THE FIRST THING HE DOES IS NOT ONLY CONFESS HIS LOVE TO YUKIHIME-SAMA, BUT ASK HER TO MARRY HIM.
IT'S ABSURD.
HE'S THE LOWEST OF THE LOW. A BAD IN-FLUENCE.
YOU THINK SO? I ACTUALLY LIKE HIM BETTER AFTER THAT.
IT'S MUCH NICER THAN IF HE WERE SLOW AND WISHY-WASHY ABOUT IT. EVEN IF SHE DID DUMP HIM.
DUMP HIM... DID SHE REALLY?

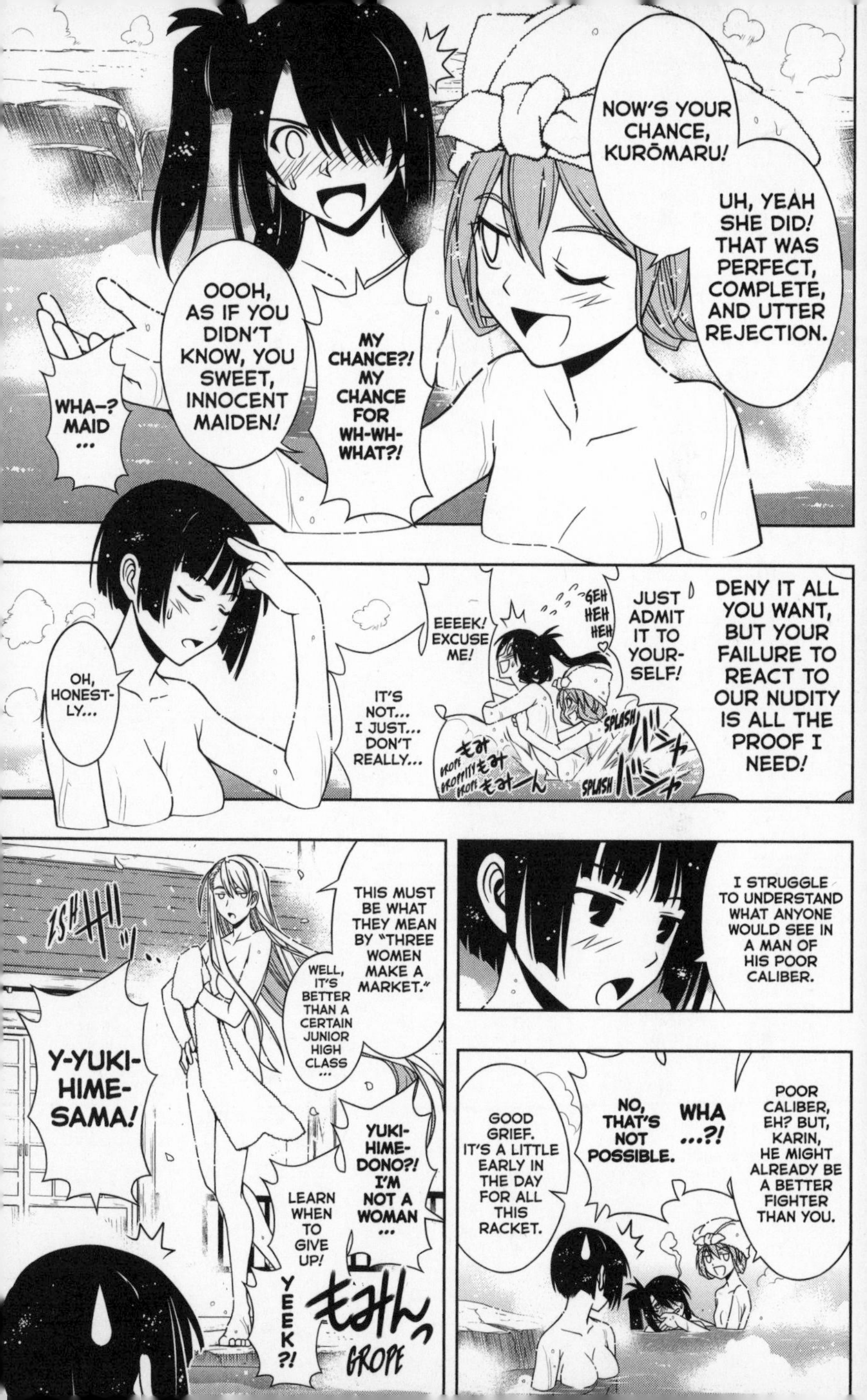
NOW'S YOUR CHANCE, KURŌMARU!
UH, YEAH SHE DID! THAT WAS PERFECT, COMPLETE, AND UTTER REJECTION.
MY CHANCE?! MY CHANCE FOR WH-WH-WHAT?!
OOOH, AS IF YOU DIDN'T KNOW, YOU SWEET, INNOCENT MAIDEN!
WHA–? MAID ...
DENY IT ALL YOU WANT, BUT YOUR FAILURE TO REACT TO OUR NUDITY IS ALL THE PROOF I NEED!
JUST ADMIT IT TO YOUR-SELF!
GEH HEH HEH ♥
EEEEK! EXCUSE ME!
SPLASH バシャ
SPLASH バシャ
GROPE もみ
GROPPITY もみ
GROPE もみーん
IT'S NOT... I JUST... DON'T REALLY...
OH, HONEST-LY...
I STRUGGLE TO UNDERSTAND WHAT ANYONE WOULD SEE IN A MAN OF HIS POOR CALIBER.
POOR CALIBER, EH? BUT, KARIN, HE MIGHT ALREADY BE A BETTER FIGHTER THAN YOU.
WHA ...?!
NO, THAT'S NOT POSSIBLE.
GOOD GRIEF. IT'S A LITTLE EARLY IN THE DAY FOR ALL THIS RACKET.
THIS MUST BE WHAT THEY MEAN BY "THREE WOMEN MAKE A MARKET."
WELL, IT'S BETTER THAN A CERTAIN JUNIOR HIGH CLASS ...
Y-YUKI-HIME-SAMA!
YUKI-HIME-DONO?! I'M NOT A WOMAN ...
LEARN WHEN TO GIVE UP!
YEEK?!
もみん
GROPE

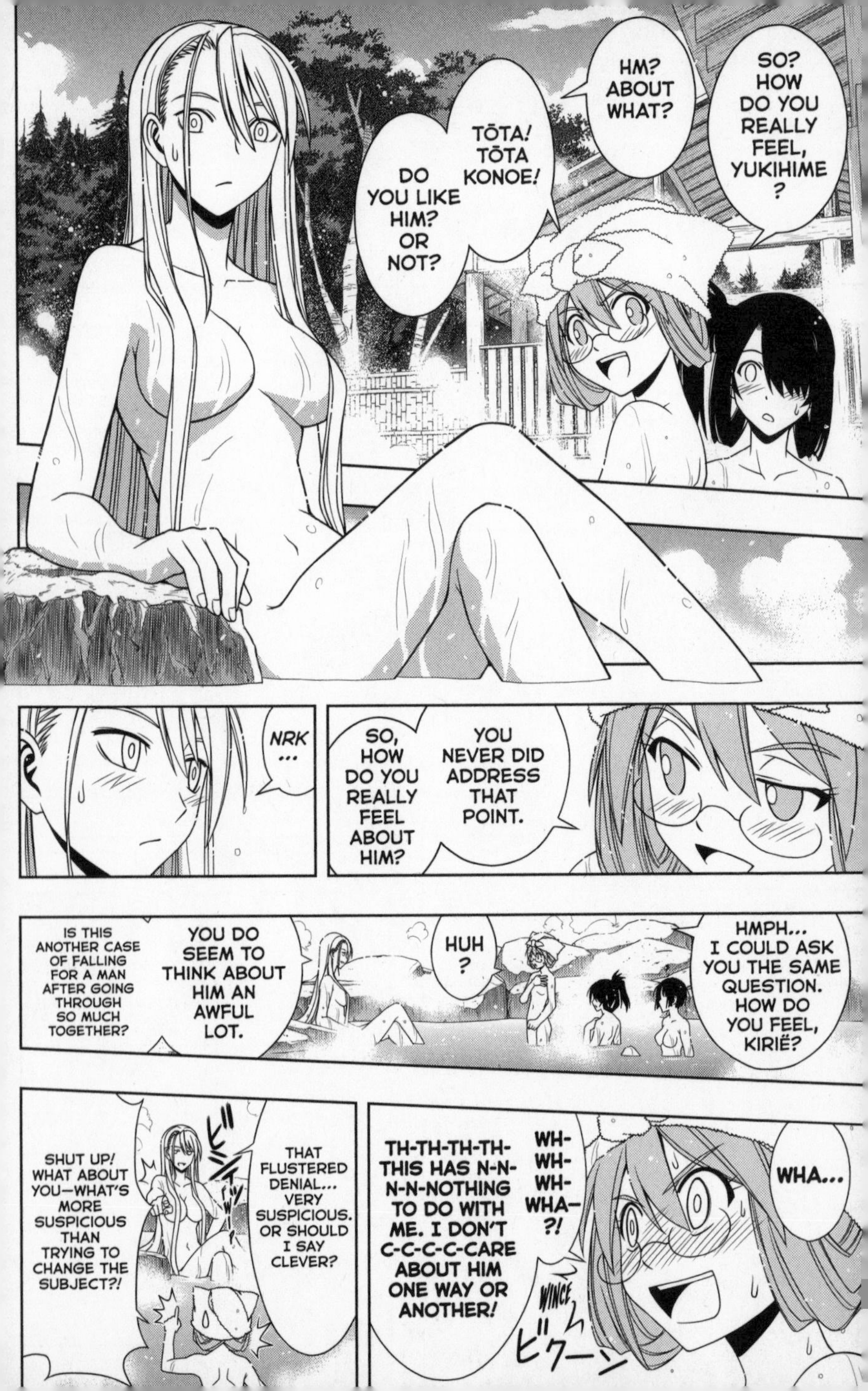
SO? HOW DO YOU REALLY FEEL, YUKIHIME?
HM? ABOUT WHAT?
TŌTA! TŌTA KONOE!
DO YOU LIKE HIM? OR NOT?
YOU NEVER DID ADDRESS THAT POINT.
SO, HOW DO YOU REALLY FEEL ABOUT HIM?
NRK...
HMPH... I COULD ASK YOU THE SAME QUESTION. HOW DO YOU FEEL, KIRIË?
HUH?
YOU DO SEEM TO THINK ABOUT HIM AN AWFUL LOT.
IS THIS ANOTHER CASE OF FALLING FOR A MAN AFTER GOING THROUGH SO MUCH TOGETHER?
WHA...
WH-WH-WH-WHA-?!
TH-TH-TH-TH-THIS HAS N-N-N-N-NOTHING TO DO WITH ME. I DON'T C-C-C-C-CARE ABOUT HIM ONE WAY OR ANOTHER!
WINCE
THAT FLUSTERED DENIAL... VERY SUSPICIOUS. OR SHOULD I SAY CLEVER?
SHUT UP! WHAT ABOUT YOU—WHAT'S MORE SUSPICIOUS THAN TRYING TO CHANGE THE SUBJECT?!

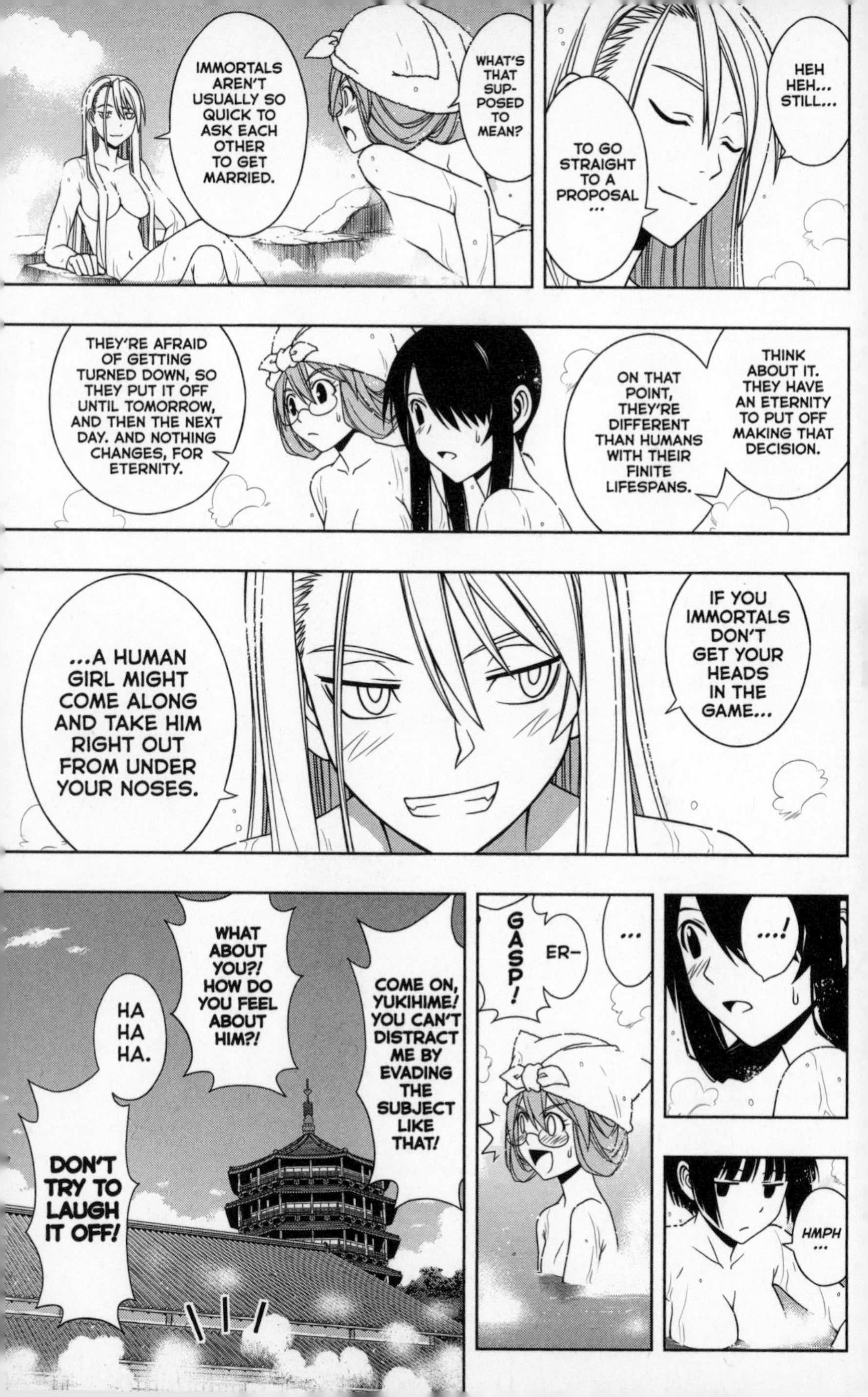
HEH HEH... STILL...
TO GO STRAIGHT TO A PROPOSAL...
WHAT'S THAT SUP-POSED TO MEAN?
IMMORTALS AREN'T USUALLY SO QUICK TO ASK EACH OTHER TO GET MARRIED.
THINK ABOUT IT. THEY HAVE AN ETERNITY TO PUT OFF MAKING THAT DECISION.
ON THAT POINT, THEY'RE DIFFERENT THAN HUMANS WITH THEIR FINITE LIFESPANS.
THEY'RE AFRAID OF GETTING TURNED DOWN, SO THEY PUT IT OFF UNTIL TOMORROW, AND THEN THE NEXT DAY. AND NOTHING CHANGES, FOR ETERNITY.
IF YOU IMMORTALS DON'T GET YOUR HEADS IN THE GAME...
...A HUMAN GIRL MIGHT COME ALONG AND TAKE HIM RIGHT OUT FROM UNDER YOUR NOSES.
...!
HMPH...
...
ER–
GASP!
COME ON, YUKIHIME! YOU CAN'T DISTRACT ME BY EVADING THE SUBJECT LIKE THAT!
WHAT ABOUT YOU?! HOW DO YOU FEEL ABOUT HIM?!
HA HA HA.
DON'T TRY TO LAUGH IT OFF!

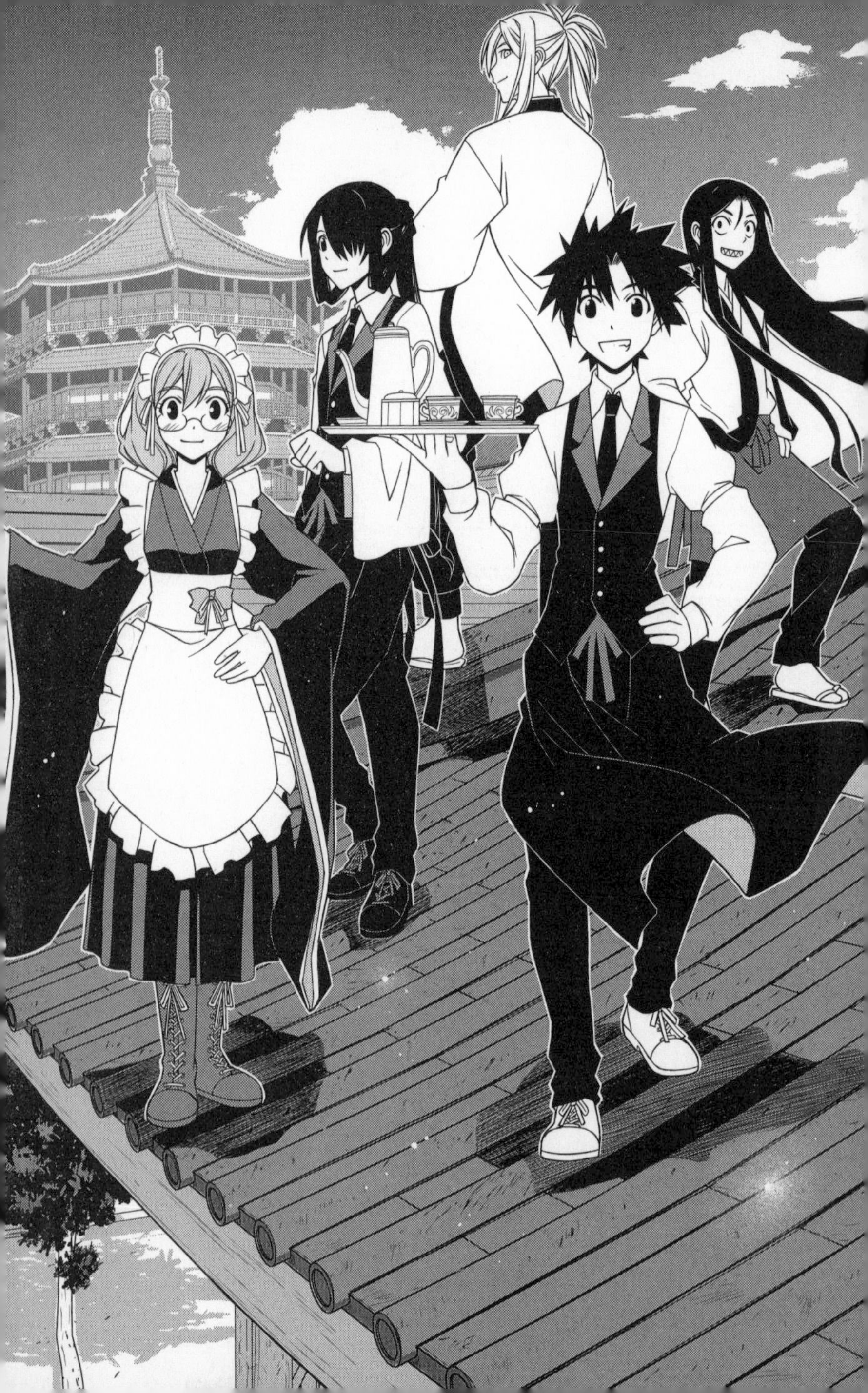

## STAGE 97: UNEXPECTED GUEST

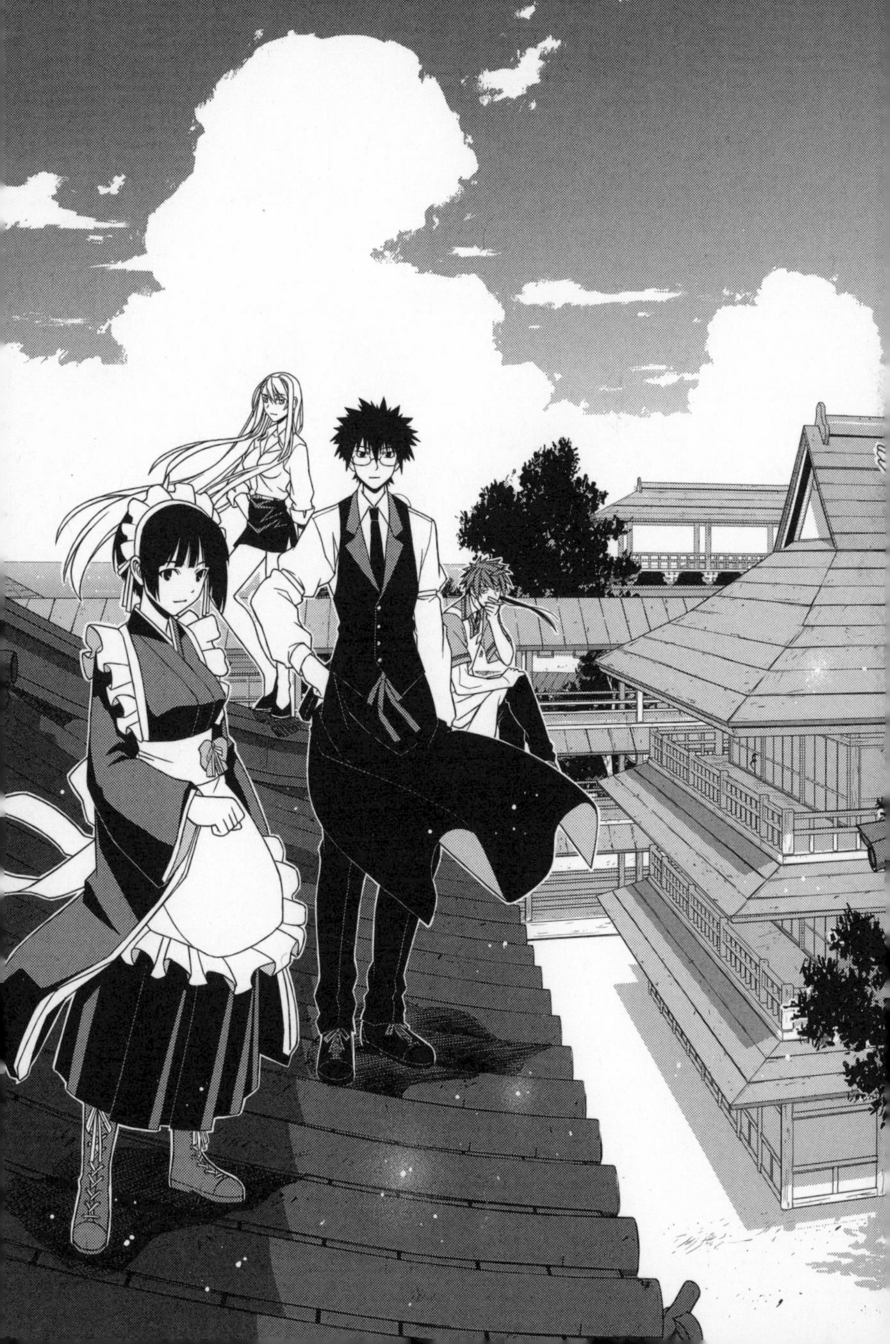

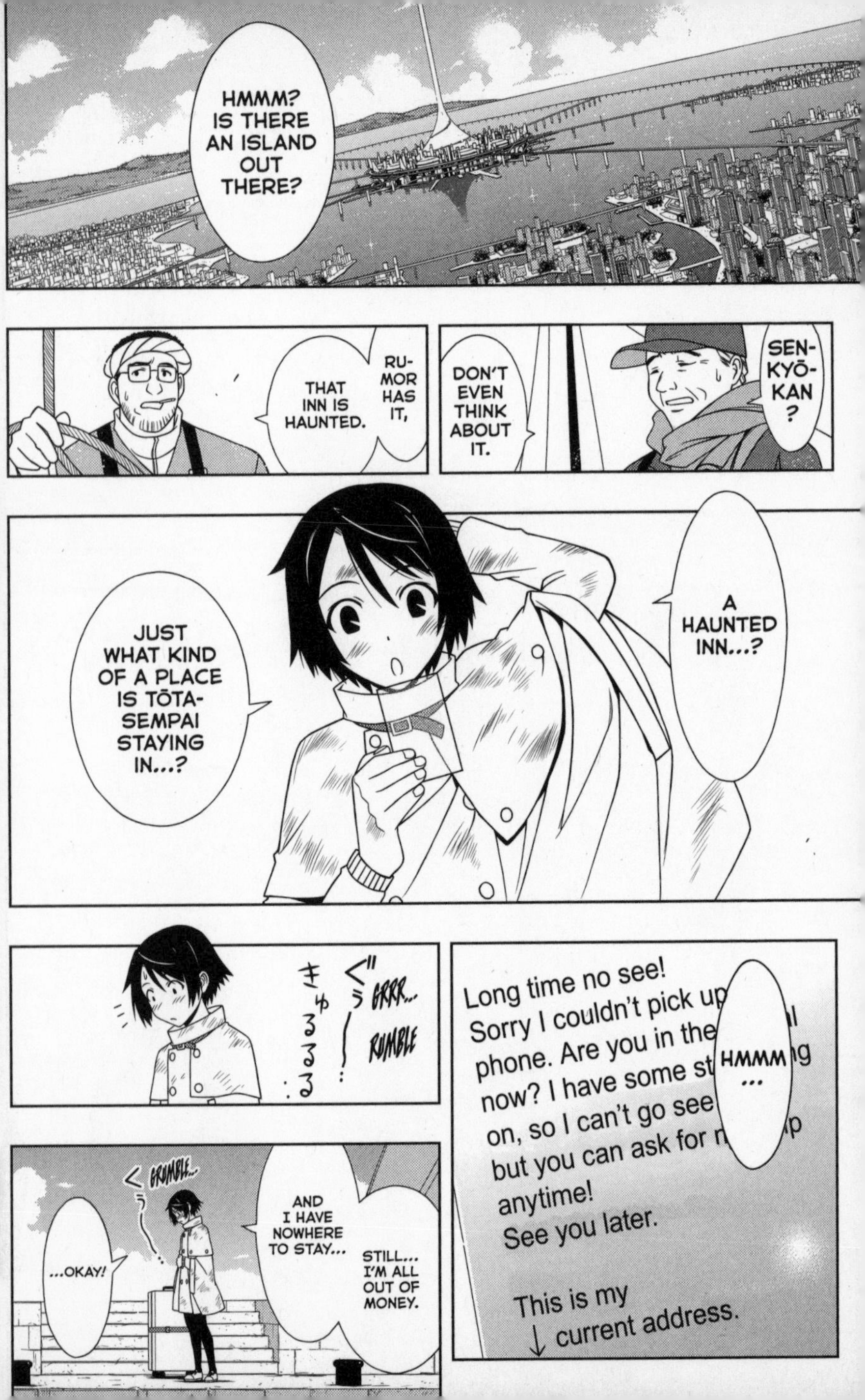
HMMM? IS THERE AN ISLAND OUT THERE?
SEN-KYŌ-KAN?
DON'T EVEN THINK ABOUT IT.
RU-MOR HAS IT,
THAT INN IS HAUNTED.
A HAUNTED INN...?
JUST WHAT KIND OF A PLACE IS TŌTA-SEMPAI STAYING IN...?
Long time no see!
Sorry I couldn't pick up
phone. Are you in the
now? I have some st
on, so I can't go see
but you can ask for
anytime!
See you later.
This is my
↓ current address.
HMMM...
ぐぅ～…
GRRR...
きゅるるるる
RUMBLE
STILL... I'M ALL OUT OF MONEY.
AND I HAVE NOWHERE TO STAY...
くぅ～…
GRUMBLE...
...OKAY!

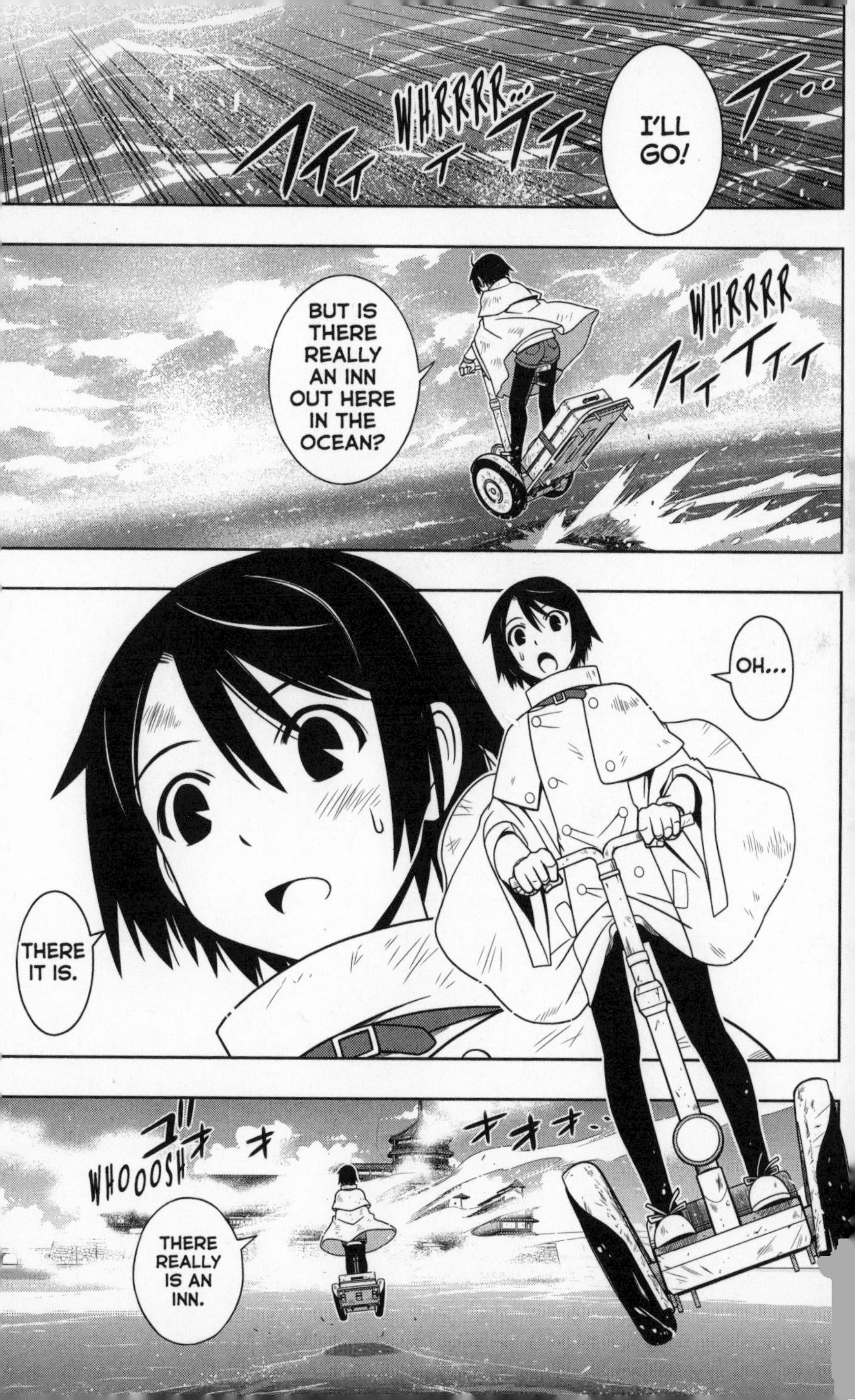
I'LL GO!
WHRRRR...
WHRRRR
BUT IS THERE REALLY AN INN OUT HERE IN THE OCEAN?
OH...
THERE IT IS.
WHOOOSH
THERE REALLY IS AN INN.

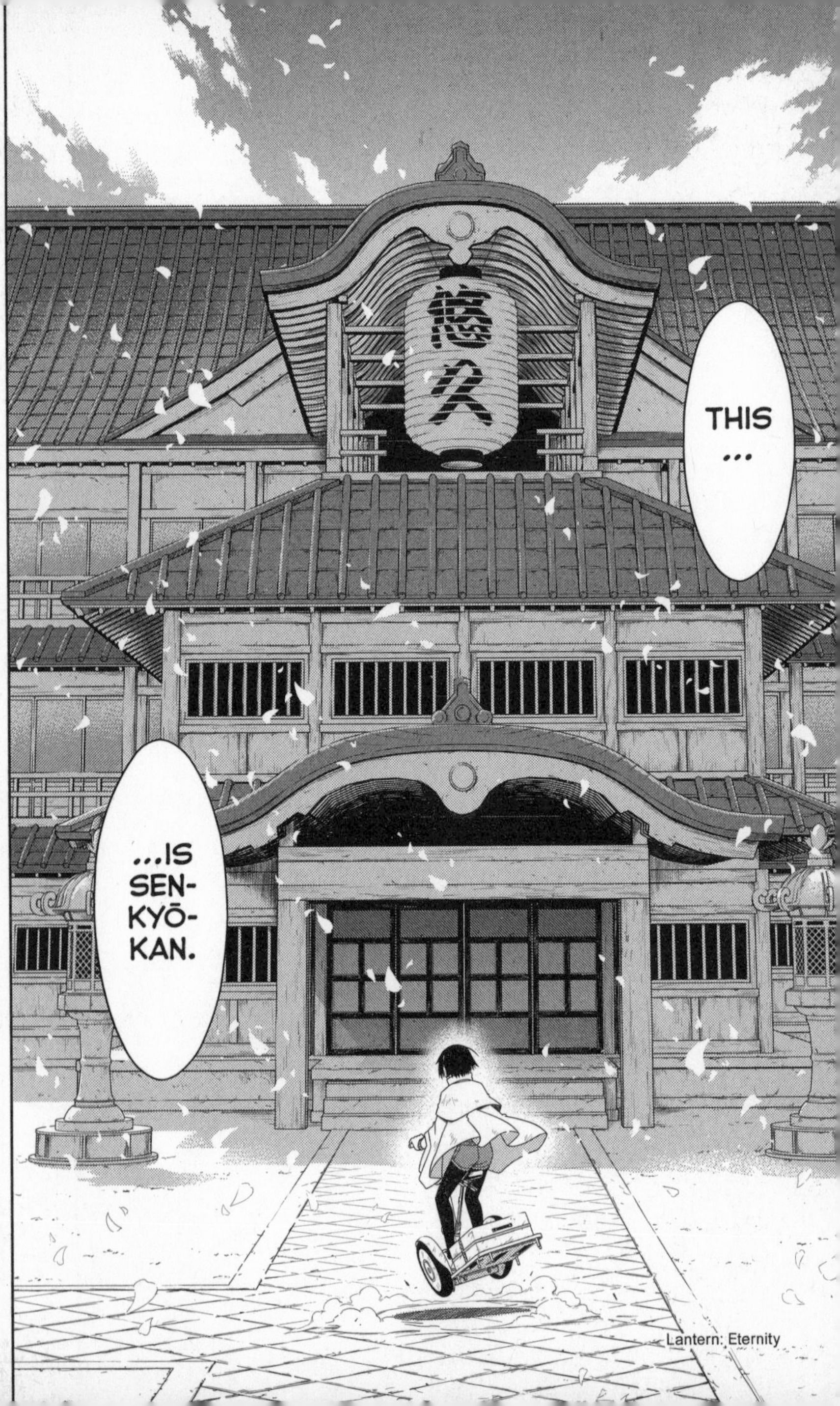
THIS...
...IS SEN-KYŌ-KAN.
Lantern: Eternity

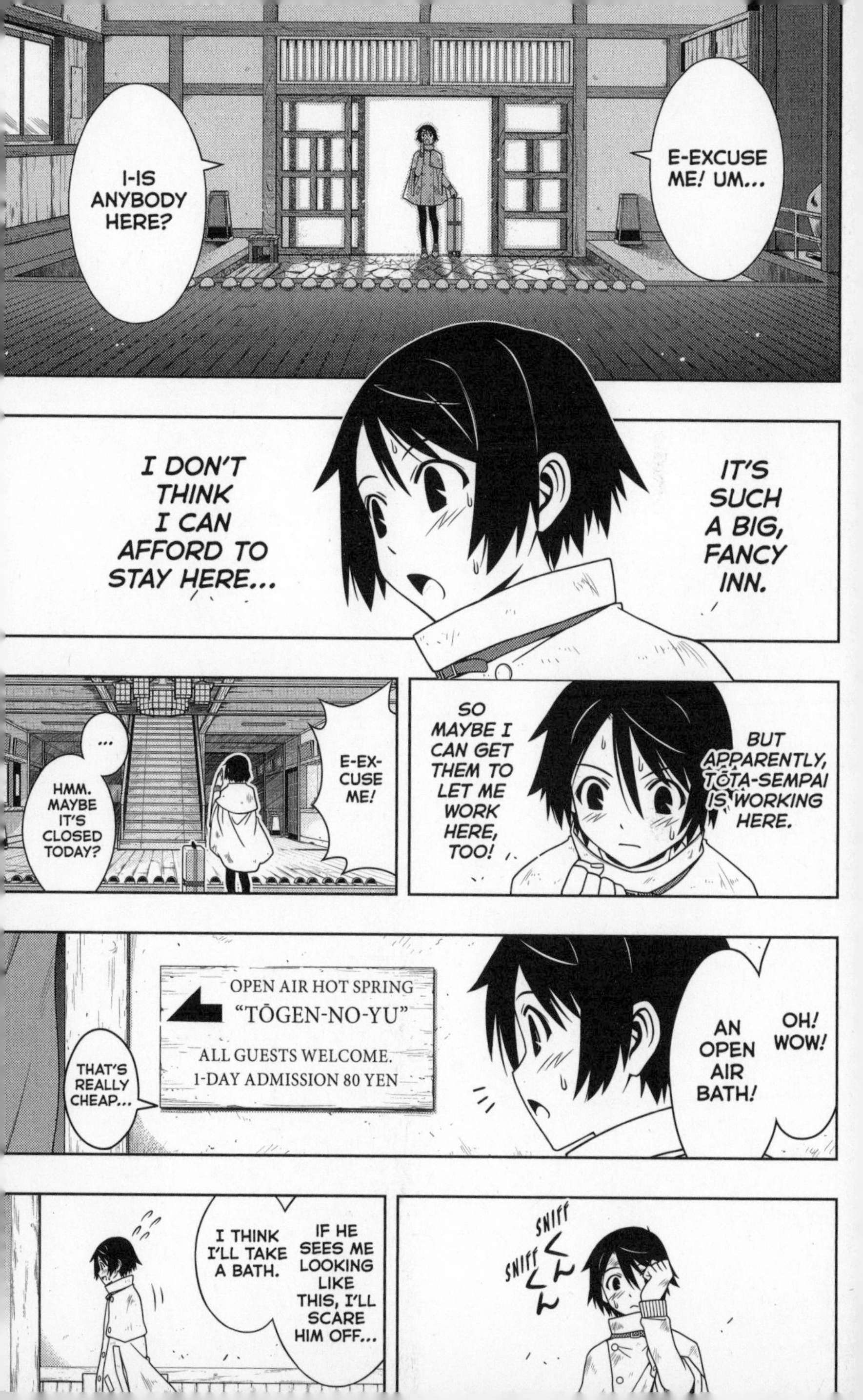
E-EXCUSE ME! UM...
I-IS ANYBODY HERE?
IT'S SUCH A BIG, FANCY INN.
I DON'T THINK I CAN AFFORD TO STAY HERE...
BUT APPARENTLY, TŌTA-SEMPAI IS WORKING HERE.
SO MAYBE I CAN GET THEM TO LET ME WORK HERE, TOO!
E-EXCUSE ME!
...
HMM. MAYBE IT'S CLOSED TODAY?
OH! WOW!
AN OPEN AIR BATH!
OPEN AIR HOT SPRING
"TŌGEN-NO-YU"
ALL GUESTS WELCOME.
1-DAY ADMISSION 80 YEN
THAT'S REALLY CHEAP...
SNIFF
くん
SNIFF
くん
IF HE SEES ME LOOKING LIKE THIS, I'LL SCARE HIM OFF...
I THINK I'LL TAKE A BATH.

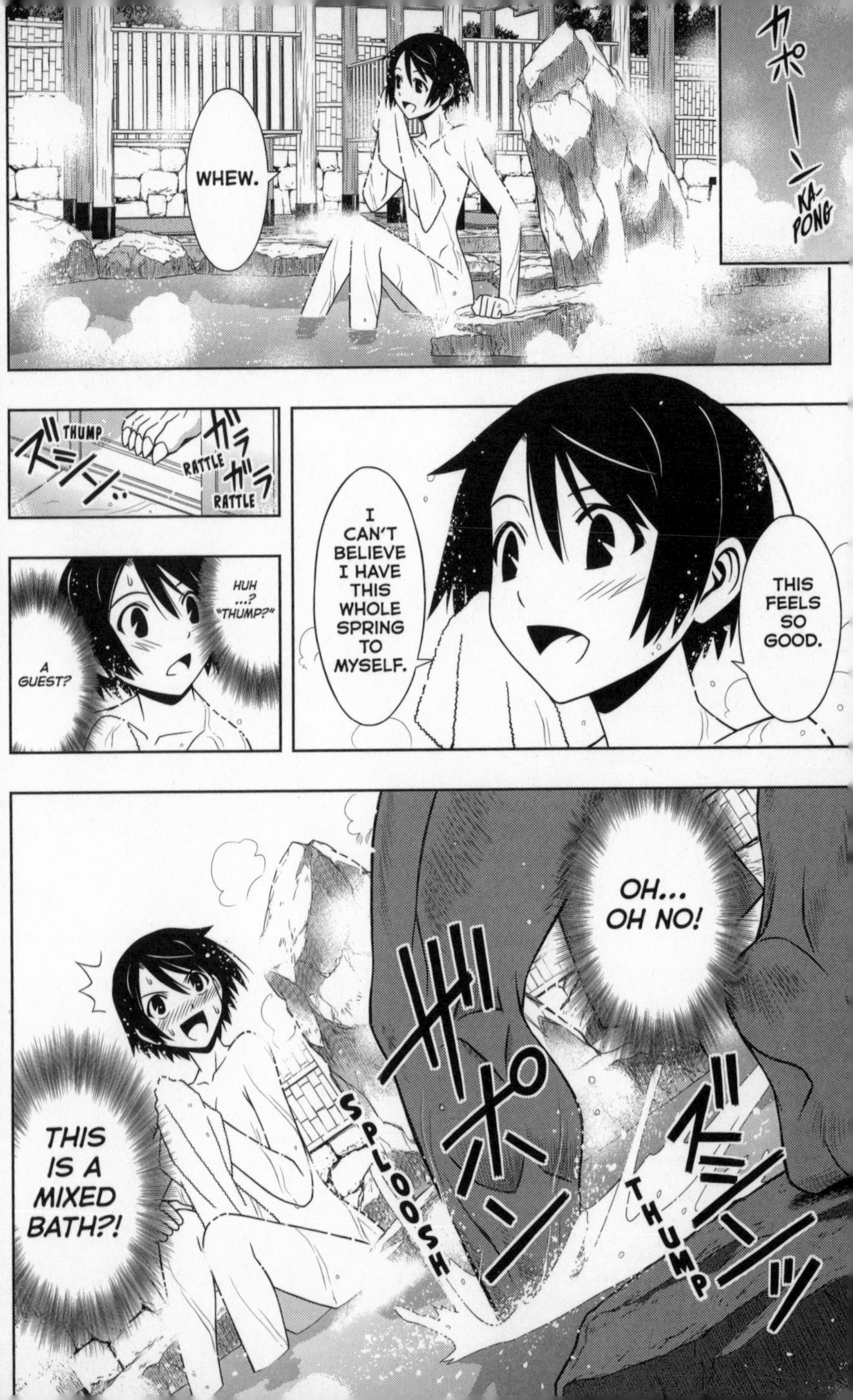
カポーン
KA-PONG
WHEW.
THIS FEELS SO GOOD.
I CAN'T BELIEVE I HAVE THIS WHOLE SPRING TO MYSELF.
ガラ ガラ
RATTLE RATTLE
ズシン
THUMP
HUH ...? "THUMP?"
A GUEST?
OH... OH NO!
ズシーン
THUMP
ザポーン
SPLOOSH
THIS IS A MIXED BATH?!

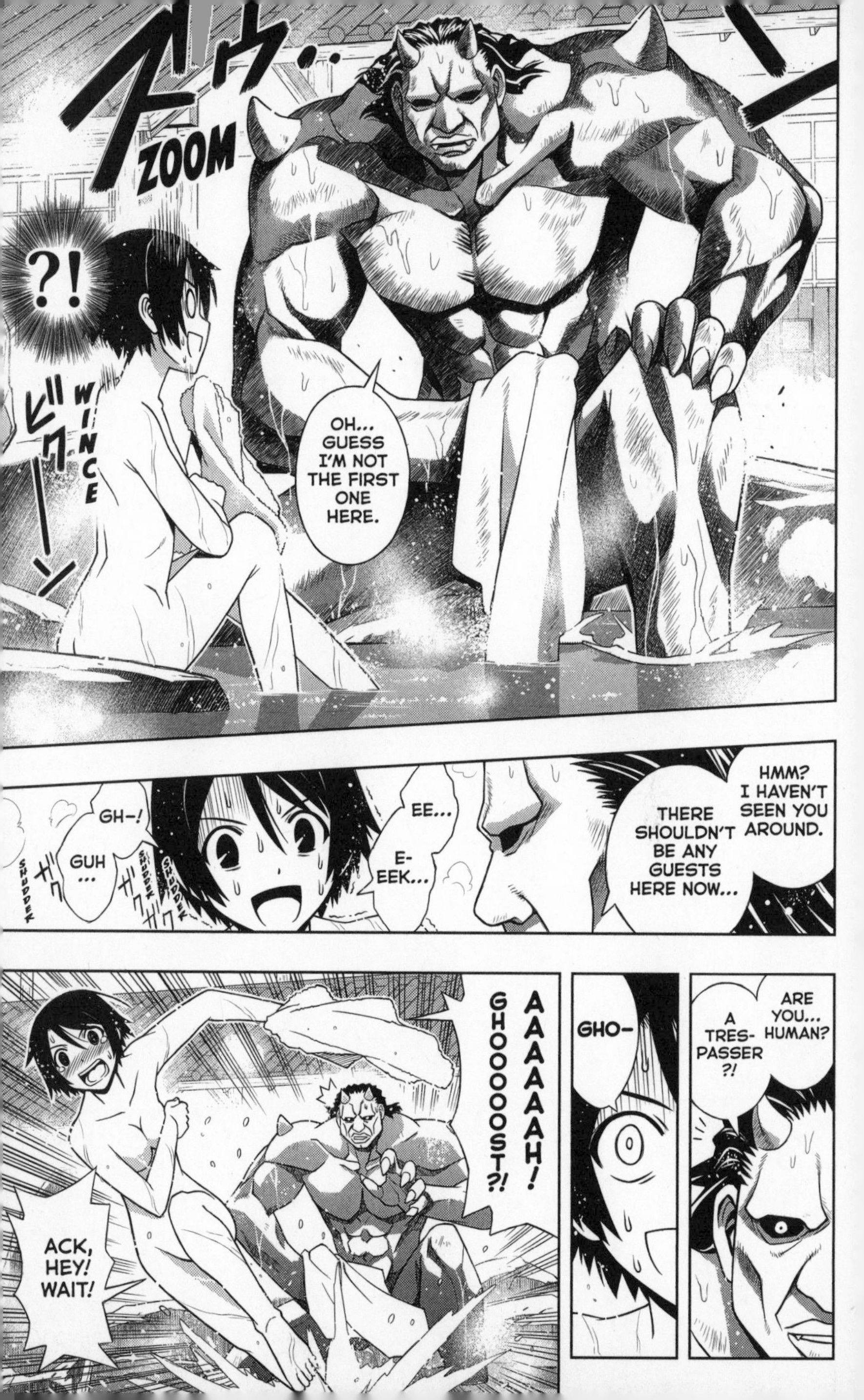
ZOOM
?!
WINCE
OH... GUESS I'M NOT THE FIRST ONE HERE.
HMM? I HAVEN'T SEEN YOU AROUND.
THERE SHOULDN'T BE ANY GUESTS HERE NOW...
EE...
E-EEK...
SHUDDER
SHUDDER
SHUDDER
GH-!
GUH...
ARE YOU... HUMAN?
A TRES-PASSER?!
GHO-
AAAAAAAH!
GHOOOOOST?!
ACK, HEY! WAIT!

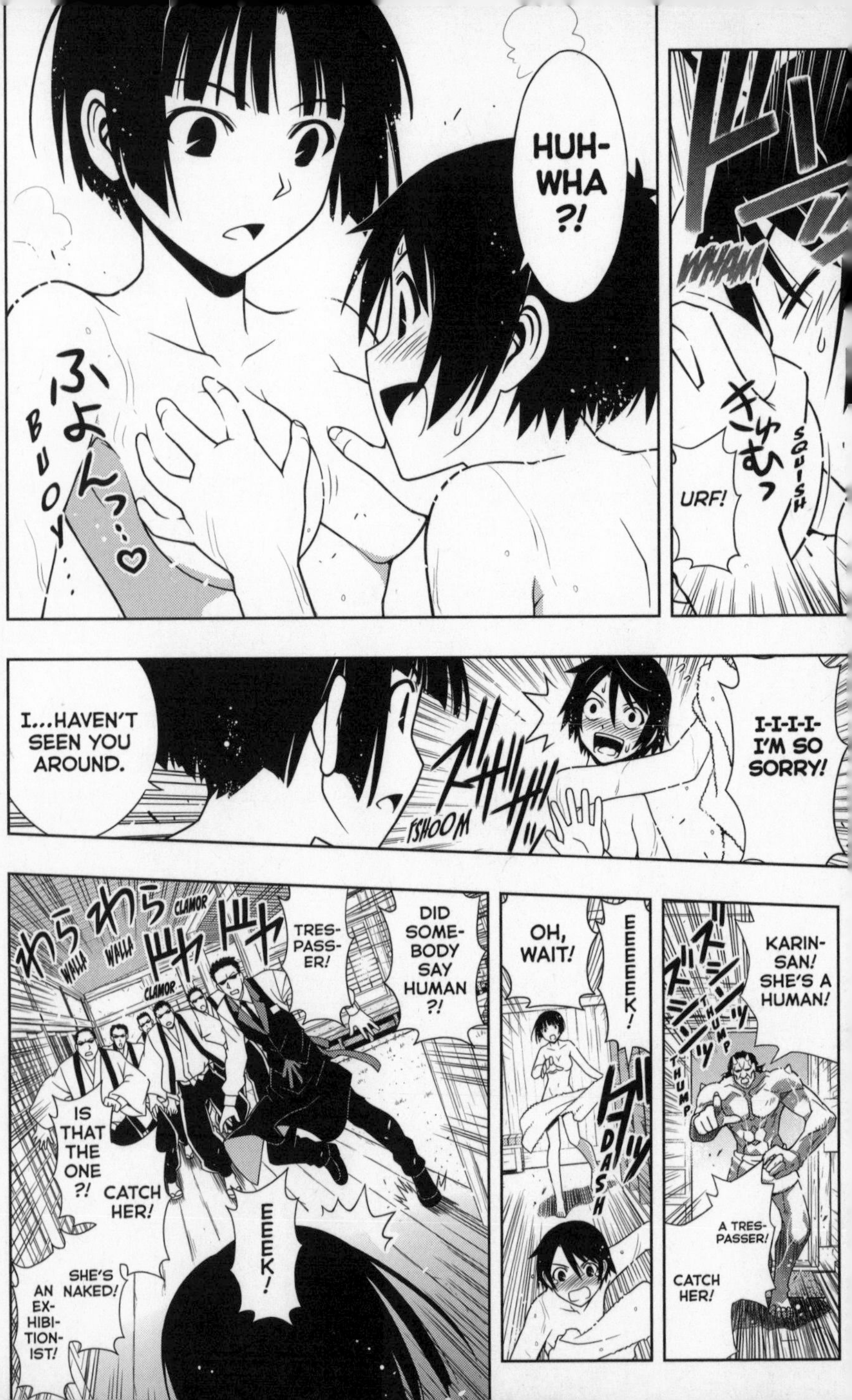

ぎゅむっ
SQUISH
URF!
HUH-WHA?!
ふよんっ…♡
BUOY...
I-I-I-I-I'M SO SORRY!
TSHOOM
I...HAVEN'T SEEN YOU AROUND.
KARIN-SAN! SHE'S A HUMAN!
THUMP
THUMP
A TRESPASSER!
CATCH HER!
EEEEEK!
OH, WAIT!
DASH
DID SOMEBODY SAY HUMAN?!
TRES-PASSER!
わらわら
WALLA WALLA
CLAMOR
CLAMOR
IS THAT THE ONE?!
CATCH HER!
EEEK!
SHE'S NAKED!
AN EXHIBITIONIST!

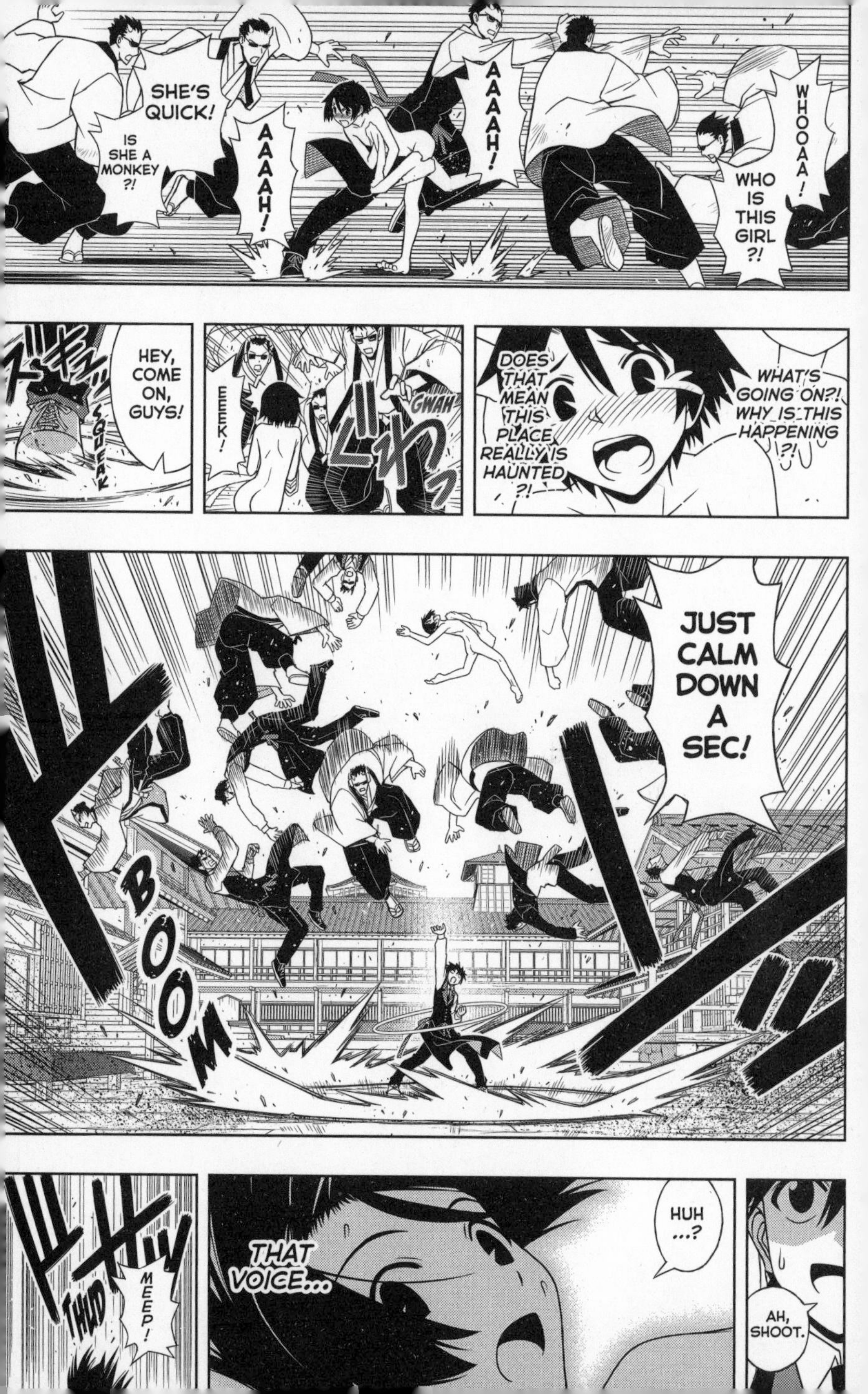
WHOOAAA!
WHO IS THIS GIRL?!
AAAAH!
AAAAH!
SHE'S QUICK!
IS SHE A MONKEY?!
WHAT'S GOING ON?! WHY IS THIS HAPPENING?!
DOES THAT MEAN THIS PLACE REALLY IS HAUNTED?!
GWAH
EEEK!
HEY, COME ON, GUYS!
SQUEAK
JUST CALM DOWN A SEC!
BOOM
AH, SHOOT.
HUH...?
THAT VOICE...
MEEP!
THUD

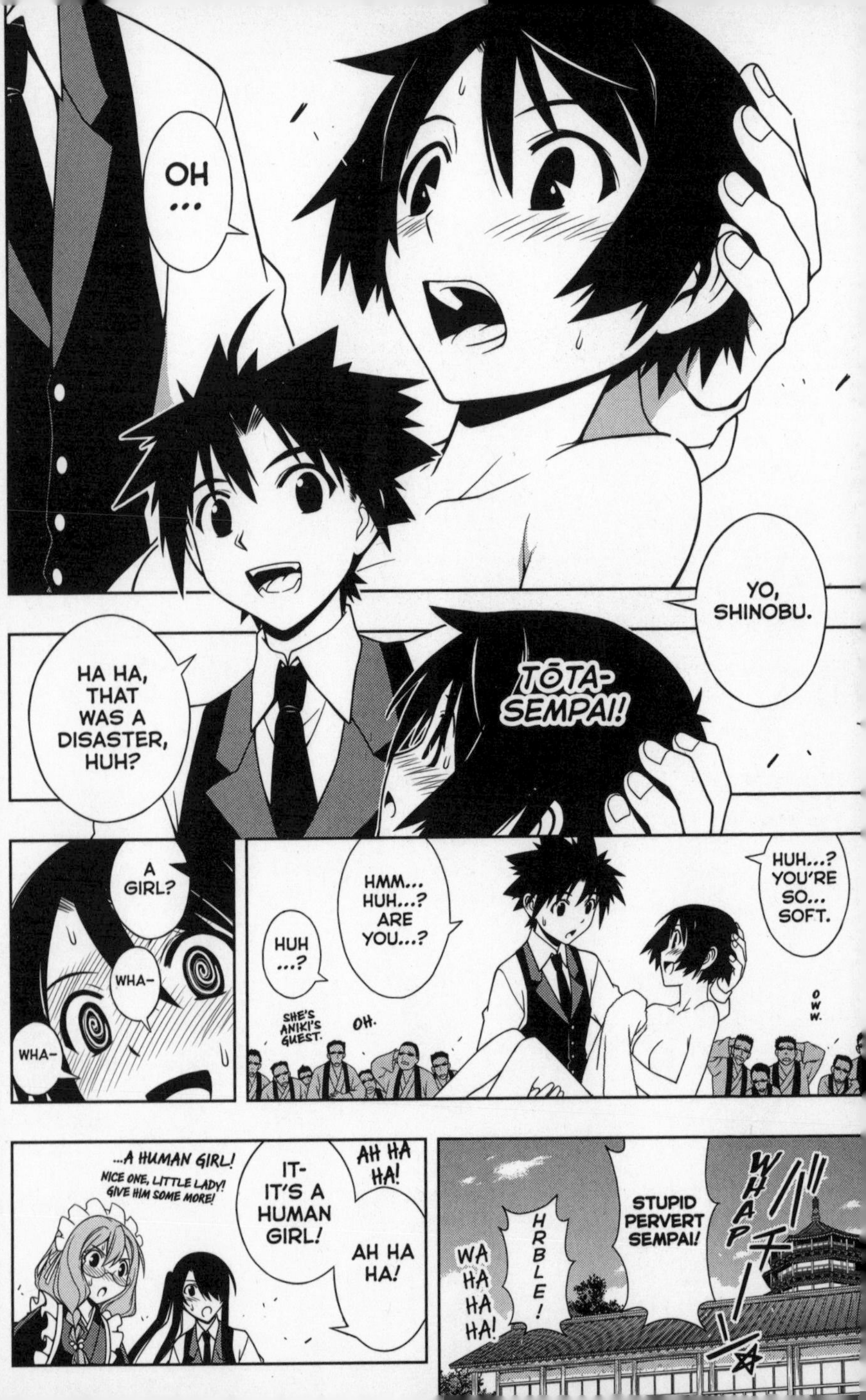
OH ...
YO, SHINOBU.
TŌTA-SEMPAI!
HA HA, THAT WAS A DISASTER, HUH?
HUH...? YOU'RE SO... SOFT.
OWW.
HMM... HUH...? ARE YOU...?
HUH ...?
OH.
SHE'S ANIKI'S GUEST.
A GIRL?
WHA-
WHA-
WHAP
STUPID PERVERT SEMPAI!
HRBLE!
WA HA HA HA HA!
AH HA HA!
IT- IT'S A HUMAN GIRL!
AH HA HA!
...A HUMAN GIRL!
NICE ONE, LITTLE LADY! GIVE HIM SOME MORE!

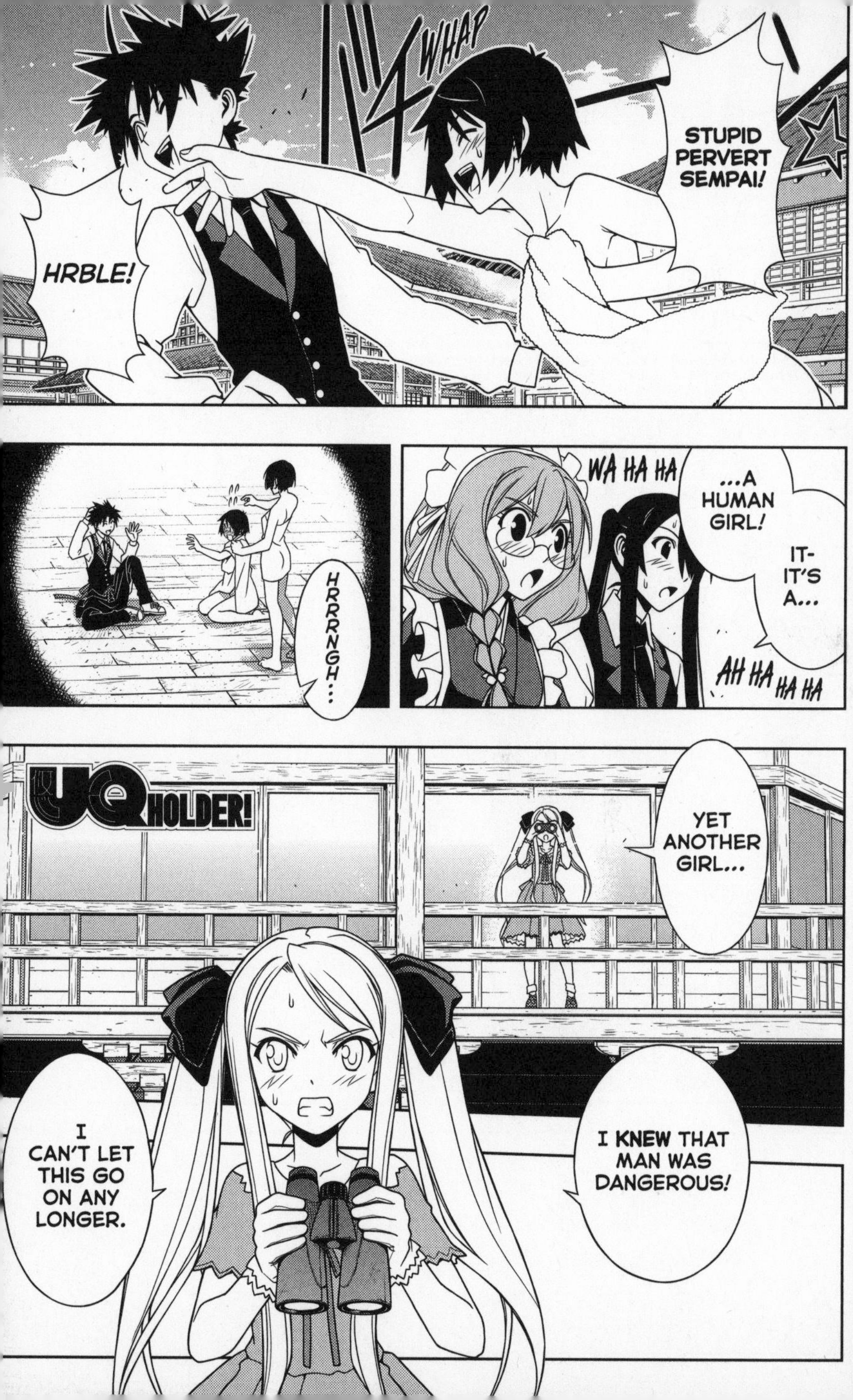
WHAP
STUPID PERVERT SEMPAI!
HRBLE!
IT- IT'S A...
...A HUMAN GIRL!
WA HA HA
AH HA HA HA HA
HRRRNGH...
UQ HOLDER!
YET ANOTHER GIRL...
I KNEW THAT MAN WAS DANGEROUS!
I CAN'T LET THIS GO ON ANY LONGER.

# STAGE 98: BE OUR GUEST!

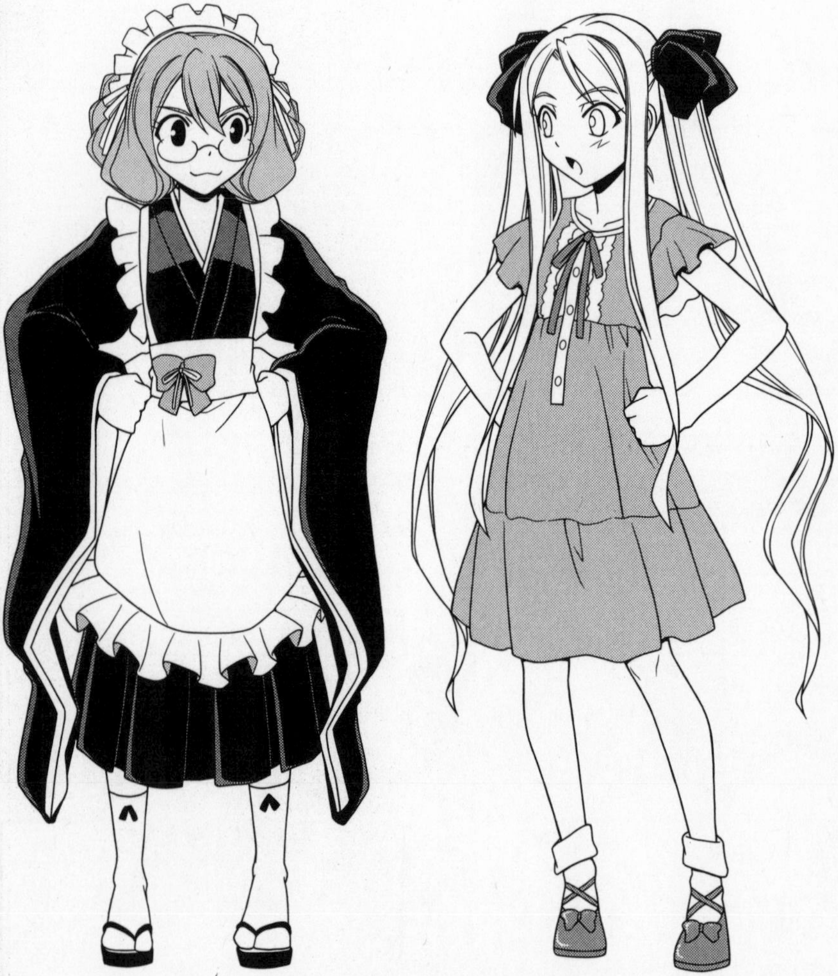

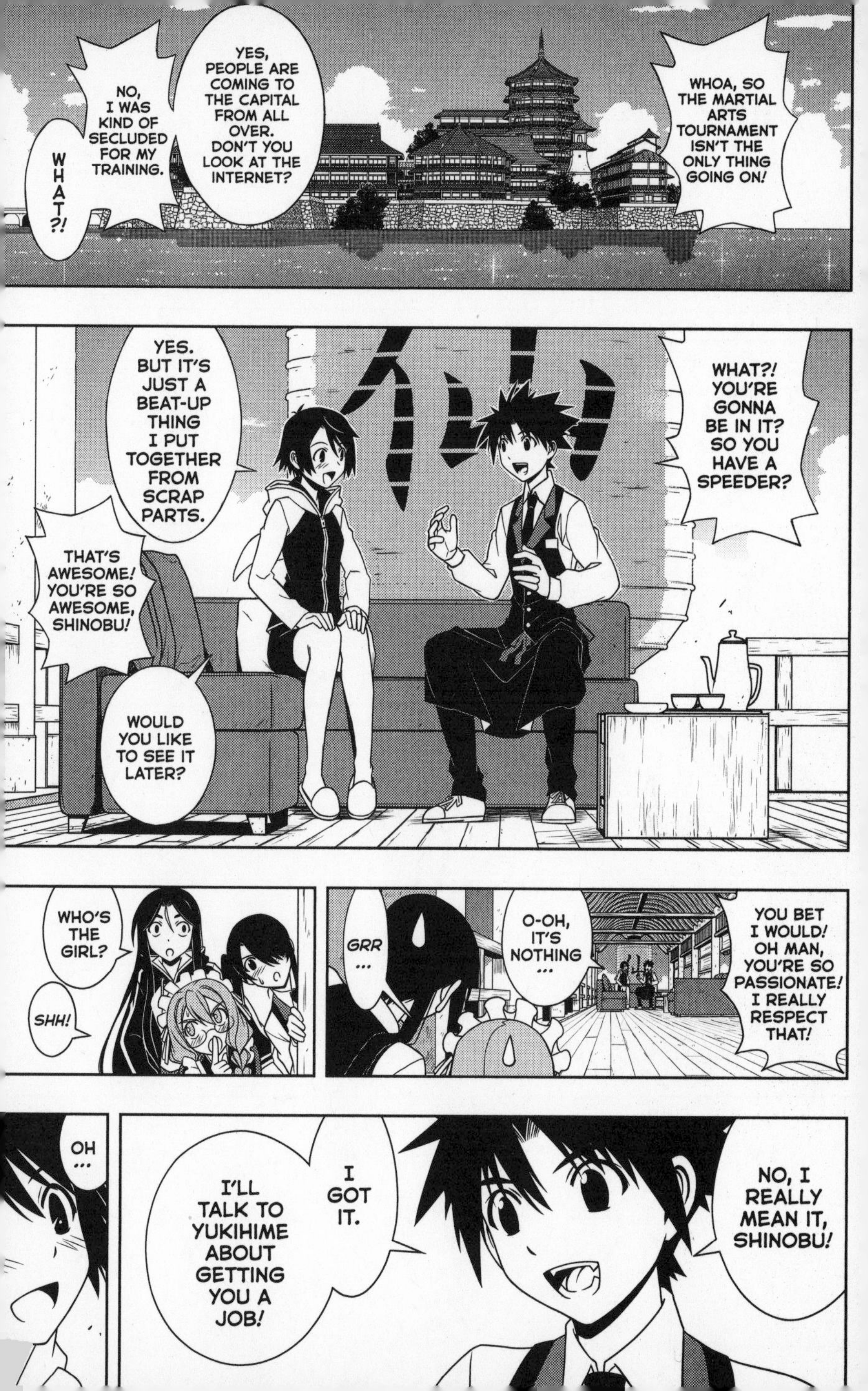
WHOA, SO THE MARTIAL ARTS TOURNAMENT ISN'T THE ONLY THING GOING ON!
YES, PEOPLE ARE COMING TO THE CAPITAL FROM ALL OVER. DON'T YOU LOOK AT THE INTERNET?
NO, I WAS KIND OF SECLUDED FOR MY TRAINING.
WHAT?!
WHAT?! YOU'RE GONNA BE IN IT? SO YOU HAVE A SPEEDER?
YES. BUT IT'S JUST A BEAT-UP THING I PUT TOGETHER FROM SCRAP PARTS.
THAT'S AWESOME! YOU'RE SO AWESOME, SHINOBU!
WOULD YOU LIKE TO SEE IT LATER?
YOU BET I WOULD! OH MAN, YOU'RE SO PASSIONATE! I REALLY RESPECT THAT!
O-OH, IT'S NOTHING...
GRR...
WHO'S THE GIRL?
SHH!
NO, I REALLY MEAN IT, SHINOBU!
I GOT IT.
I'LL TALK TO YUKIHIME ABOUT GETTING YOU A JOB!
OH...

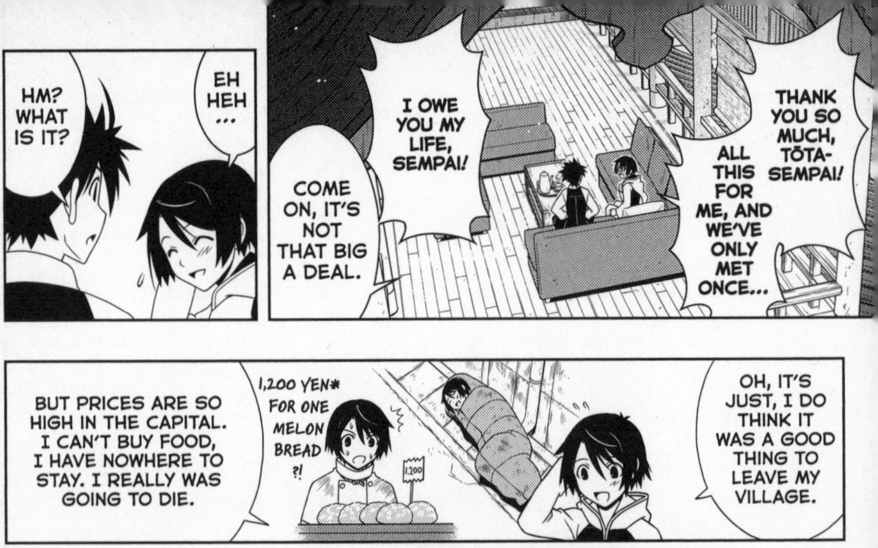
THANK YOU SO MUCH, TŌTA-SEMPAI!
ALL THIS FOR ME, AND WE'VE ONLY MET ONCE...
I OWE YOU MY LIFE, SEMPAI!
COME ON, IT'S NOT THAT BIG A DEAL.
EH HEH ...
HM? WHAT IS IT?
OH, IT'S JUST, I DO THINK IT WAS A GOOD THING TO LEAVE MY VILLAGE.
1,200
1,200 YEN* FOR ONE MELON BREAD ?!
BUT PRICES ARE SO HIGH IN THE CAPITAL. I CAN'T BUY FOOD, I HAVE NOWHERE TO STAY. I REALLY WAS GOING TO DIE.

*1,200 yen = approx. $12 USD.

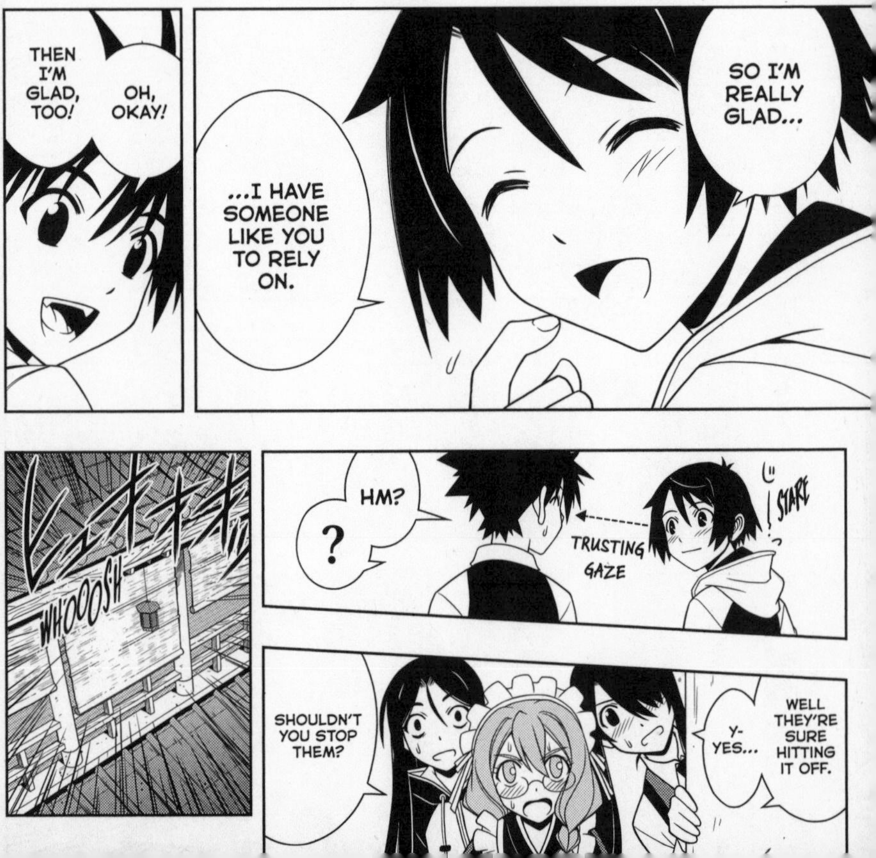
SO I'M REALLY GLAD...
...I HAVE SOMEONE LIKE YOU TO RELY ON.
OH, OKAY!
THEN I'M GLAD, TOO!
STARE
TRUSTING GAZE
HM?
?
WELL THEY'RE SURE HITTING IT OFF.
Y-YES...
SHOULDN'T YOU STOP THEM?
WHOOOSH

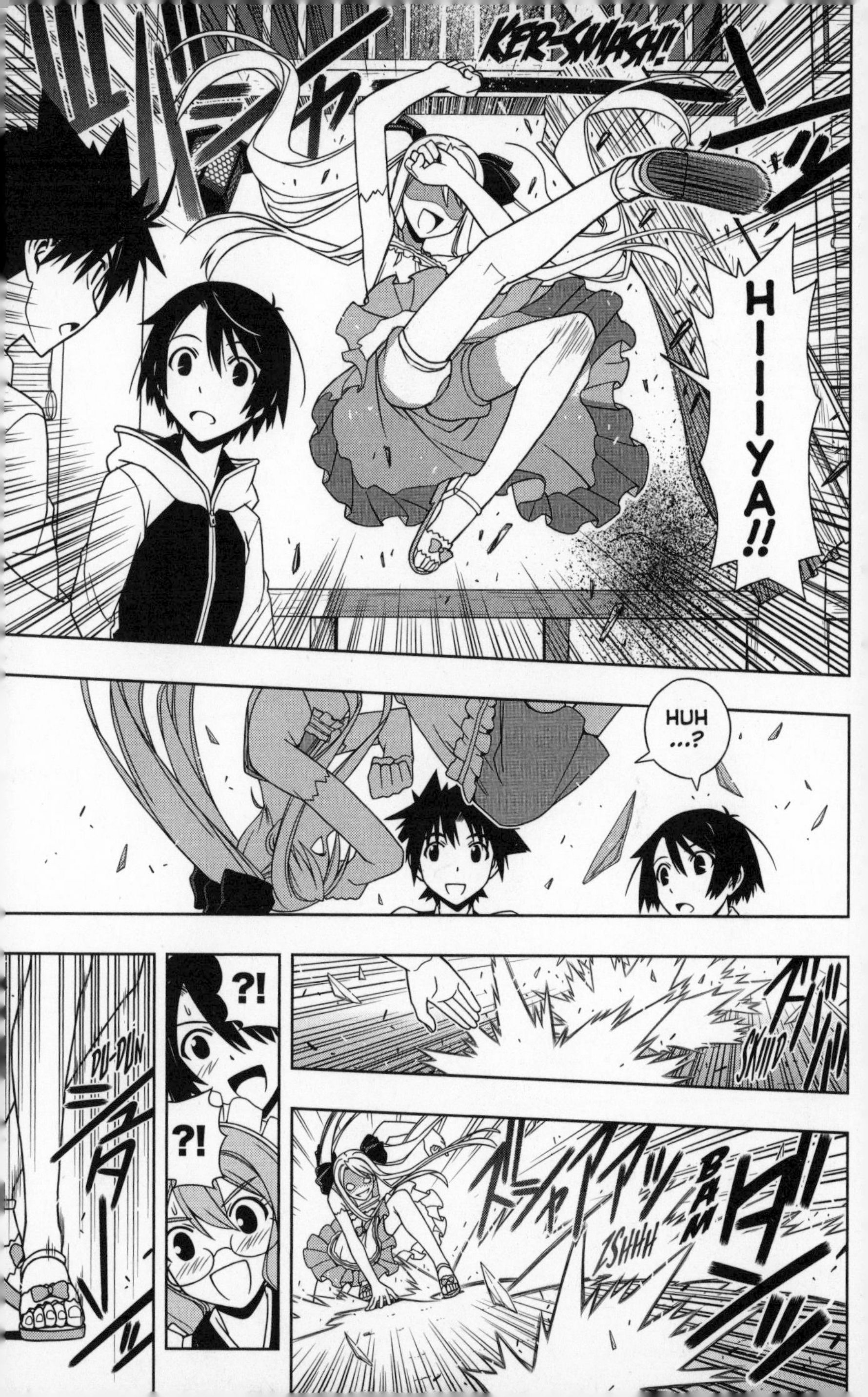
KER-SMASH!
HIIIYA!!
HUH ...?
SKID
BAM
TSHHH
?!
?!
DU-DUN

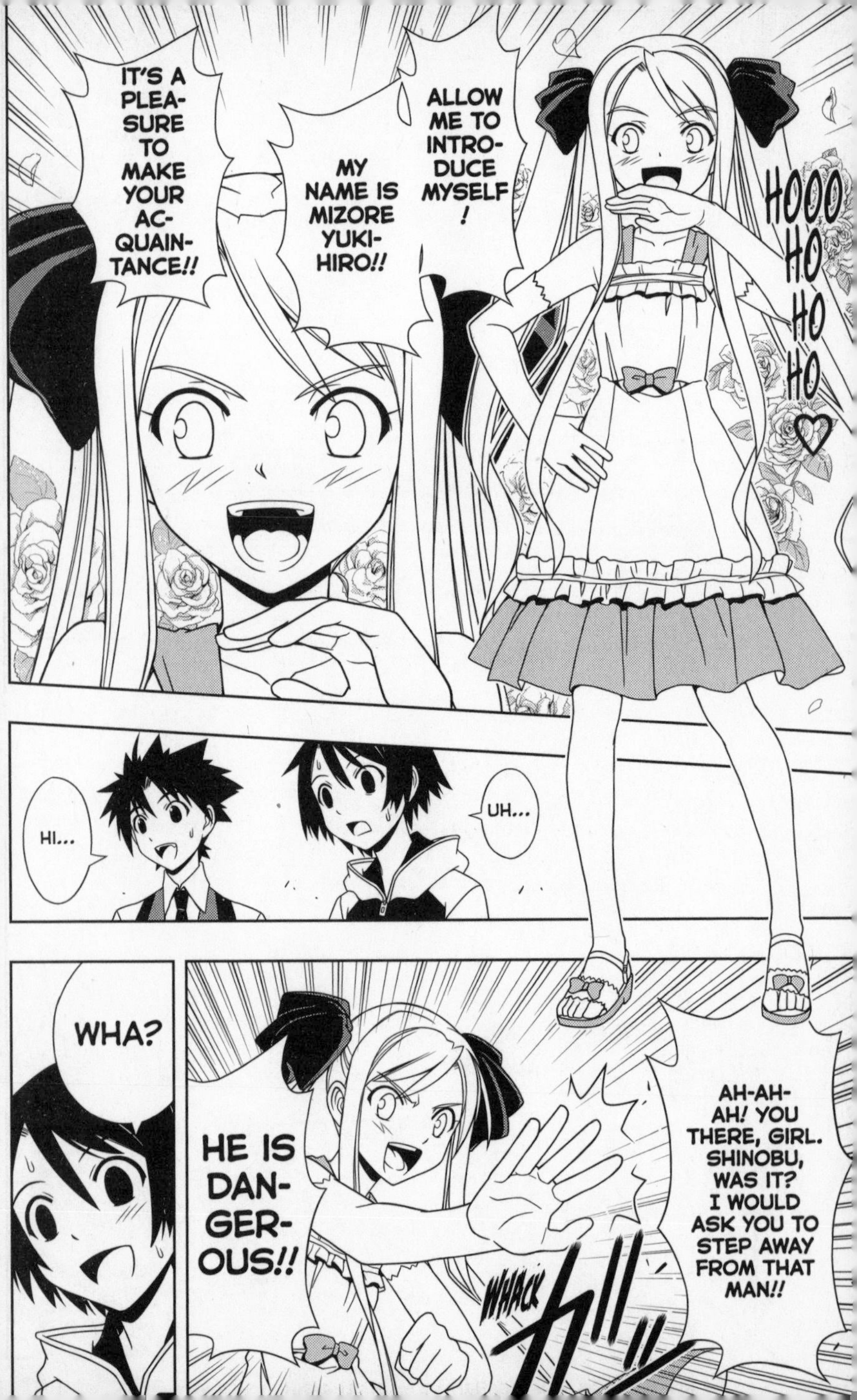
HOOOHOHOHO♡
ALLOW ME TO INTRODUCE MYSELF!
MY NAME IS MIZORE YUKIHIRO!!
IT'S A PLEASURE TO MAKE YOUR ACQUAINTANCE!!
UH...
HI...
AH-AH-AH! YOU THERE, GIRL. SHINOBU, WAS IT? I WOULD ASK YOU TO STEP AWAY FROM THAT MAN!!
WHACK
HE IS DANGEROUS!!
WHA?

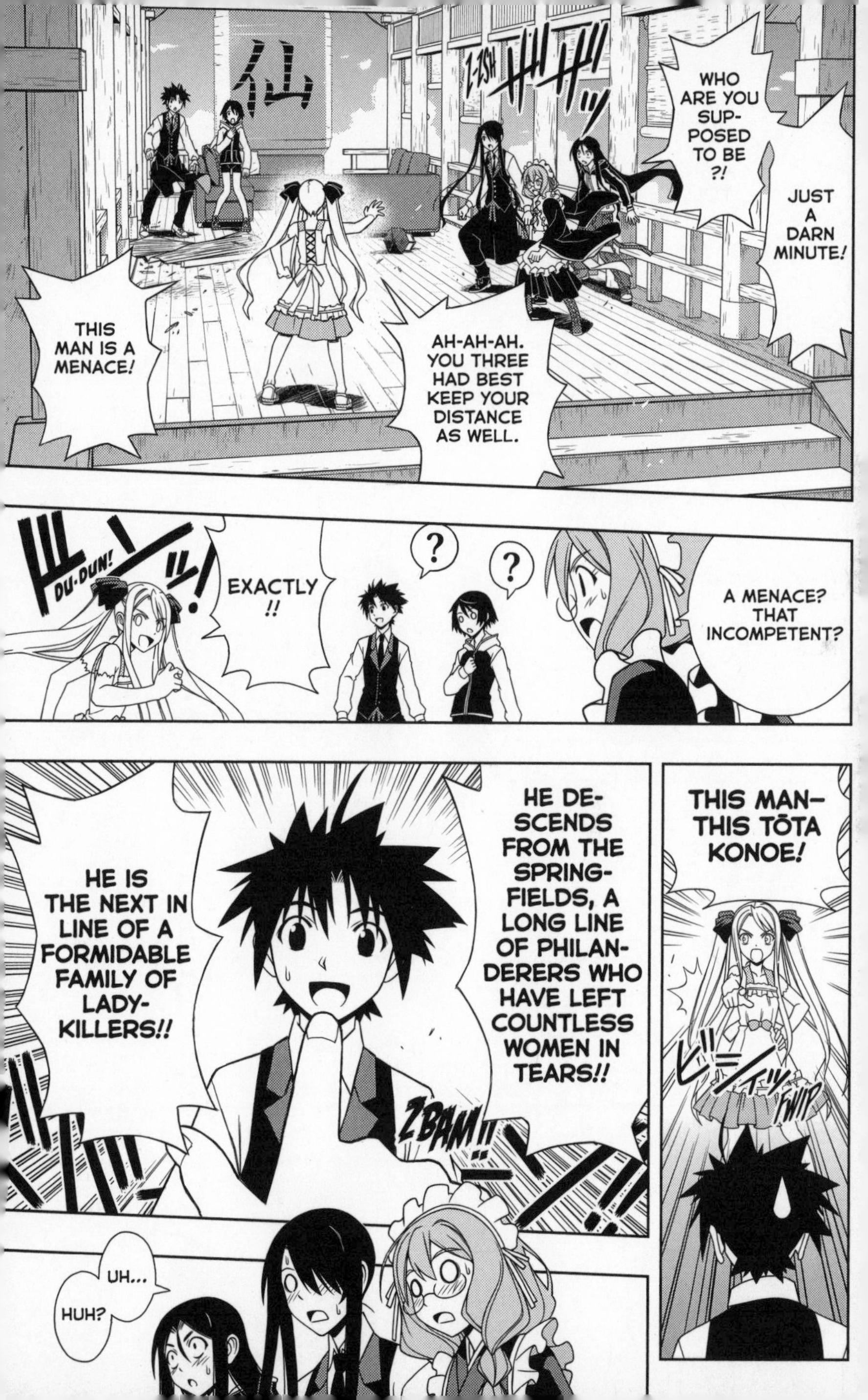
WHO ARE YOU SUPPOSED TO BE ?!
JUST A DARN MINUTE!
Z-ZSH
AH-AH-AH. YOU THREE HAD BEST KEEP YOUR DISTANCE AS WELL.
THIS MAN IS A MENACE!
A MENACE? THAT INCOMPETENT?
?
?
EXACTLY !!
DU-DUN!
THIS MAN— THIS TŌTA KONOE!
FWIP
HE DESCENDS FROM THE SPRINGFIELDS, A LONG LINE OF PHILANDERERS WHO HAVE LEFT COUNTLESS WOMEN IN TEARS!!
HE IS THE NEXT IN LINE OF A FORMIDABLE FAMILY OF LADY-KILLERS!!
ZBAM!!
UH...
HUH?

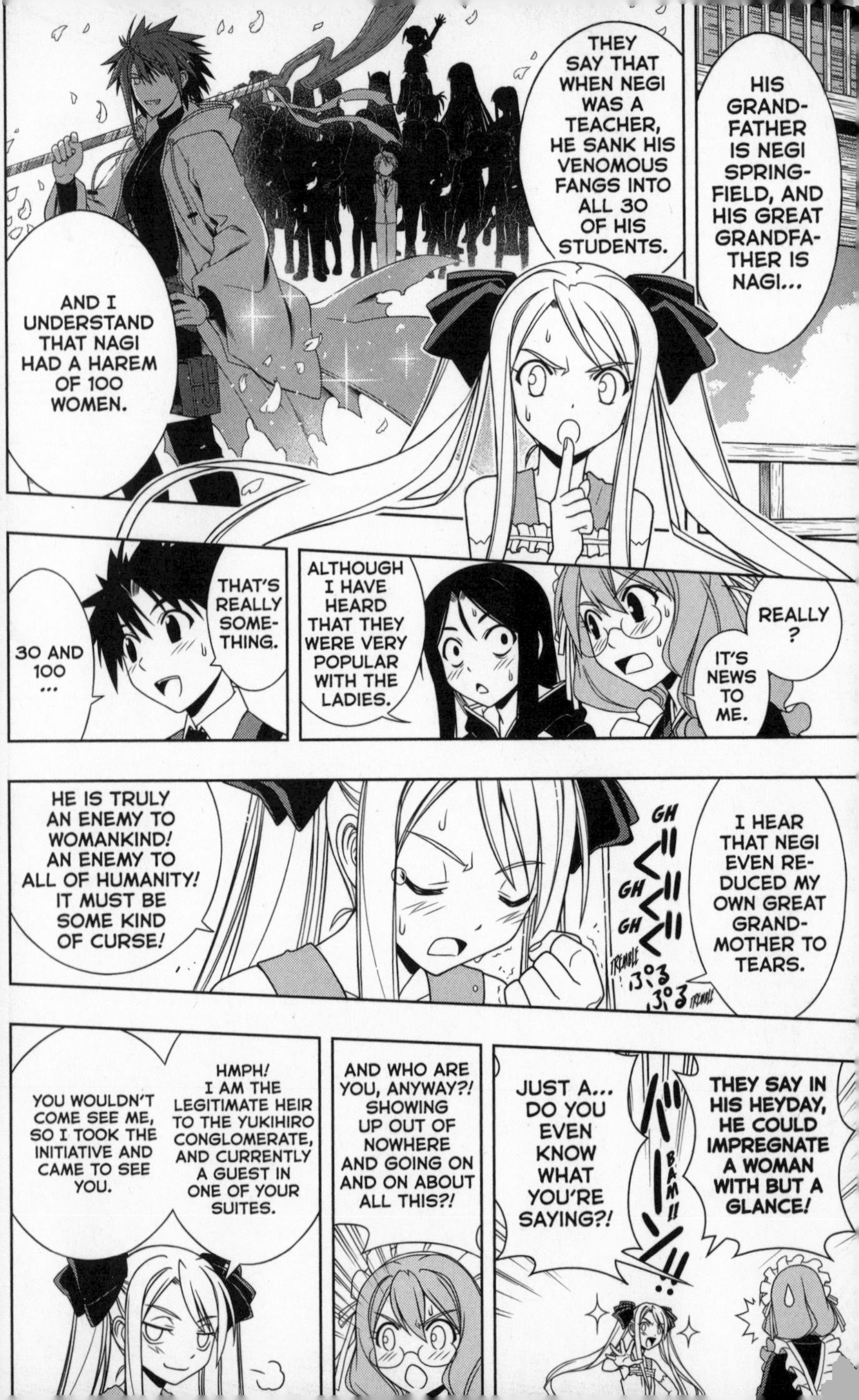
HIS GRANDFATHER IS NEGI SPRINGFIELD, AND HIS GREAT GRANDFATHER IS NAGI...
THEY SAY THAT WHEN NEGI WAS A TEACHER, HE SANK HIS VENOMOUS FANGS INTO ALL 30 OF HIS STUDENTS.
AND I UNDERSTAND THAT NAGI HAD A HAREM OF 100 WOMEN.
REALLY? IT'S NEWS TO ME.
ALTHOUGH I HAVE HEARD THAT THEY WERE VERY POPULAR WITH THE LADIES.
THAT'S REALLY SOMETHING.
30 AND 100...
I HEAR THAT NEGI EVEN REDUCED MY OWN GREAT GRANDMOTHER TO TEARS.
GH GH GH
TREMBLE TREMBLE
HE IS TRULY AN ENEMY TO WOMANKIND! AN ENEMY TO ALL OF HUMANITY! IT MUST BE SOME KIND OF CURSE!
THEY SAY IN HIS HEYDAY, HE COULD IMPREGNATE A WOMAN WITH BUT A GLANCE!
BAM!!
JUST A... DO YOU EVEN KNOW WHAT YOU'RE SAYING?!
AND WHO ARE YOU, ANYWAY?! SHOWING UP OUT OF NOWHERE AND GOING ON AND ON ABOUT ALL THIS?!
HMPH! I AM THE LEGITIMATE HEIR TO THE YUKIHIRO CONGLOMERATE, AND CURRENTLY A GUEST IN ONE OF YOUR SUITES.
YOU WOULDN'T COME SEE ME, SO I TOOK THE INITIATIVE AND CAME TO SEE YOU.

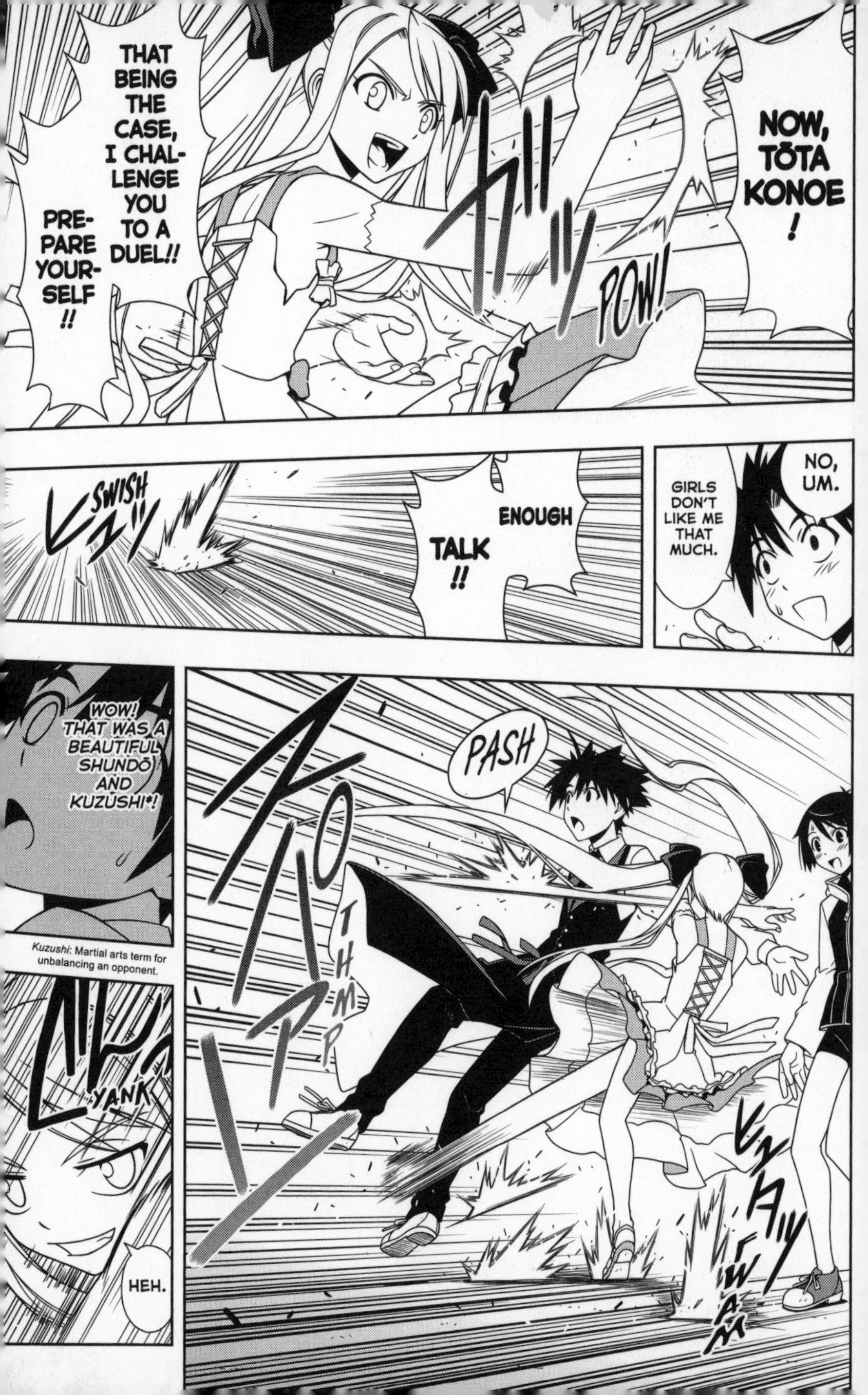
NOW, TŌTA KONOE!
POW!
THAT BEING THE CASE, I CHALLENGE YOU TO A DUEL!!
PREPARE YOURSELF!!
NO, UM.
GIRLS DON'T LIKE ME THAT MUCH.
ENOUGH TALK!!
SWISH
PASH
THUMP
WHAM
WOW! THAT WAS A BEAUTIFUL SHUNDŌ AND KUZUSHI*!
YANK
HEH.
*Kuzushi*: Martial arts term for unbalancing an opponent.

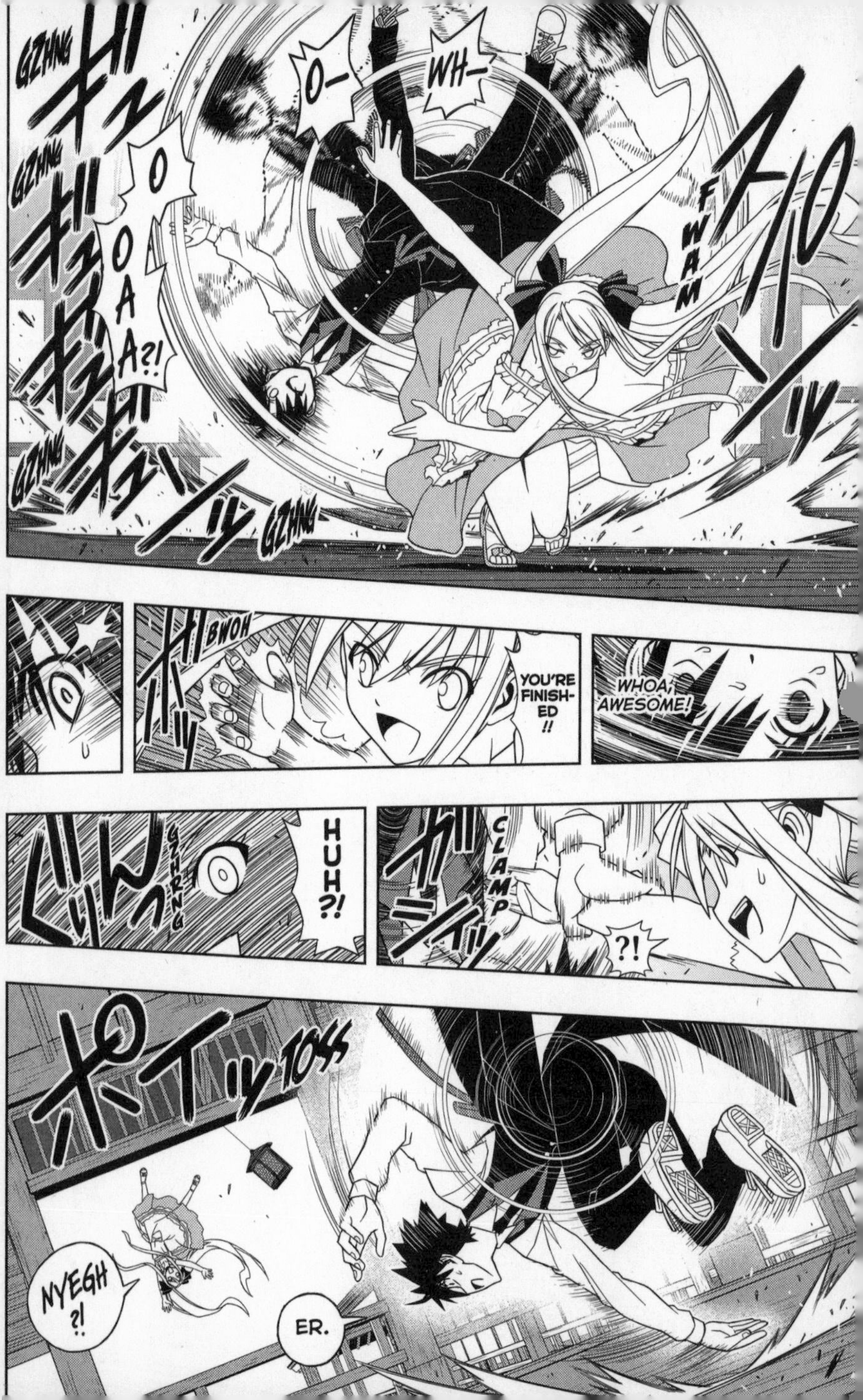
FWAM
WH—
O—
O
OAAA?!
GZHNG
GZHNG
GZHNG
GZHNG
WHOA, AWESOME!
YOU'RE FINISH-ED!!
BWOH
CLAMP
?!
HUH?!
GZHRNG
TOSS
ER.
NYEGH?!

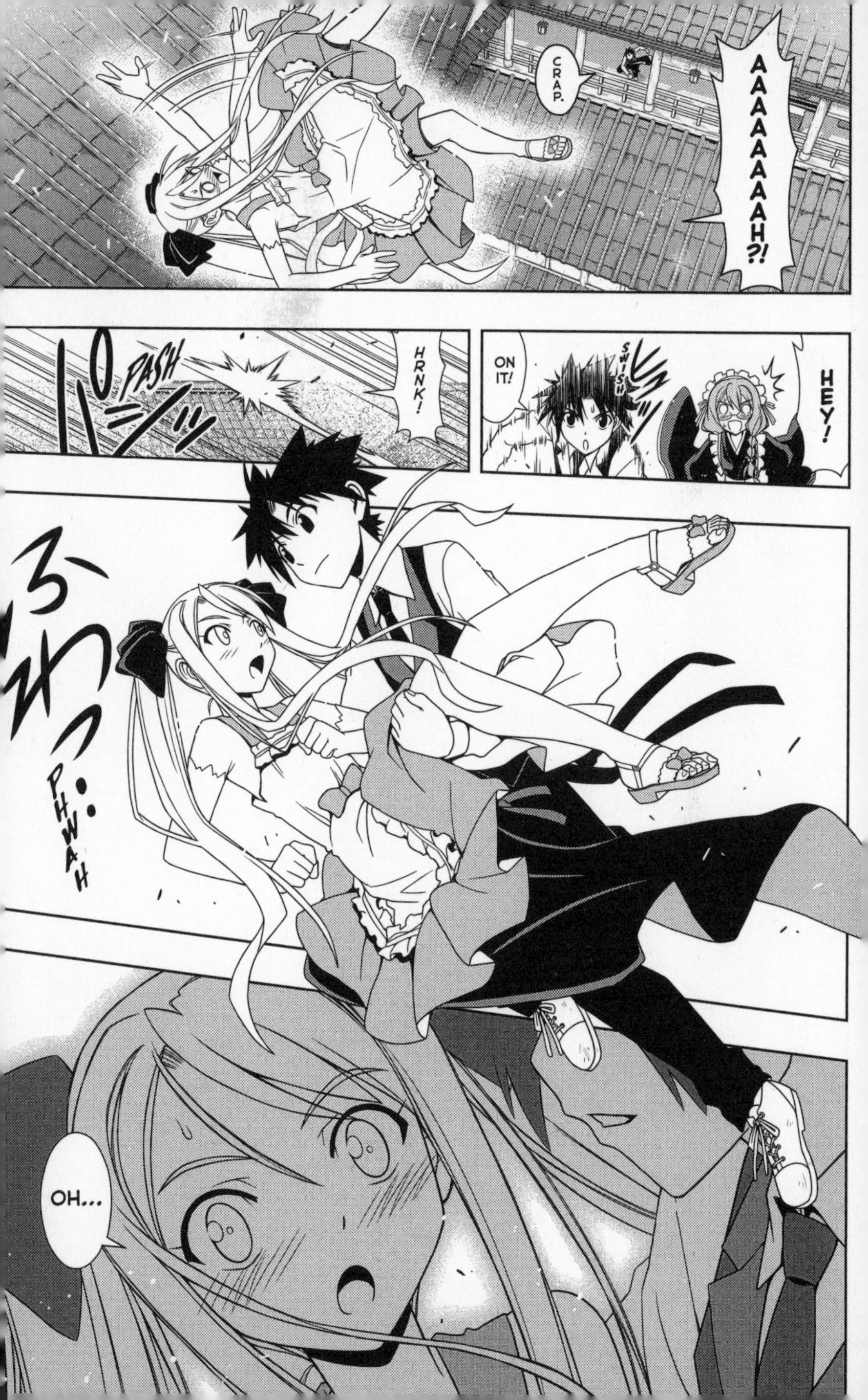
AAAAAAAAAH?!
CRAP.
HEY!
SWISH
ON IT!
HRNK!
PASH
ふわっ
PHWAH
OH...

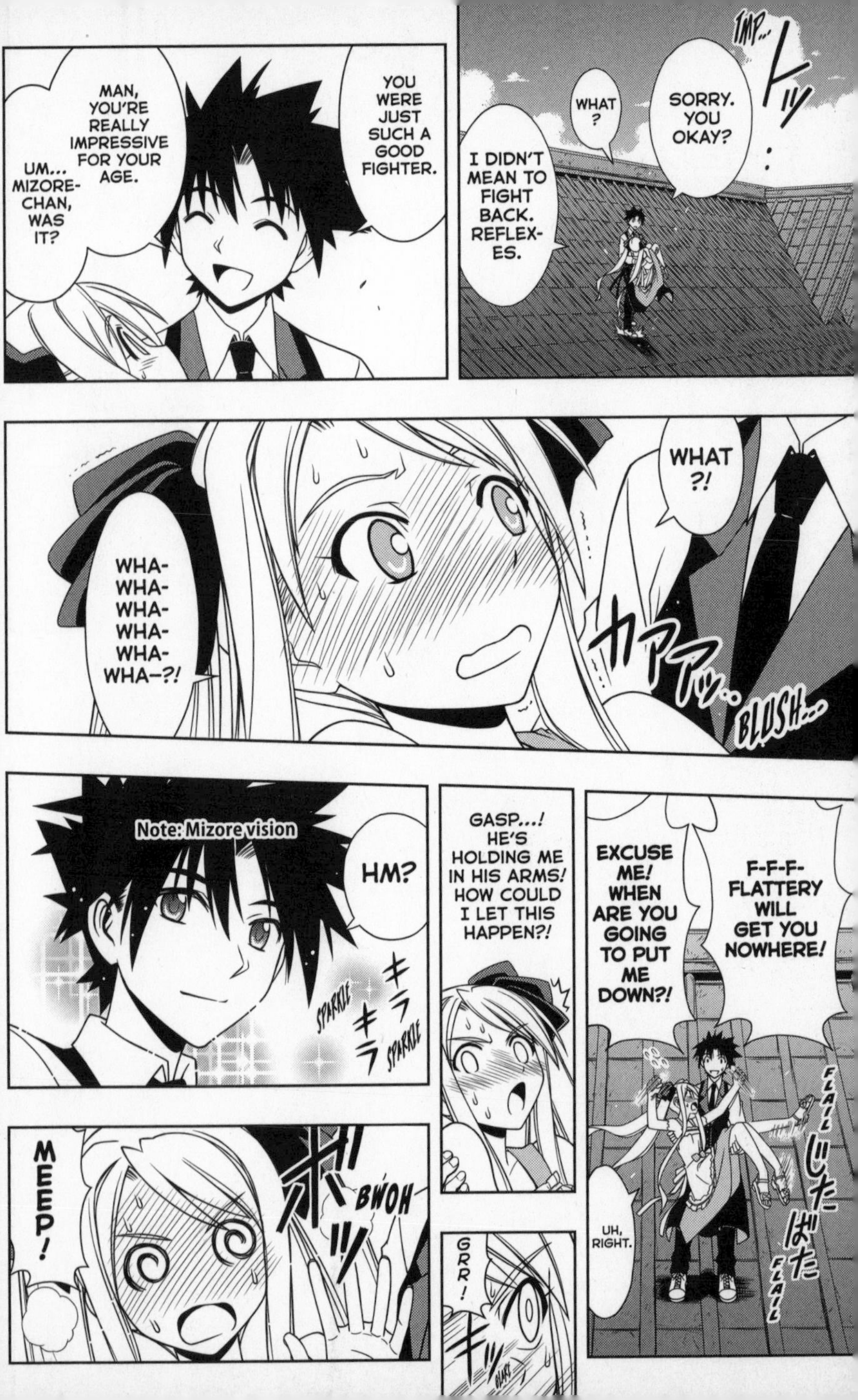

IMP...
SORRY. YOU OKAY?
WHAT?
I DIDN'T MEAN TO FIGHT BACK. REFLEXES.
YOU WERE JUST SUCH A GOOD FIGHTER.
MAN, YOU'RE REALLY IMPRESSIVE FOR YOUR AGE.
UM... MIZORE-CHAN, WAS IT?
WHAT?!
BLUSH...
WHA-WHA-WHA-WHA-WHA-WHA-?!
F-F-F-FLATTERY WILL GET YOU NOWHERE!
EXCUSE ME! WHEN ARE YOU GOING TO PUT ME DOWN?!
UH, RIGHT.
FLAIL
FLAIL
GASP...! HE'S HOLDING ME IN HIS ARMS! HOW COULD I LET THIS HAPPEN?!
HM?
Note: Mizore vision
SPARKLE
SPARKLE
GRR!
BWOH
MEEP!

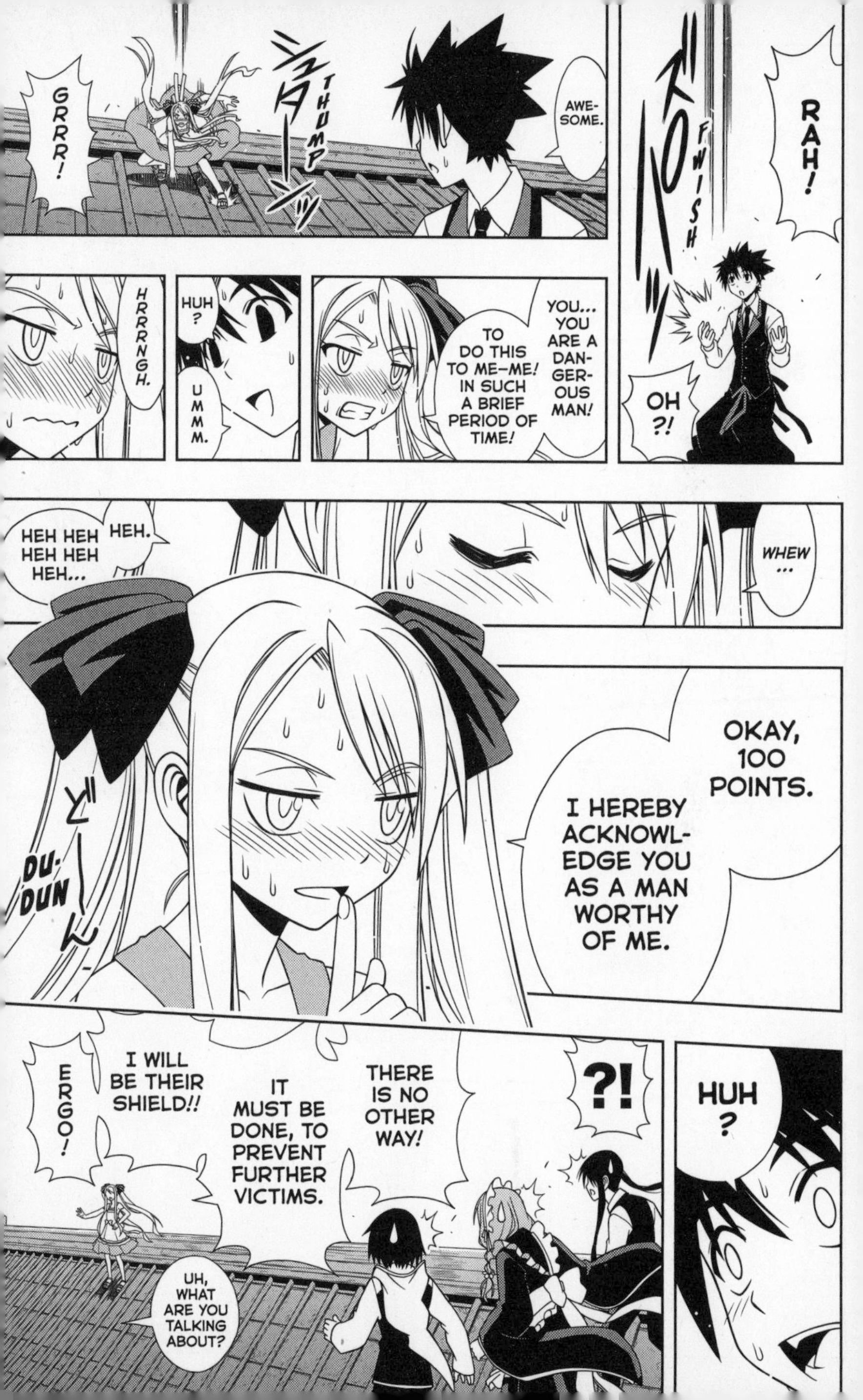
RAH!
FWISH
OH?!
AWE-SOME.
THUMP
GRRR!
YOU... YOU ARE A DAN-GER-OUS MAN!
TO DO THIS TO ME—ME! IN SUCH A BRIEF PERIOD OF TIME!
HUH?
UMMM.
HRRRNGH.
WHEW...
HEH.
HEH HEH HEH HEH HEH...
OKAY, 100 POINTS.
I HEREBY ACKNOWL-EDGE YOU AS A MAN WORTHY OF ME.
DU-DUN
HUH?
?!
THERE IS NO OTHER WAY!
IT MUST BE DONE, TO PREVENT FURTHER VICTIMS.
I WILL BE THEIR SHIELD!!
ERGO!
UH, WHAT ARE YOU TALKING ABOUT?

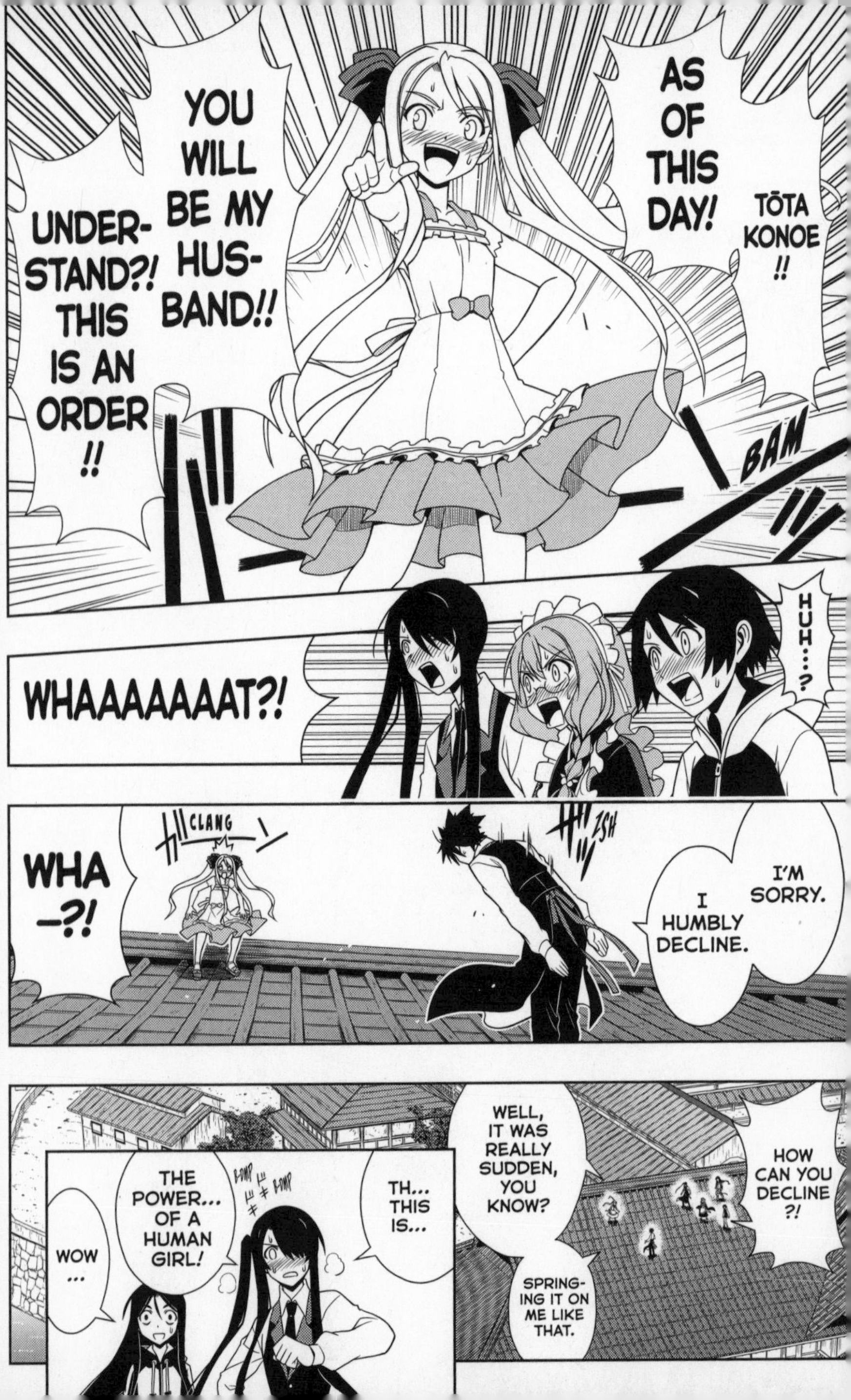
TŌTA KONOE!!
AS OF THIS DAY!
YOU WILL BE MY HUSBAND!!
UNDERSTAND?! THIS IS AN ORDER!!
BAM
HUH...?
WHAAAAAAAT?!
I'M SORRY.
I HUMBLY DECLINE.
ZSH
CLANG
WHA-?!
HOW CAN YOU DECLINE?!
WELL, IT WAS REALLY SUDDEN, YOU KNOW?
SPRINGING IT ON ME LIKE THAT.
TH... THIS IS...
BOMP BOMP
THE POWER... OF A HUMAN GIRL!
WOW...

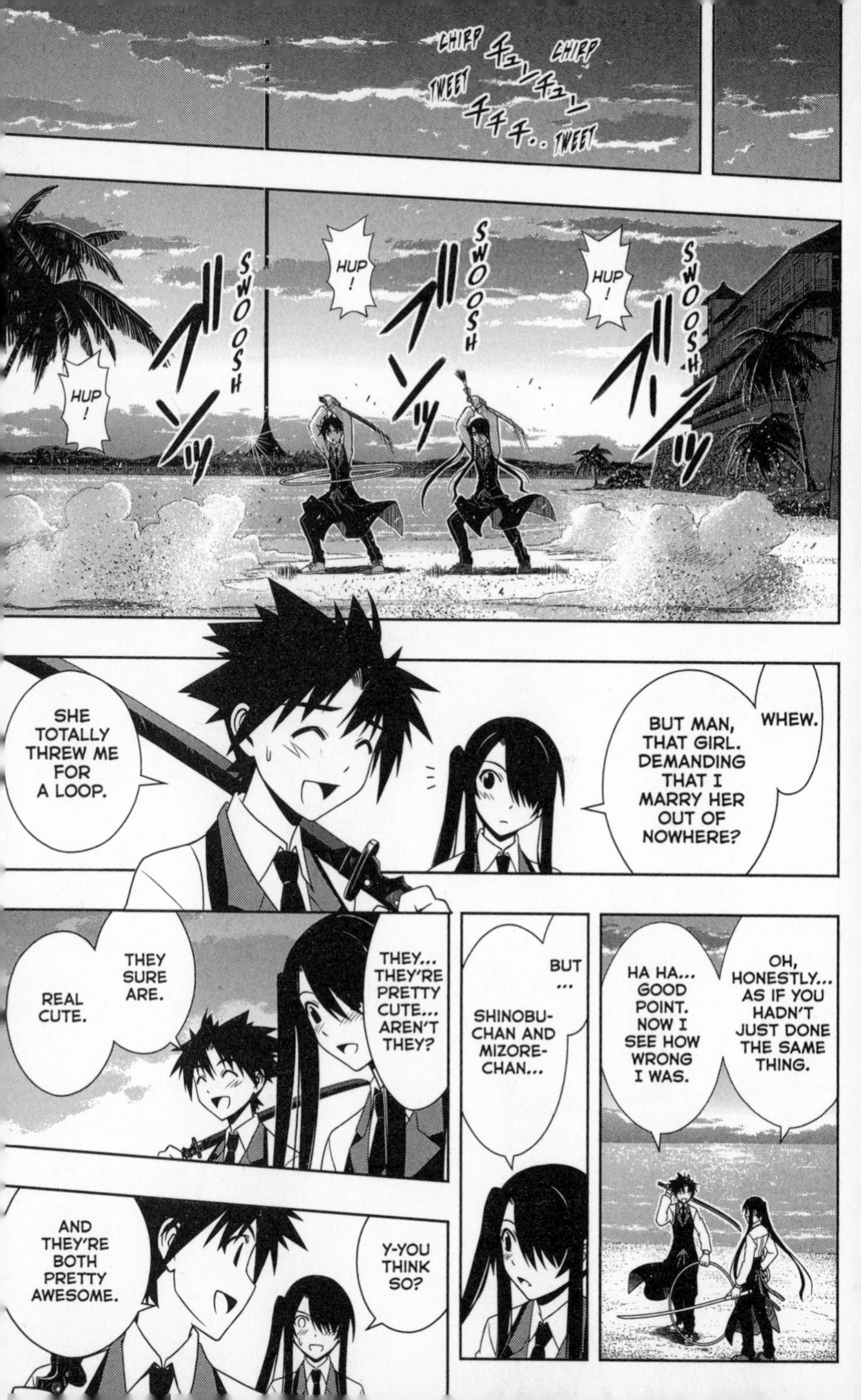
CHIRP
チュンチュン
CHIRP
TWEET
チチチ..
TWEET
SWOOSH
HUP!
SWOOSH
HUP!
SWOOSH
HUP!
WHEW.
BUT MAN, THAT GIRL. DEMANDING THAT I MARRY HER OUT OF NOWHERE?
SHE TOTALLY THREW ME FOR A LOOP.
OH, HONESTLY... AS IF YOU HADN'T JUST DONE THE SAME THING.
HA HA... GOOD POINT. NOW I SEE HOW WRONG I WAS.
BUT ...
SHINOBU-CHAN AND MIZORE-CHAN...
THEY... THEY'RE PRETTY CUTE... AREN'T THEY?
THEY SURE ARE.
REAL CUTE.
Y-YOU THINK SO?
AND THEY'RE BOTH PRETTY AWESOME.

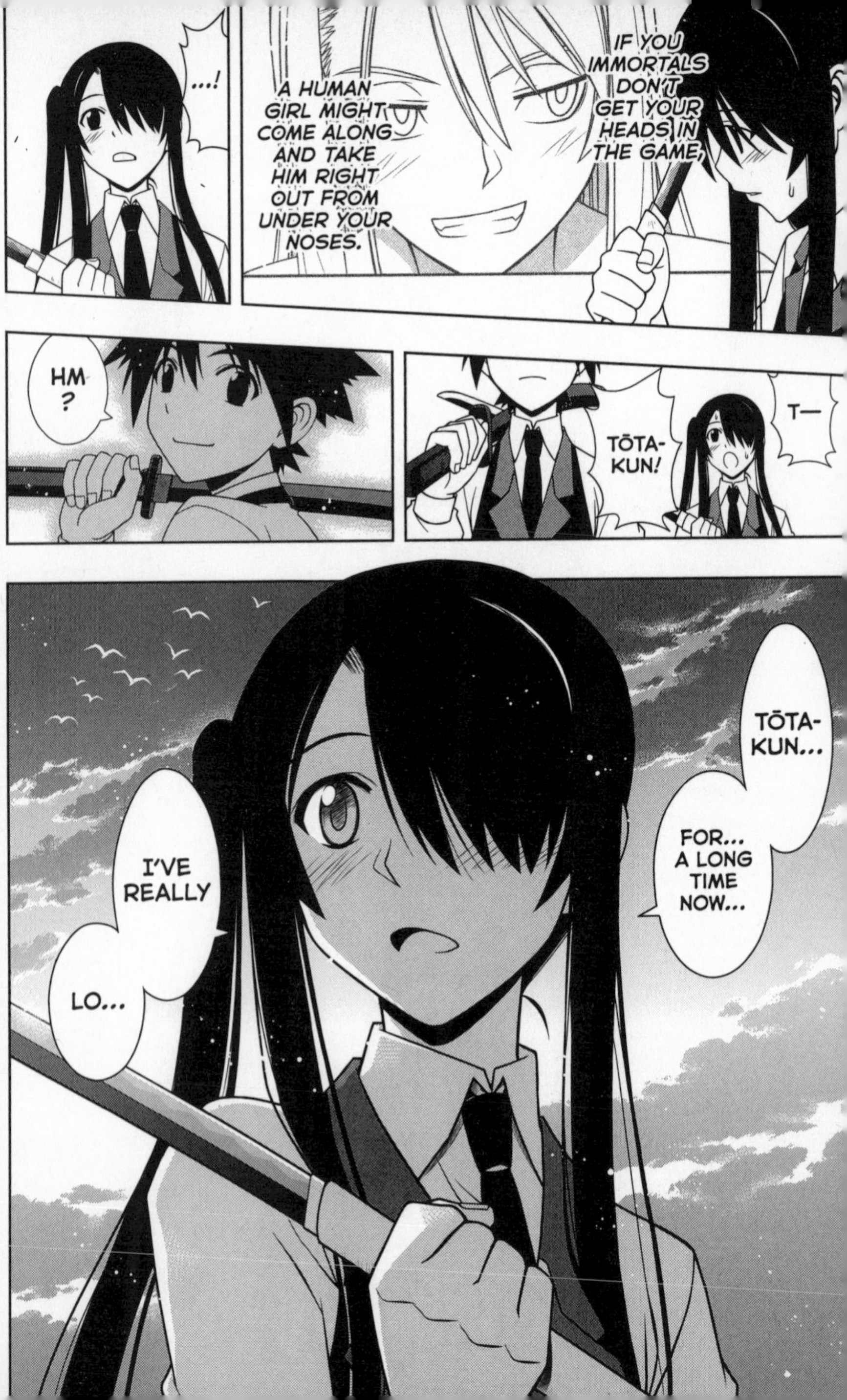
IF YOU IMMORTALS DON'T GET YOUR HEADS IN THE GAME,
A HUMAN GIRL MIGHT COME ALONG AND TAKE HIM RIGHT OUT FROM UNDER YOUR NOSES.
...!
T—
TŌTA-KUN!
HM?
TŌTA-KUN...
FOR... A LONG TIME NOW...
I'VE REALLY
LO...

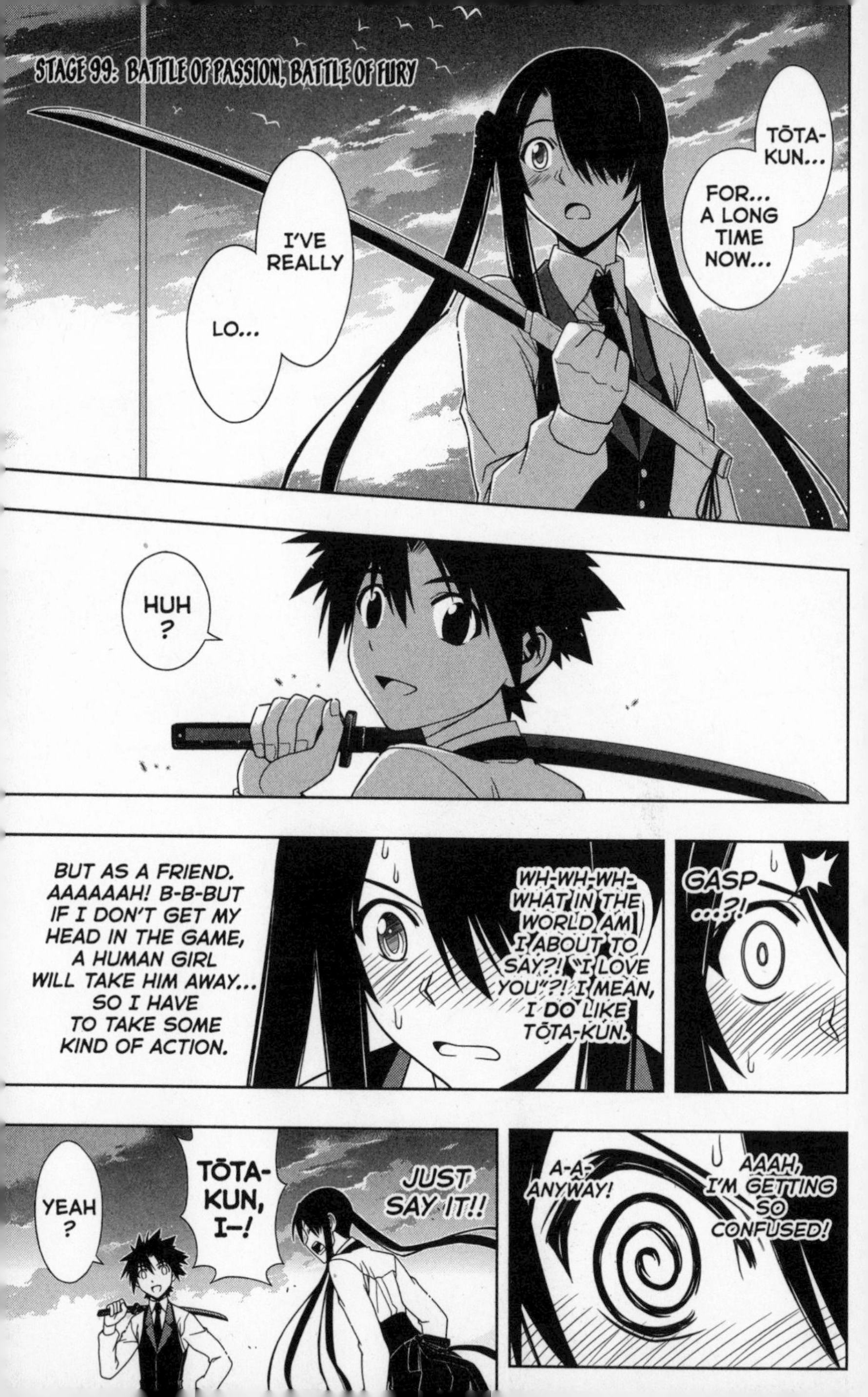
STAGE 99: BATTLE OF PASSION, BATTLE OF FURY
TŌTA-KUN... FOR... A LONG TIME NOW...
I'VE REALLY LO...
HUH?
GASP ...?!
WH-WH-WH-WHAT IN THE WORLD AM I ABOUT TO SAY?! "I LOVE YOU"?! I MEAN, I DO LIKE TŌTA-KUN.
BUT AS A FRIEND. AAAAAAH! B-B-BUT IF I DON'T GET MY HEAD IN THE GAME, A HUMAN GIRL WILL TAKE HIM AWAY... SO I HAVE TO TAKE SOME KIND OF ACTION.
AAAH, I'M GETTING SO CONFUSED!
A-A-ANYWAY!
JUST SAY IT!!
TŌTA-KUN, I–!
YEAH?

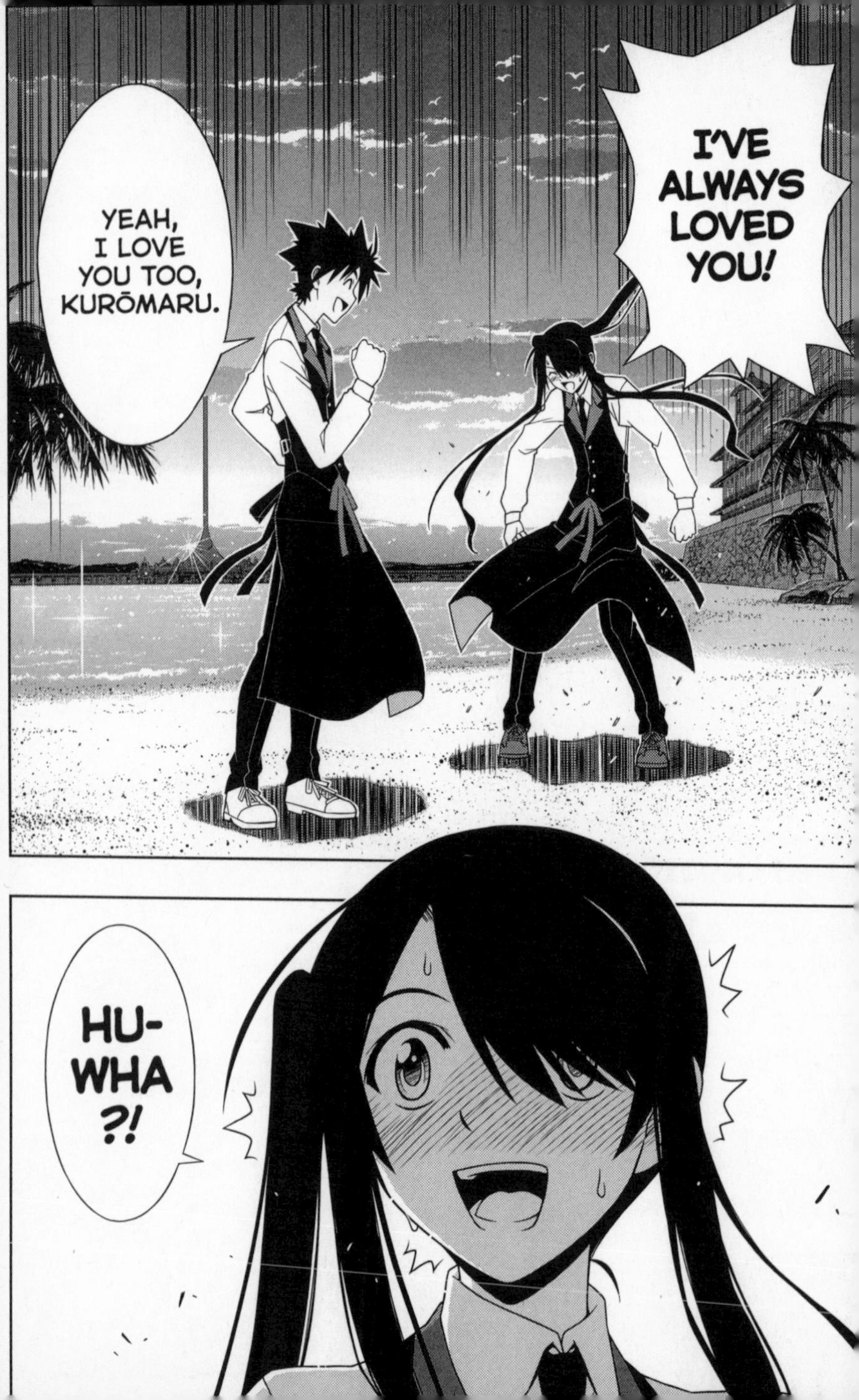
I'VE ALWAYS LOVED YOU!
YEAH, I LOVE YOU TOO, KURŌMARU.
HU-WHA?!

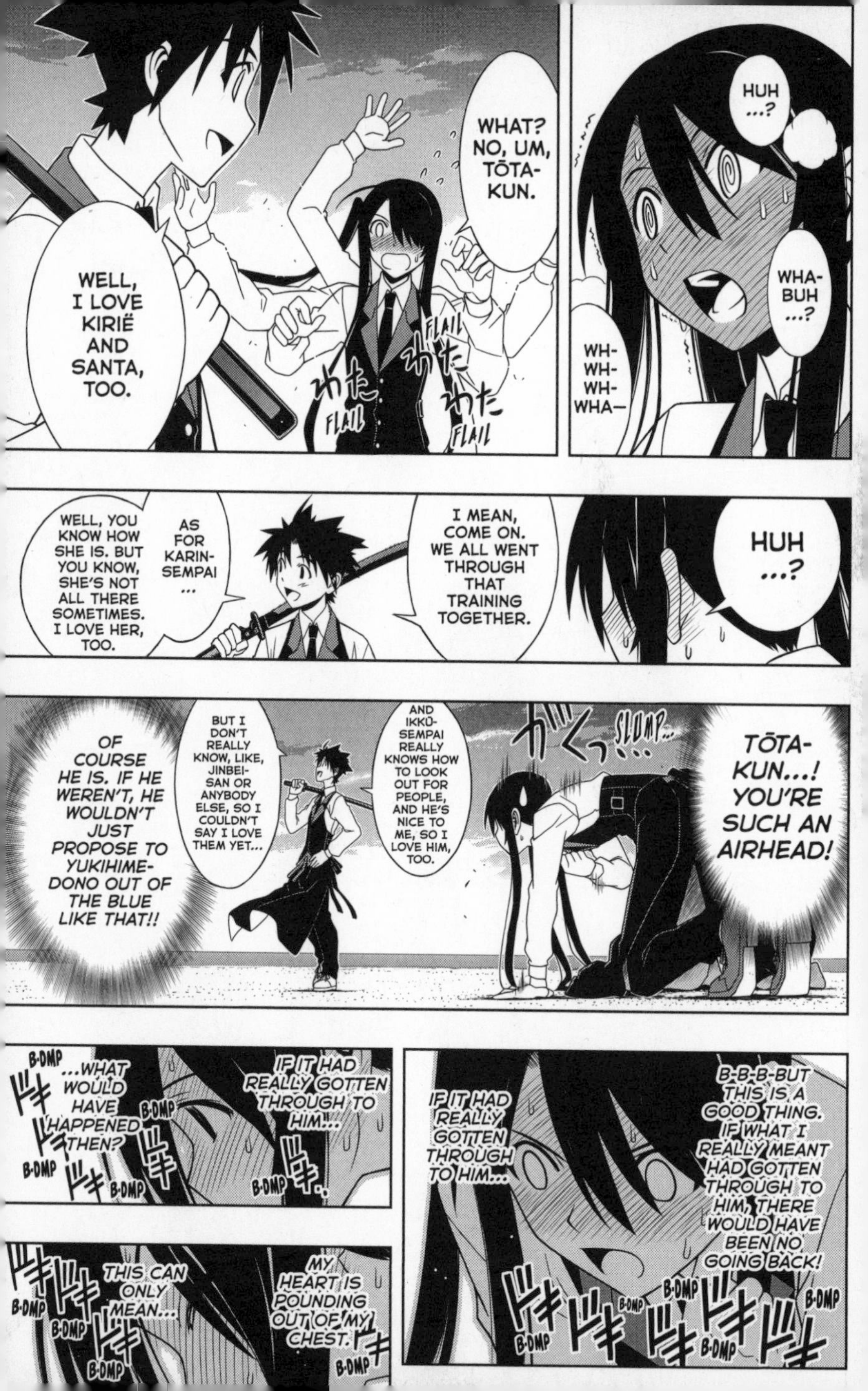
HUH ...?
WHA-BUH ...?
WH-WH-WH-WHA—
WHAT? NO, UM, TŌTA-KUN.
FLAIL わた FLAIL わた FLAIL わた FLAIL
WELL, I LOVE KIRIË AND SANTA, TOO.
HUH ...?
I MEAN, COME ON. WE ALL WENT THROUGH THAT TRAINING TOGETHER.
AS FOR KARIN-SEMPAI ...
WELL, YOU KNOW HOW SHE IS. BUT YOU KNOW, SHE'S NOT ALL THERE SOMETIMES. I LOVE HER, TOO.
TŌTA-KUN...! YOU'RE SUCH AN AIRHEAD!
がくっ SLUMP...
AND IKKŪ-SEMPAI REALLY KNOWS HOW TO LOOK OUT FOR PEOPLE, AND HE'S NICE TO ME, SO I LOVE HIM, TOO.
BUT I DON'T REALLY KNOW, LIKE, JINBEI-SAN OR ANYBODY ELSE, SO I COULDN'T SAY I LOVE THEM YET...
OF COURSE HE IS. IF HE WEREN'T, HE WOULDN'T JUST PROPOSE TO YUKIHIME-DONO OUT OF THE BLUE LIKE THAT!!
B-B-B-BUT THIS IS A GOOD THING. IF WHAT I REALLY MEANT HAD GOTTEN THROUGH TO HIM, THERE WOULD HAVE BEEN NO GOING BACK!
IF IT HAD REALLY GOTTEN THROUGH TO HIM...
ドキ B-DMP ドキ B-DMP ドキ B-DMP ドキ B-DMP
IF IT HAD REALLY GOTTEN THROUGH TO HIM...
...WHAT WOULD HAVE HAPPENED THEN?
ドキ B-DMP ドキ B-DMP ドキ B-DMP ドキ B-DMP
MY HEART IS POUNDING OUT OF MY CHEST.
THIS CAN ONLY MEAN...
ドキ B-DMP ドキ B-DMP ドキ B-DMP

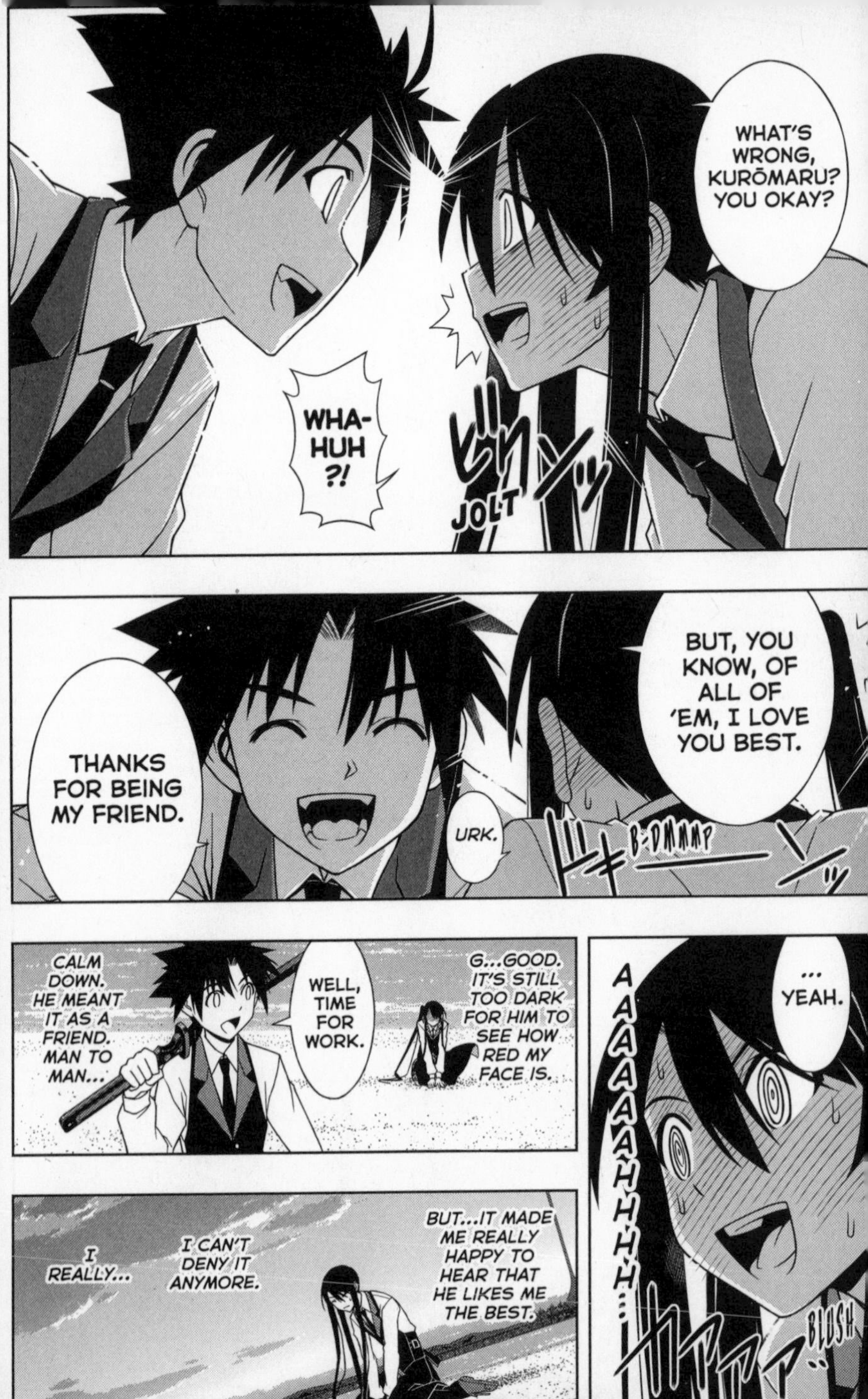
WHAT'S WRONG, KURŌMARU? YOU OKAY?
WHA-HUH ?!
JOLT
BUT, YOU KNOW, OF ALL OF 'EM, I LOVE YOU BEST.
B-DMMMP
URK.
THANKS FOR BEING MY FRIEND.
... YEAH.
AAAAAAAHHHH...
BLUSH
G...GOOD. IT'S STILL TOO DARK FOR HIM TO SEE HOW RED MY FACE IS.
WELL, TIME FOR WORK.
CALM DOWN. HE MEANT IT AS A FRIEND. MAN TO MAN...
BUT...IT MADE ME REALLY HAPPY TO HEAR THAT HE LIKES ME THE BEST.
I CAN'T DENY IT ANYMORE.
I REALLY...

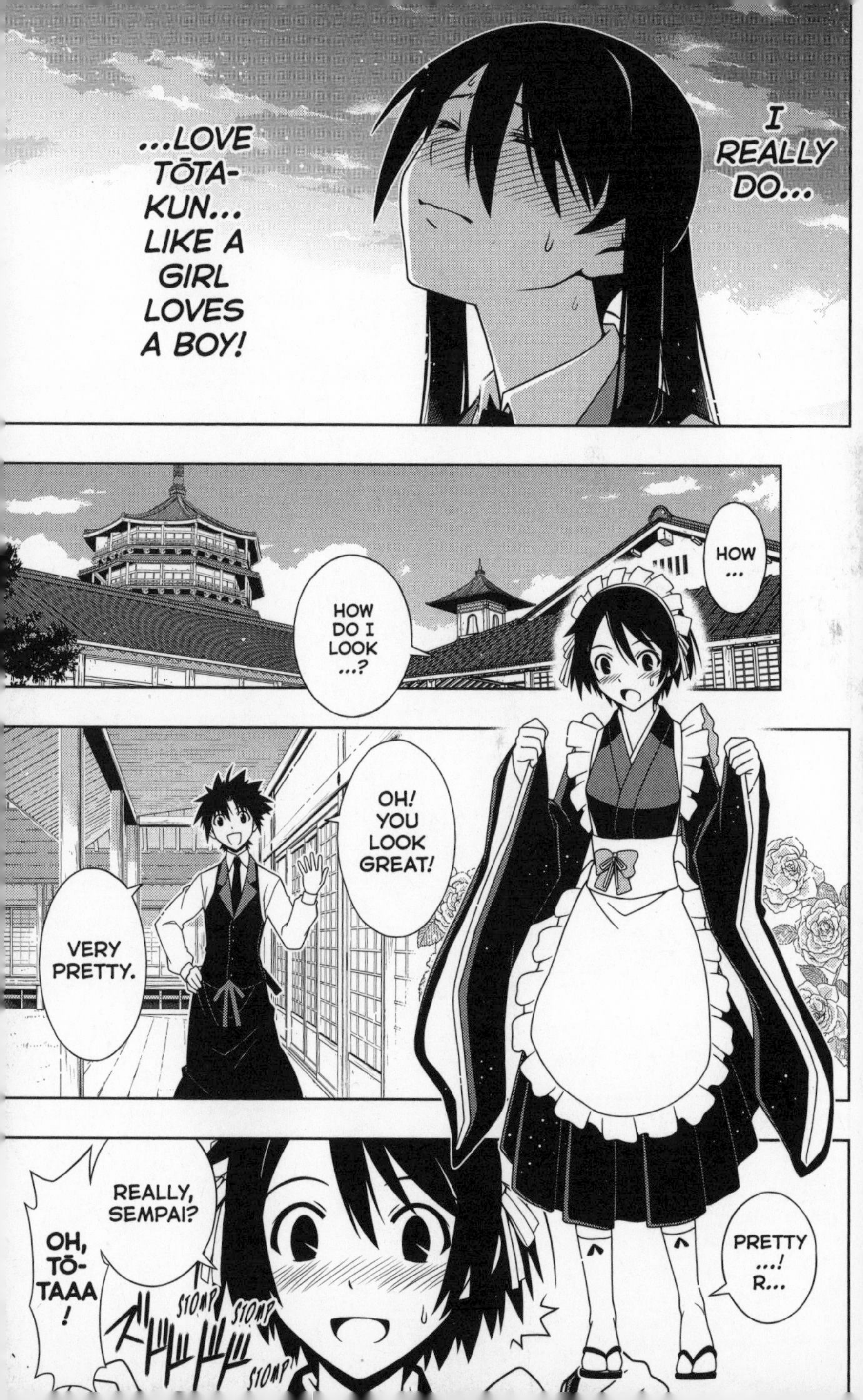
I REALLY DO...
...LOVE TŌTA-KUN... LIKE A GIRL LOVES A BOY!
HOW...
HOW DO I LOOK...?
OH! YOU LOOK GREAT!
VERY PRETTY.
PRETTY...! R...
REALLY, SEMPAI?
OH, TŌ-TAAA!
STOMP
STOMP
STOMP

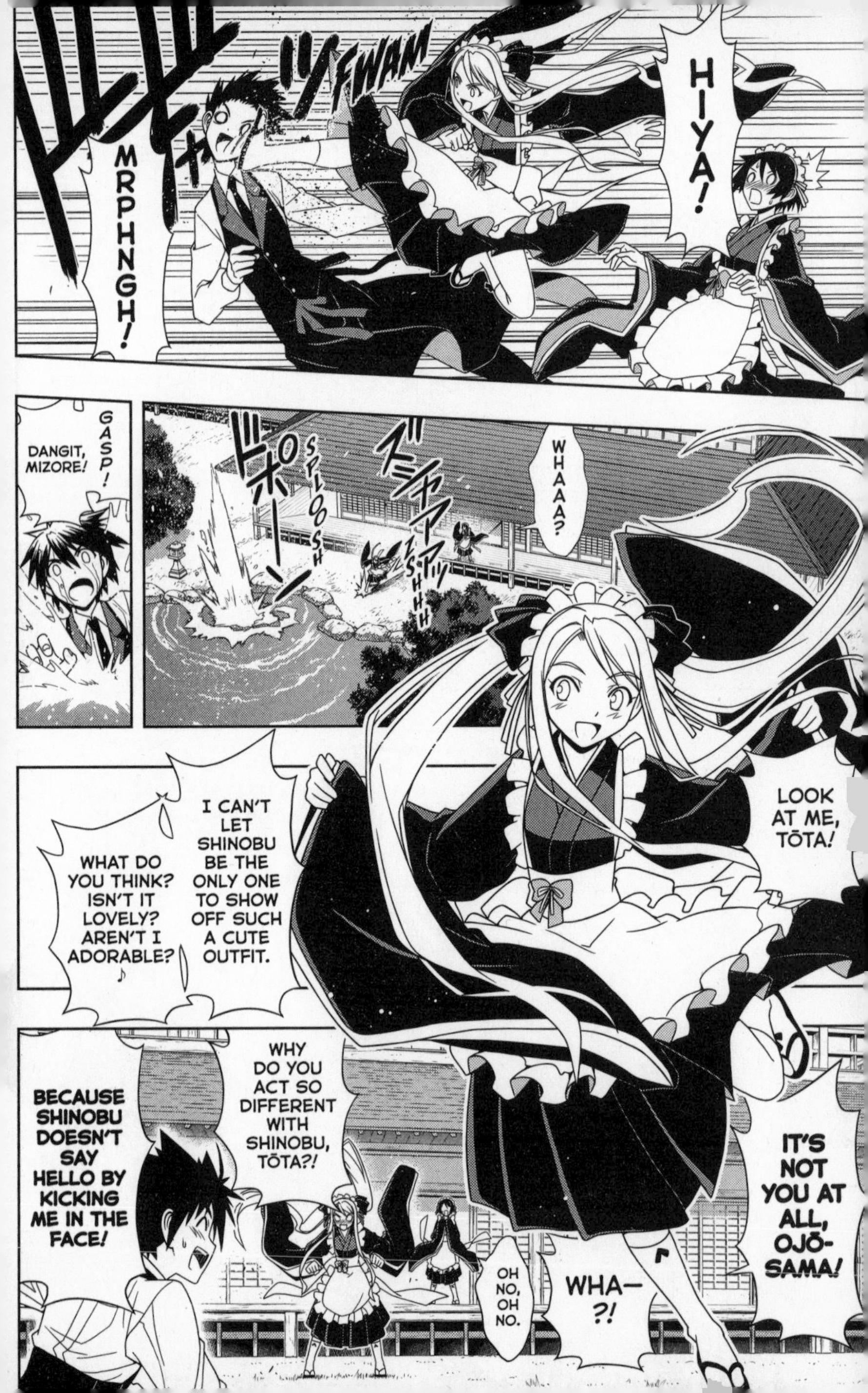
HIYA!
FWAM
MRPHNGH!
WHAAA?
ZSHHH
SPLOOSH
GASP!
DANGIT, MIZORE!
LOOK AT ME, TŌTA!
I CAN'T LET SHINOBU BE THE ONLY ONE TO SHOW OFF SUCH A CUTE OUTFIT.
WHAT DO YOU THINK? ISN'T IT LOVELY? AREN'T I ADORABLE? ♪
IT'S NOT YOU AT ALL, OJŌ-SAMA!
WHA—?!
OH NO, OH NO.
WHY DO YOU ACT SO DIFFERENT WITH SHINOBU, TŌTA?!
BECAUSE SHINOBU DOESN'T SAY HELLO BY KICKING ME IN THE FACE!

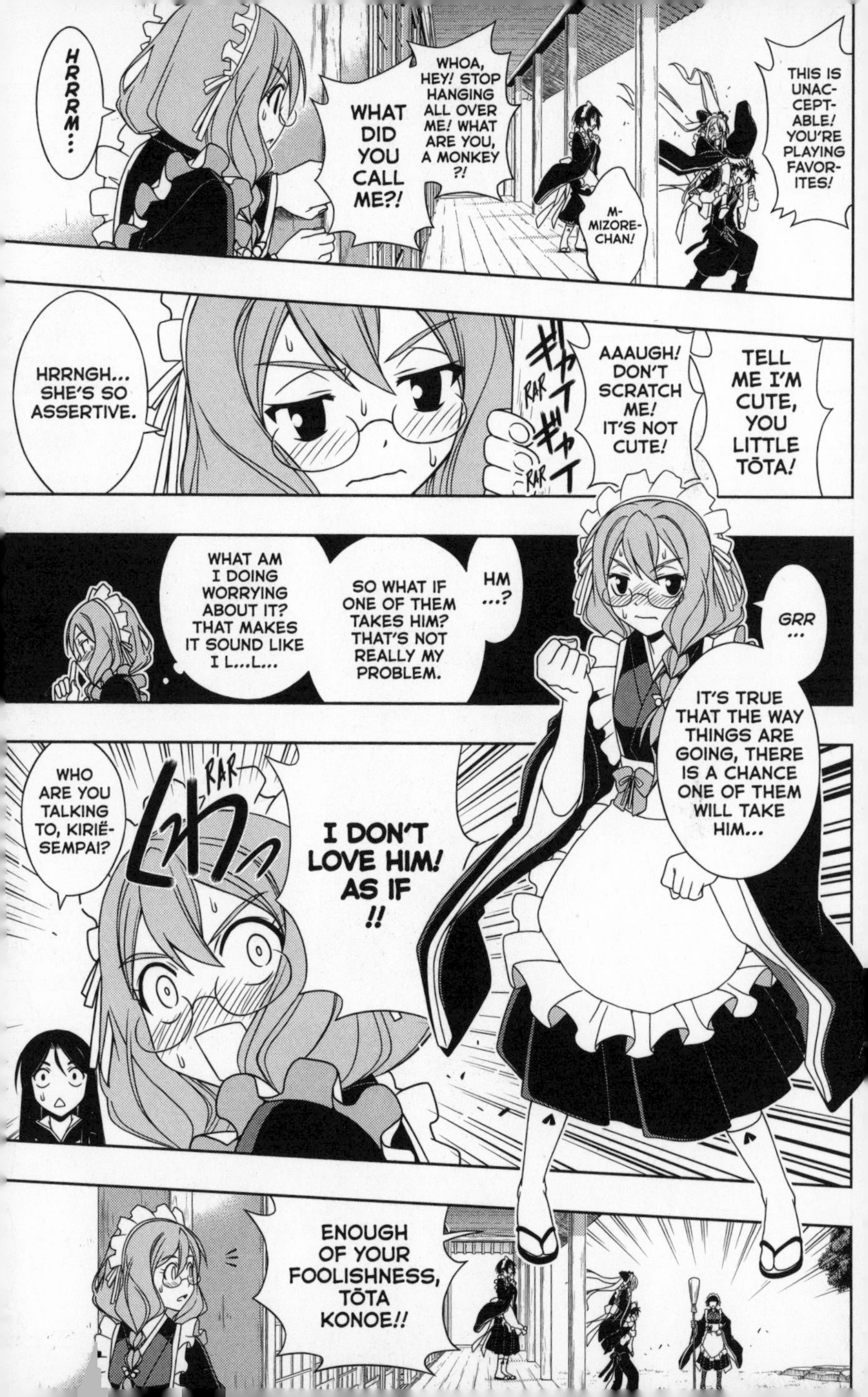

THIS IS UNACCEPTABLE! YOU'RE PLAYING FAVORITES!
WHOA, HEY! STOP HANGING ALL OVER ME! WHAT ARE YOU, A MONKEY?!
M-MIZORE-CHAN!
WHAT DID YOU CALL ME?!
HRRRM...
TELL ME I'M CUTE, YOU LITTLE TŌTA!
AAAUGH! DON'T SCRATCH ME! IT'S NOT CUTE!
RAR
RAR
HRRNGH... SHE'S SO ASSERTIVE.
GRR...
IT'S TRUE THAT THE WAY THINGS ARE GOING, THERE IS A CHANCE ONE OF THEM WILL TAKE HIM...
HM...?
SO WHAT IF ONE OF THEM TAKES HIM? THAT'S NOT REALLY MY PROBLEM.
WHAT AM I DOING WORRYING ABOUT IT? THAT MAKES IT SOUND LIKE I L...L...
I DON'T LOVE HIM! AS IF!!
RAR
WHO ARE YOU TALKING TO, KIRIË-SEMPAI?
ENOUGH OF YOUR FOOLISHNESS, TŌTA KONOE!!

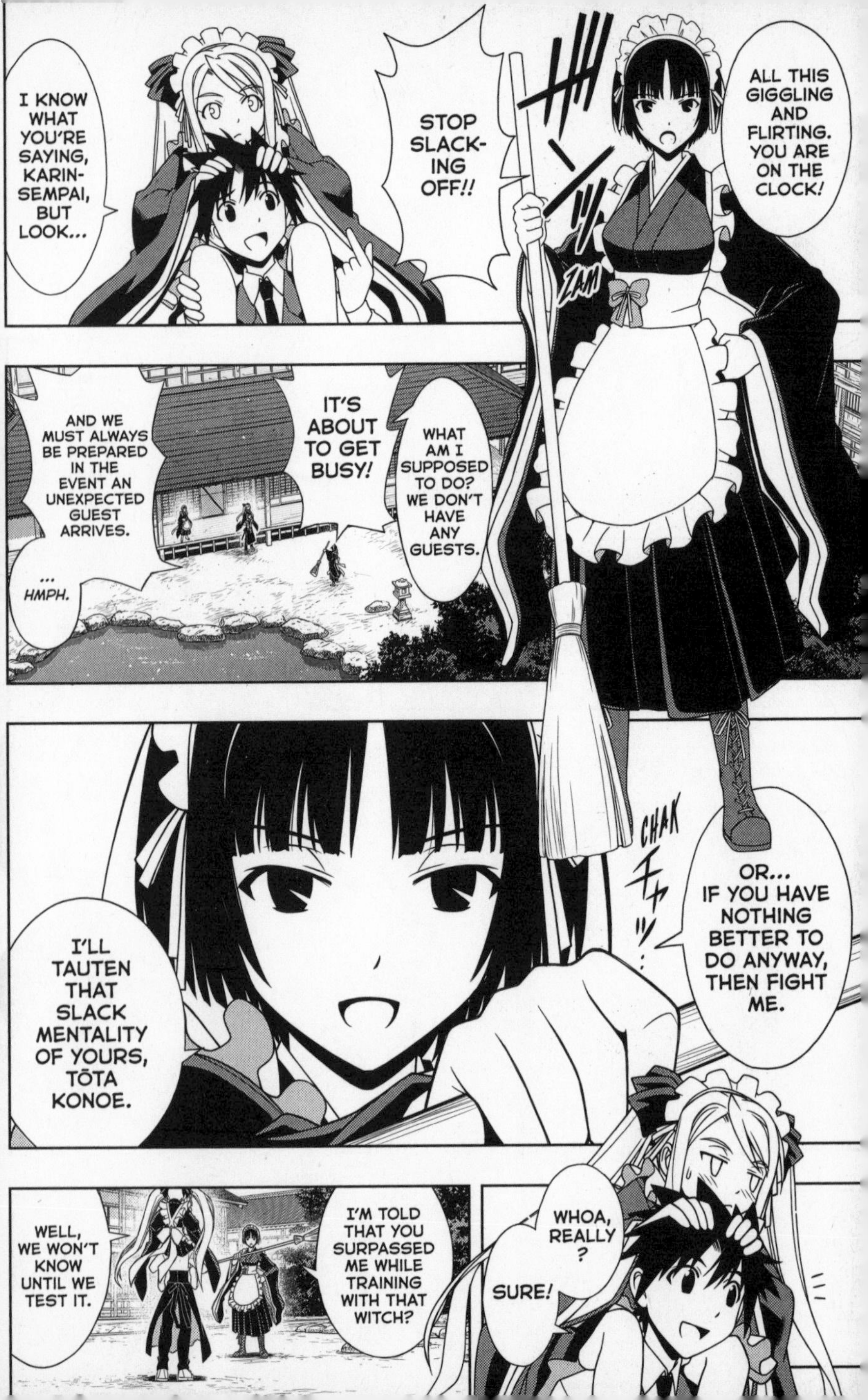
ALL THIS GIGGLING AND FLIRTING. YOU ARE ON THE CLOCK!
ZAM
STOP SLACKING OFF!!
I KNOW WHAT YOU'RE SAYING, KARIN-SEMPAI, BUT LOOK...
WHAT AM I SUPPOSED TO DO? WE DON'T HAVE ANY GUESTS.
IT'S ABOUT TO GET BUSY!
AND WE MUST ALWAYS BE PREPARED IN THE EVENT AN UNEXPECTED GUEST ARRIVES.
... HMPH.
CHAK
OR... IF YOU HAVE NOTHING BETTER TO DO ANYWAY, THEN FIGHT ME.
I'LL TAUTEN THAT SLACK MENTALITY OF YOURS, TŌTA KONOE.
WHOA, REALLY?
SURE!
I'M TOLD THAT YOU SURPASSED ME WHILE TRAINING WITH THAT WITCH?
WELL, WE WON'T KNOW UNTIL WE TEST IT.

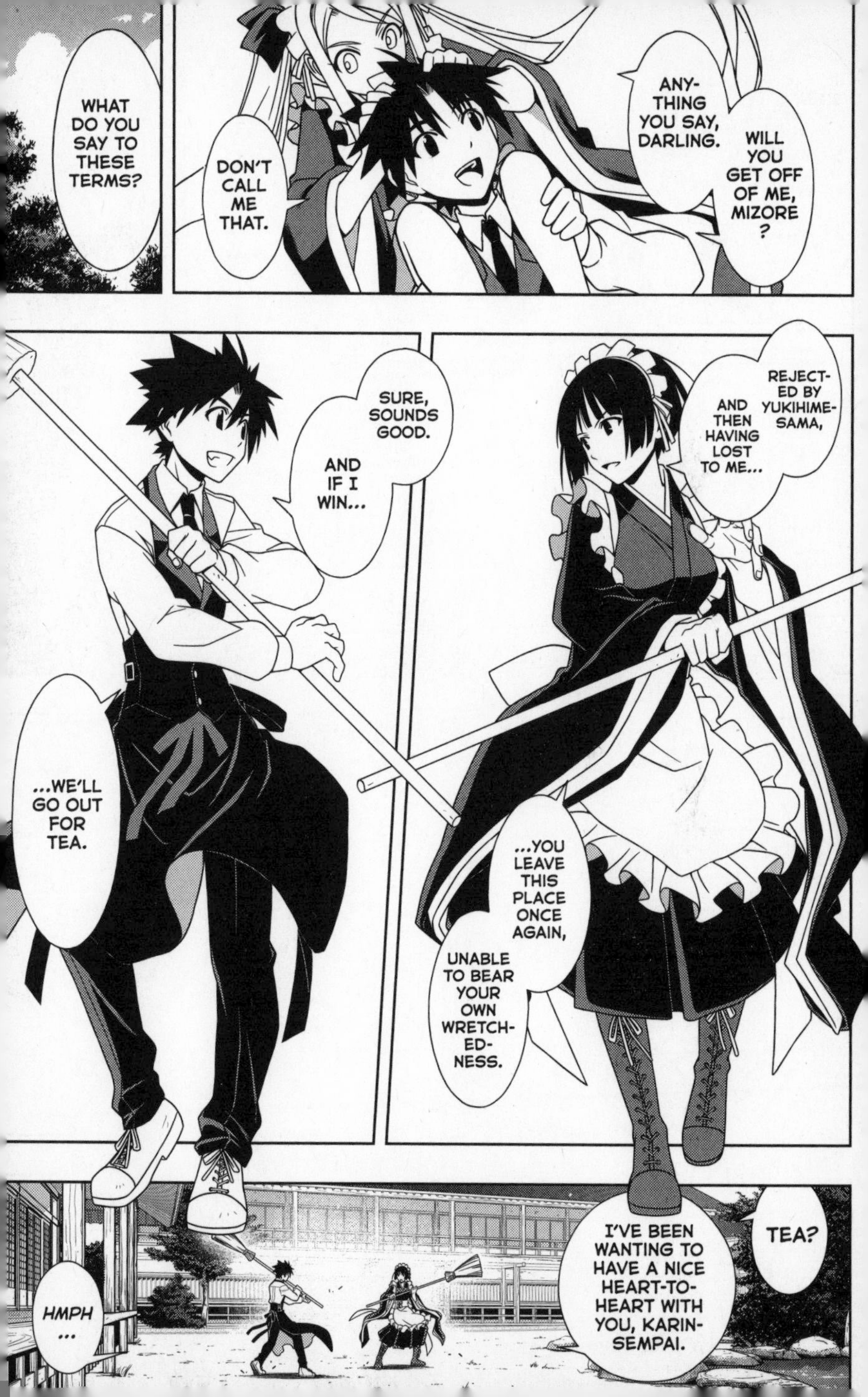
WILL YOU GET OFF OF ME, MIZORE?
ANYTHING YOU SAY, DARLING.
DON'T CALL ME THAT.
WHAT DO YOU SAY TO THESE TERMS?
REJECTED BY YUKIHIME-SAMA,
AND THEN HAVING LOST TO ME...
...YOU LEAVE THIS PLACE ONCE AGAIN,
UNABLE TO BEAR YOUR OWN WRETCHEDNESS.
SURE, SOUNDS GOOD.
AND IF I WIN...
...WE'LL GO OUT FOR TEA.
TEA?
I'VE BEEN WANTING TO HAVE A NICE HEART-TO-HEART WITH YOU, KARIN-SEMPAI.
HMPH...

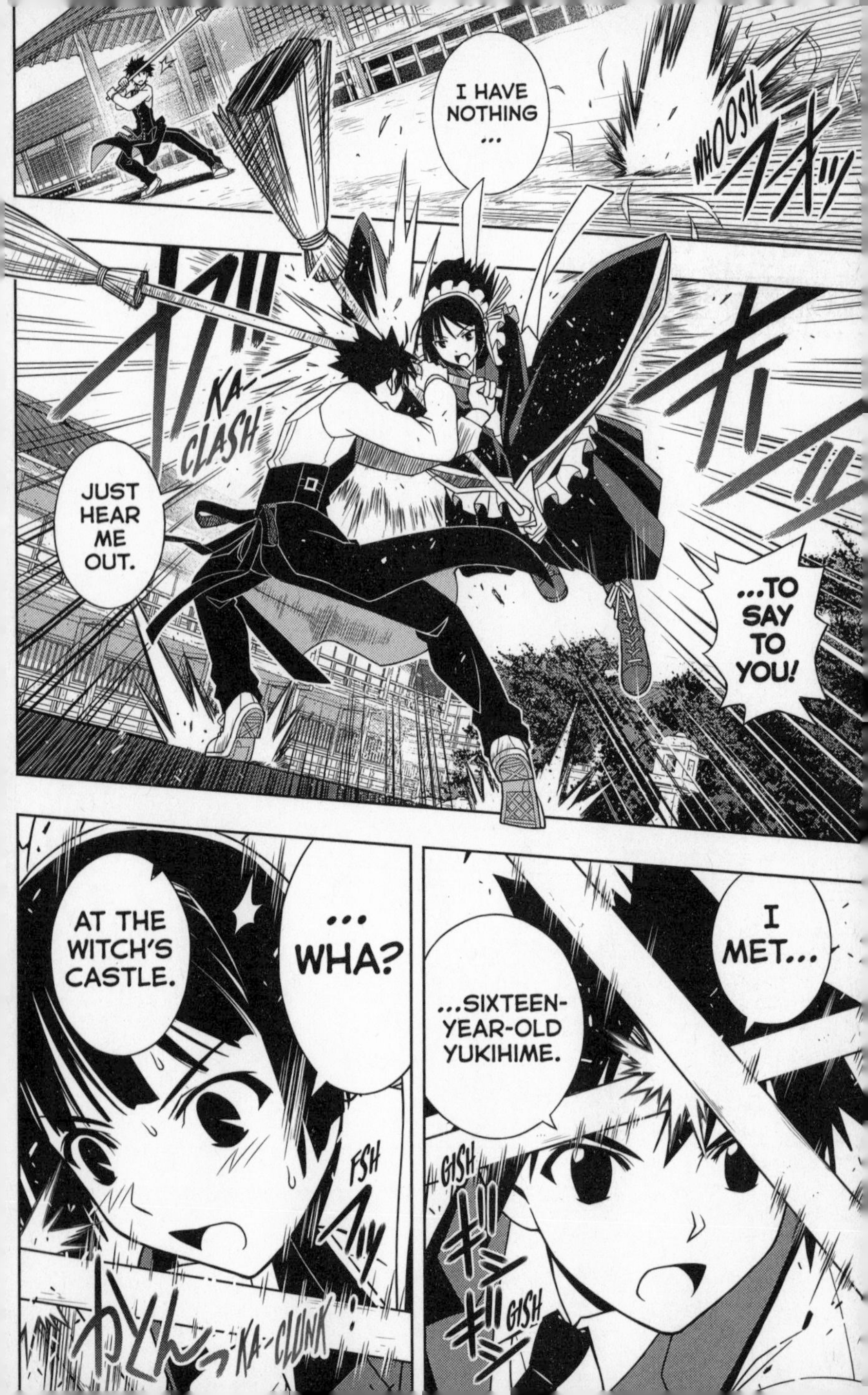

I HAVE NOTHING ...
WHOOSH
...TO SAY TO YOU!
KA-CLASH
JUST HEAR ME OUT.
I MET...
...SIXTEEN-YEAR-OLD YUKIHIME.
GISH
GISH
... WHA?
AT THE WITCH'S CASTLE.
FSH
KA-CLUNK

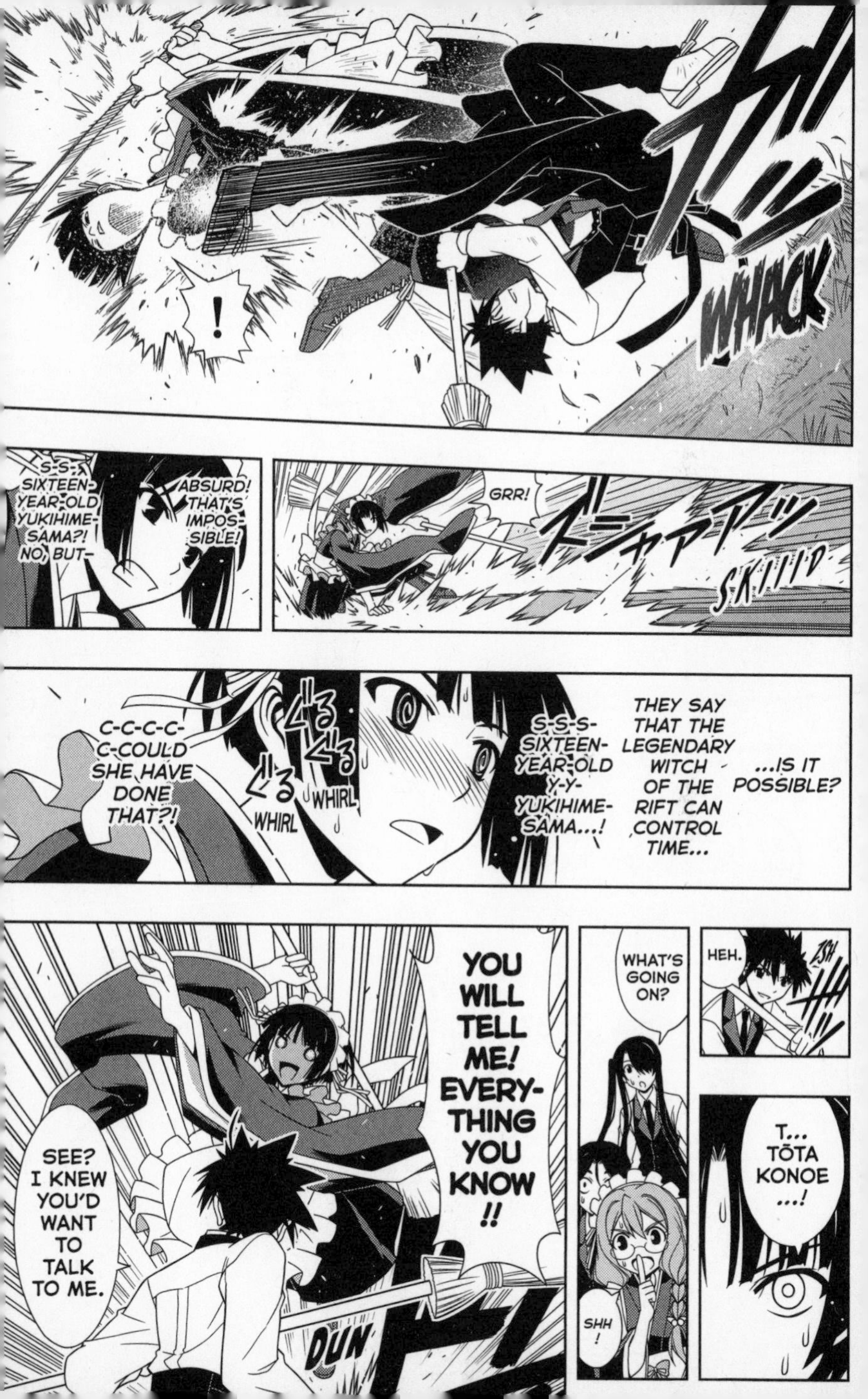
WHACK
!
GRR!
ズシャアアッ
SKIIID
ABSURD! THAT'S IMPOSSIBLE!
S-S-SIXTEEN-YEAR-OLD YUKIHIME-SAMA?! NO, BUT-
...IS IT POSSIBLE?
THEY SAY THAT THE LEGENDARY WITCH OF THE RIFT CAN CONTROL TIME...
S-S-S-SIXTEEN-YEAR-OLD Y-Y-YUKIHIME-SAMA...!
ぐるぐるぐる
WHIRL
WHIRL
C-C-C-C-C-COULD SHE HAVE DONE THAT?!
HEH.
TSH
T... TŌTA KONOE ...!
WHAT'S GOING ON?
SHH!
YOU WILL TELL ME! EVERYTHING YOU KNOW!!
SEE? I KNEW YOU'D WANT TO TALK TO ME.
DUN

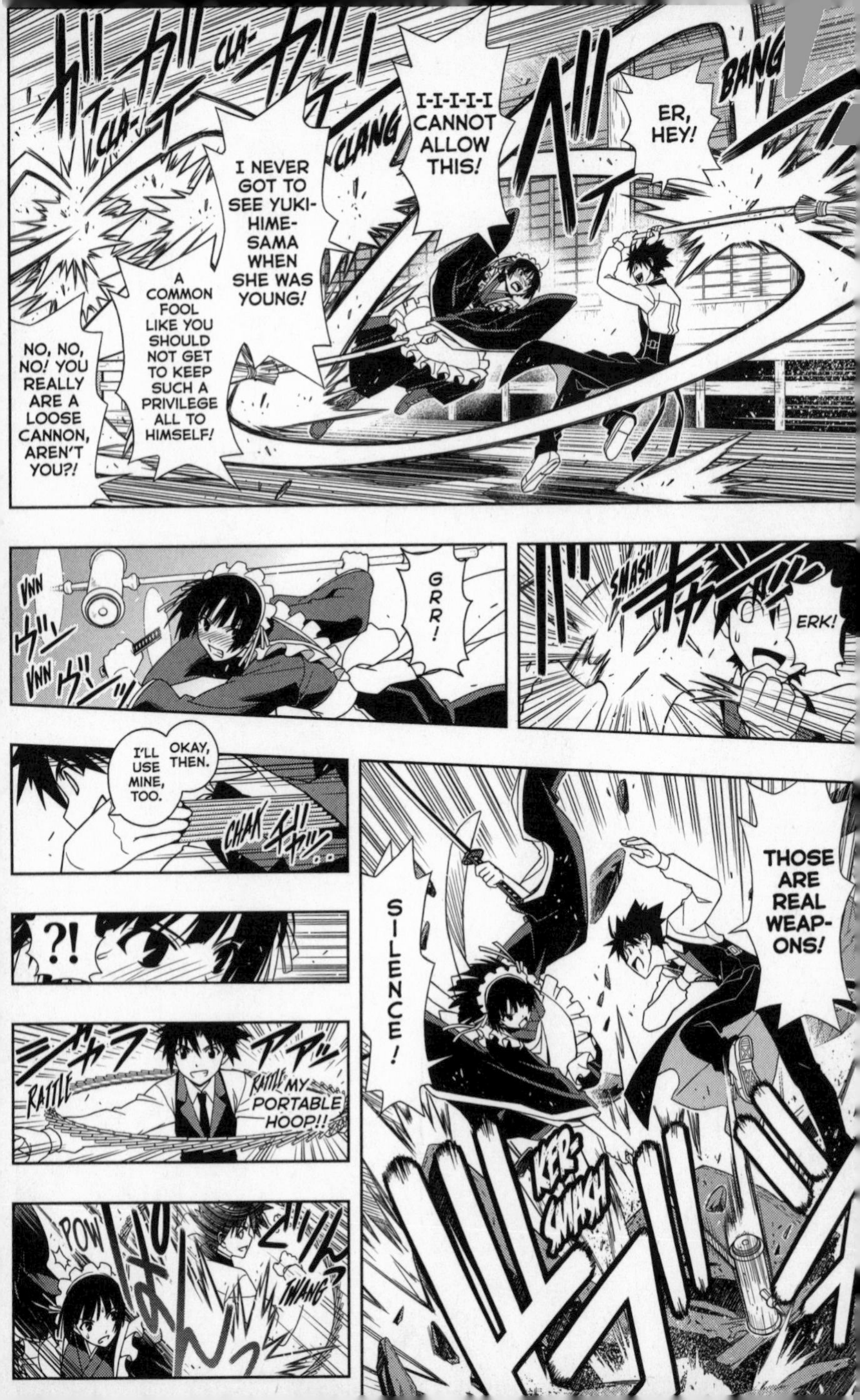
BANG
ER, HEY!
I-I-I-I-I CANNOT ALLOW THIS!
CLANG
I NEVER GOT TO SEE YUKI-HIME-SAMA WHEN SHE WAS YOUNG!
CLA-
CLA-
A COMMON FOOL LIKE YOU SHOULD NOT GET TO KEEP SUCH A PRIVILEGE ALL TO HIMSELF!
NO, NO, NO! YOU REALLY ARE A LOOSE CANNON, AREN'T YOU?!
SMASH
ERK!
GRR!
VNN
VNN
THOSE ARE REAL WEAPONS!
SILENCE!
KER-SMASH
OKAY, THEN.
I'LL USE MINE, TOO.
CHAK
?!
RATTLE
RATTLE
MY PORTABLE HOOP!!
POW
TWANG

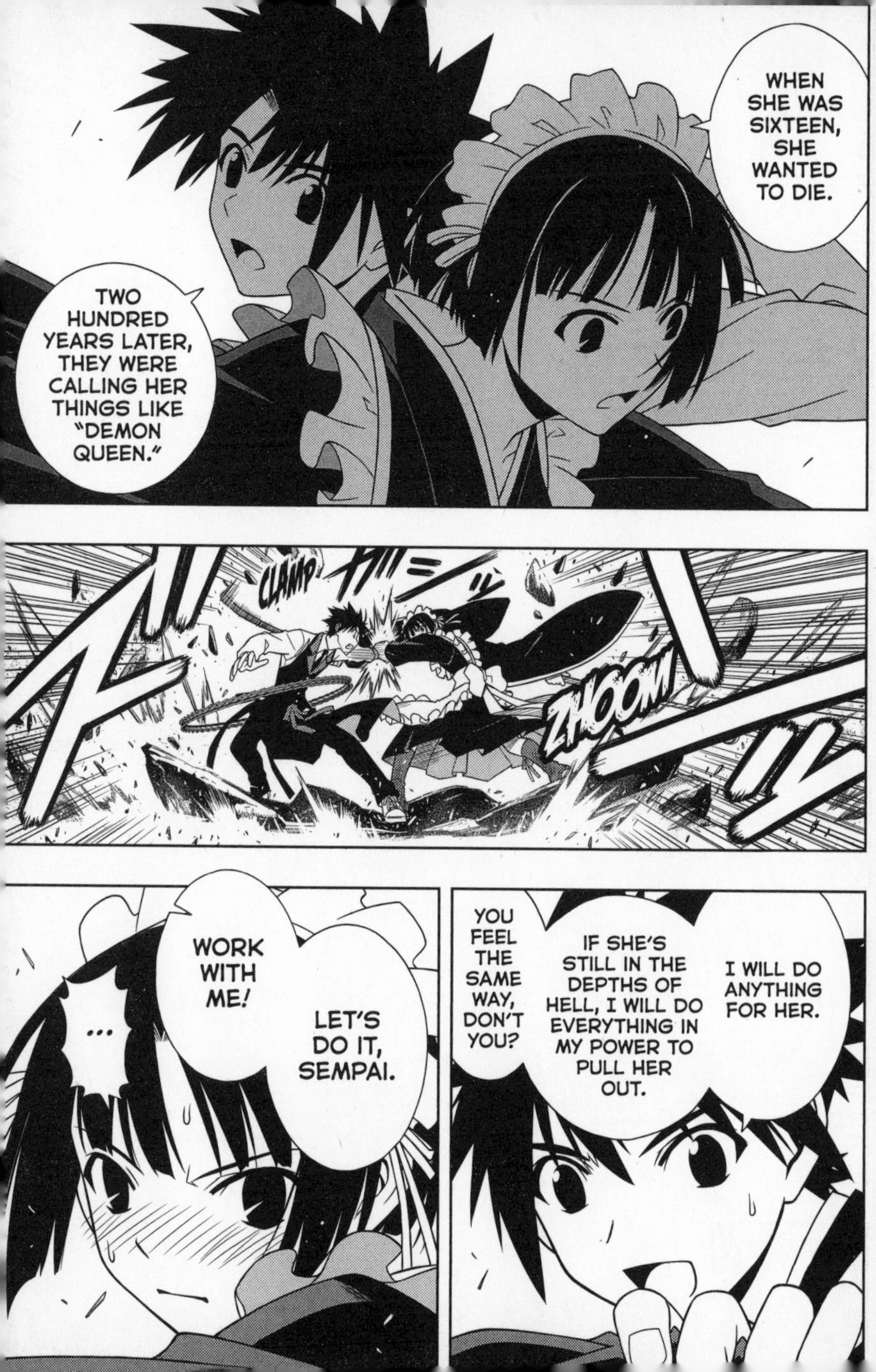
WHEN SHE WAS SIXTEEN, SHE WANTED TO DIE.
TWO HUNDRED YEARS LATER, THEY WERE CALLING HER THINGS LIKE "DEMON QUEEN."
CLAMP
ZHOOM
I WILL DO ANYTHING FOR HER.
IF SHE'S STILL IN THE DEPTHS OF HELL, I WILL DO EVERYTHING IN MY POWER TO PULL HER OUT.
YOU FEEL THE SAME WAY, DON'T YOU?
LET'S DO IT, SEMPAI.
WORK WITH ME!
...

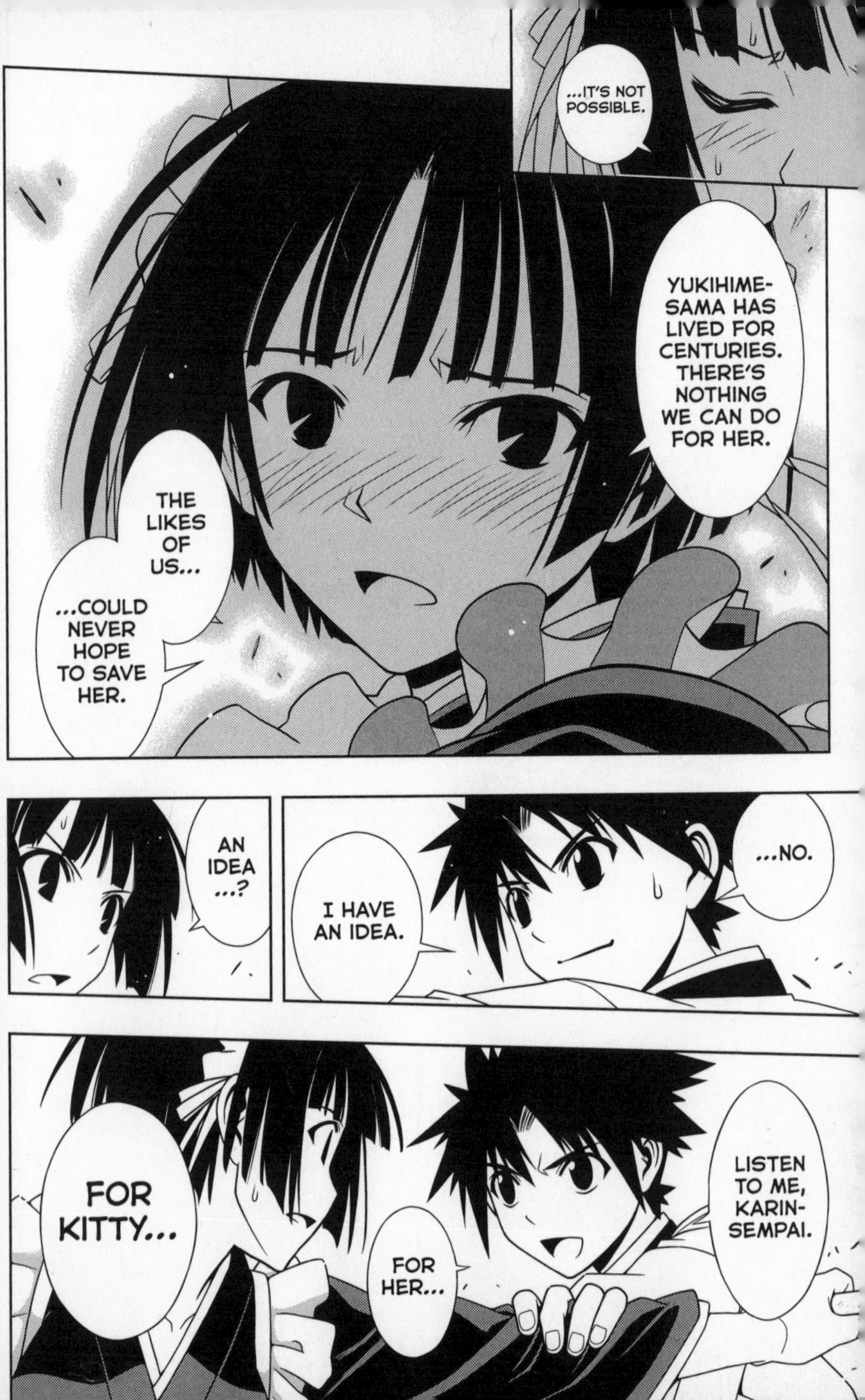
...IT'S NOT POSSIBLE.
YUKIHIME-SAMA HAS LIVED FOR CENTURIES. THERE'S NOTHING WE CAN DO FOR HER.
THE LIKES OF US...
...COULD NEVER HOPE TO SAVE HER.
...NO.
I HAVE AN IDEA.
AN IDEA...?
LISTEN TO ME, KARIN-SEMPAI.
FOR HER...
FOR KITTY...

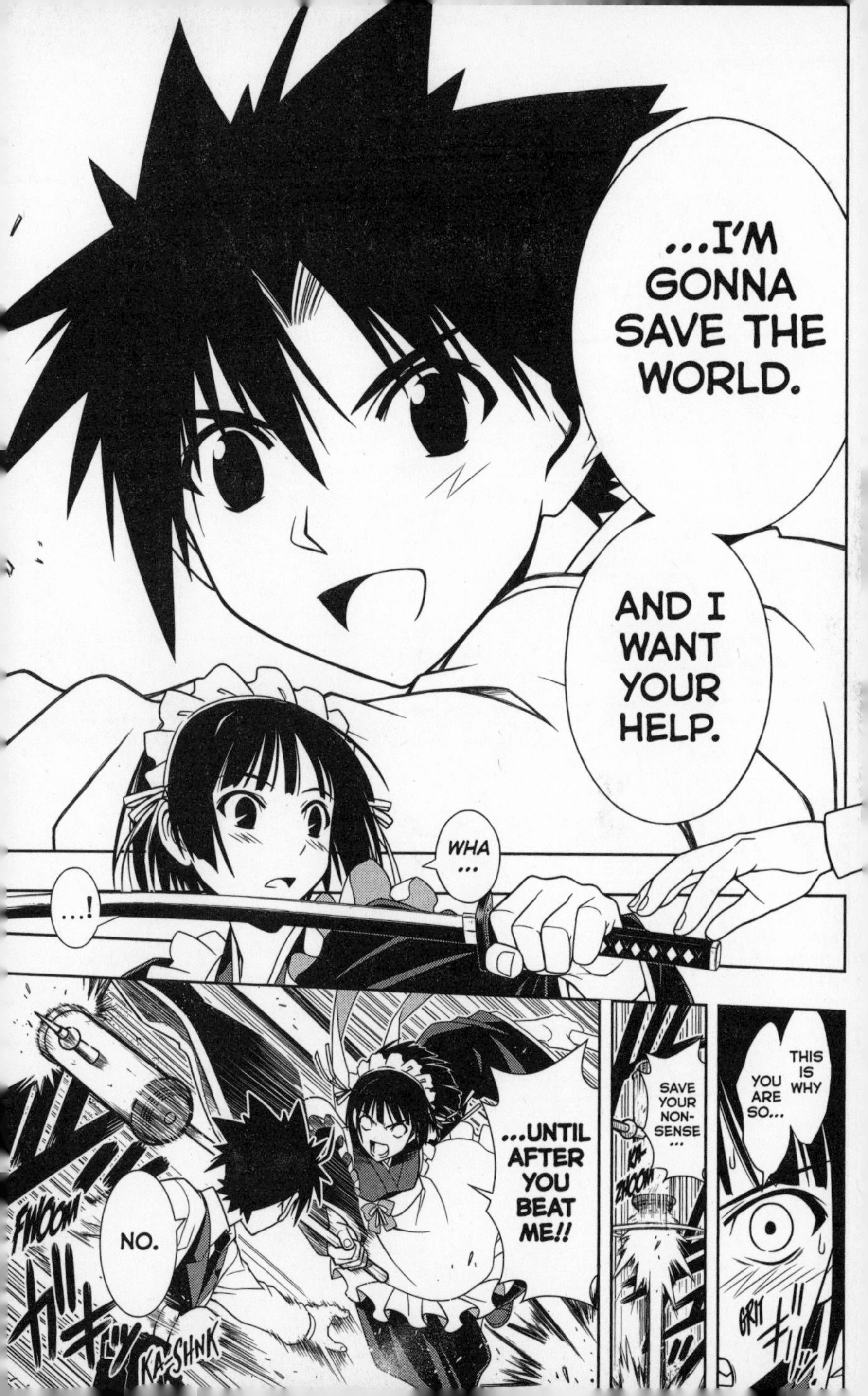
...I'M GONNA SAVE THE WORLD.
AND I WANT YOUR HELP.
WHA...
...!
THIS IS WHY YOU ARE SO...
SAVE YOUR NON-SENSE...
KA-ZHOOM
...UNTIL AFTER YOU BEAT ME!!
NO.
FWOOM
KA-SHNK

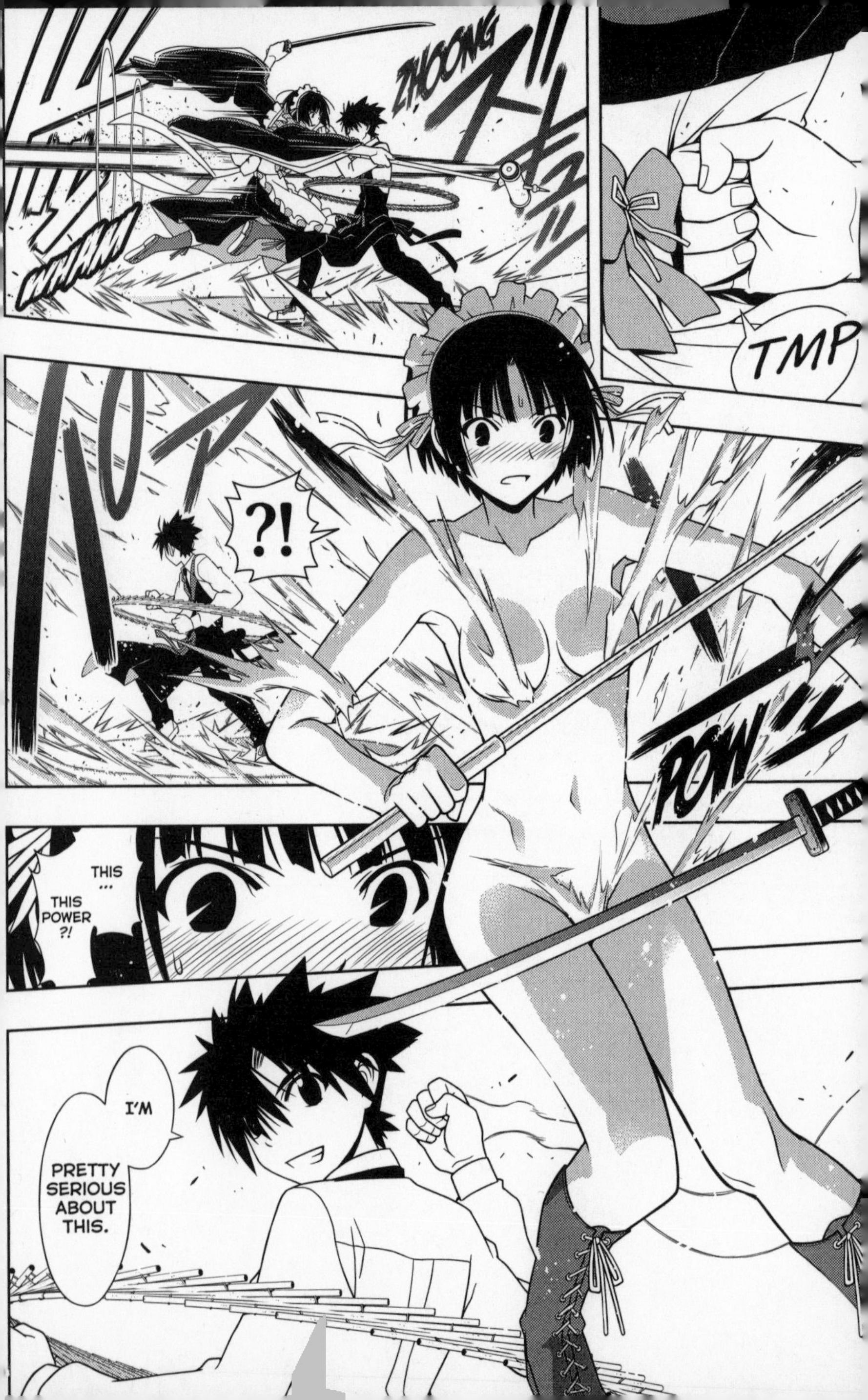
TMP
ZHOONG
?!
POW
THIS ... THIS POWER ?!
I'M PRETTY SERIOUS ABOUT THIS.

悠UQ HOLDER!

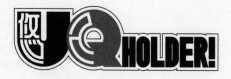

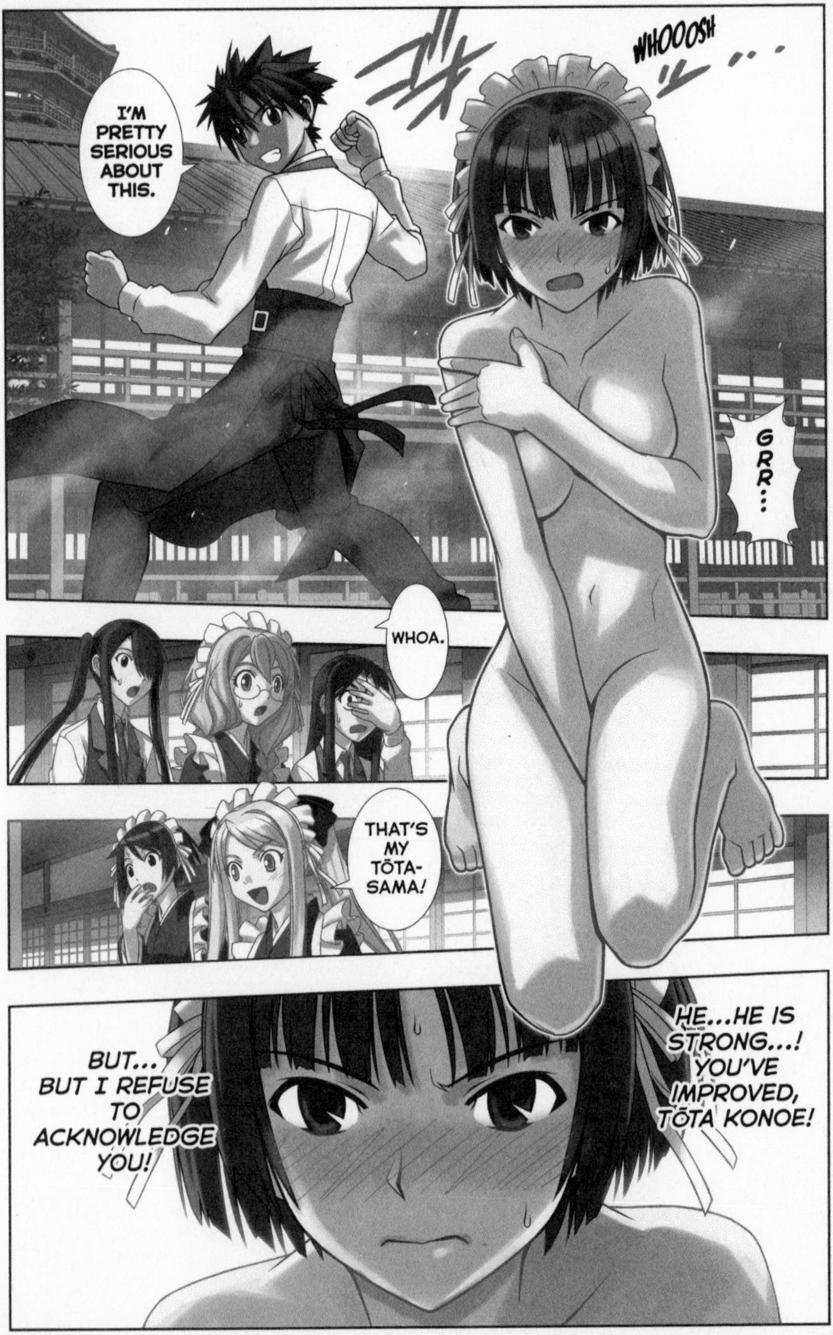
WHOOOSH
GRR...
I'M PRETTY SERIOUS ABOUT THIS.
WHOA.
THAT'S MY TŌTA-SAMA!
HE...HE IS STRONG...! YOU'VE IMPROVED, TŌTA KONOE!
BUT... BUT I REFUSE TO ACKNOWLEDGE YOU!

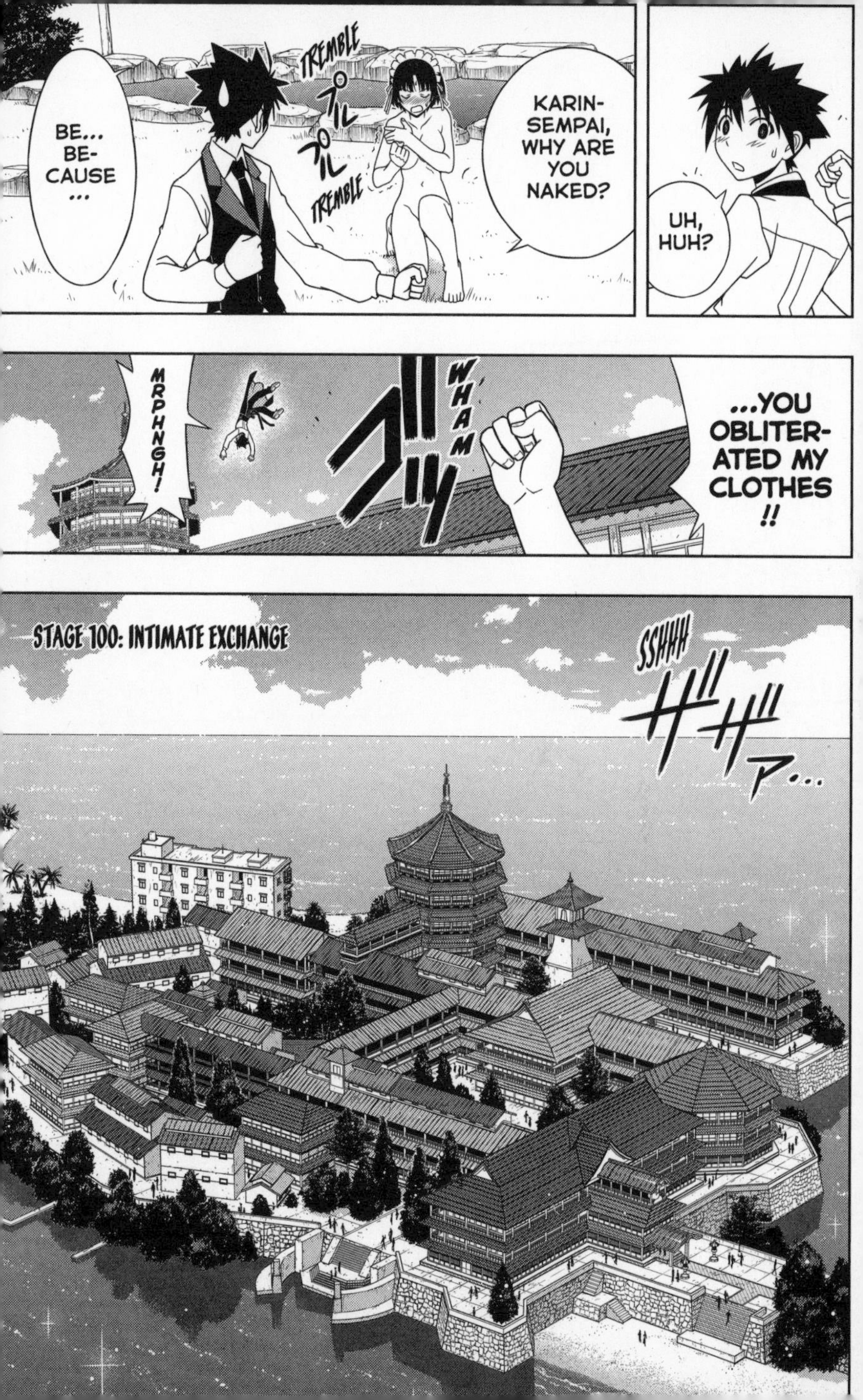
UH, HUH?
KARIN-SEMPAI, WHY ARE YOU NAKED?
TREMBLE
プル
プル
TREMBLE
BE... BE-CAUSE...
...YOU OBLITER-ATED MY CLOTHES!!
WHAM
ゴッ
MRPHNGH!
STAGE 100: INTIMATE EXCHANGE
SSHHH
ザザァ...

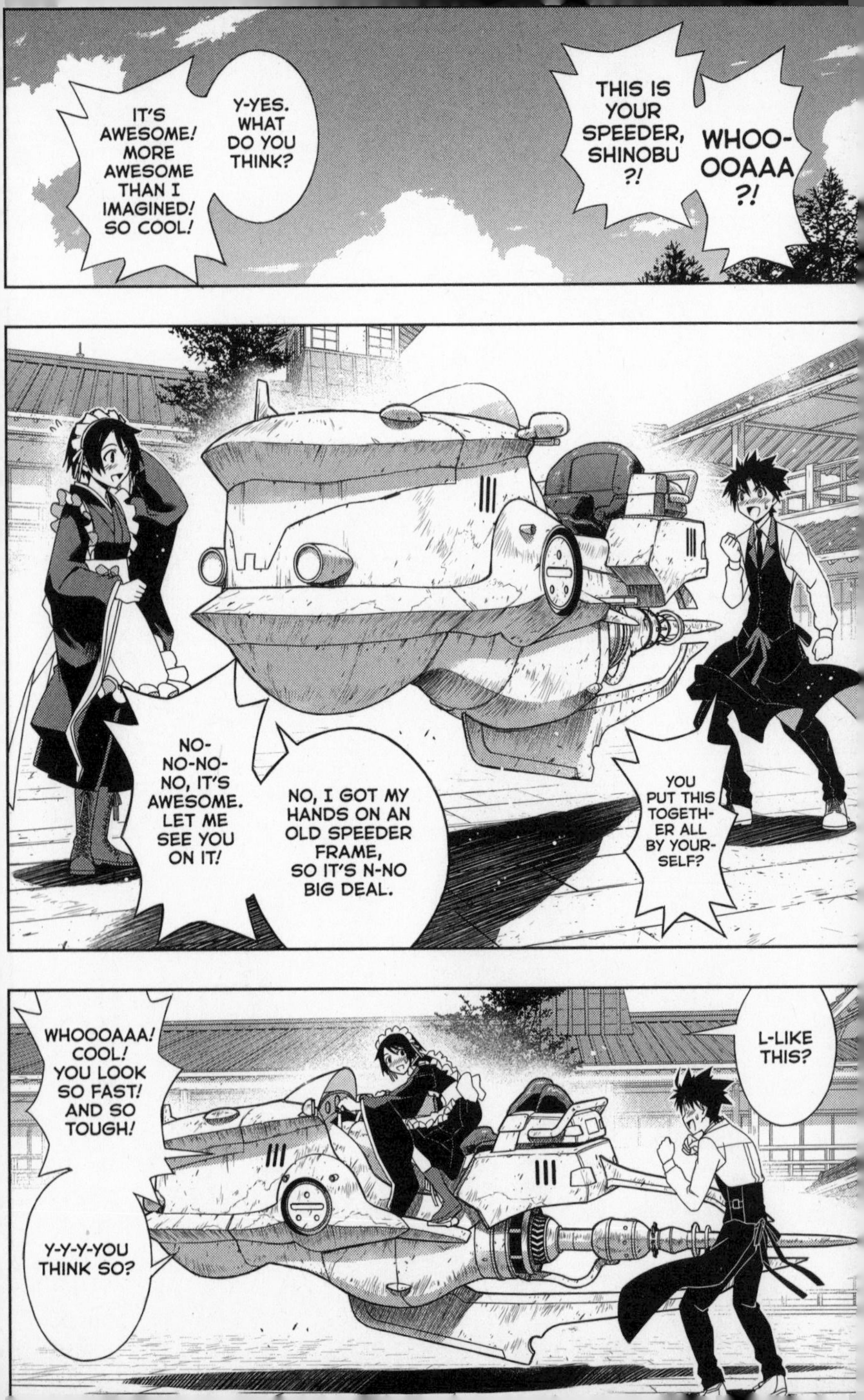
WHOO-OOAAA?!
THIS IS YOUR SPEEDER, SHINOBU?!
Y-YES. WHAT DO YOU THINK?
IT'S AWESOME! MORE AWESOME THAN I IMAGINED! SO COOL!
YOU PUT THIS TOGETH-ER ALL BY YOUR-SELF?
NO, I GOT MY HANDS ON AN OLD SPEEDER FRAME, SO IT'S N-NO BIG DEAL.
NO-NO-NO-NO, IT'S AWESOME. LET ME SEE YOU ON IT!
L-LIKE THIS?
WHOOOOAAA! COOL! YOU LOOK SO FAST! AND SO TOUGH!
Y-Y-Y-YOU THINK SO?

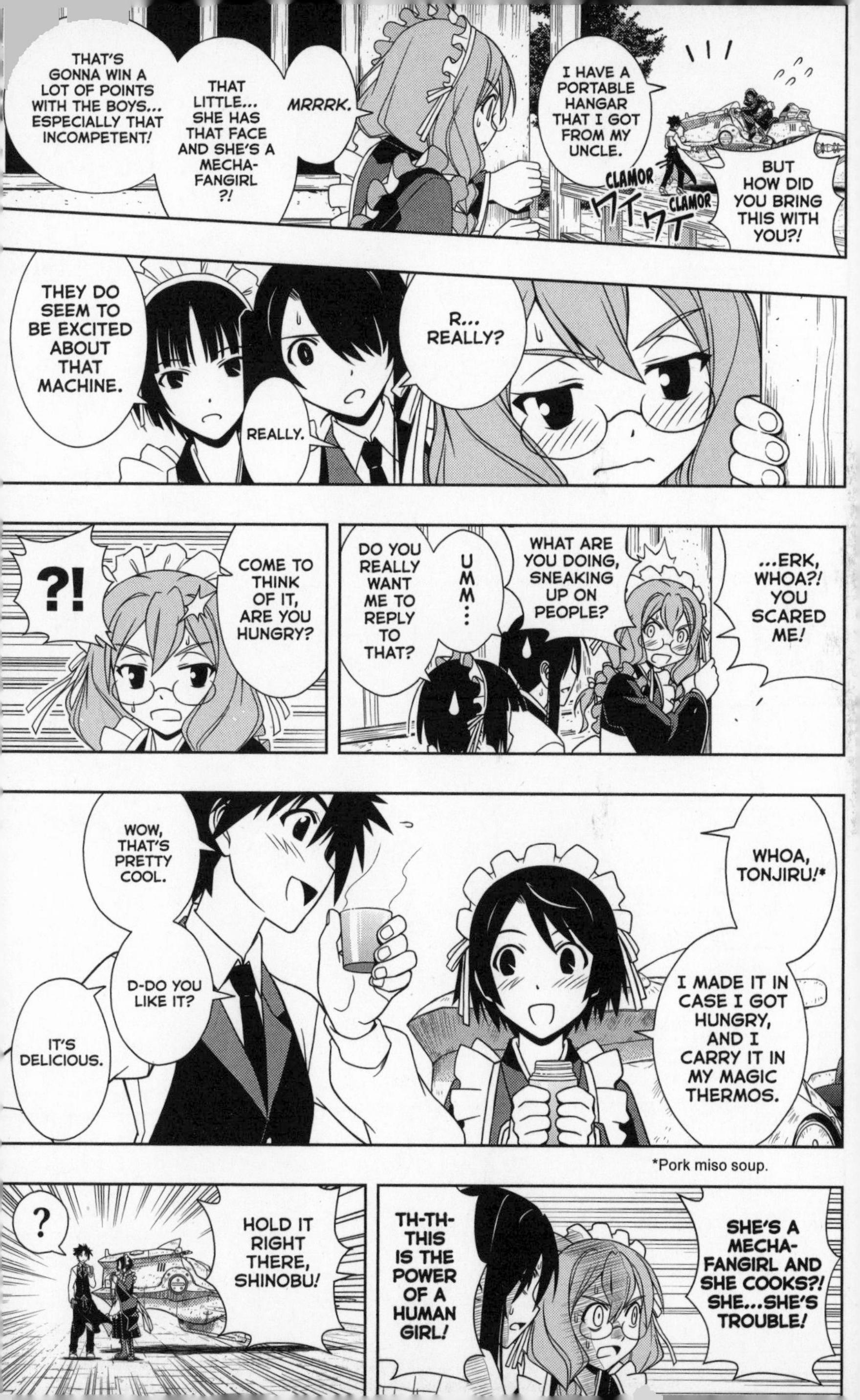
BUT HOW DID YOU BRING THIS WITH YOU?!
I HAVE A PORTABLE HANGAR THAT I GOT FROM MY UNCLE.
CLAMOR
CLAMOR
MRRRK.
THAT LITTLE... SHE HAS THAT FACE AND SHE'S A MECHA-FANGIRL ?!
THAT'S GONNA WIN A LOT OF POINTS WITH THE BOYS... ESPECIALLY THAT INCOMPETENT!
R... REALLY?
THEY DO SEEM TO BE EXCITED ABOUT THAT MACHINE.
REALLY.
...ERK, WHOA?! YOU SCARED ME!
WHAT ARE YOU DOING, SNEAKING UP ON PEOPLE?
UMM...
DO YOU REALLY WANT ME TO REPLY TO THAT?
?!
COME TO THINK OF IT, ARE YOU HUNGRY?
WHOA, TONJIRU!*
I MADE IT IN CASE I GOT HUNGRY, AND I CARRY IT IN MY MAGIC THERMOS.
WOW, THAT'S PRETTY COOL.
D-DO YOU LIKE IT?
IT'S DELICIOUS.
SHE'S A MECHA-FANGIRL AND SHE COOKS?! SHE...SHE'S TROUBLE!
TH-TH-THIS IS THE POWER OF A HUMAN GIRL!
HOLD IT RIGHT THERE, SHINOBU!
?

*Pork miso soup.

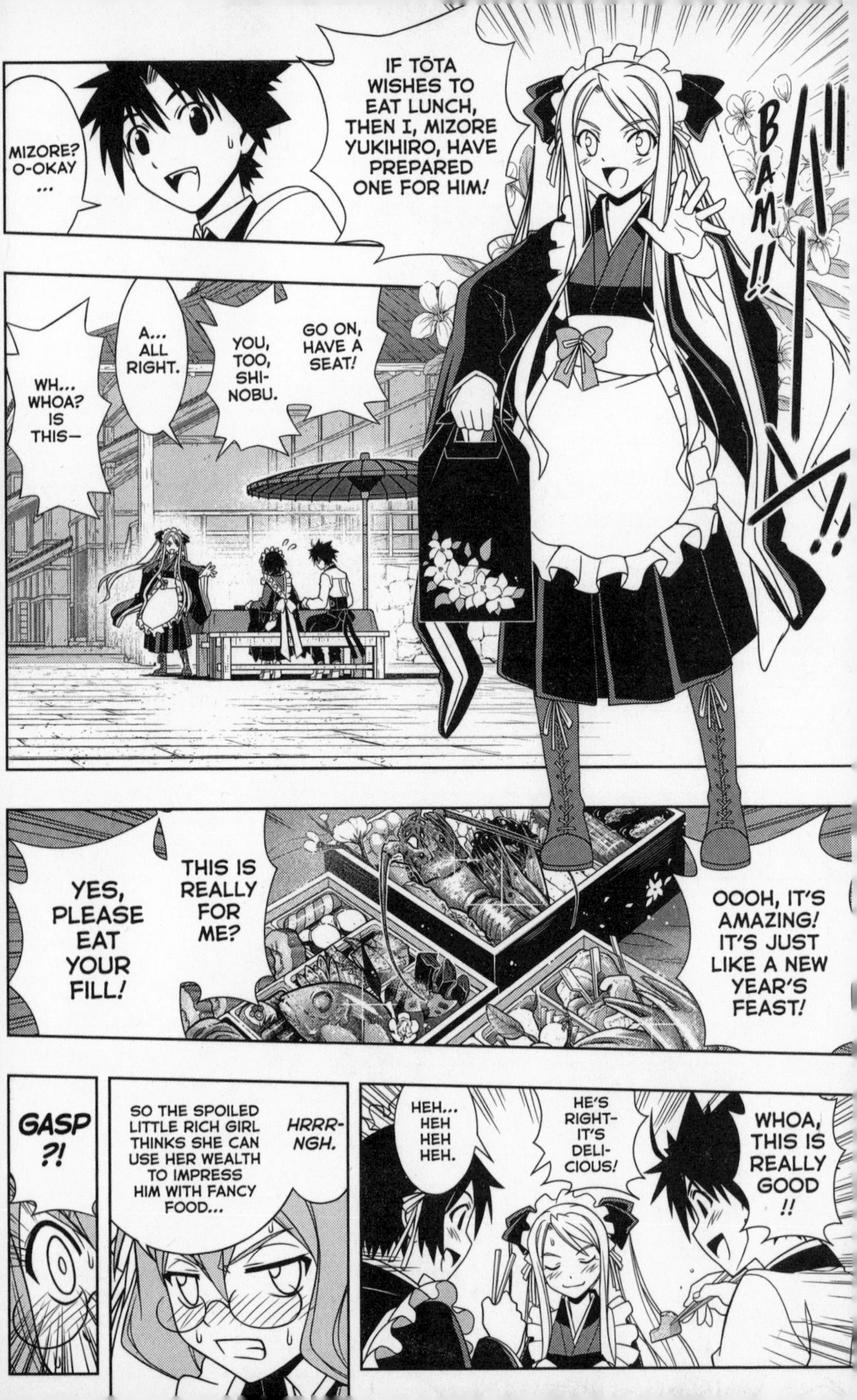
IF TŌTA WISHES TO EAT LUNCH, THEN I, MIZORE YUKIHIRO, HAVE PREPARED ONE FOR HIM!
BAM!!
MIZORE? O-OKAY ...
GO ON, HAVE A SEAT!
YOU, TOO, SHI-NOBU.
A... ALL RIGHT.
WH... WHOA? IS THIS—
OOOH, IT'S AMAZING! IT'S JUST LIKE A NEW YEAR'S FEAST!
THIS IS REALLY FOR ME?
YES, PLEASE EAT YOUR FILL!
WHOA, THIS IS REALLY GOOD !!
HE'S RIGHT- IT'S DELI-CIOUS!
HEH... HEH HEH HEH.
HRRR-NGH.
SO THE SPOILED LITTLE RICH GIRL THINKS SHE CAN USE HER WEALTH TO IMPRESS HIM WITH FANCY FOOD...
GASP ?!

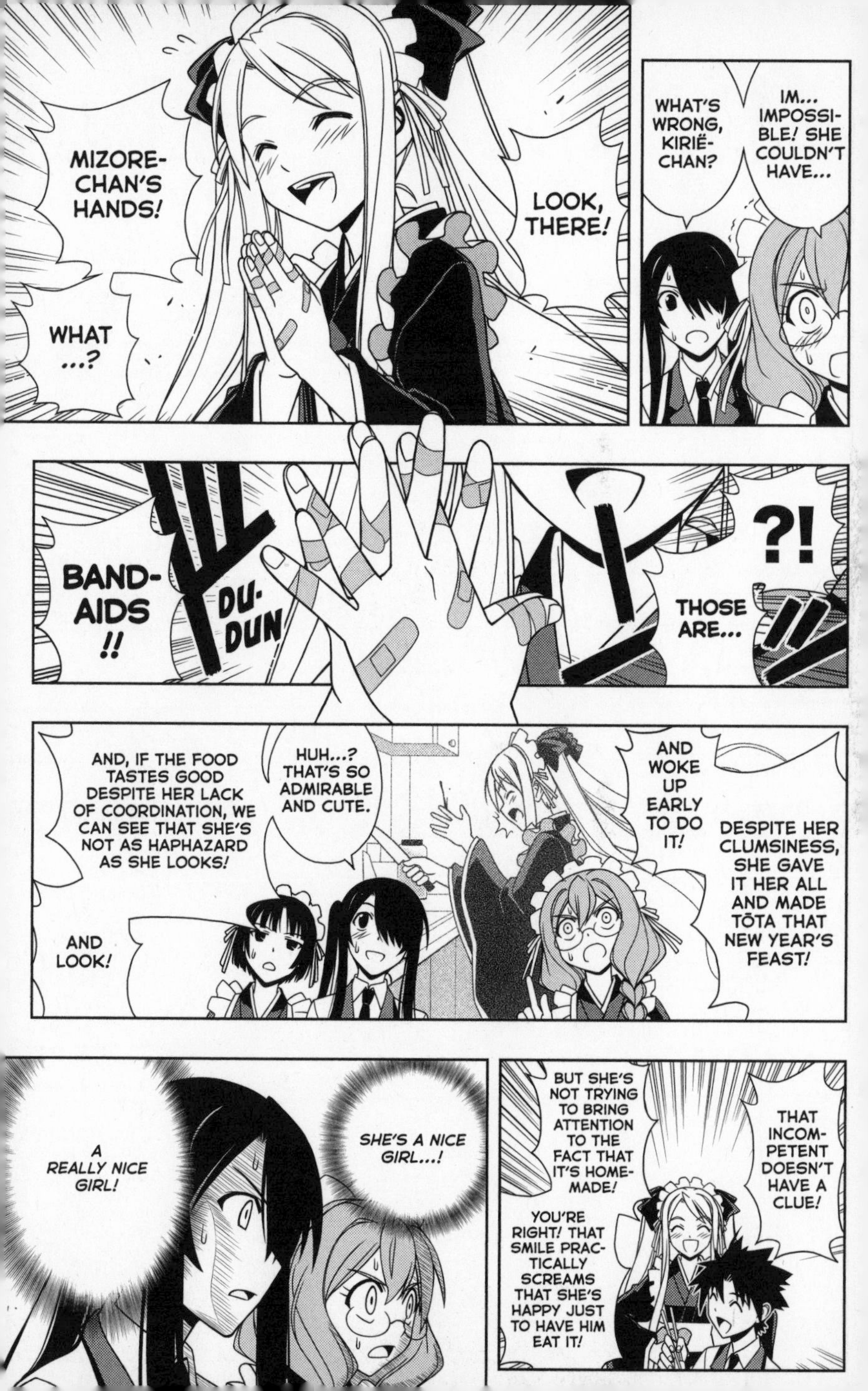
IM... IMPOSSIBLE! SHE COULDN'T HAVE...
WHAT'S WRONG, KIRIË-CHAN?
LOOK, THERE!
MIZORE-CHAN'S HANDS!
WHAT ...?
?!
THOSE ARE...
DU-DUN
BAND-AIDS !!
DESPITE HER CLUMSINESS, SHE GAVE IT HER ALL AND MADE TŌTA THAT NEW YEAR'S FEAST!
AND WOKE UP EARLY TO DO IT!
HUH...? THAT'S SO ADMIRABLE AND CUTE.
AND, IF THE FOOD TASTES GOOD DESPITE HER LACK OF COORDINATION, WE CAN SEE THAT SHE'S NOT AS HAPHAZARD AS SHE LOOKS!
AND LOOK!
THAT INCOMPETENT DOESN'T HAVE A CLUE!
BUT SHE'S NOT TRYING TO BRING ATTENTION TO THE FACT THAT IT'S HOMEMADE!
YOU'RE RIGHT! THAT SMILE PRACTICALLY SCREAMS THAT SHE'S HAPPY JUST TO HAVE HIM EAT IT!
SHE'S A NICE GIRL...!
A REALLY NICE GIRL!

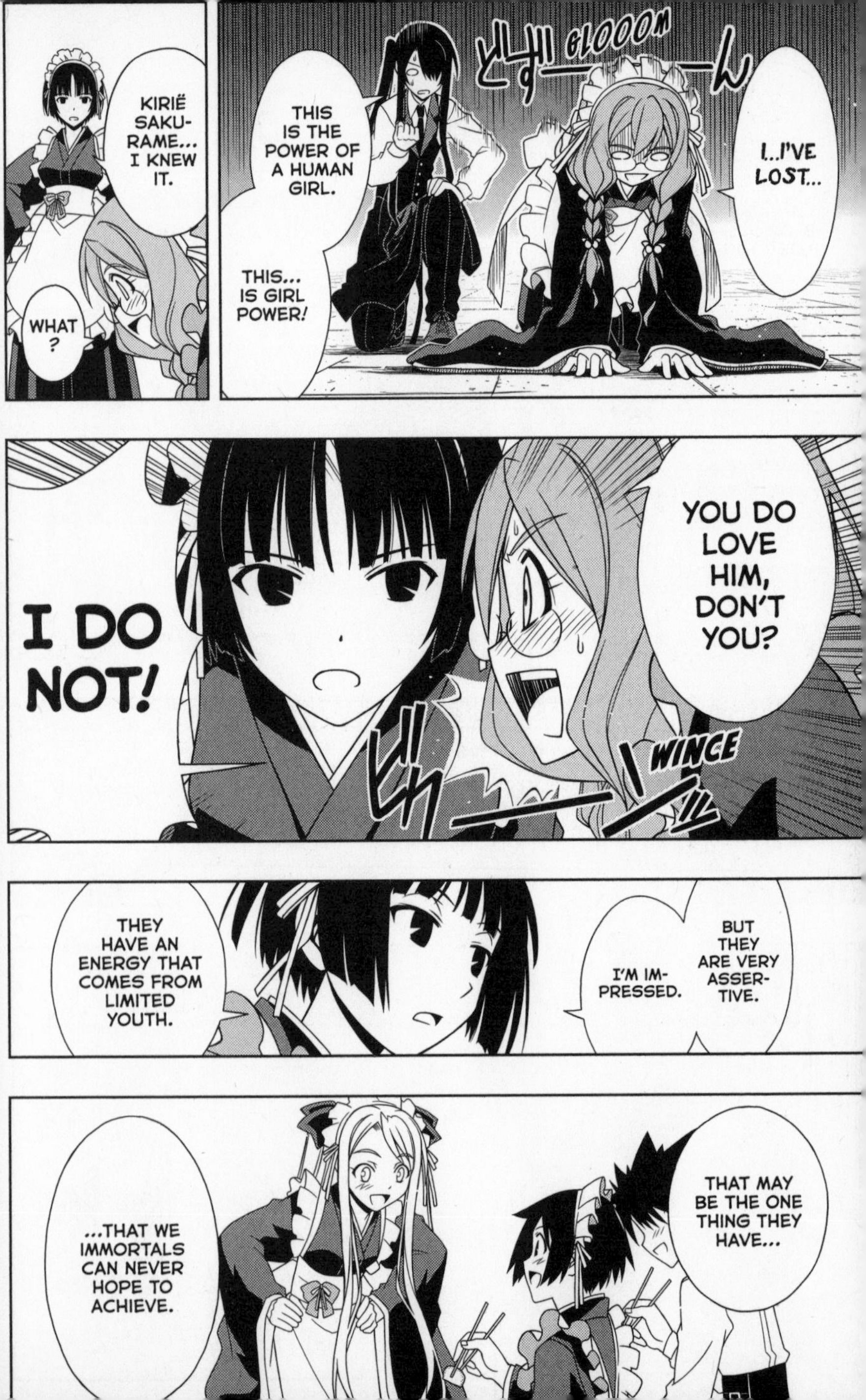
どすーーーん GLOOOM
I...I'VE LOST...
THIS IS THE POWER OF A HUMAN GIRL.
THIS... IS GIRL POWER!
KIRIË SAKURAME... I KNEW IT.
WHAT?
YOU DO LOVE HIM, DON'T YOU?
I DO NOT!
WINCE
BUT THEY ARE VERY ASSERTIVE.
I'M IMPRESSED.
THEY HAVE AN ENERGY THAT COMES FROM LIMITED YOUTH.
THAT MAY BE THE ONE THING THEY HAVE...
...THAT WE IMMORTALS CAN NEVER HOPE TO ACHIEVE.

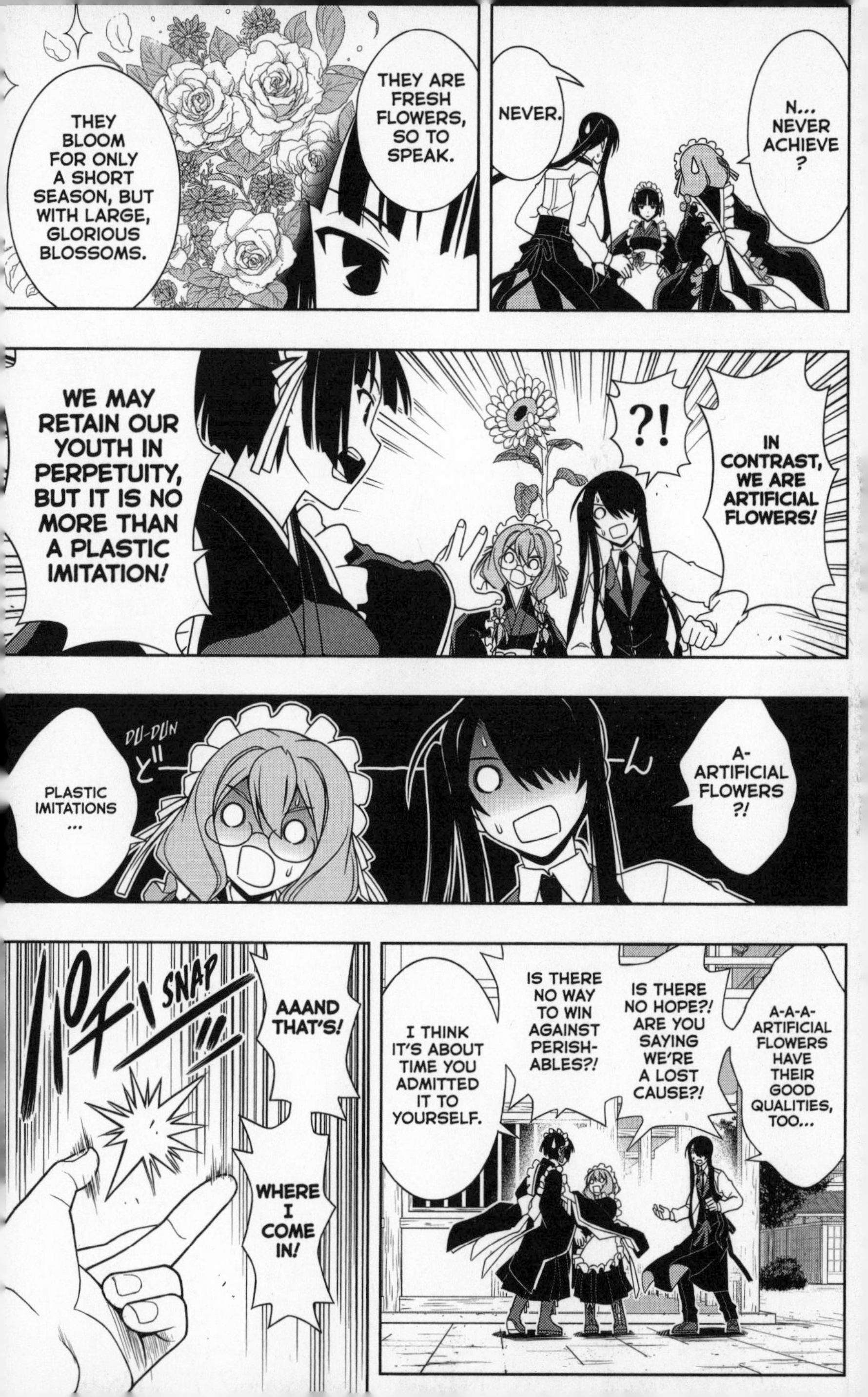
N... NEVER ACHIEVE?
NEVER.
THEY ARE FRESH FLOWERS, SO TO SPEAK.
THEY BLOOM FOR ONLY A SHORT SEASON, BUT WITH LARGE, GLORIOUS BLOSSOMS.
IN CONTRAST, WE ARE ARTIFICIAL FLOWERS!
?!
WE MAY RETAIN OUR YOUTH IN PERPETUITY, BUT IT IS NO MORE THAN A PLASTIC IMITATION!
A- ARTIFICIAL FLOWERS?!
DU-DUN
PLASTIC IMITATIONS...
A-A-A- ARTIFICIAL FLOWERS HAVE THEIR GOOD QUALITIES, TOO...
IS THERE NO HOPE?! ARE YOU SAYING WE'RE A LOST CAUSE?!
IS THERE NO WAY TO WIN AGAINST PERISH- ABLES?!
I THINK IT'S ABOUT TIME YOU ADMITTED IT TO YOURSELF.
AAAND THAT'S!
SNAP
WHERE I COME IN!

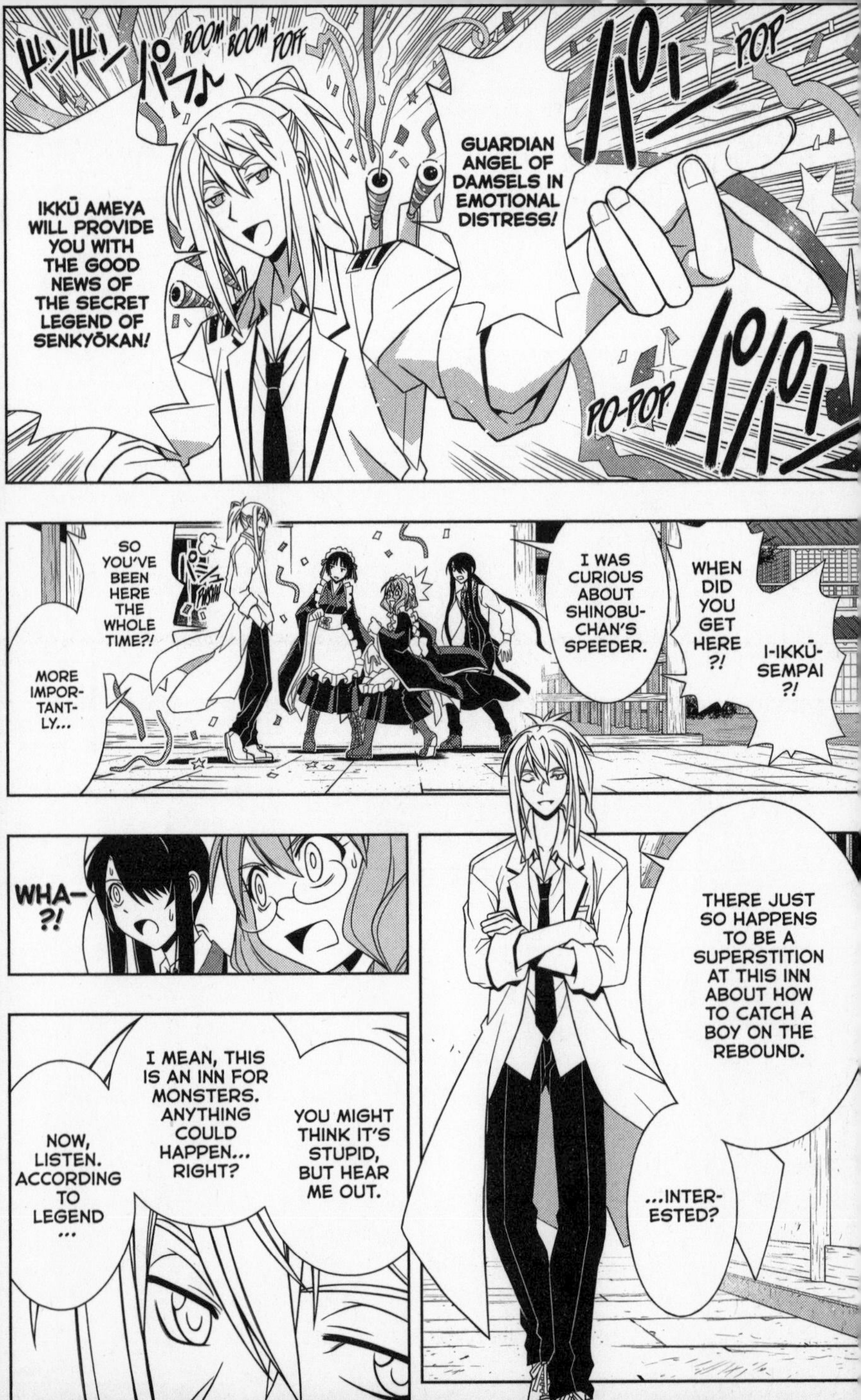
パー
POP
パパパ
PO-POP
GUARDIAN ANGEL OF DAMSELS IN EMOTIONAL DISTRESS!
ドンドン
BOOM BOOM
パフ♪
POFF
IKKŪ AMEYA WILL PROVIDE YOU WITH THE GOOD NEWS OF THE SECRET LEGEND OF SENKYŌKAN!
I-IKKŪ-SEMPAI?!
WHEN DID YOU GET HERE?!
I WAS CURIOUS ABOUT SHINOBU-CHAN'S SPEEDER.
SO YOU'VE BEEN HERE THE WHOLE TIME?!
MORE IMPORTANTLY...
THERE JUST SO HAPPENS TO BE A SUPERSTITION AT THIS INN ABOUT HOW TO CATCH A BOY ON THE REBOUND.
...INTERESTED?
WHA-?!
YOU MIGHT THINK IT'S STUPID, BUT HEAR ME OUT.
I MEAN, THIS IS AN INN FOR MONSTERS. ANYTHING COULD HAPPEN... RIGHT?
NOW, LISTEN. ACCORDING TO LEGEND...

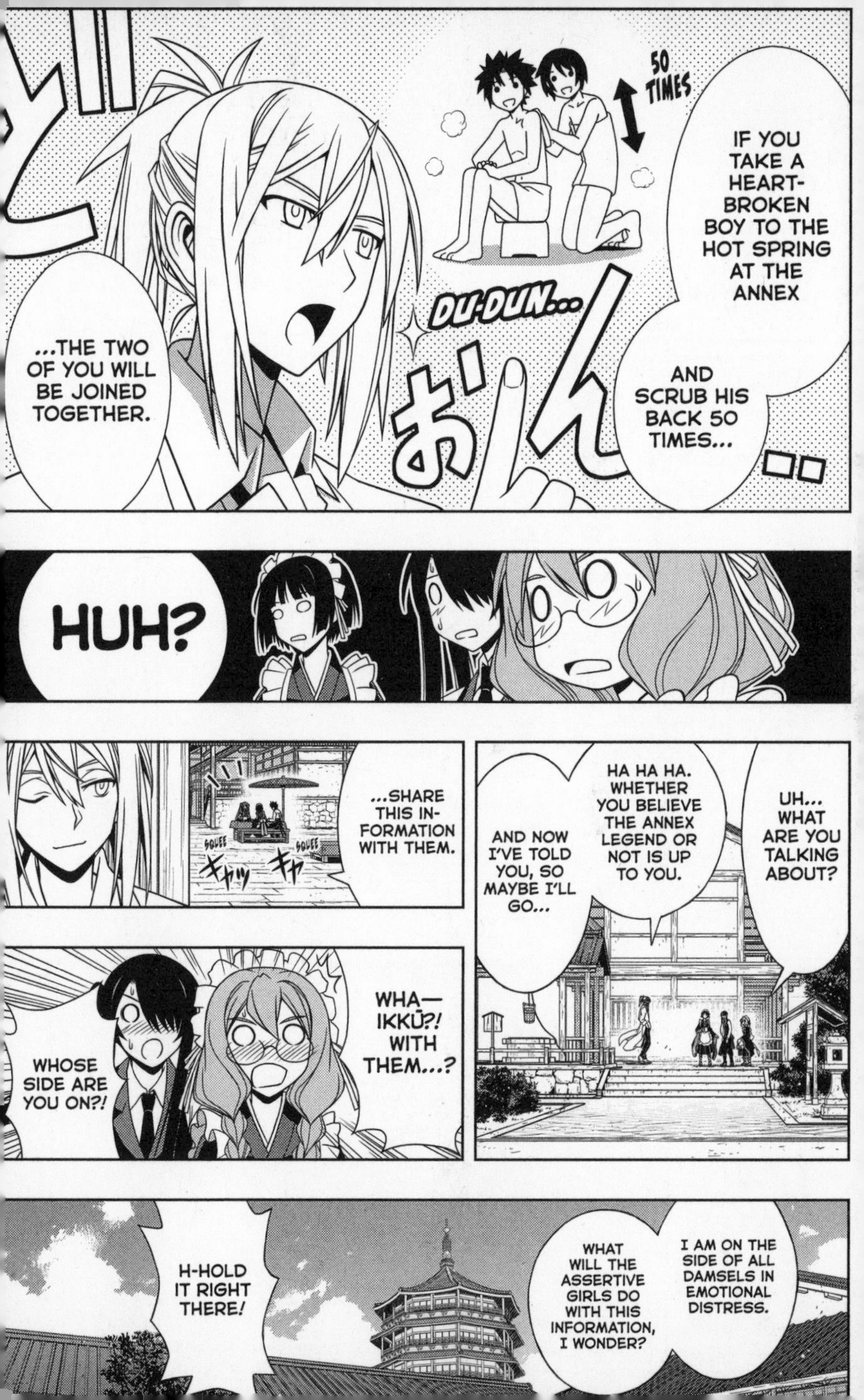
IF YOU TAKE A HEART-BROKEN BOY TO THE HOT SPRING AT THE ANNEX
AND SCRUB HIS BACK 50 TIMES...
50 TIMES
DU-DUN...
...THE TWO OF YOU WILL BE JOINED TOGETHER.
HUH?
UH... WHAT ARE YOU TALKING ABOUT?
HA HA HA. WHETHER YOU BELIEVE THE ANNEX LEGEND OR NOT IS UP TO YOU.
AND NOW I'VE TOLD YOU, SO MAYBE I'LL GO...
...SHARE THIS INFORMATION WITH THEM.
SQUEE
SQUEE
WHA— IKKŪ?! WITH THEM...?
WHOSE SIDE ARE YOU ON?!
I AM ON THE SIDE OF ALL DAMSELS IN EMOTIONAL DISTRESS.
WHAT WILL THE ASSERTIVE GIRLS DO WITH THIS INFORMATION, I WONDER?
H-HOLD IT RIGHT THERE!

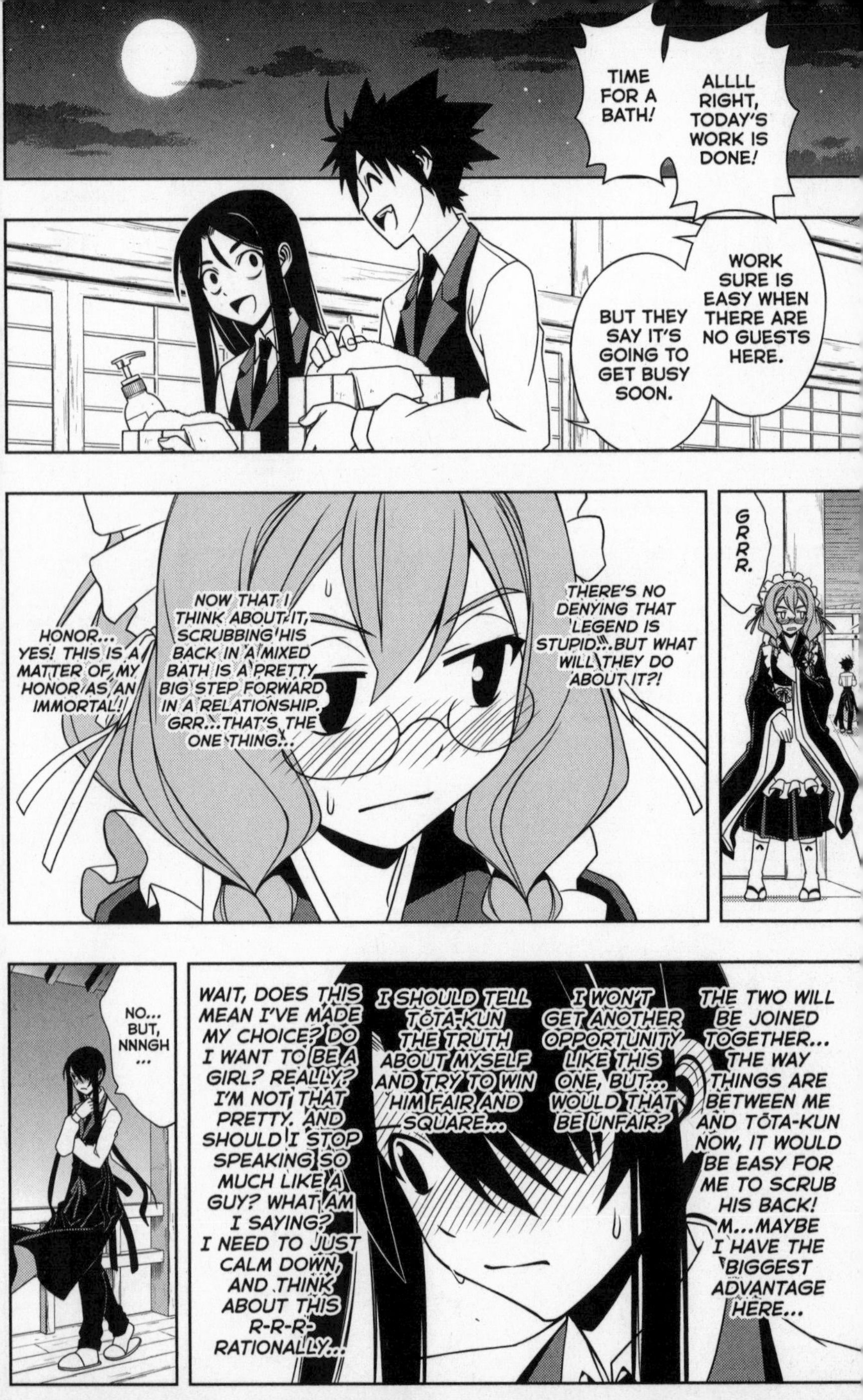
ALLLL RIGHT, TODAY'S WORK IS DONE!
TIME FOR A BATH!
WORK SURE IS EASY WHEN THERE ARE NO GUESTS HERE.
BUT THEY SAY IT'S GOING TO GET BUSY SOON.
GRRR.
THERE'S NO DENYING THAT LEGEND IS STUPID... BUT WHAT WILL THEY DO ABOUT IT?!
NOW THAT I THINK ABOUT IT, SCRUBBING HIS BACK IN A MIXED BATH IS A PRETTY BIG STEP FORWARD IN A RELATIONSHIP. GRR... THAT'S THE ONE THING...
HONOR... YES! THIS IS A MATTER OF MY HONOR AS AN IMMORTAL!
THE TWO WILL BE JOINED TOGETHER... THE WAY THINGS ARE BETWEEN ME AND TŌTA-KUN NOW, IT WOULD BE EASY FOR ME TO SCRUB HIS BACK! M... MAYBE I HAVE THE BIGGEST ADVANTAGE HERE...
I WON'T GET ANOTHER OPPORTUNITY LIKE THIS ONE, BUT... WOULD THAT BE UNFAIR?
I SHOULD TELL TŌTA-KUN THE TRUTH ABOUT MYSELF AND TRY TO WIN HIM FAIR AND SQUARE...
WAIT, DOES THIS MEAN I'VE MADE MY CHOICE? DO I WANT TO BE A GIRL? REALLY? I'M NOT THAT PRETTY. AND SHOULD I STOP SPEAKING SO MUCH LIKE A GUY? WHAT AM I SAYING? I NEED TO JUST CALM DOWN, AND THINK ABOUT THIS R-R-R-RATIONALLY...
NO... BUT, NNNGH...

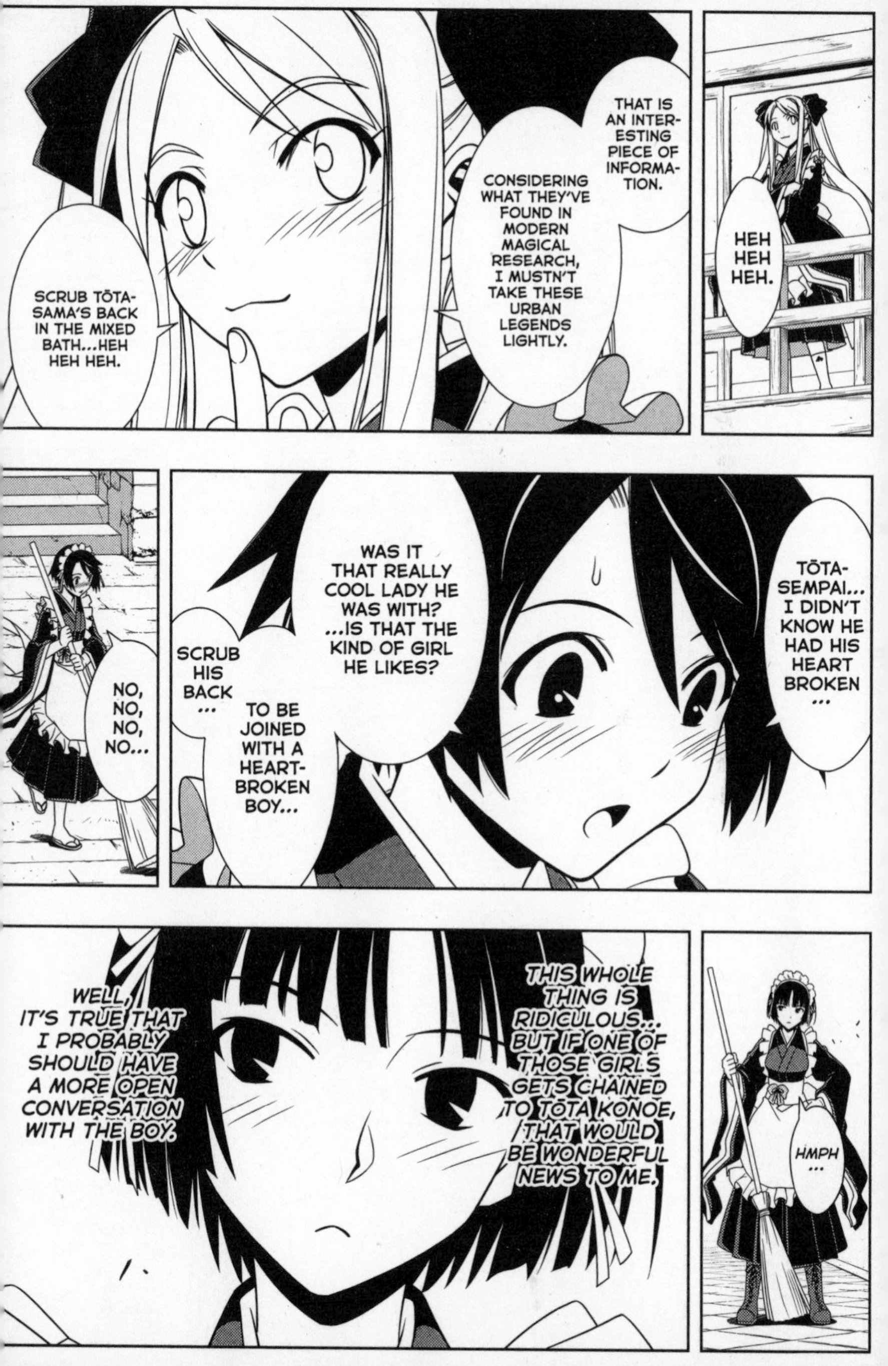
HEH HEH HEH.
THAT IS AN INTERESTING PIECE OF INFORMATION.
CONSIDERING WHAT THEY'VE FOUND IN MODERN MAGICAL RESEARCH, I MUSTN'T TAKE THESE URBAN LEGENDS LIGHTLY.
SCRUB TŌTA-SAMA'S BACK IN THE MIXED BATH...HEH HEH HEH.
TŌTA-SEMPAI... I DIDN'T KNOW HE HAD HIS HEART BROKEN...
WAS IT THAT REALLY COOL LADY HE WAS WITH? ...IS THAT THE KIND OF GIRL HE LIKES?
TO BE JOINED WITH A HEART-BROKEN BOY...
SCRUB HIS BACK...
NO, NO, NO, NO...
HMPH...
THIS WHOLE THING IS RIDICULOUS... BUT IF ONE OF THOSE GIRLS GETS CHAINED TO TŌTA KONOE, THAT WOULD BE WONDERFUL NEWS TO ME.
WELL, IT'S TRUE THAT I PROBABLY SHOULD HAVE A MORE OPEN CONVERSATION WITH THE BOY.

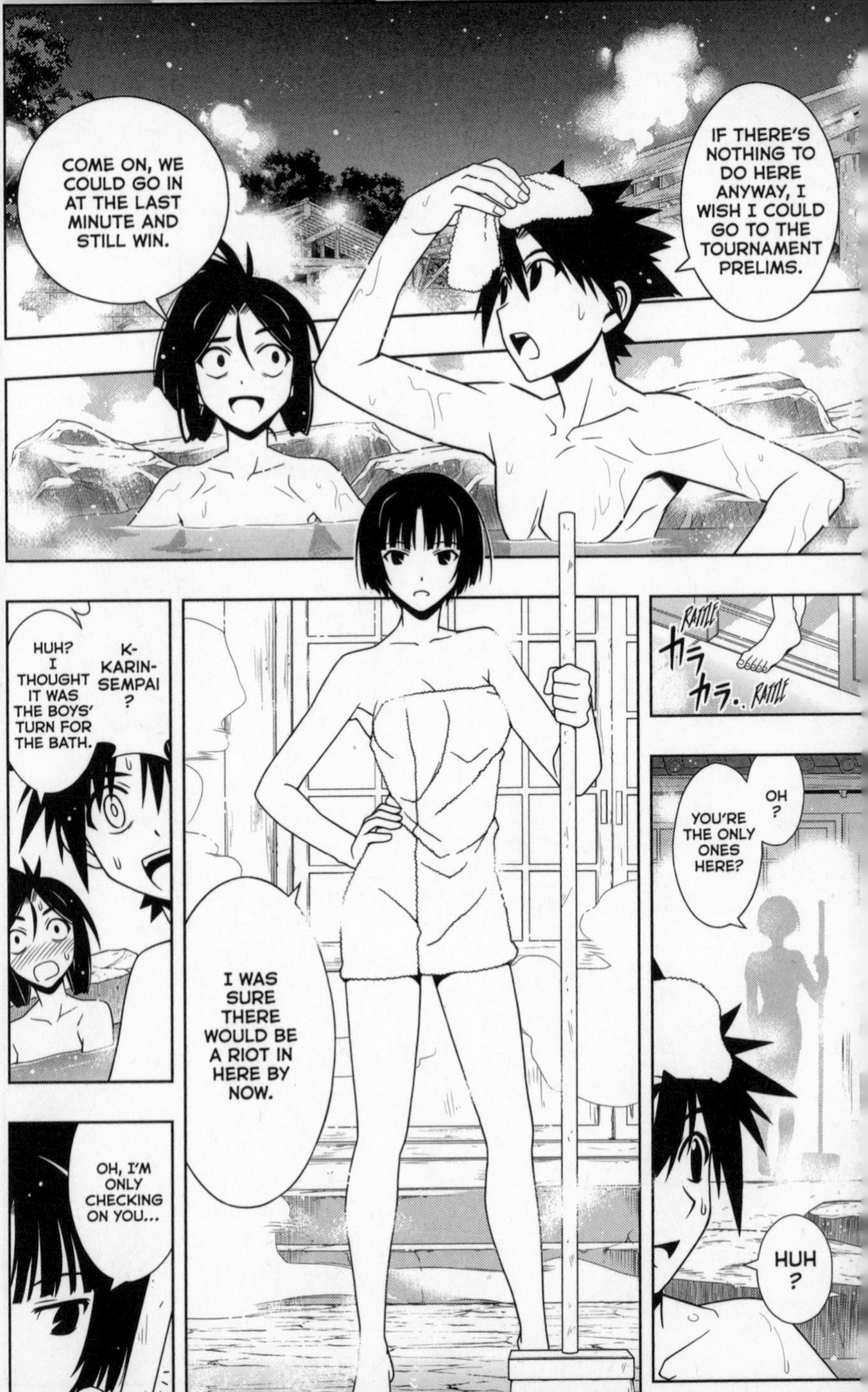

IF THERE'S NOTHING TO DO HERE ANYWAY, I WISH I COULD GO TO THE TOURNAMENT PRELIMS.
COME ON, WE COULD GO IN AT THE LAST MINUTE AND STILL WIN.
RATTLE
カラ
カラ..
RATTLE
OH?
YOU'RE THE ONLY ONES HERE?
HUH?
I WAS SURE THERE WOULD BE A RIOT IN HERE BY NOW.
K-KARIN-SEMPAI?
HUH? I THOUGHT IT WAS THE BOYS' TURN FOR THE BATH.
OH, I'M ONLY CHECKING ON YOU...

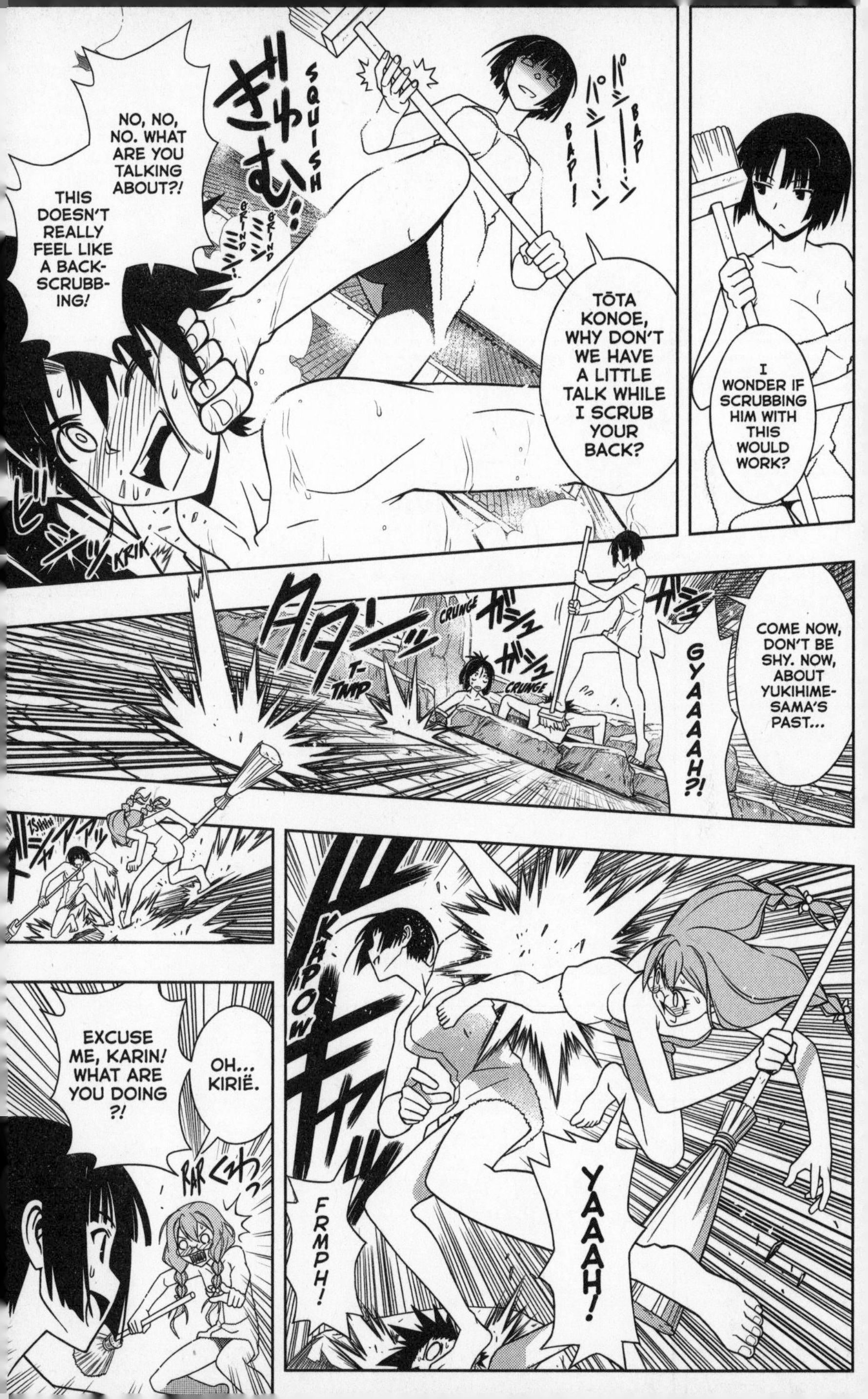
I WONDER IF SCRUBBING HIM WITH THIS WOULD WORK?
TŌTA KONOE, WHY DON'T WE HAVE A LITTLE TALK WHILE I SCRUB YOUR BACK?
BAP BAP!
SQUISH
GRIND GRIND
NO, NO, NO. WHAT ARE YOU TALKING ABOUT?!
THIS DOESN'T REALLY FEEL LIKE A BACK-SCRUBBING!
KRIK
COME NOW, DON'T BE SHY. NOW, ABOUT YUKIHIME-SAMA'S PAST...
GYAAAAAH?!
CRUNGE
CRUNGE
T-TMP
KAPOW
YAAAH!
FRMPH!
OH... KIRIË.
EXCUSE ME, KARIN! WHAT ARE YOU DOING?!
RAR

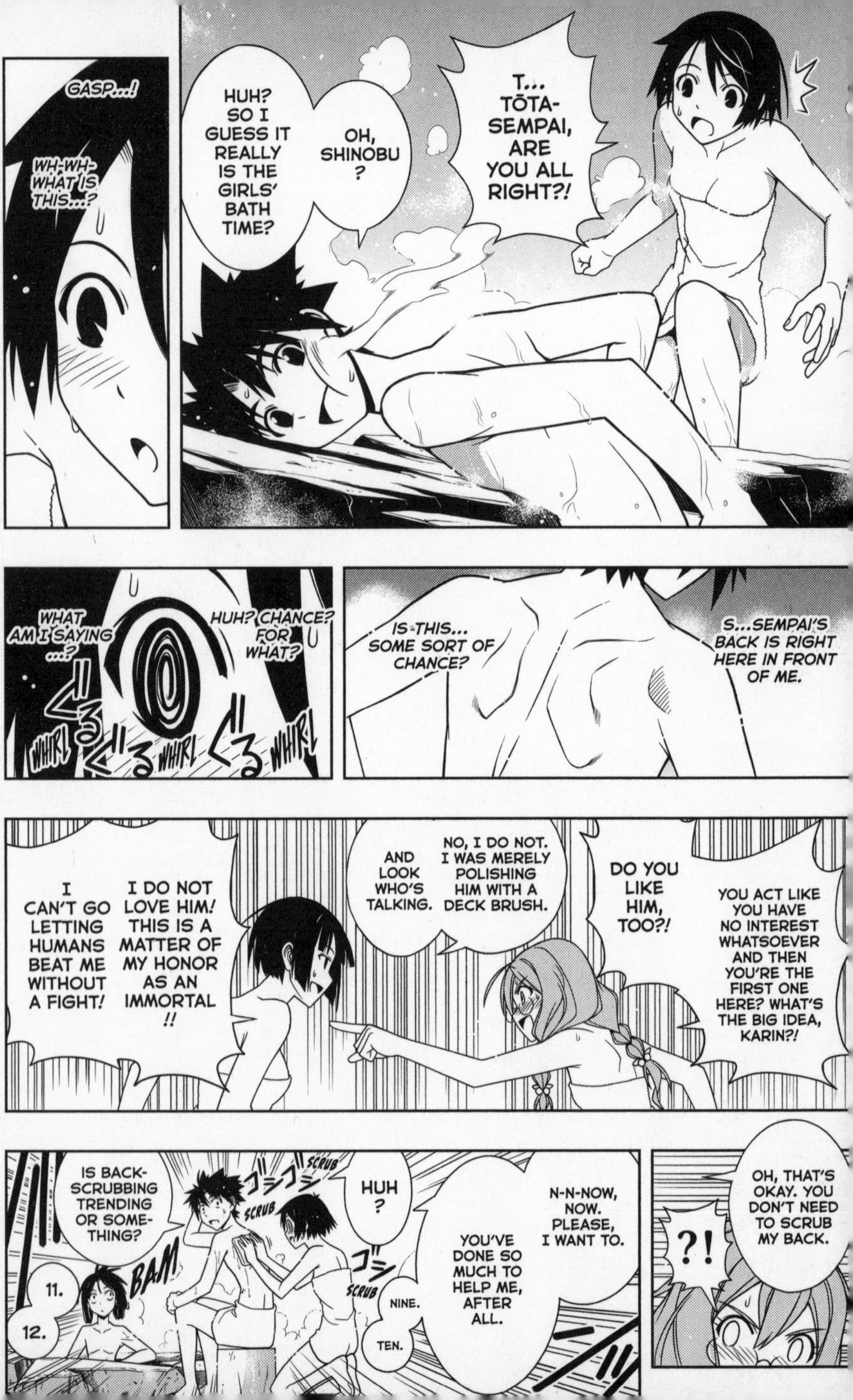
T... TŌTA-SEMPAI, ARE YOU ALL RIGHT?!
OH, SHINOBU?
HUH? SO I GUESS IT REALLY IS THE GIRLS' BATH TIME?
GASP...!
WH-WH-WHAT IS THIS...?
S...SEMPAI'S BACK IS RIGHT HERE IN FRONT OF ME.
IS THIS... SOME SORT OF CHANCE?
HUH? CHANCE? FOR WHAT?
WHAT AM I SAYING...?
WHIRL
WHIRL
WHIRL
YOU ACT LIKE YOU HAVE NO INTEREST WHATSOEVER AND THEN YOU'RE THE FIRST ONE HERE? WHAT'S THE BIG IDEA, KARIN?!
DO YOU LIKE HIM, TOO?!
NO, I DO NOT. I WAS MERELY POLISHING HIM WITH A DECK BRUSH.
AND LOOK WHO'S TALKING.
I DO NOT LOVE HIM! THIS IS A MATTER OF MY HONOR AS AN IMMORTAL!!
I CAN'T GO LETTING HUMANS BEAT ME WITHOUT A FIGHT!
OH, THAT'S OKAY. YOU DON'T NEED TO SCRUB MY BACK.
?!
N-N-NOW, NOW. PLEASE, I WANT TO.
YOU'VE DONE SO MUCH TO HELP ME, AFTER ALL.
HUH?
SCRUB
SCRUB
SCRUB
NINE.
TEN.
IS BACK-SCRUBBING TRENDING OR SOMETHING?
BAM
11.
12.

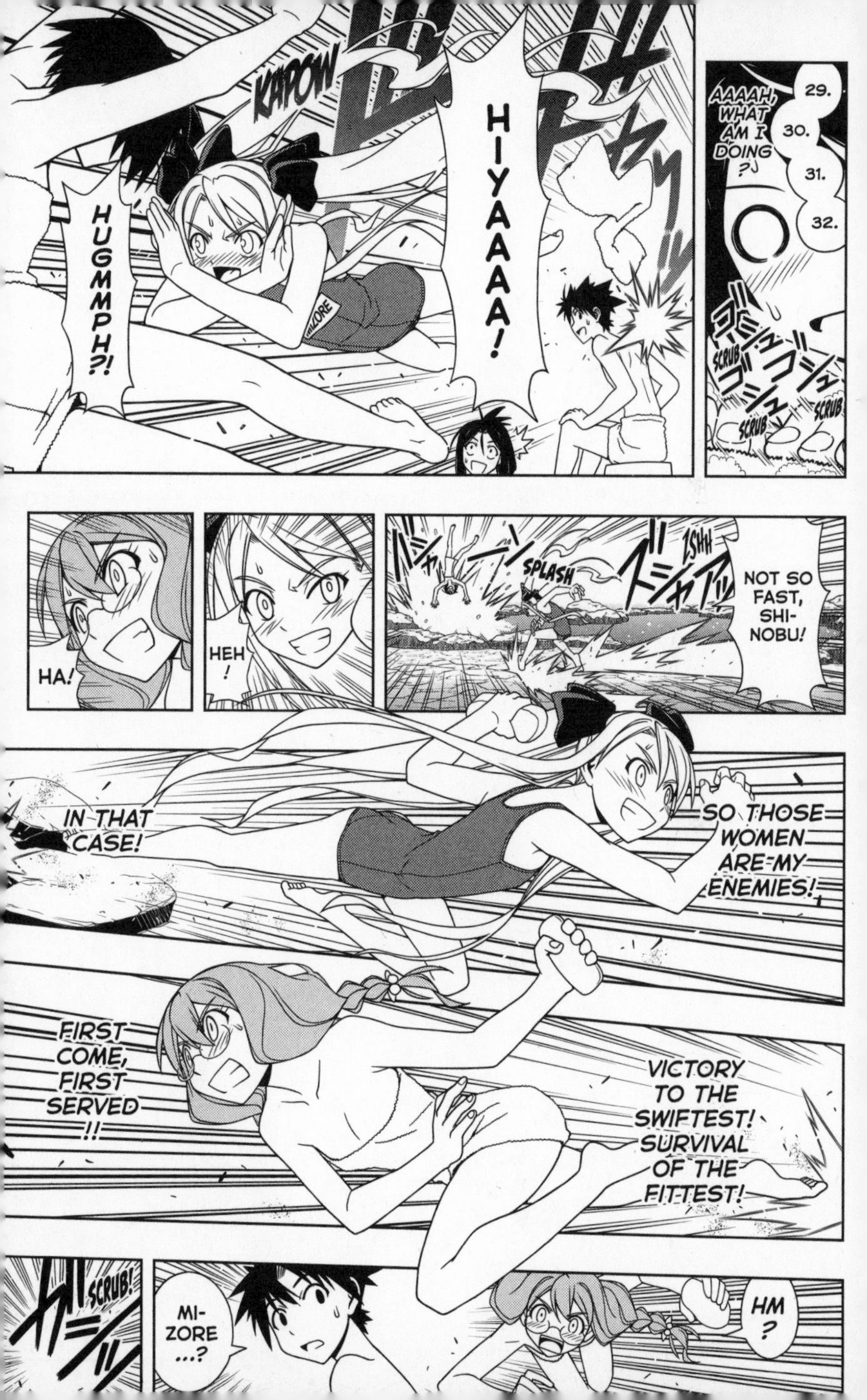
29.
30.
31.
32.
AAAAH, WHAT AM I DOING?
SCRUB
SCRUB
SCRUB
KAPOW
HIYAAAAA!
MIZORE
HUGMMPH?!
NOT SO FAST, SHI-NOBU!
ZSHH
SPLASH
HEH!
HA!
SO THOSE WOMEN ARE MY ENEMIES!
IN THAT CASE!
VICTORY TO THE SWIFTEST! SURVIVAL OF THE FITTEST!
FIRST COME, FIRST SERVED!!
HM?
MI-ZORE...?
SCRUB!

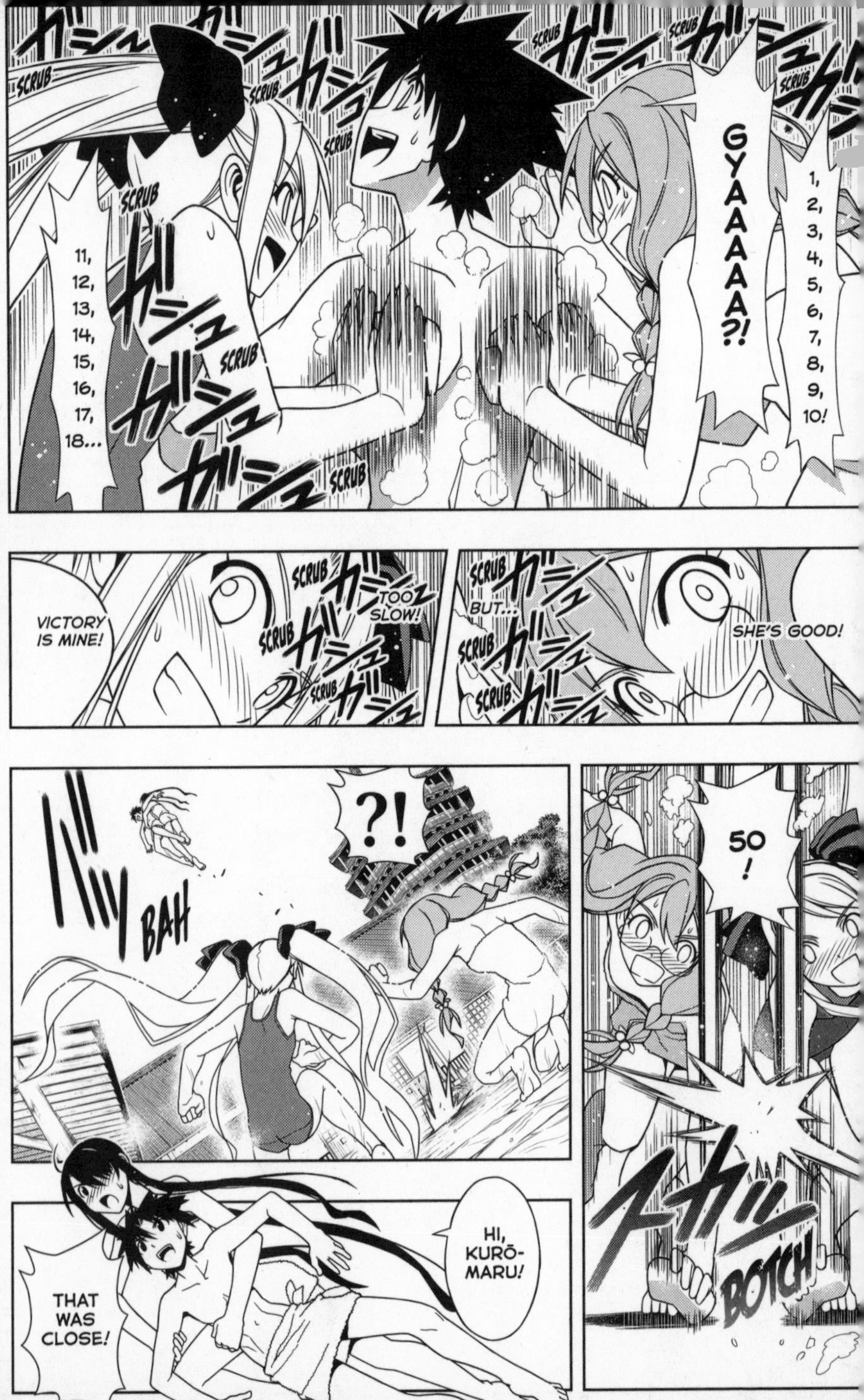
1, 2, 3, 4, 5, 6, 7, 8, 9, 10!
GYAAAAAA?!
SCRUB
SCRUB
SCRUB
SCRUB
SCRUB
SCRUB
SCRUB
SCRUB
SCRUB
11, 12, 13, 14, 15, 16, 17, 18...
SHE'S GOOD!
BUT...
SCRUB
SCRUB
SCRUB
TOO SLOW!
SCRUB
SCRUB
SCRUB
VICTORY IS MINE!
50!
BOTCH
?!
BAH
HI, KURŌMARU!
THAT WAS CLOSE!

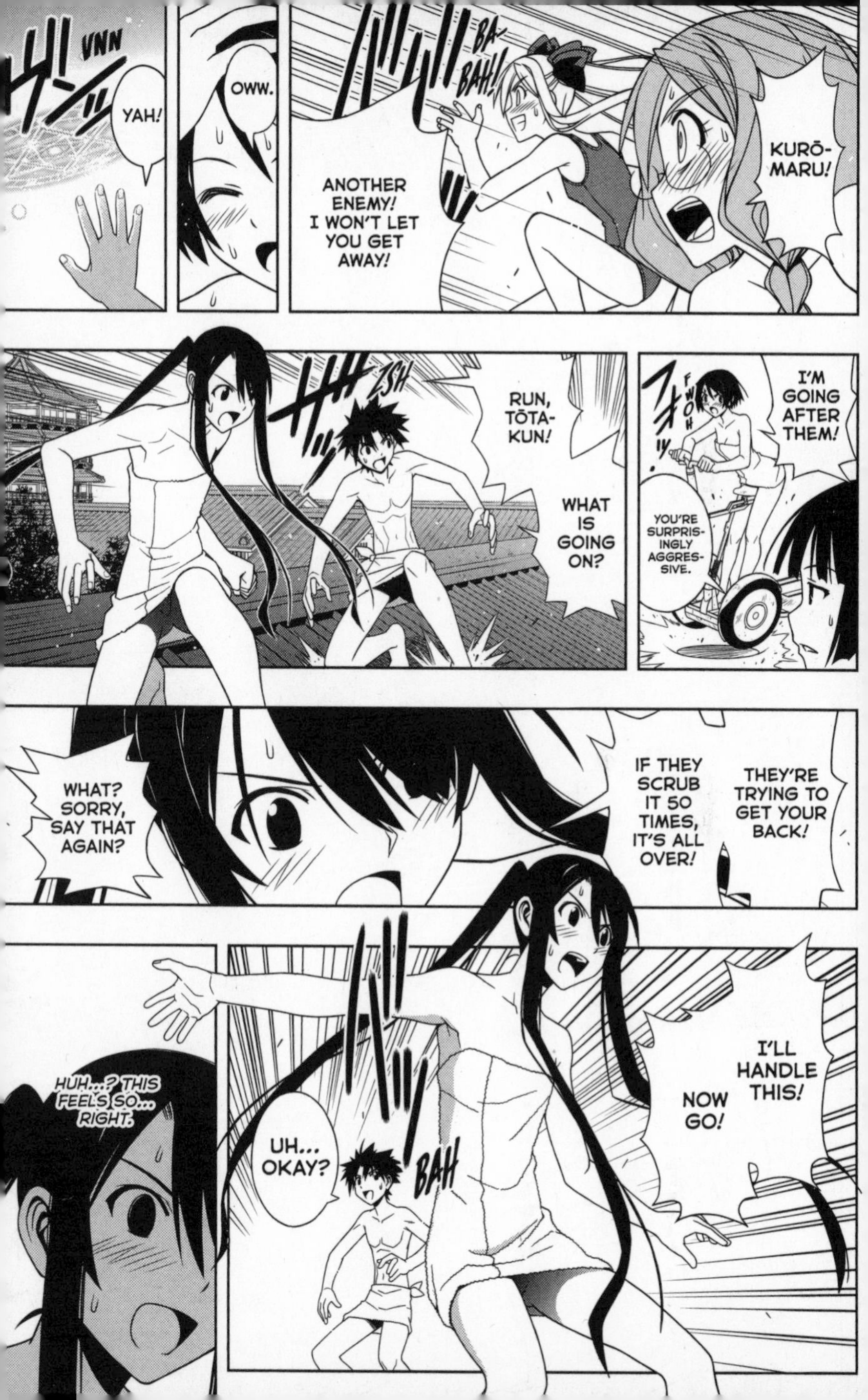
KURŌ-MARU!
BA-BAH!!
ANOTHER ENEMY! I WON'T LET YOU GET AWAY!
OWW.
VNN
YAH!
I'M GOING AFTER THEM!
FWOH
YOU'RE SURPRISINGLY AGGRESSIVE.
ZSH
RUN, TŌTA-KUN!
WHAT IS GOING ON?
THEY'RE TRYING TO GET YOUR BACK!
IF THEY SCRUB IT 50 TIMES, IT'S ALL OVER!
WHAT? SORRY, SAY THAT AGAIN?
I'LL HANDLE THIS!
NOW GO!
BAH
UH... OKAY?
HUH...? THIS FEELS SO... RIGHT.

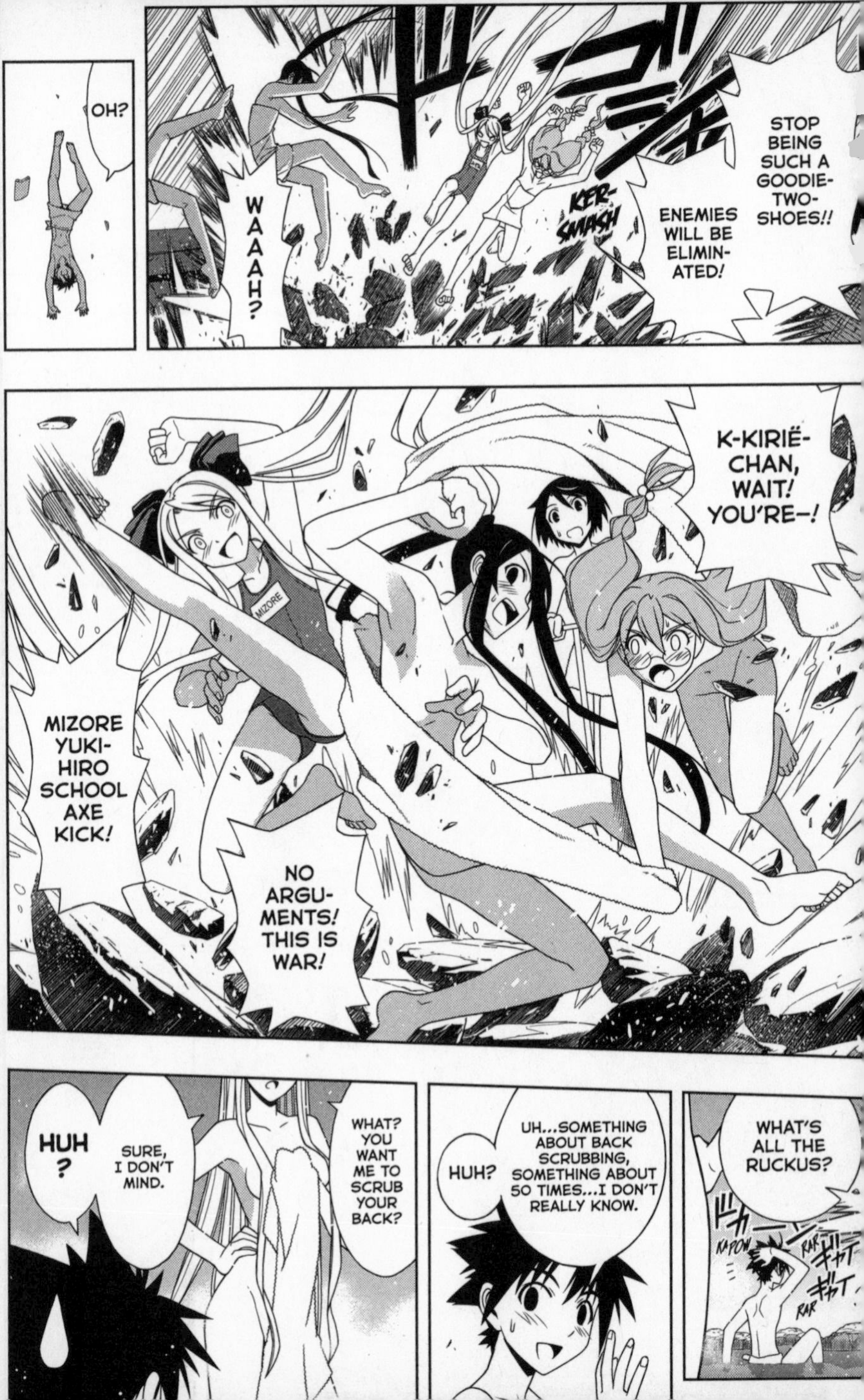
STOP BEING SUCH A GOODIE-TWO-SHOES!!
ENEMIES WILL BE ELIMINATED!
KER-SMASH
WAAAAH?
OH?
K-KIRIË-CHAN, WAIT! YOU'RE–!
NO ARGUMENTS! THIS IS WAR!
MIZORE YUKIHIRO SCHOOL AXE KICK!
WHAT'S ALL THE RUCKUS?
KAPOW
RAR
RAR
UH...SOMETHING ABOUT BACK SCRUBBING, SOMETHING ABOUT 50 TIMES...I DON'T REALLY KNOW.
HUH?
WHAT? YOU WANT ME TO SCRUB YOUR BACK?
SURE, I DON'T MIND.
HUH?

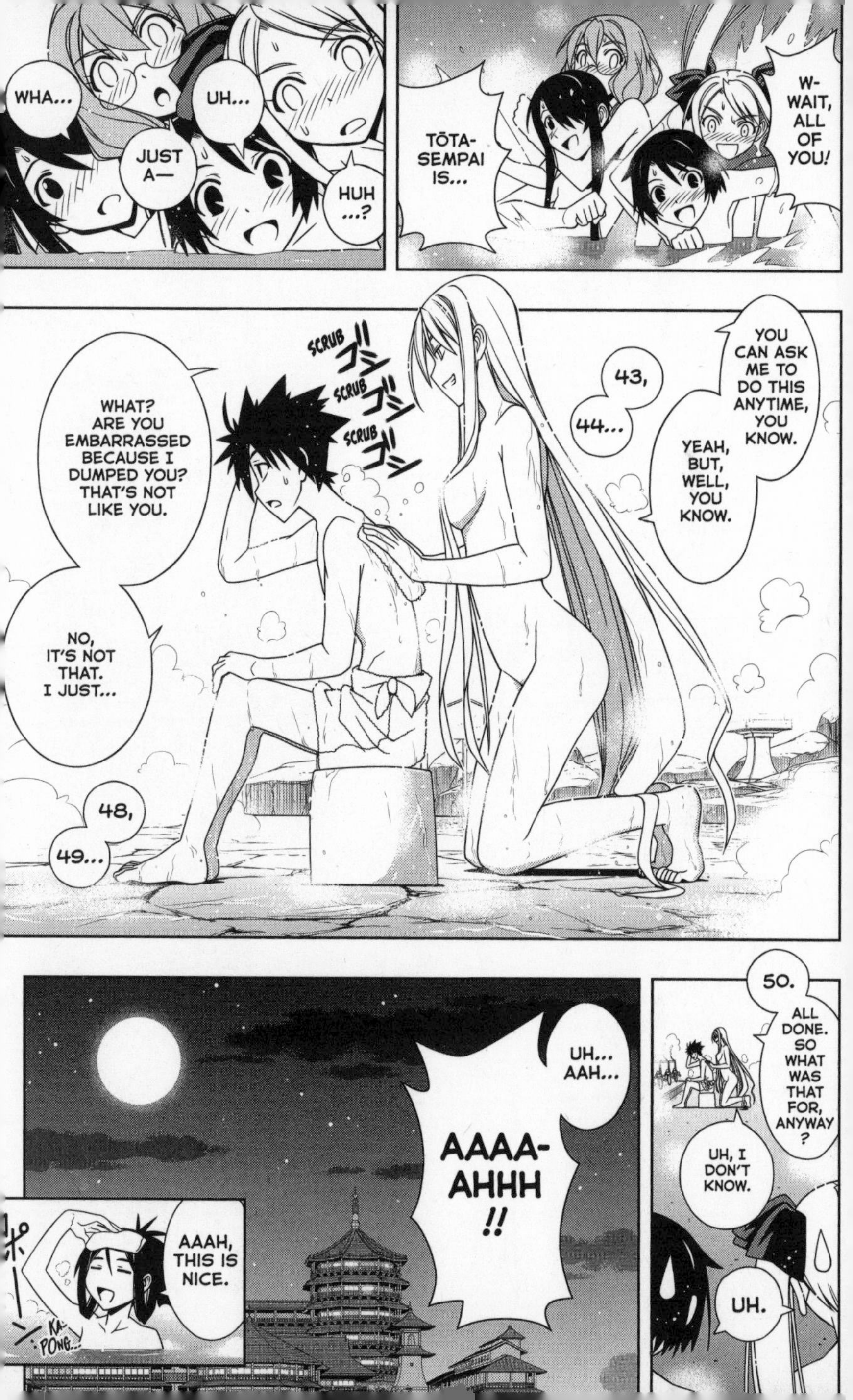
W-WAIT, ALL OF YOU!
TŌTA-SEMPAI IS...
UH...
HUH...?
JUST A—
WHA...
YOU CAN ASK ME TO DO THIS ANYTIME, YOU KNOW.
43, 44...
YEAH, BUT, WELL, YOU KNOW.
SCRUB
SCRUB
SCRUB
WHAT? ARE YOU EMBARRASSED BECAUSE I DUMPED YOU? THAT'S NOT LIKE YOU.
NO, IT'S NOT THAT. I JUST...
48, 49...
50.
ALL DONE. SO WHAT WAS THAT FOR, ANYWAY?
UH, I DON'T KNOW.
UH.
UH... AAH...
AAAA-AHHH!!
AAAH, THIS IS NICE.
KA-PONG...!

UQ
HOLDER!

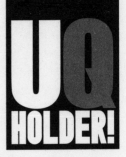

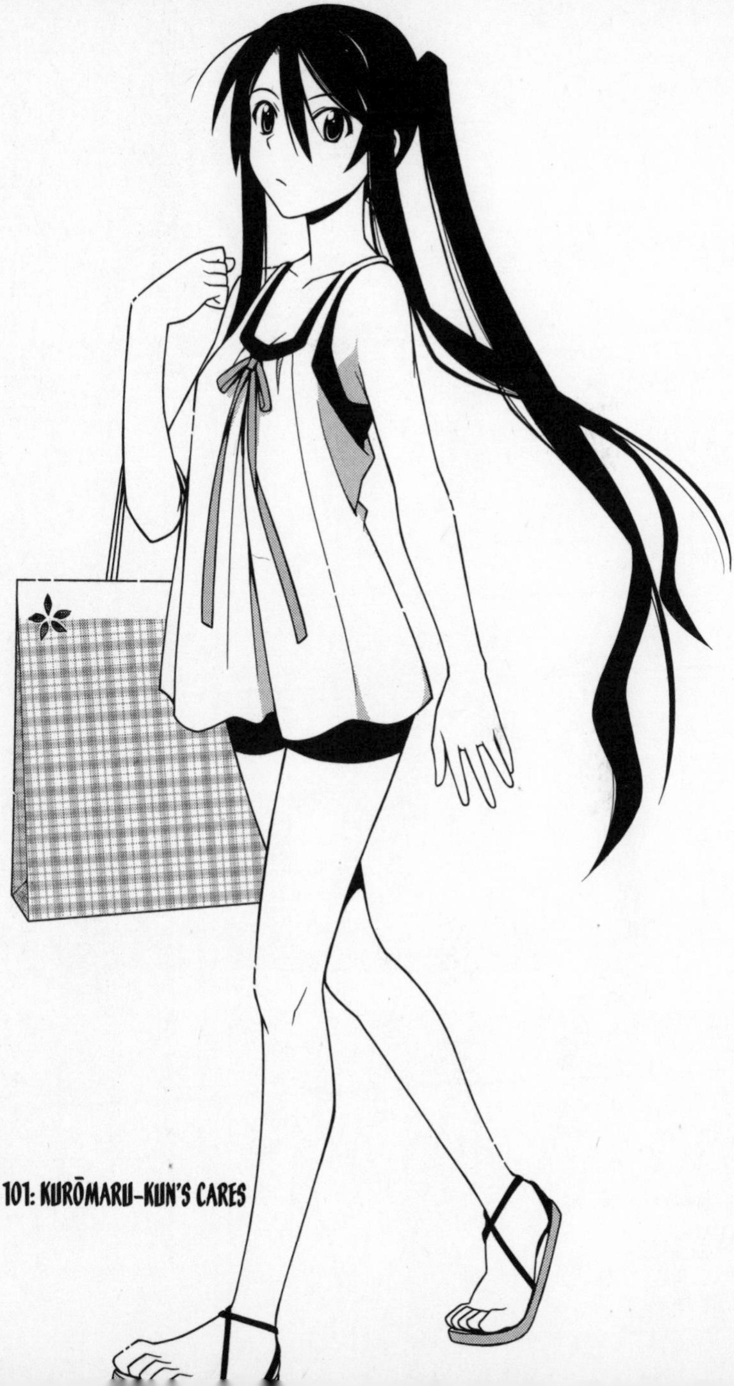

## STAGE 101: KURŌMARU-KUN'S CARES

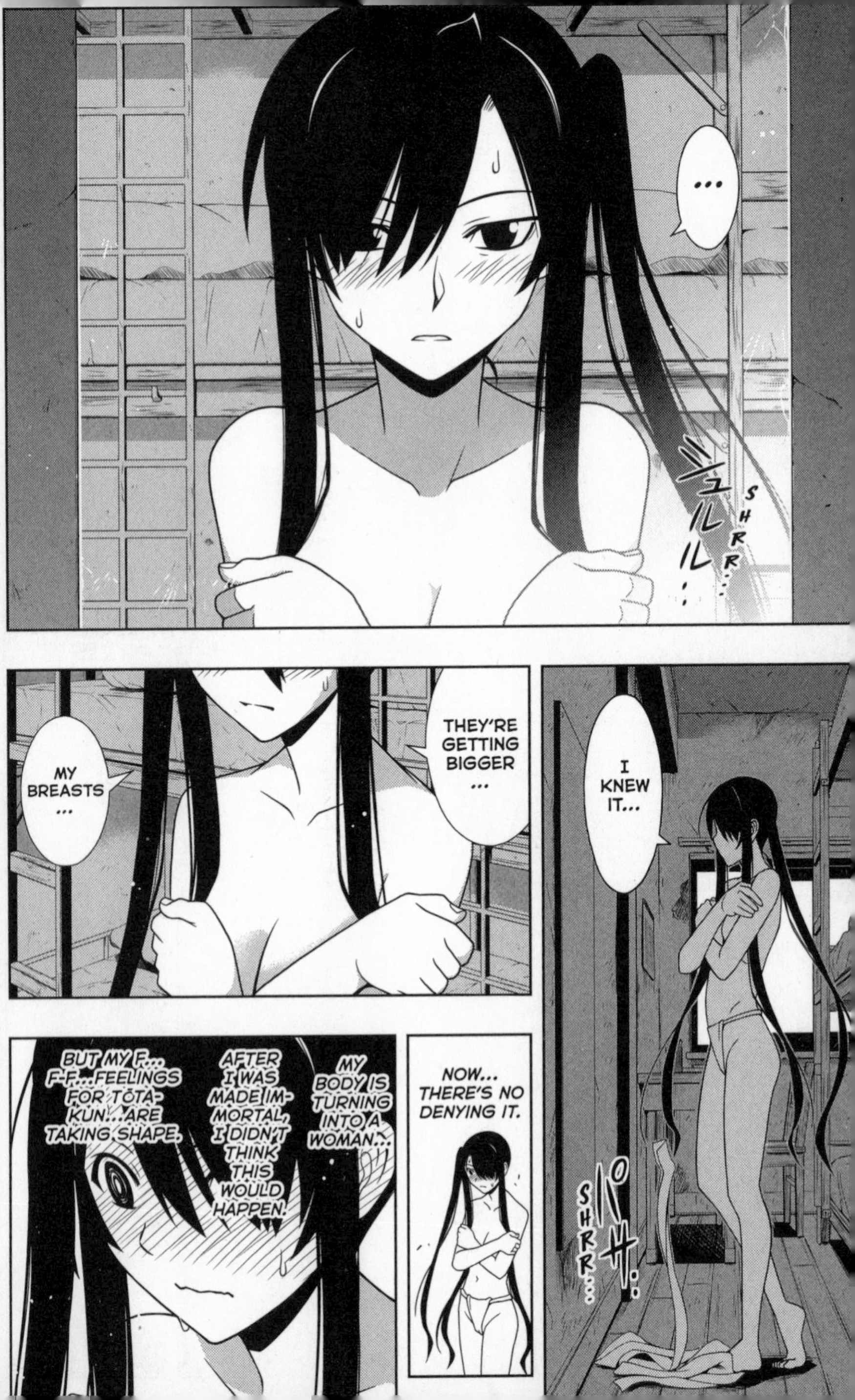
...
SHRR...
I KNEW IT...
SHRR...
MY BREASTS...
THEY'RE GETTING BIGGER...
NOW... THERE'S NO DENYING IT.
MY BODY IS TURNING INTO A WOMAN...
AFTER I WAS MADE IMMORTAL, I DIDN'T THINK THIS WOULD HAPPEN.
BUT MY F... F-F...FEELINGS FOR TOTA-KUN...ARE TAKING SHAPE.

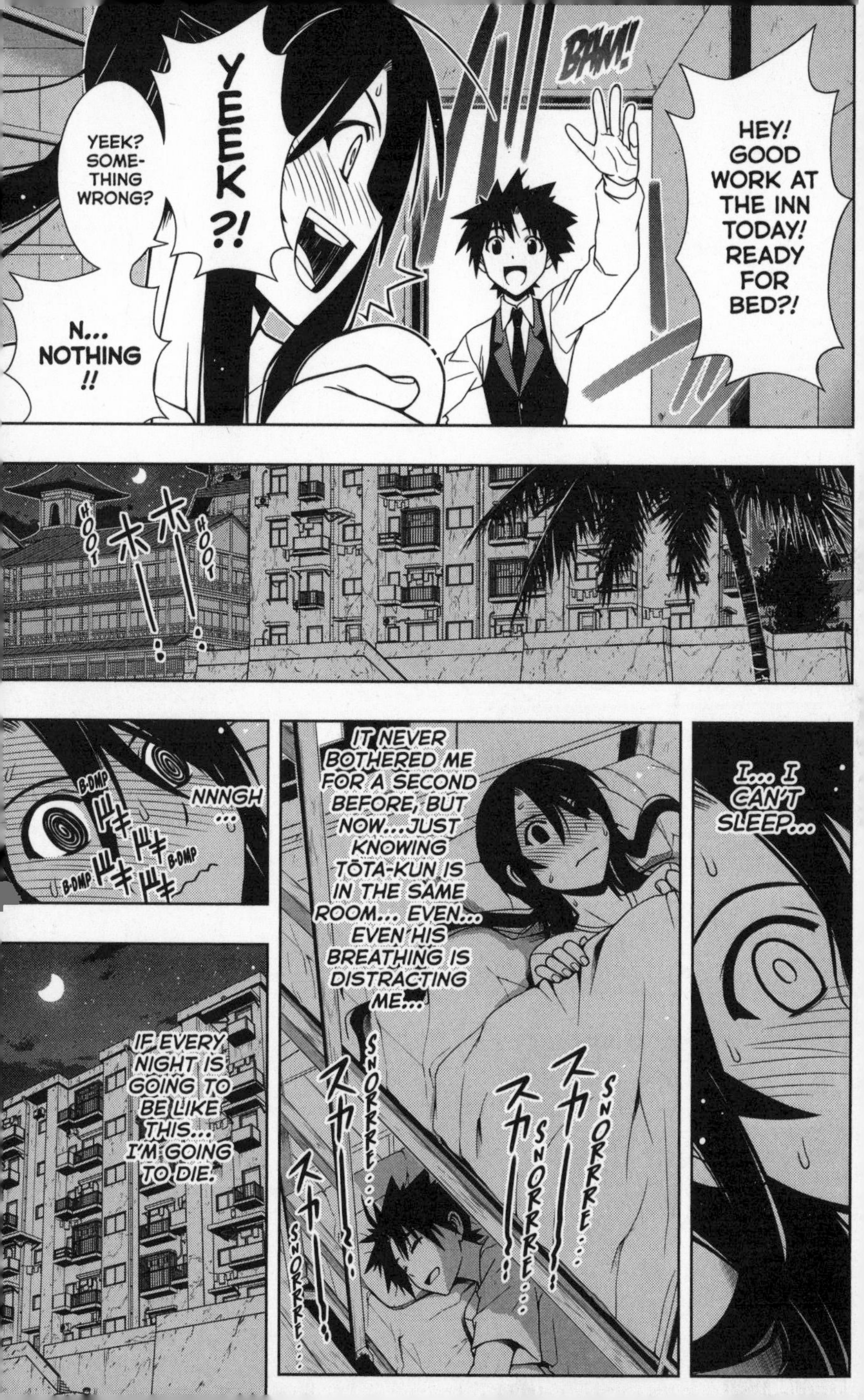
BAM!!
HEY! GOOD WORK AT THE INN TODAY! READY FOR BED?!
YEEK?!
YEEK? SOME-THING WRONG?
N... NOTHING!!
HOOT
ホーー…
HOOT
ホーー…
I... I CAN'T SLEEP...
IT NEVER BOTHERED ME FOR A SECOND BEFORE, BUT NOW...JUST KNOWING TŌTA-KUN IS IN THE SAME ROOM... EVEN... EVEN HIS BREATHING IS DISTRACTING ME...
SNORRRE...
スカーー!!
SNORRRE...
スカーー…!!
SNORRRE...
スカー~…
SNORRRE...
NNNGH...
B-DMP
ドキ
B-DMP
ドキ
B-DMP
ドキ
ドキ
IF EVERY NIGHT IS GOING TO BE LIKE THIS... I'M GOING TO DIE.

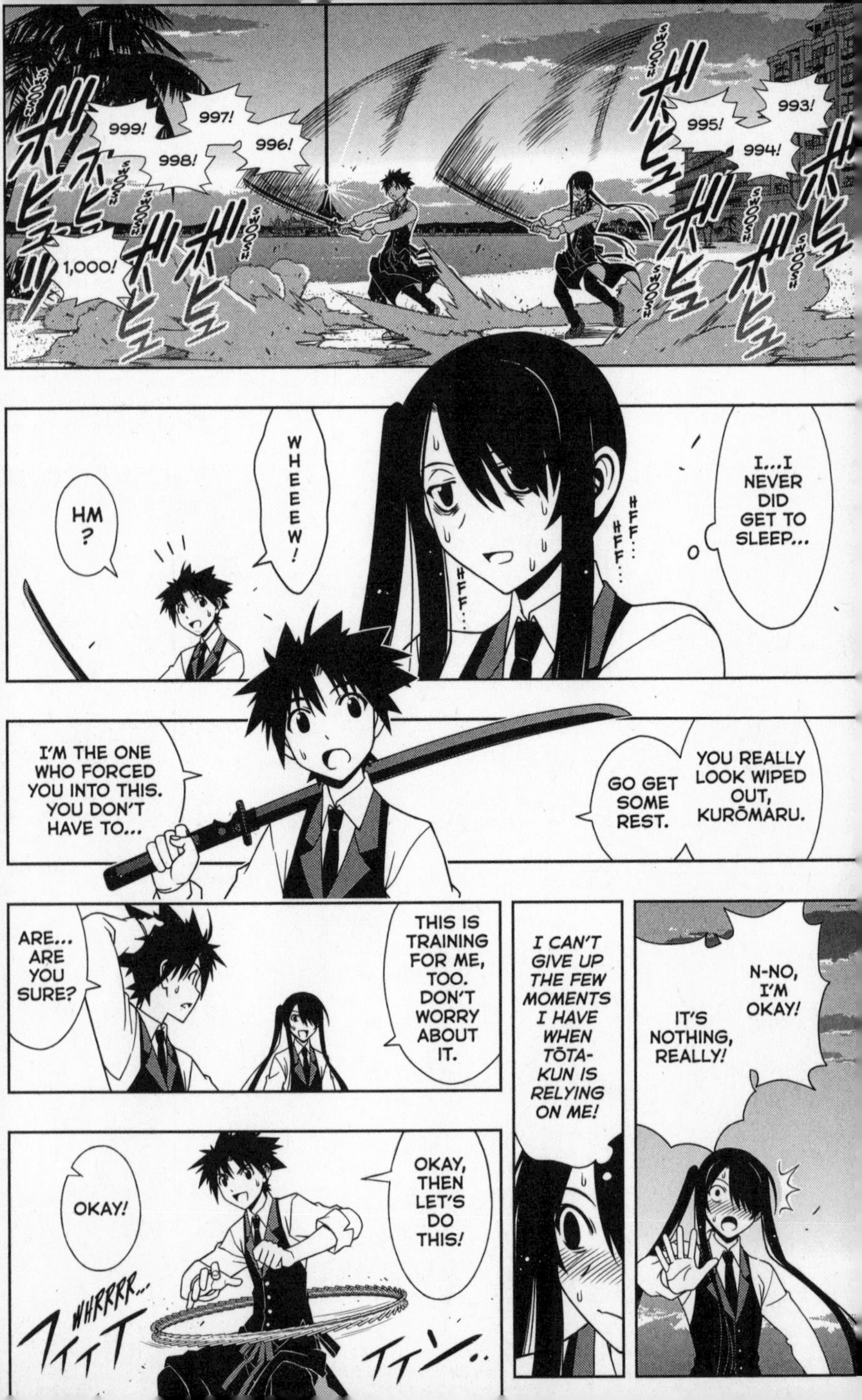
SWOOSH
993!
994!
995!
SWOOSH
SWOOSH
SWOOSH
996!
997!
998!
999!
SWOOSH
SWOOSH
SWOOSH
SWOOSH
1,000!
I...I NEVER DID GET TO SLEEP...
HFF... HFF... HFF...
WHEEEEW!
HM?
YOU REALLY LOOK WIPED OUT, KURŌMARU.
GO GET SOME REST.
I'M THE ONE WHO FORCED YOU INTO THIS. YOU DON'T HAVE TO...
N-NO, I'M OKAY!
IT'S NOTHING, REALLY!
I CAN'T GIVE UP THE FEW MOMENTS I HAVE WHEN TŌTA-KUN IS RELYING ON ME!
THIS IS TRAINING FOR ME, TOO. DON'T WORRY ABOUT IT.
ARE... ARE YOU SURE?
OKAY, THEN LET'S DO THIS!
OKAY!
WHRRRR...

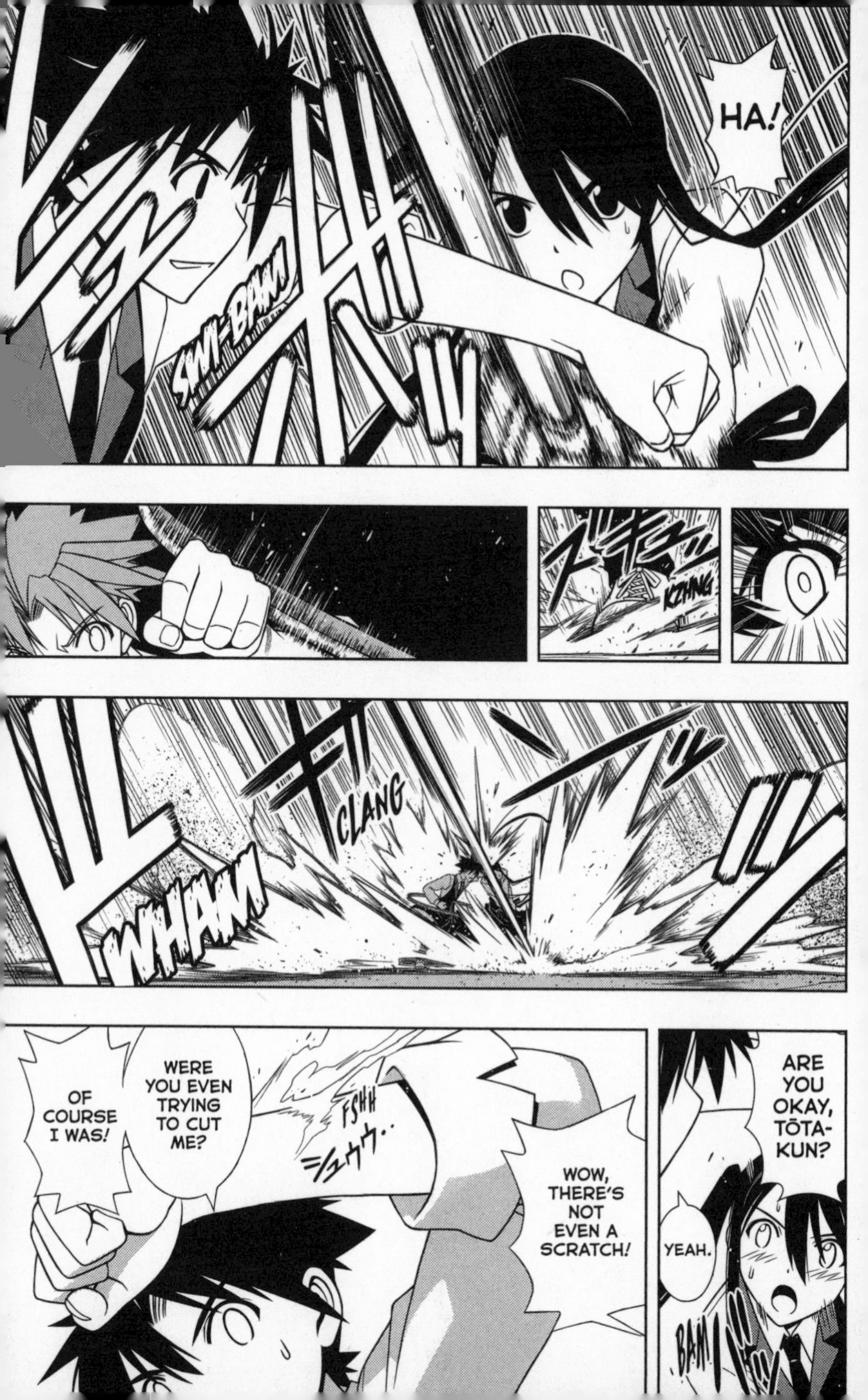
HA!
SWI-BANN
KZHNG
CLANG
WHAM
ARE YOU OKAY, TŌTA-KUN?
YEAH.
BAM!
WOW, THERE'S NOT EVEN A SCRATCH!
FSHH
シュウウ..
WERE YOU EVEN TRYING TO CUT ME?
OF COURSE I WAS!

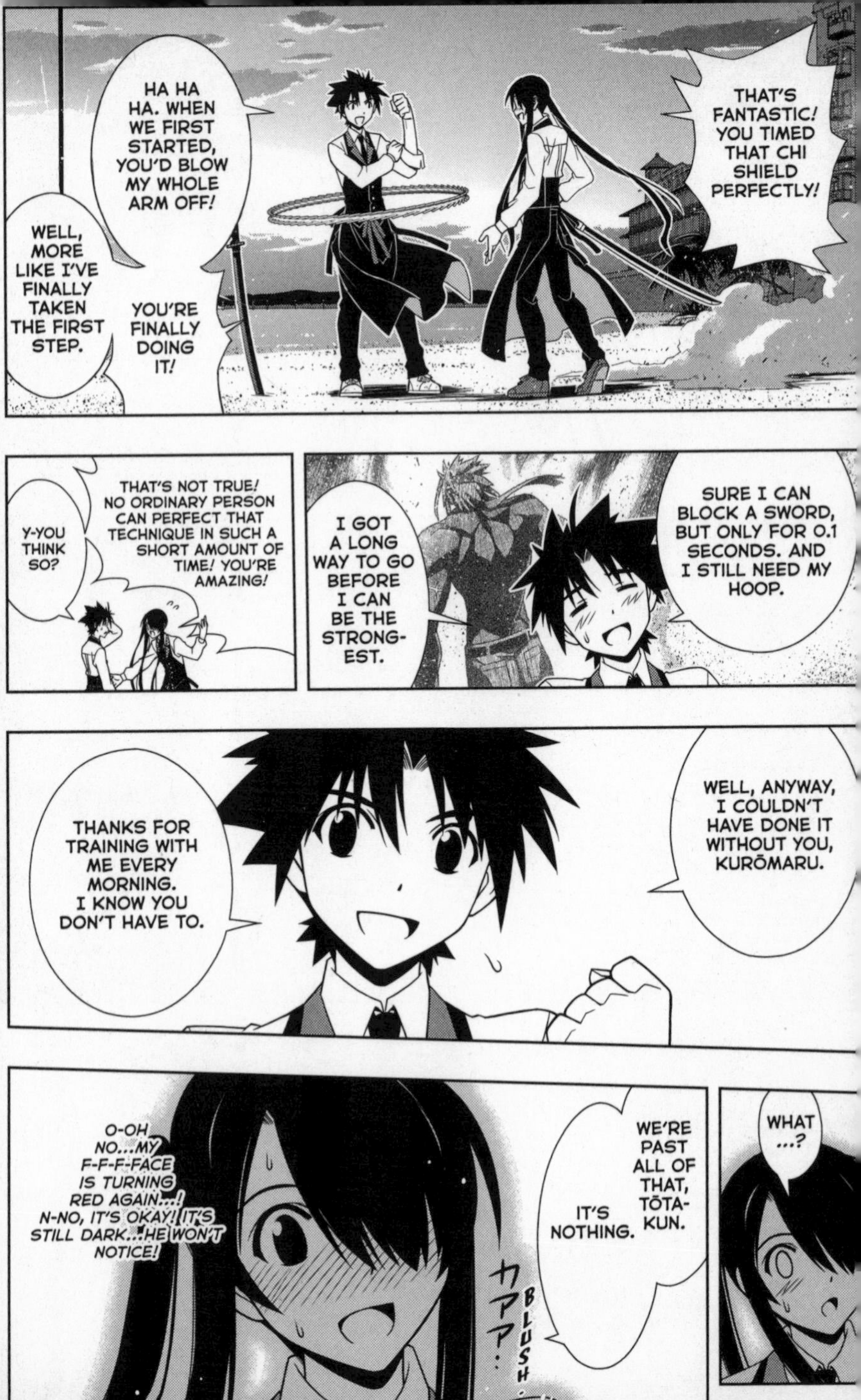
THAT'S FANTASTIC! YOU TIMED THAT CHI SHIELD PERFECTLY!
HA HA HA. WHEN WE FIRST STARTED, YOU'D BLOW MY WHOLE ARM OFF!
YOU'RE FINALLY DOING IT!
WELL, MORE LIKE I'VE FINALLY TAKEN THE FIRST STEP.
SURE I CAN BLOCK A SWORD, BUT ONLY FOR 0.1 SECONDS. AND I STILL NEED MY HOOP.
I GOT A LONG WAY TO GO BEFORE I CAN BE THE STRONG-EST.
THAT'S NOT TRUE! NO ORDINARY PERSON CAN PERFECT THAT TECHNIQUE IN SUCH A SHORT AMOUNT OF TIME! YOU'RE AMAZING!
Y-YOU THINK SO?
WELL, ANYWAY, I COULDN'T HAVE DONE IT WITHOUT YOU, KURŌMARU.
THANKS FOR TRAINING WITH ME EVERY MORNING. I KNOW YOU DON'T HAVE TO.
WHAT ...?
WE'RE PAST ALL OF THAT, TŌTA-KUN.
IT'S NOTHING.
カァァ
BLUSH...
O-OH NO...MY F-F-F-FACE IS TURNING RED AGAIN...! N-NO, IT'S OKAY! IT'S STILL DARK...HE WON'T NOTICE!

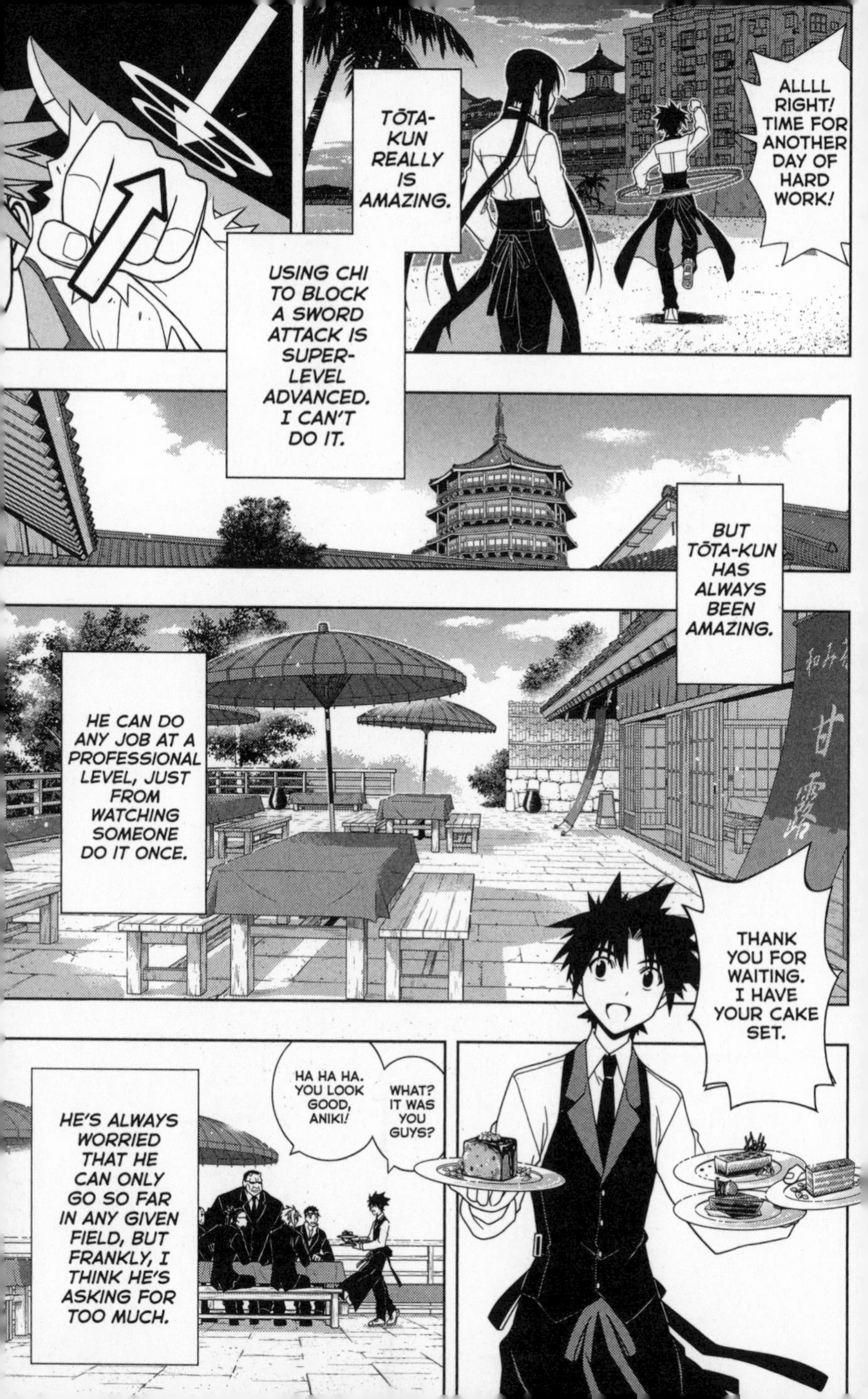
ALLLL RIGHT! TIME FOR ANOTHER DAY OF HARD WORK!
TŌTA-KUN REALLY IS AMAZING.
USING CHI TO BLOCK A SWORD ATTACK IS SUPER-LEVEL ADVANCED. I CAN'T DO IT.
BUT TŌTA-KUN HAS ALWAYS BEEN AMAZING.
HE CAN DO ANY JOB AT A PROFESSIONAL LEVEL, JUST FROM WATCHING SOMEONE DO IT ONCE.
THANK YOU FOR WAITING. I HAVE YOUR CAKE SET.
HA HA HA. YOU LOOK GOOD, ANIKI!
WHAT? IT WAS YOU GUYS?
HE'S ALWAYS WORRIED THAT HE CAN ONLY GO SO FAR IN ANY GIVEN FIELD, BUT FRANKLY, I THINK HE'S ASKING FOR TOO MUCH.

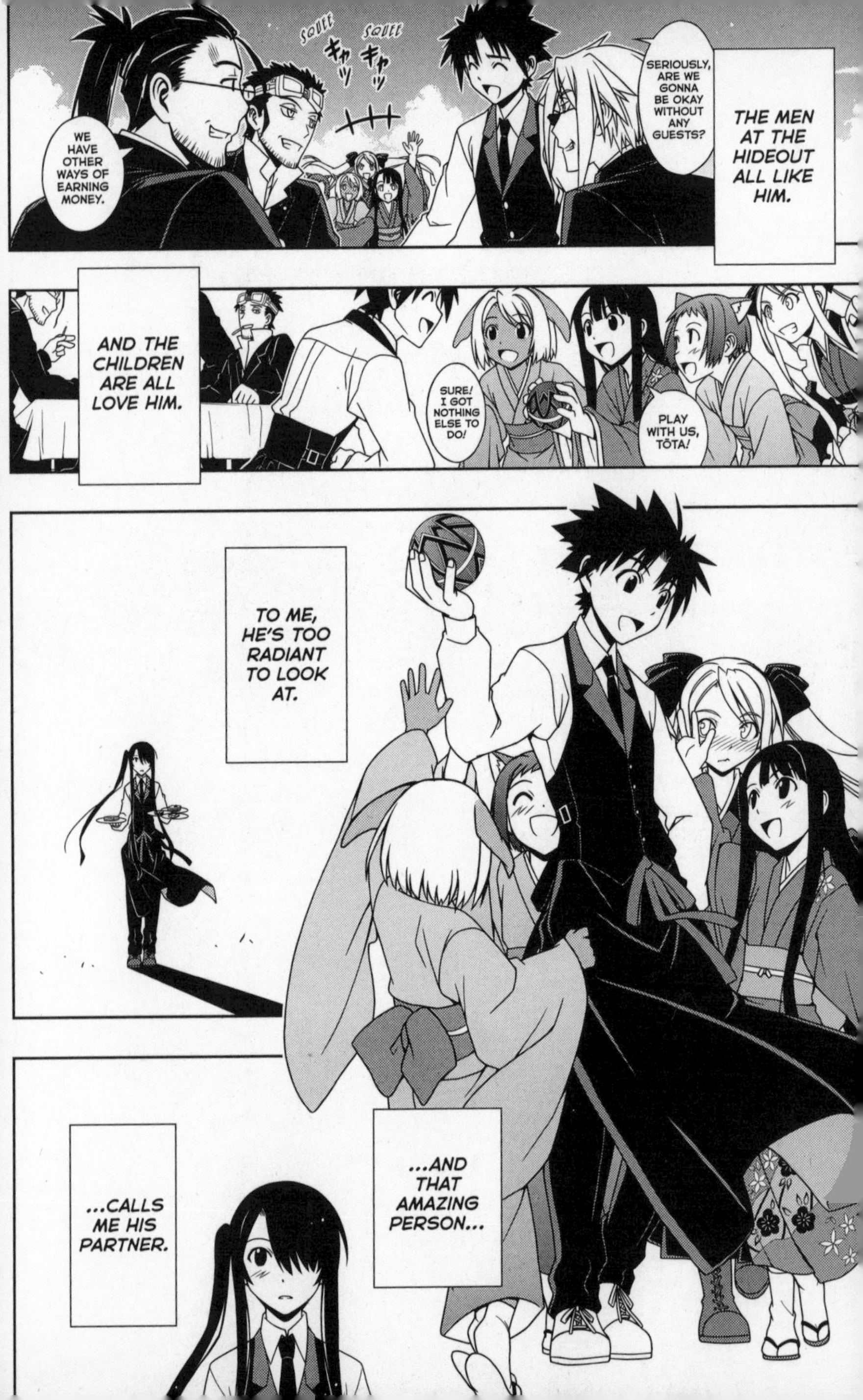
THE MEN AT THE HIDEOUT ALL LIKE HIM.
SERIOUSLY, ARE WE GONNA BE OKAY WITHOUT ANY GUESTS?
SQUEE キャッ
SQUEE キャッ
WE HAVE OTHER WAYS OF EARNING MONEY.
PLAY WITH US, TŌTA!
SURE! I GOT NOTHING ELSE TO DO!
AND THE CHILDREN ARE ALL LOVE HIM.
TO ME, HE'S TOO RADIANT TO LOOK AT.
...AND THAT AMAZING PERSON...
...CALLS ME HIS PARTNER.

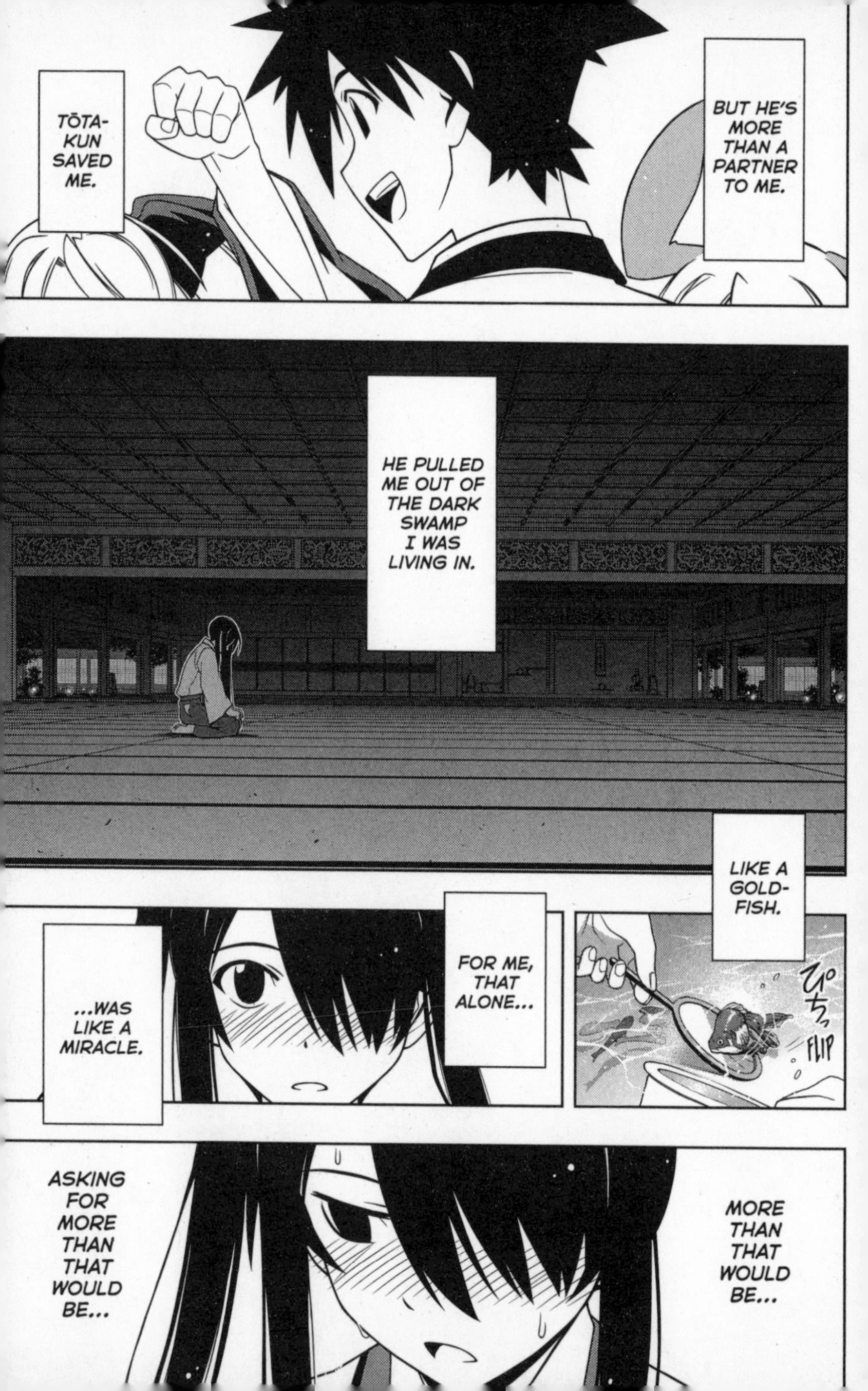
BUT HE'S MORE THAN A PARTNER TO ME.
TŌTA-KUN SAVED ME.
HE PULLED ME OUT OF THE DARK SWAMP I WAS LIVING IN.
LIKE A GOLD-FISH.
ぴちっ
FLIP
FOR ME, THAT ALONE...
...WAS LIKE A MIRACLE.
MORE THAN THAT WOULD BE...
ASKING FOR MORE THAN THAT WOULD BE...

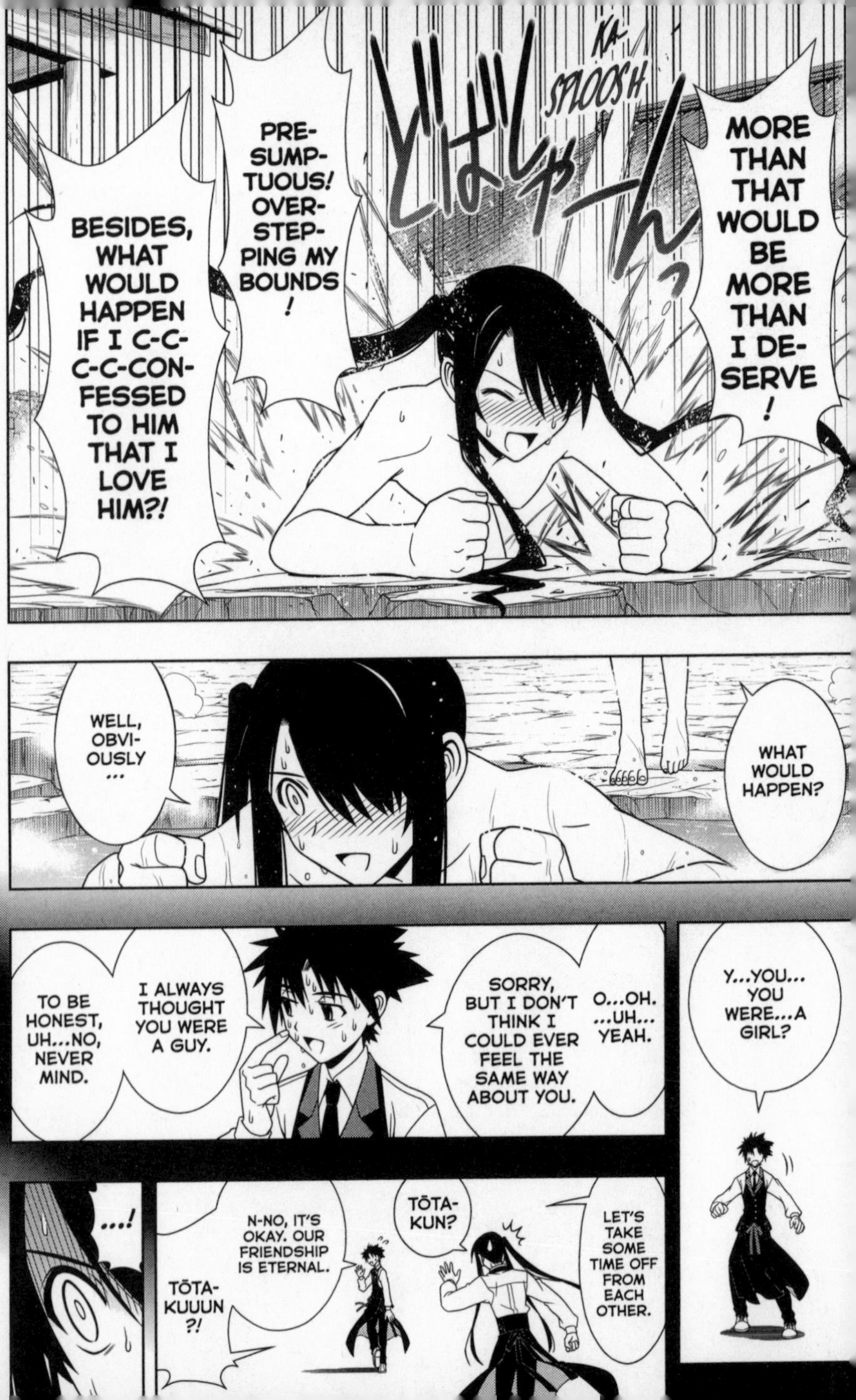
MORE THAN THAT WOULD BE MORE THAN I DESERVE!
どばしゃーん
KA-SPLOOSH
PRESUMPTUOUS! OVERSTEPPING MY BOUNDS!
BESIDES, WHAT WOULD HAPPEN IF I C-C-C-C-CONFESSED TO HIM THAT I LOVE HIM?!
WHAT WOULD HAPPEN?
WELL, OBVIOUSLY...
Y...YOU... YOU WERE...A GIRL?
O...OH. ...UH... YEAH.
SORRY, BUT I DON'T THINK I COULD EVER FEEL THE SAME WAY ABOUT YOU.
I ALWAYS THOUGHT YOU WERE A GUY.
TO BE HONEST, UH...NO, NEVER MIND.
LET'S TAKE SOME TIME OFF FROM EACH OTHER.
TŌTA-KUN?
N-NO, IT'S OKAY. OUR FRIENDSHIP IS ETERNAL.
TŌTA-KUUUN?!
...!

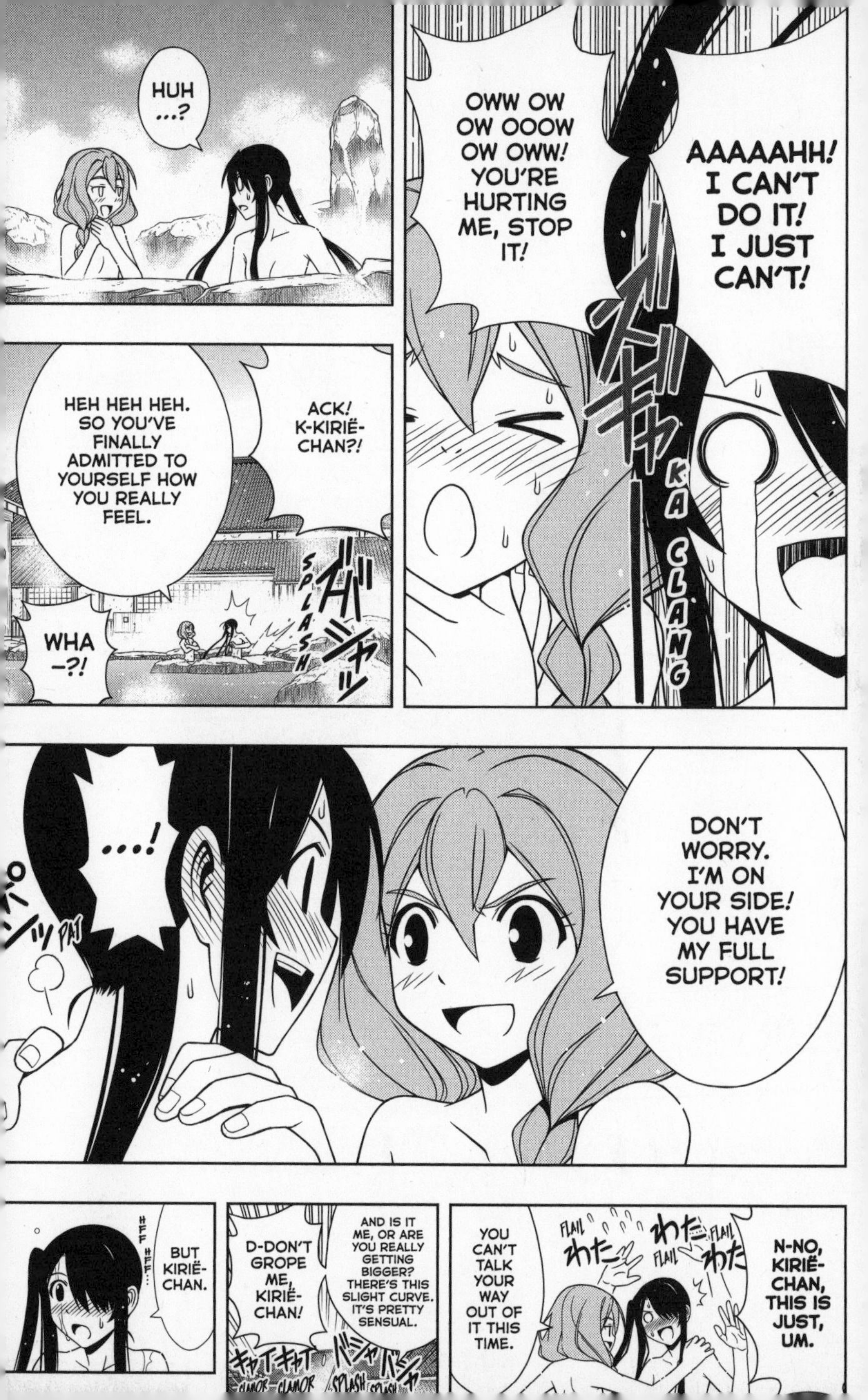
AAAAAHH! I CAN'T DO IT! I JUST CAN'T!
OWW OW OW OOOW OW OWW! YOU'RE HURTING ME, STOP IT!
KA CLANG
HUH ...?
ACK! K-KIRIË-CHAN?!
HEH HEH HEH. SO YOU'VE FINALLY ADMITTED TO YOURSELF HOW YOU REALLY FEEL.
SPLASH
WHA-?!
DON'T WORRY. I'M ON YOUR SIDE! YOU HAVE MY FULL SUPPORT!
...!
PAT
N-NO, KIRIË-CHAN, THIS IS JUST, UM.
FLAIL
FLAIL
FLAIL
YOU CAN'T TALK YOUR WAY OUT OF IT THIS TIME.
AND IS IT ME, OR ARE YOU REALLY GETTING BIGGER? THERE'S THIS SLIGHT CURVE. IT'S PRETTY SENSUAL.
D-DON'T GROPE ME, KIRIË-CHAN!
SPLASH
SPLASH
CLAMOR
CLAMOR
HFF HFF...
BUT KIRIË-CHAN.

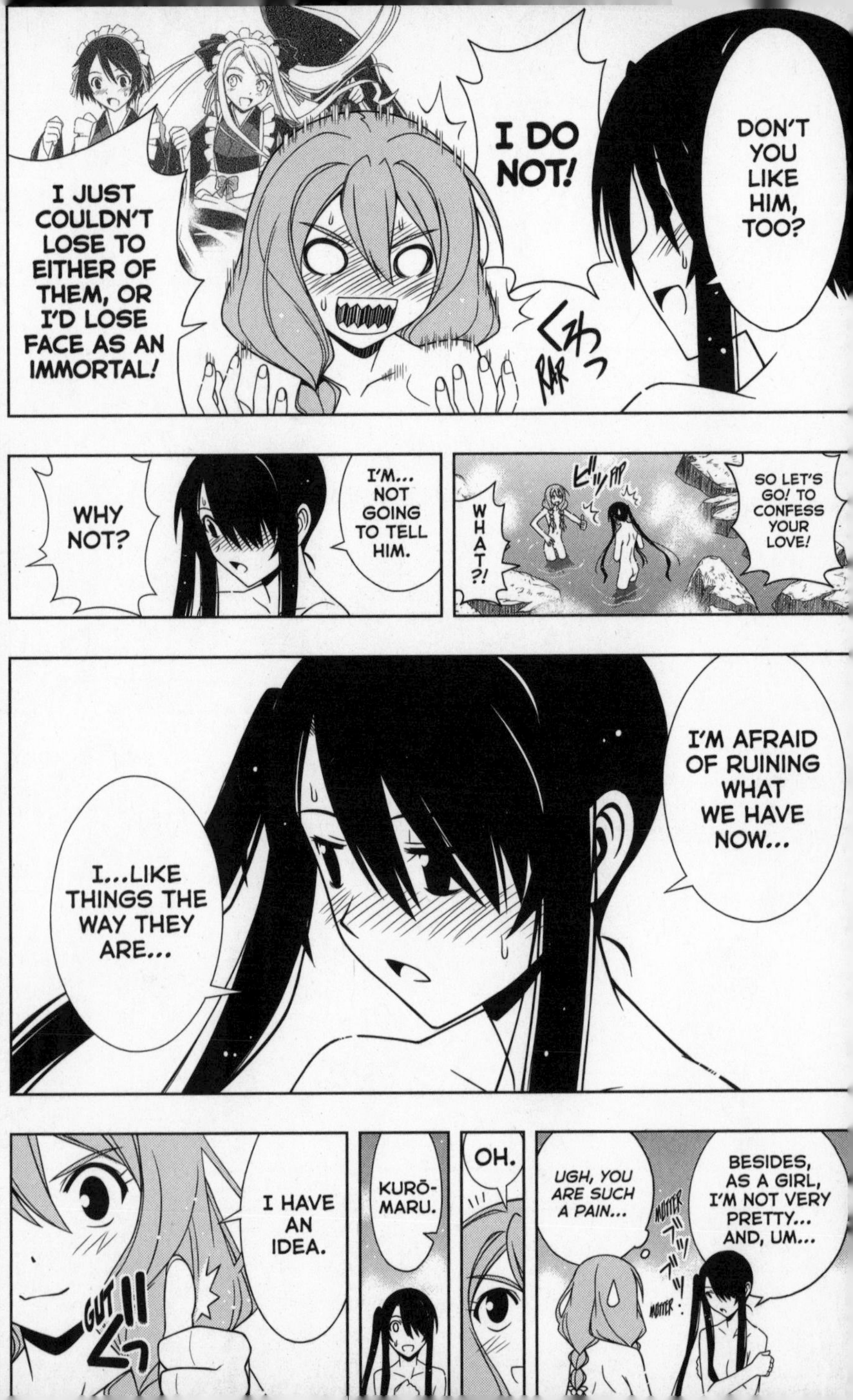
DON'T YOU LIKE HIM, TOO?
I DO NOT!
くろっ
RAR
I JUST COULDN'T LOSE TO EITHER OF THEM, OR I'D LOSE FACE AS AN IMMORTAL!
SO LET'S GO! TO CONFESS YOUR LOVE!
WHAT?!
I'M... NOT GOING TO TELL HIM.
WHY NOT?
I'M AFRAID OF RUINING WHAT WE HAVE NOW...
I...LIKE THINGS THE WAY THEY ARE...
BESIDES, AS A GIRL, I'M NOT VERY PRETTY... AND, UM...
MUTTER
MUTTER
UGH, YOU ARE SUCH A PAIN...
OH.
KURŌ-MARU.
I HAVE AN IDEA.
GUT

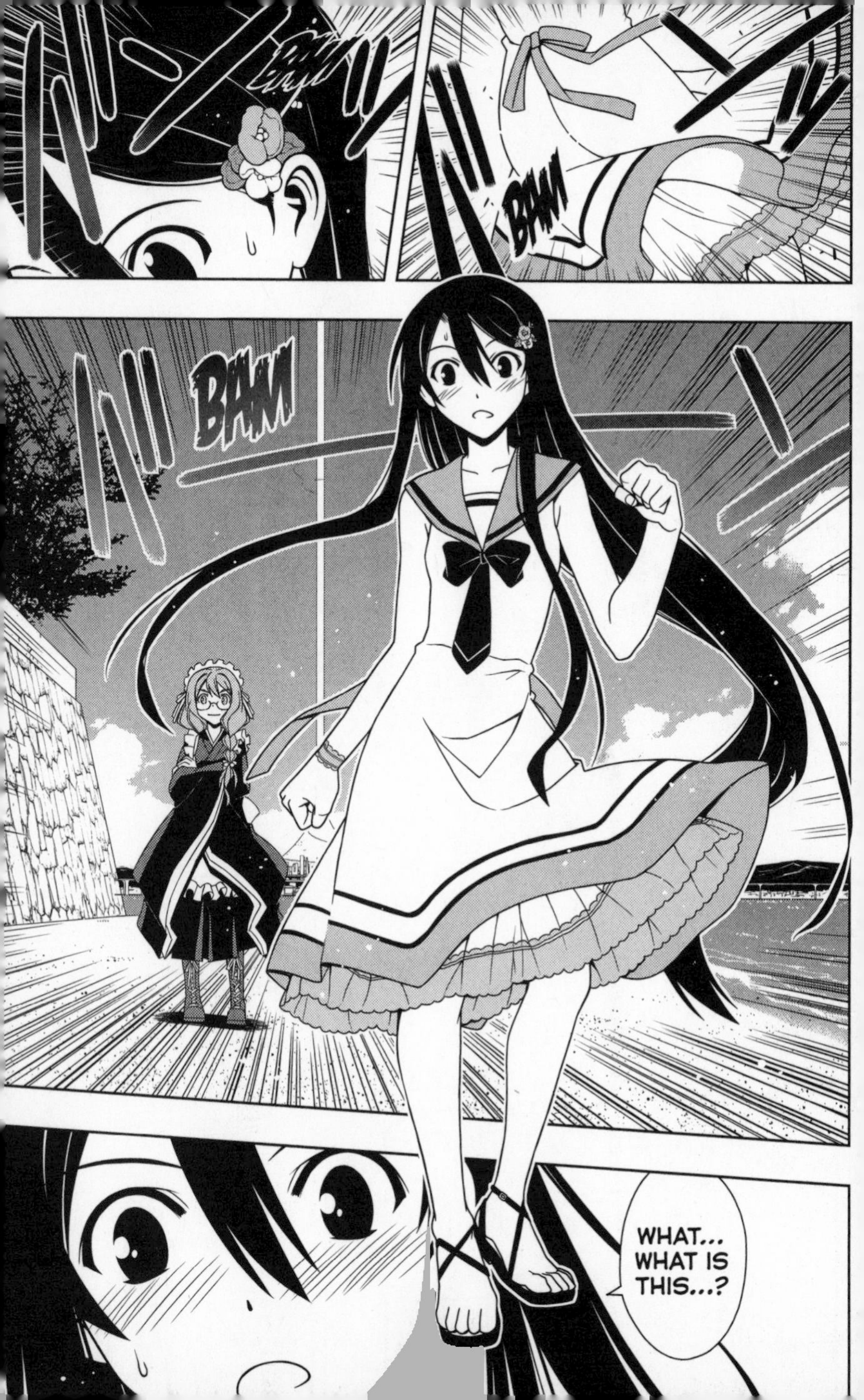
BAM
BAM
WHAT... WHAT IS THIS...?

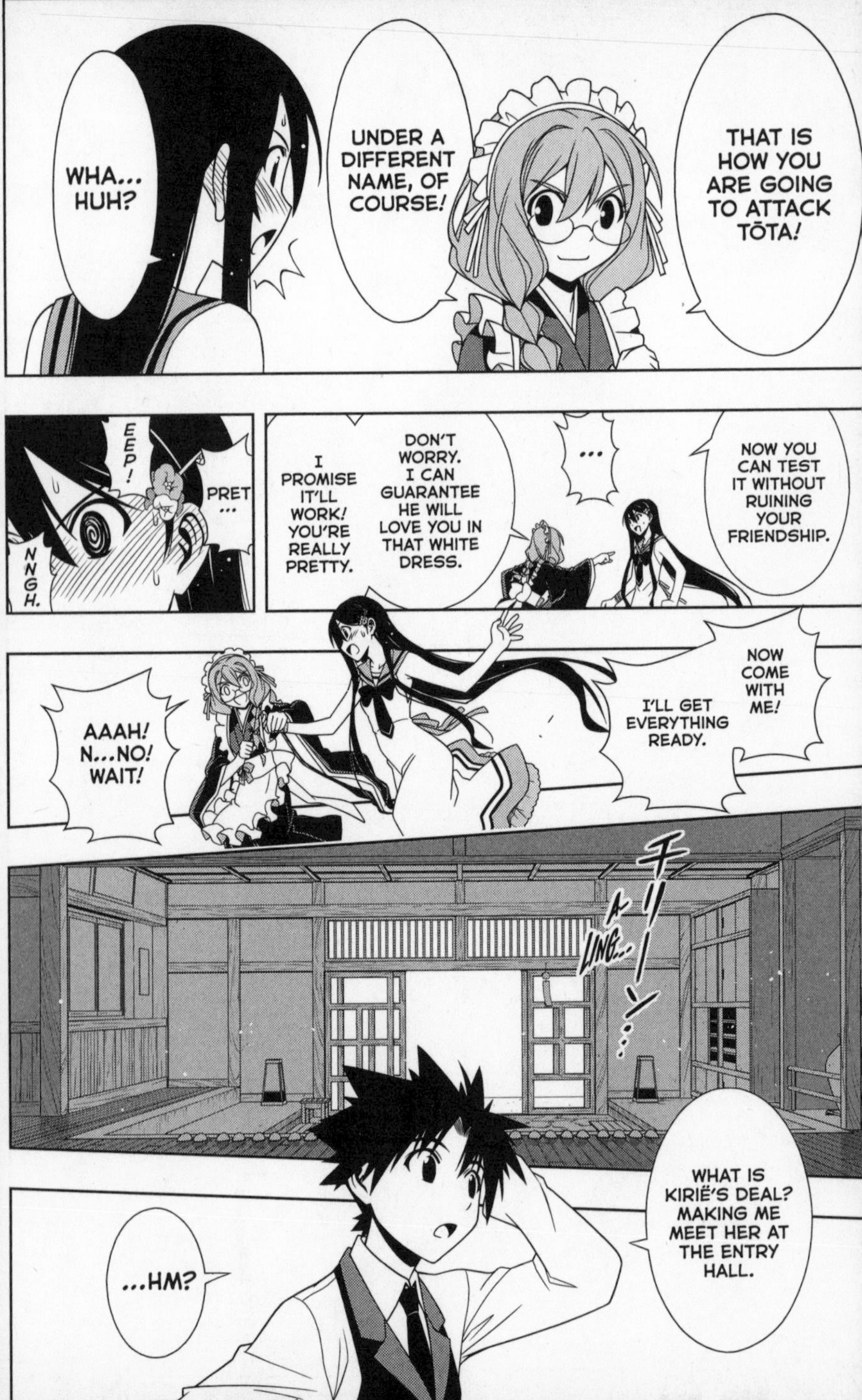
THAT IS HOW YOU ARE GOING TO ATTACK TŌTA!
UNDER A DIFFERENT NAME, OF COURSE!
WHA... HUH?
NOW YOU CAN TEST IT WITHOUT RUINING YOUR FRIENDSHIP.
...
DON'T WORRY. I CAN GUARANTEE HE WILL LOVE YOU IN THAT WHITE DRESS.
I PROMISE IT'LL WORK! YOU'RE REALLY PRETTY.
EEP!
PRET...
NNGH.
NOW COME WITH ME!
I'LL GET EVERYTHING READY.
AAAH! N...NO! WAIT!
チリーン…
A-LING...
WHAT IS KIRIË'S DEAL? MAKING ME MEET HER AT THE ENTRY HALL.
...HM?

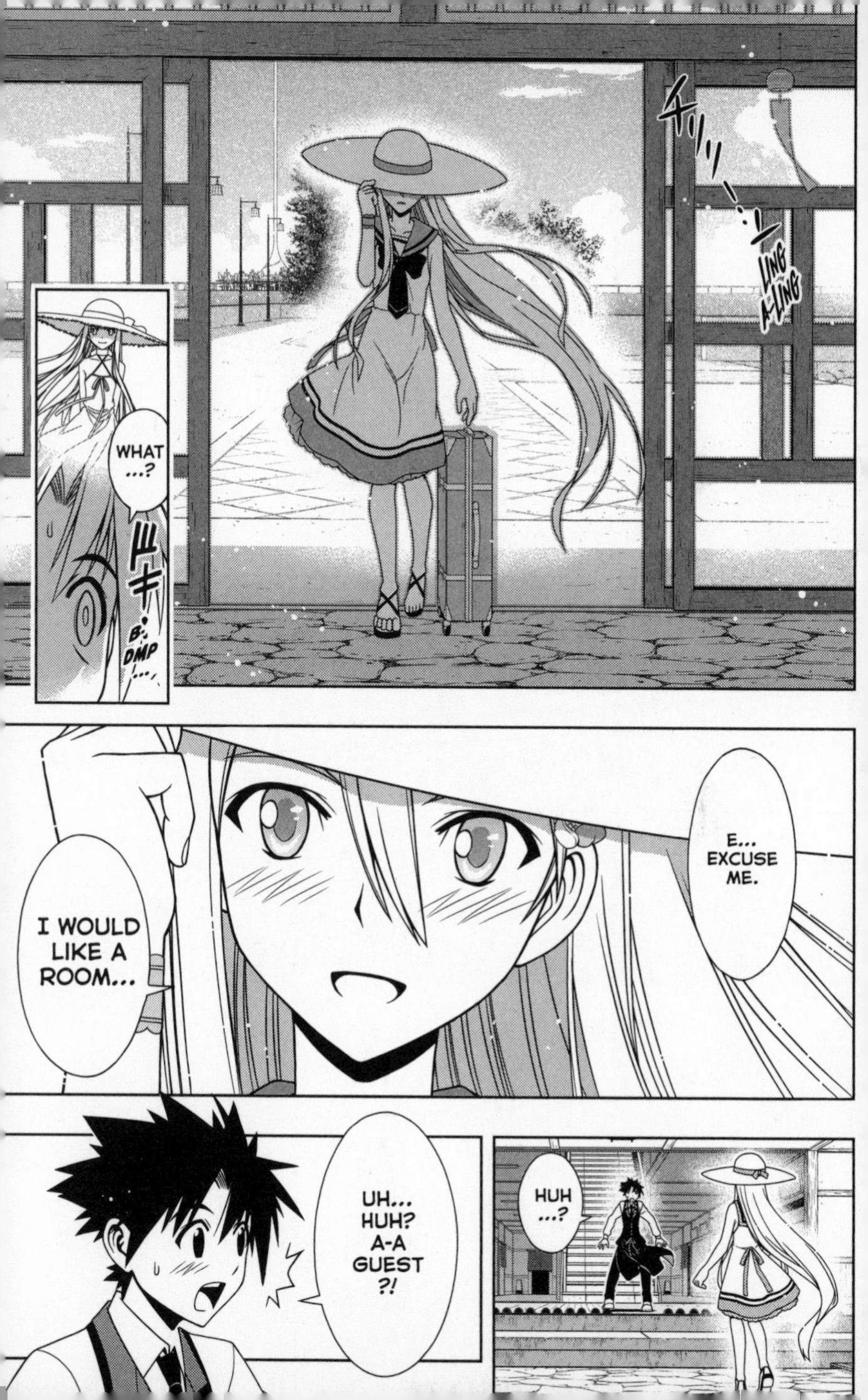
LING A-LING
WHAT ...?
B-DMP !...
E... EXCUSE ME.
I WOULD LIKE A ROOM...
HUH ...?
UH... HUH? A-A GUEST ?!

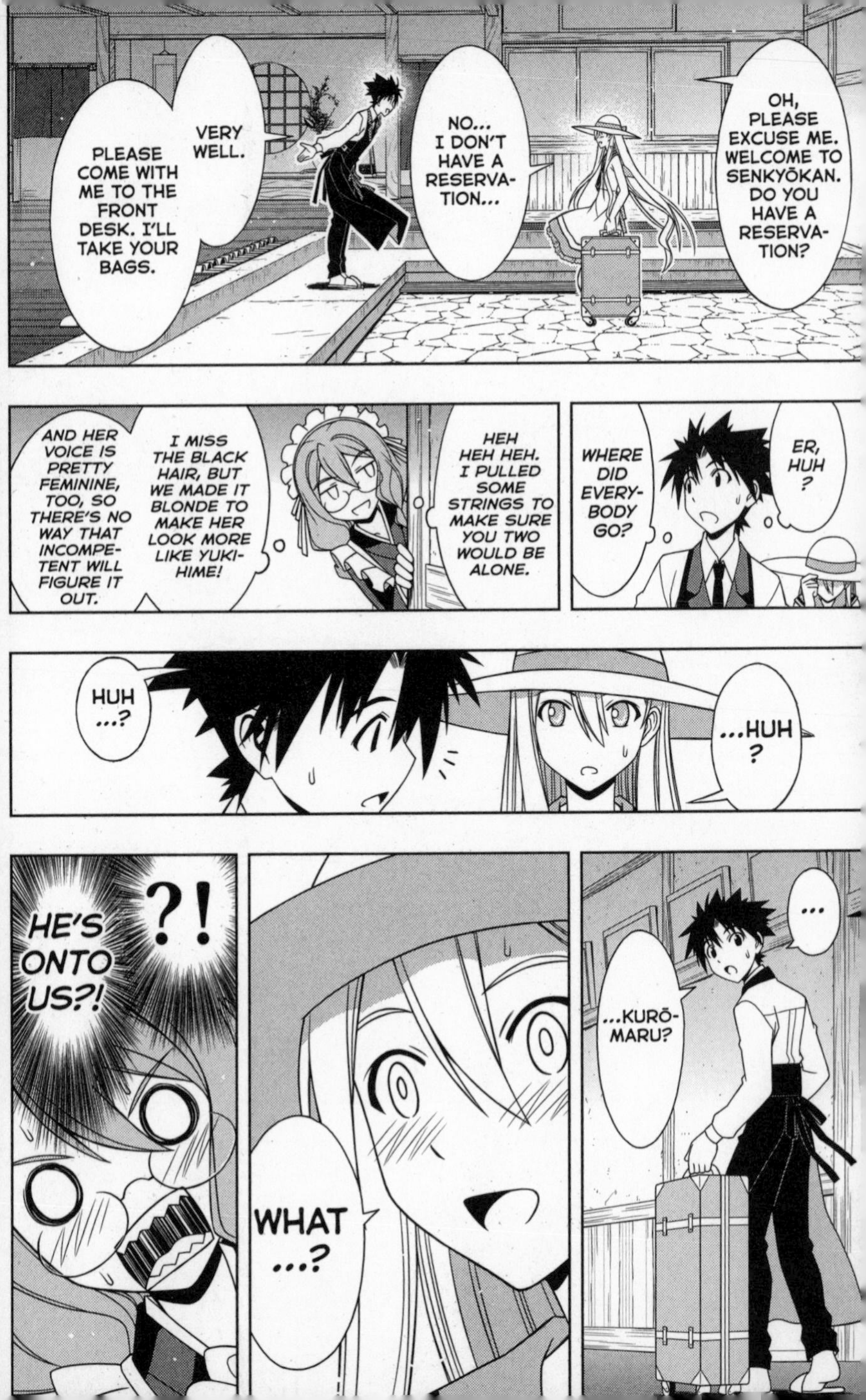
OH, PLEASE EXCUSE ME. WELCOME TO SENKYŌKAN. DO YOU HAVE A RESERVATION?
NO... I DON'T HAVE A RESERVATION...
VERY WELL.
PLEASE COME WITH ME TO THE FRONT DESK. I'LL TAKE YOUR BAGS.
ER, HUH?
WHERE DID EVERYBODY GO?
HEH HEH HEH. I PULLED SOME STRINGS TO MAKE SURE YOU TWO WOULD BE ALONE.
I MISS THE BLACK HAIR, BUT WE MADE IT BLONDE TO MAKE HER LOOK MORE LIKE YUKI-HIME!
AND HER VOICE IS PRETTY FEMININE, TOO, SO THERE'S NO WAY THAT INCOMPETENT WILL FIGURE IT OUT.
...HUH?
HUH...?
...
...KURŌMARU?
WHAT...?
?!
HE'S ONTO US?!

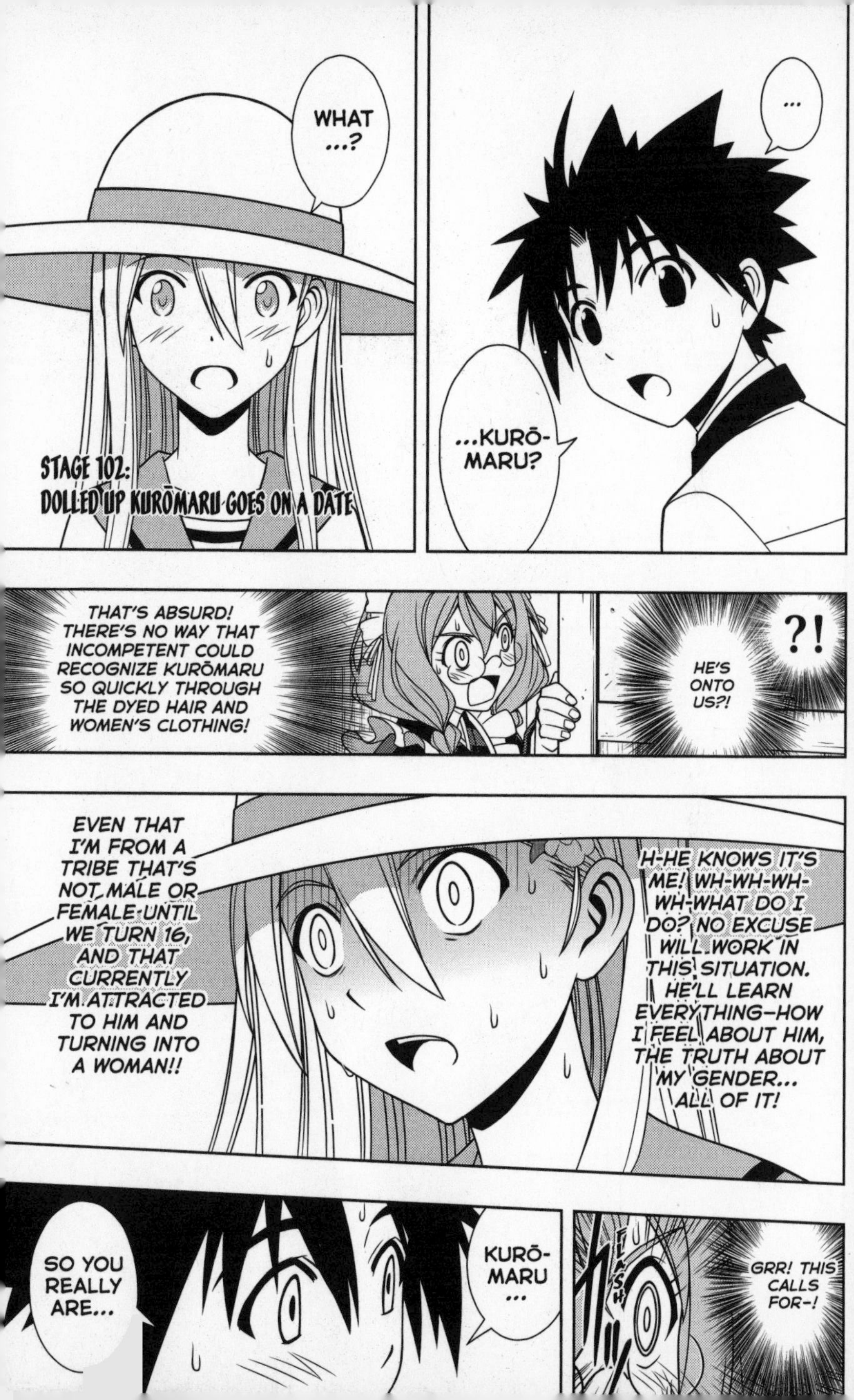
...
...KURŌ-MARU?
WHAT ...?
STAGE 102: DOLLED UP KURŌMARU GOES ON A DATE
?!
HE'S ONTO US?!
THAT'S ABSURD! THERE'S NO WAY THAT INCOMPETENT COULD RECOGNIZE KURŌMARU SO QUICKLY THROUGH THE DYED HAIR AND WOMEN'S CLOTHING!
H-HE KNOWS IT'S ME! WH-WH-WH-WH-WHAT DO I DO? NO EXCUSE WILL WORK IN THIS SITUATION. HE'LL LEARN EVERYTHING—HOW I FEEL ABOUT HIM, THE TRUTH ABOUT MY GENDER... ALL OF IT!
EVEN THAT I'M FROM A TRIBE THAT'S NOT MALE OR FEMALE UNTIL WE TURN 16, AND THAT CURRENTLY I'M ATTRACTED TO HIM AND TURNING INTO A WOMAN!!
GRR! THIS CALLS FOR-!
FLASH
KURŌ-MARU ...
SO YOU REALLY ARE...

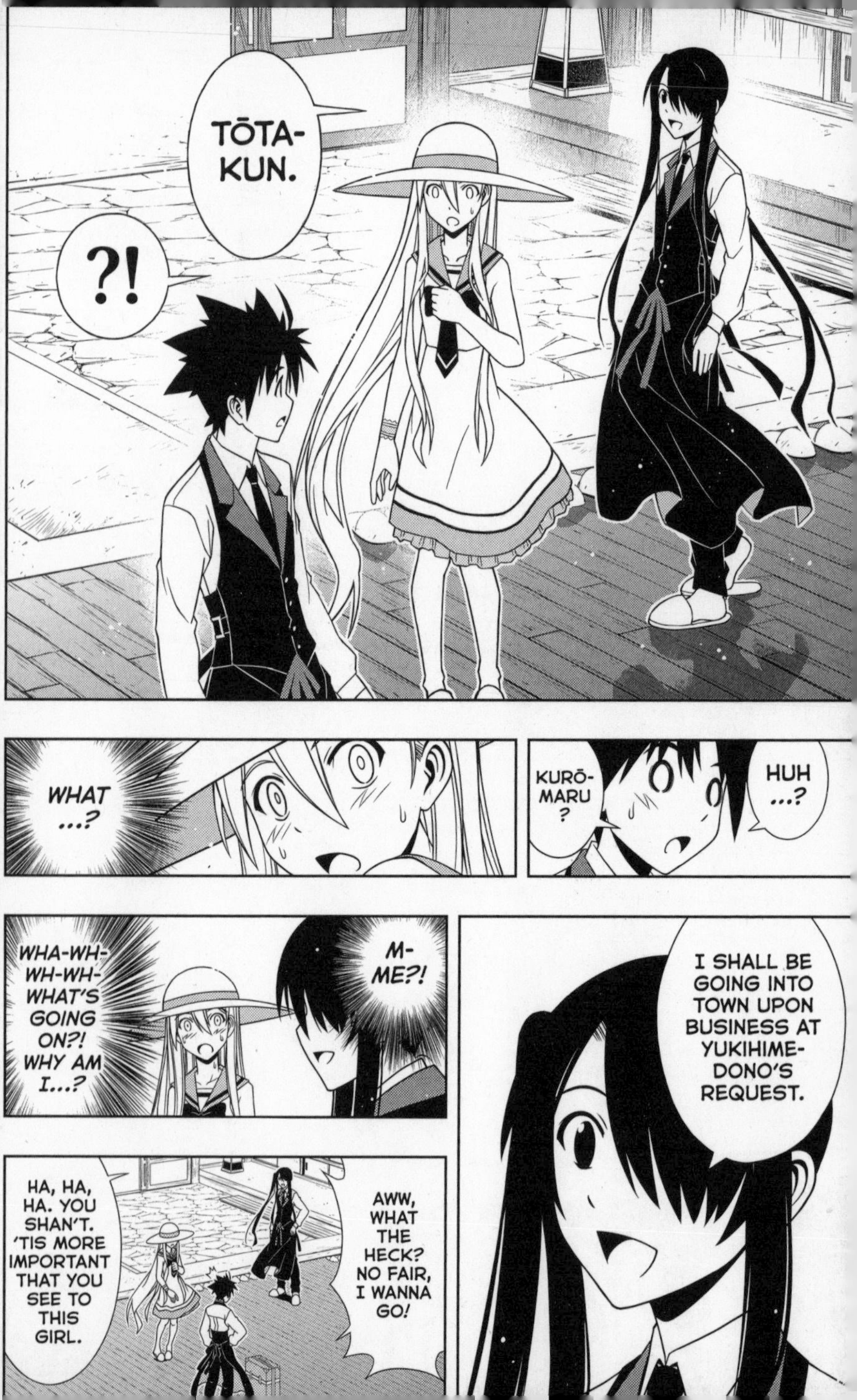
TŌTA-KUN.
?!
HUH ...?
KURŌ-MARU ?
WHAT ...?
I SHALL BE GOING INTO TOWN UPON BUSINESS AT YUKIHIME-DONO'S REQUEST.
M- ME?!
WHA-WH-WH-WH-WHAT'S GOING ON?! WHY AM I...?
AWW, WHAT THE HECK? NO FAIR, I WANNA GO!
HA, HA, HA. YOU SHAN'T. 'TIS MORE IMPORTANT THAT YOU SEE TO THIS GIRL.

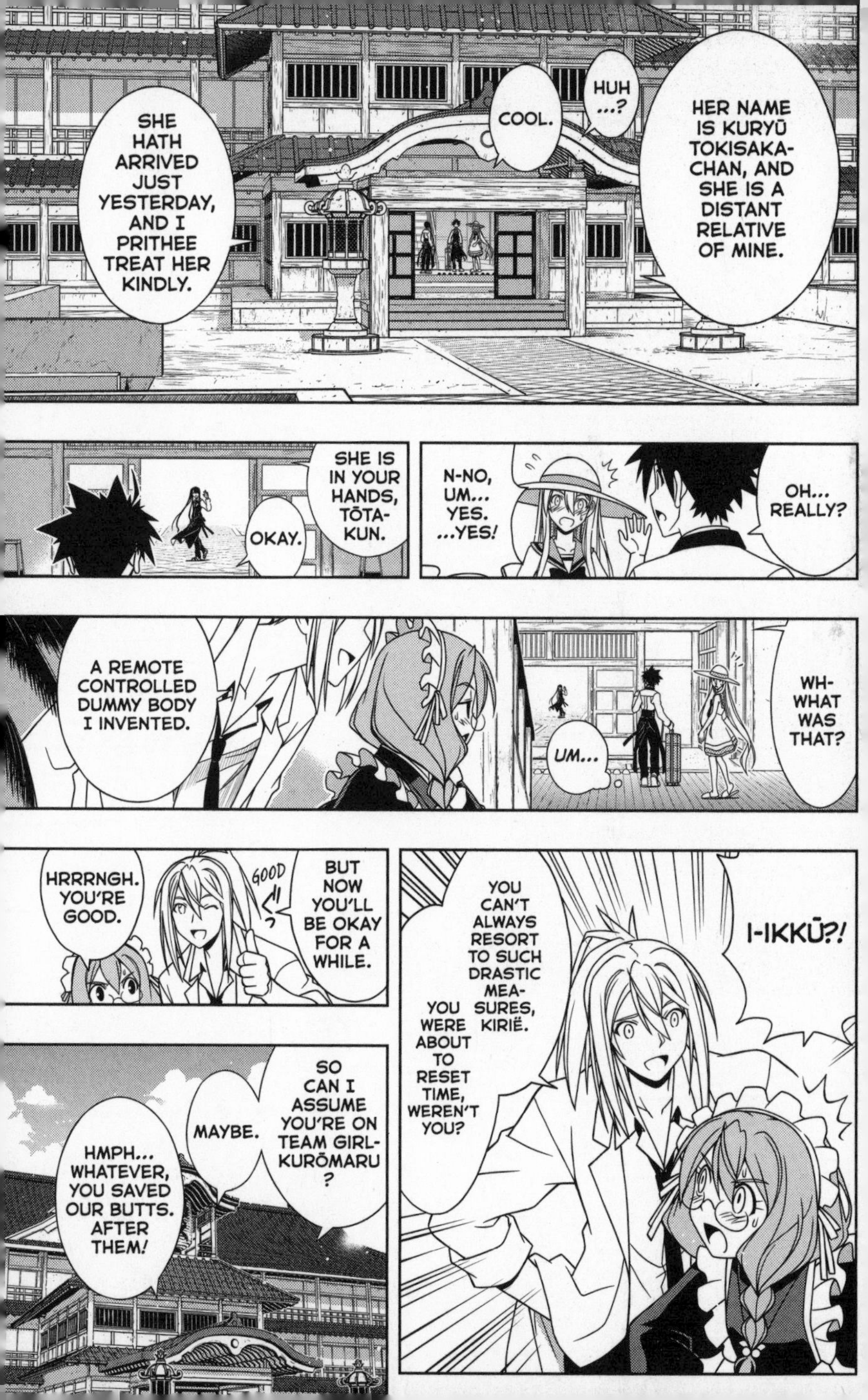
HER NAME IS KURYŪ TOKISAKA-CHAN, AND SHE IS A DISTANT RELATIVE OF MINE.
HUH ...?
COOL.
SHE HATH ARRIVED JUST YESTERDAY, AND I PRITHEE TREAT HER KINDLY.
OH... REALLY?
N-NO, UM... YES. ...YES!
SHE IS IN YOUR HANDS, TŌTA-KUN.
OKAY.
WH-WHAT WAS THAT?
UM...
A REMOTE CONTROLLED DUMMY BODY I INVENTED.
I-IKKŪ?!
YOU CAN'T ALWAYS RESORT TO SUCH DRASTIC MEA-SURES, KIRIË.
YOU WERE ABOUT TO RESET TIME, WEREN'T YOU?
BUT NOW YOU'LL BE OKAY FOR A WHILE.
GOOD
HRRRNGH. YOU'RE GOOD.
SO CAN I ASSUME YOU'RE ON TEAM GIRL-KURŌMARU ?
MAYBE.
HMPH... WHATEVER, YOU SAVED OUR BUTTS. AFTER THEM!

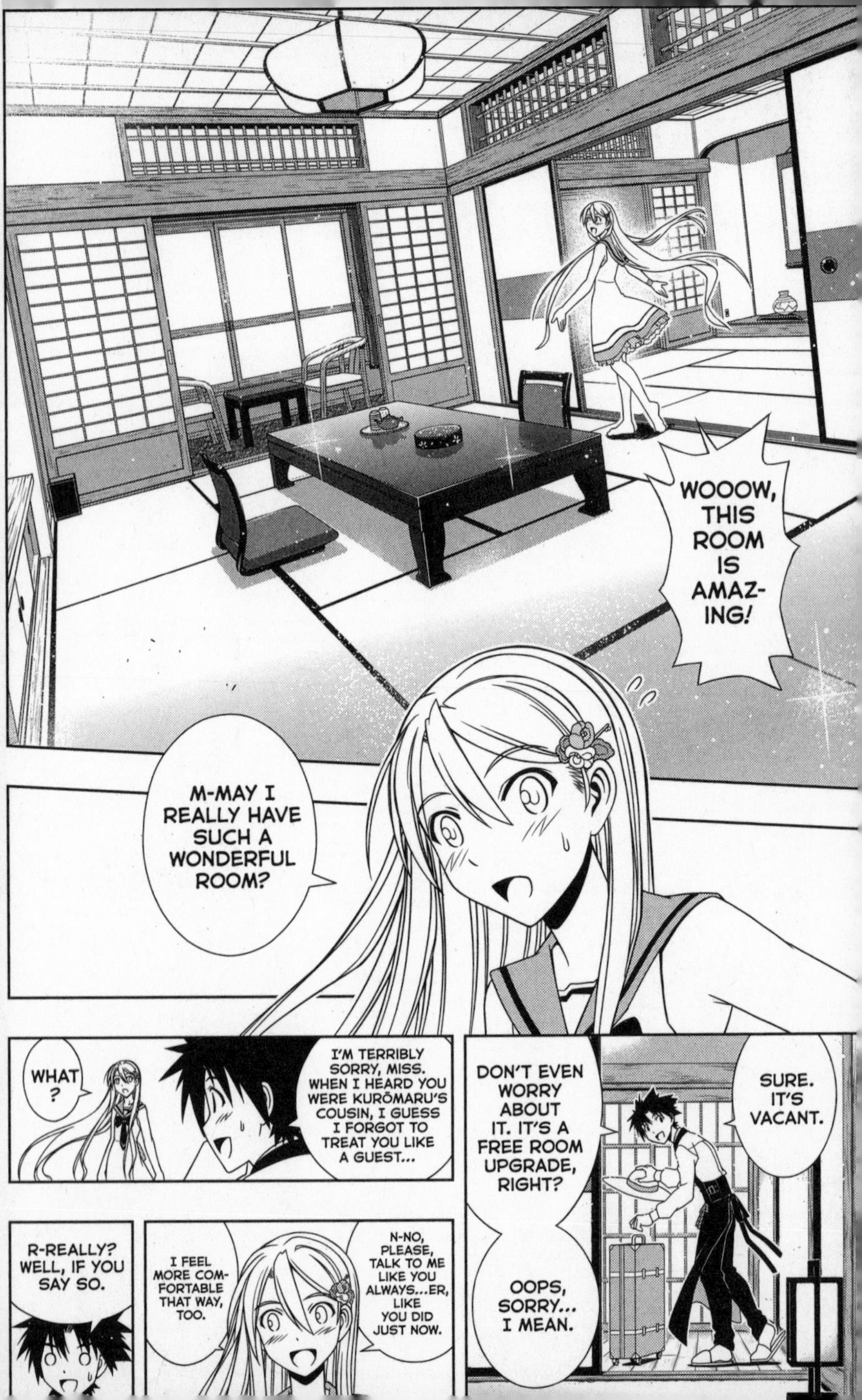
WOOOW, THIS ROOM IS AMAZING!
M-MAY I REALLY HAVE SUCH A WONDERFUL ROOM?
SURE. IT'S VACANT.
DON'T EVEN WORRY ABOUT IT. IT'S A FREE ROOM UPGRADE, RIGHT?
OOPS, SORRY... I MEAN.
I'M TERRIBLY SORRY, MISS. WHEN I HEARD YOU WERE KURŌMARU'S COUSIN, I GUESS I FORGOT TO TREAT YOU LIKE A GUEST...
WHAT?
N-NO, PLEASE, TALK TO ME LIKE YOU ALWAYS...ER, LIKE YOU DID JUST NOW.
I FEEL MORE COM-FORTABLE THAT WAY, TOO.
R-REALLY? WELL, IF YOU SAY SO.

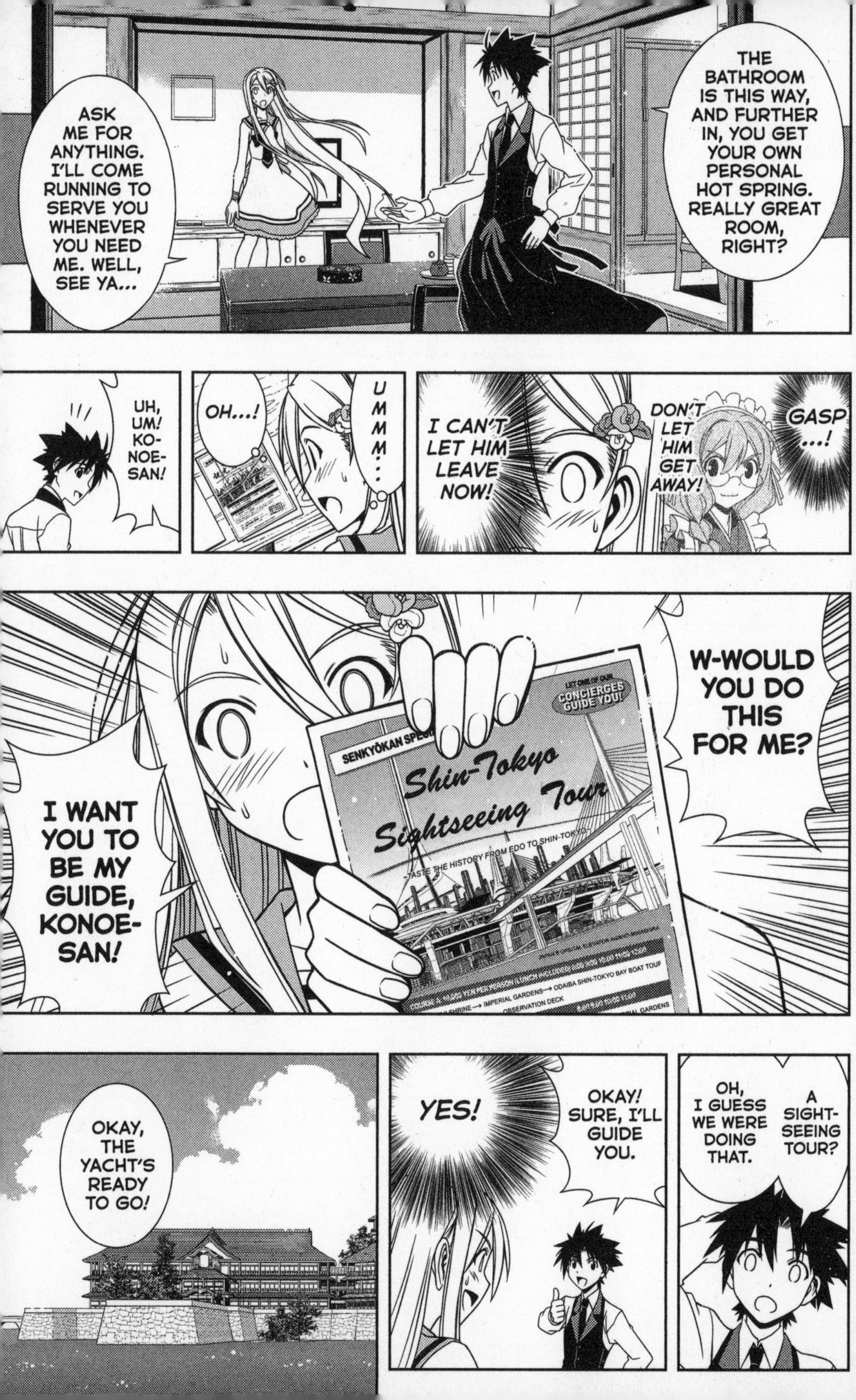
THE BATHROOM IS THIS WAY, AND FURTHER IN, YOU GET YOUR OWN PERSONAL HOT SPRING. REALLY GREAT ROOM, RIGHT?
ASK ME FOR ANYTHING. I'LL COME RUNNING TO SERVE YOU WHENEVER YOU NEED ME. WELL, SEE YA...
GASP ...!
DON'T LET HIM GET AWAY!
I CAN'T LET HIM LEAVE NOW!
UMMM...
OH...!
UH, UM! KO-NOE-SAN!
W-WOULD YOU DO THIS FOR ME?
LET ONE OF OUR CONCIERGES GUIDE YOU!
Shin-Tokyo Sightseeing Tour
-TASTE THE HISTORY FROM EDO TO SHIN-TOKYO-
I WANT YOU TO BE MY GUIDE, KONOE-SAN!
A SIGHT-SEEING TOUR?
OH, I GUESS WE WERE DOING THAT.
OKAY! SURE, I'LL GUIDE YOU.
YES!
OKAY, THE YACHT'S READY TO GO!

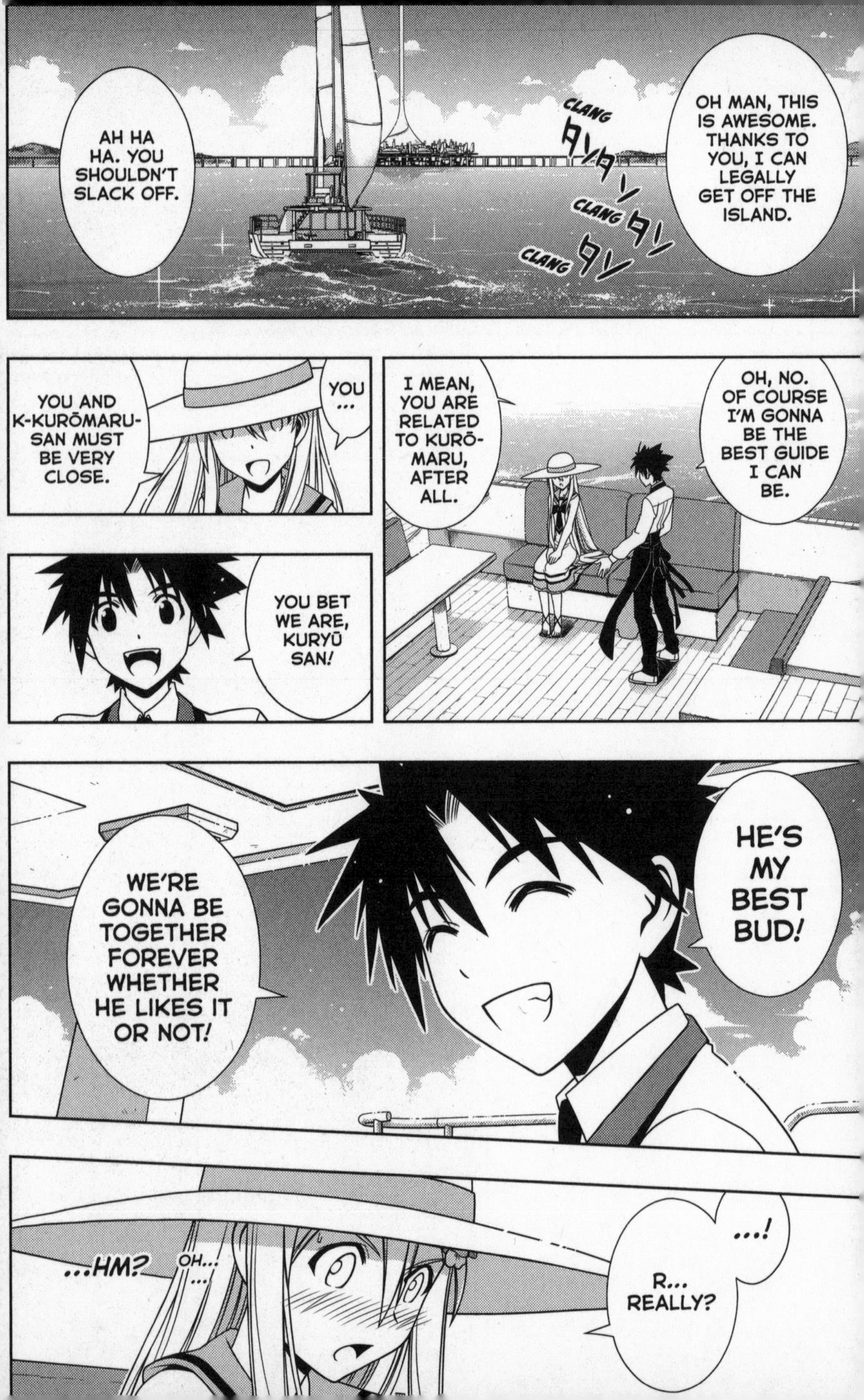
OH MAN, THIS IS AWESOME. THANKS TO YOU, I CAN LEGALLY GET OFF THE ISLAND.
CLANG
タンタン
CLANG
タン
CLANG
タン
AH HA HA. YOU SHOULDN'T SLACK OFF.
OH, NO. OF COURSE I'M GONNA BE THE BEST GUIDE I CAN BE.
I MEAN, YOU ARE RELATED TO KURŌMARU, AFTER ALL.
YOU ...
YOU AND K-KURŌMARU-SAN MUST BE VERY CLOSE.
YOU BET WE ARE, KURYŪ SAN!
HE'S MY BEST BUD!
WE'RE GONNA BE TOGETHER FOREVER WHETHER HE LIKES IT OR NOT!
...!
R... REALLY?
OH... ...
...HM?

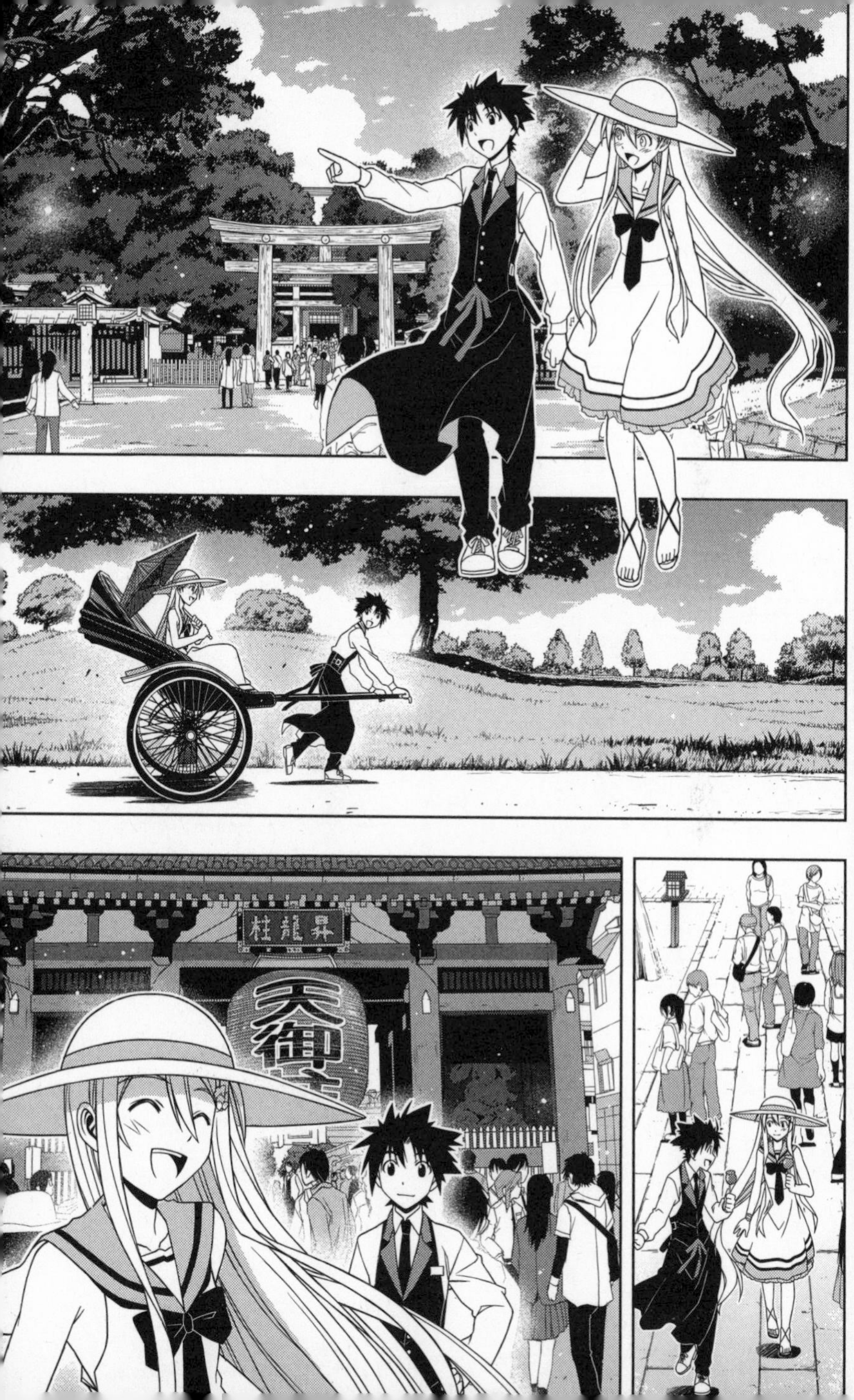
昇龍柱
天御

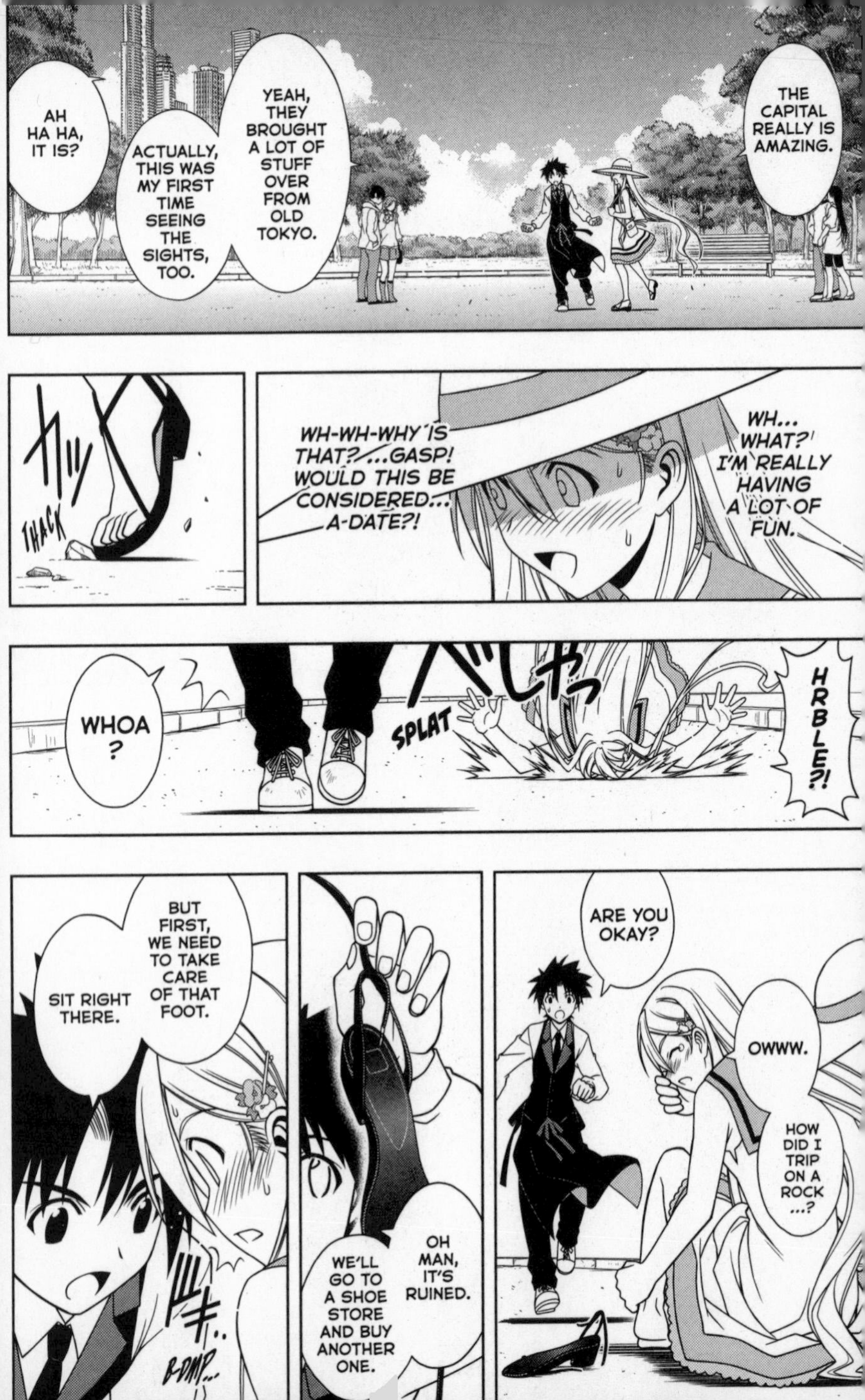
THE CAPITAL REALLY IS AMAZING.
YEAH, THEY BROUGHT A LOT OF STUFF OVER FROM OLD TOKYO.
ACTUALLY, THIS WAS MY FIRST TIME SEEING THE SIGHTS, TOO.
AH HA HA, IT IS?
WH... WHAT? I'M REALLY HAVING A LOT OF FUN.
WH-WH-WHY IS THAT? ...GASP! WOULD THIS BE CONSIDERED... A DATE?!
THACK
HRBLE?!
SPLAT
WHOA?
ARE YOU OKAY?
OWWW.
HOW DID I TRIP ON A ROCK ...?
OH MAN, IT'S RUINED.
WE'LL GO TO A SHOE STORE AND BUY ANOTHER ONE.
BUT FIRST, WE NEED TO TAKE CARE OF THAT FOOT.
SIT RIGHT THERE.
B-DMP...

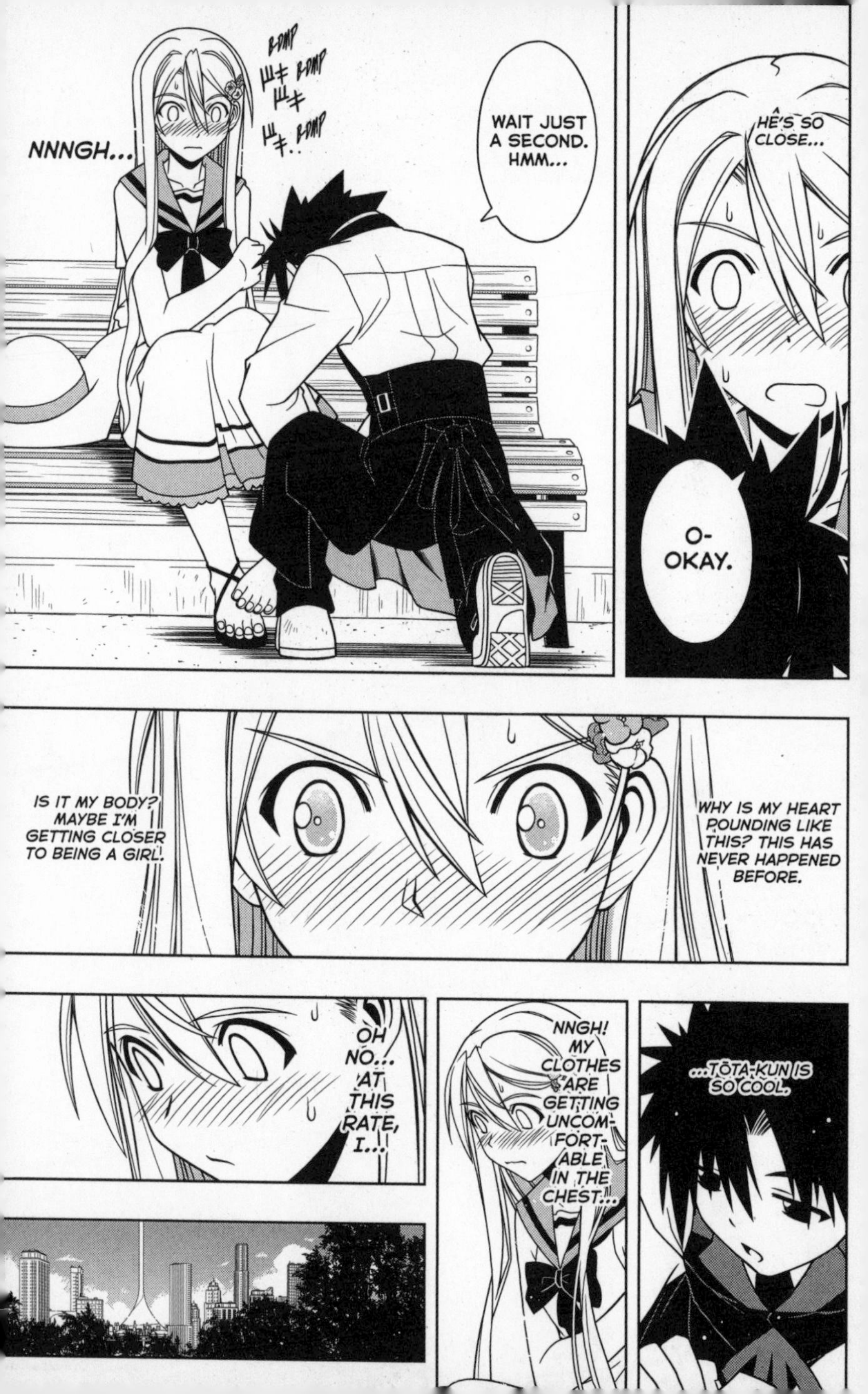
HE'S SO CLOSE...
O-OKAY.
WAIT JUST A SECOND. HMM...
B-DMP
B-DMP
B-DMP
NNNGH...
WHY IS MY HEART POUNDING LIKE THIS? THIS HAS NEVER HAPPENED BEFORE.
IS IT MY BODY? MAYBE I'M GETTING CLOSER TO BEING A GIRL.
...TŌTA-KUN IS SO COOL.
NNGH! MY CLOTHES ARE GETTING UNCOMFORTABLE IN THE CHEST...
OH NO... AT THIS RATE, I...

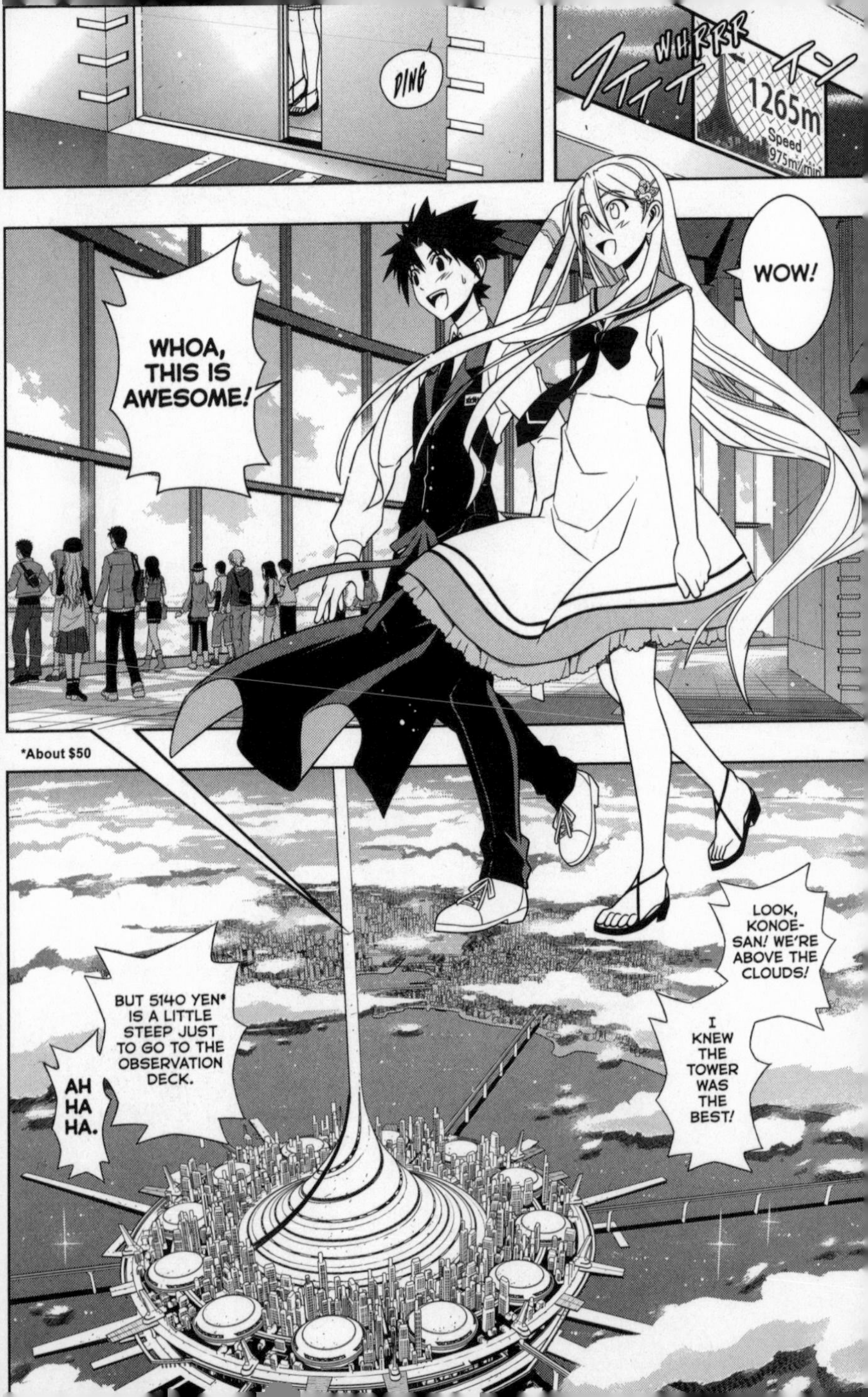
WHRRR
1265m
Speed
975m/min
DING
WOW!
WHOA, THIS IS AWESOME!
LOOK, KONOE-SAN! WE'RE ABOVE THE CLOUDS!
I KNEW THE TOWER WAS THE BEST!
BUT 5140 YEN* IS A LITTLE STEEP JUST TO GO TO THE OBSERVATION DECK.
AH HA HA.

*About $50

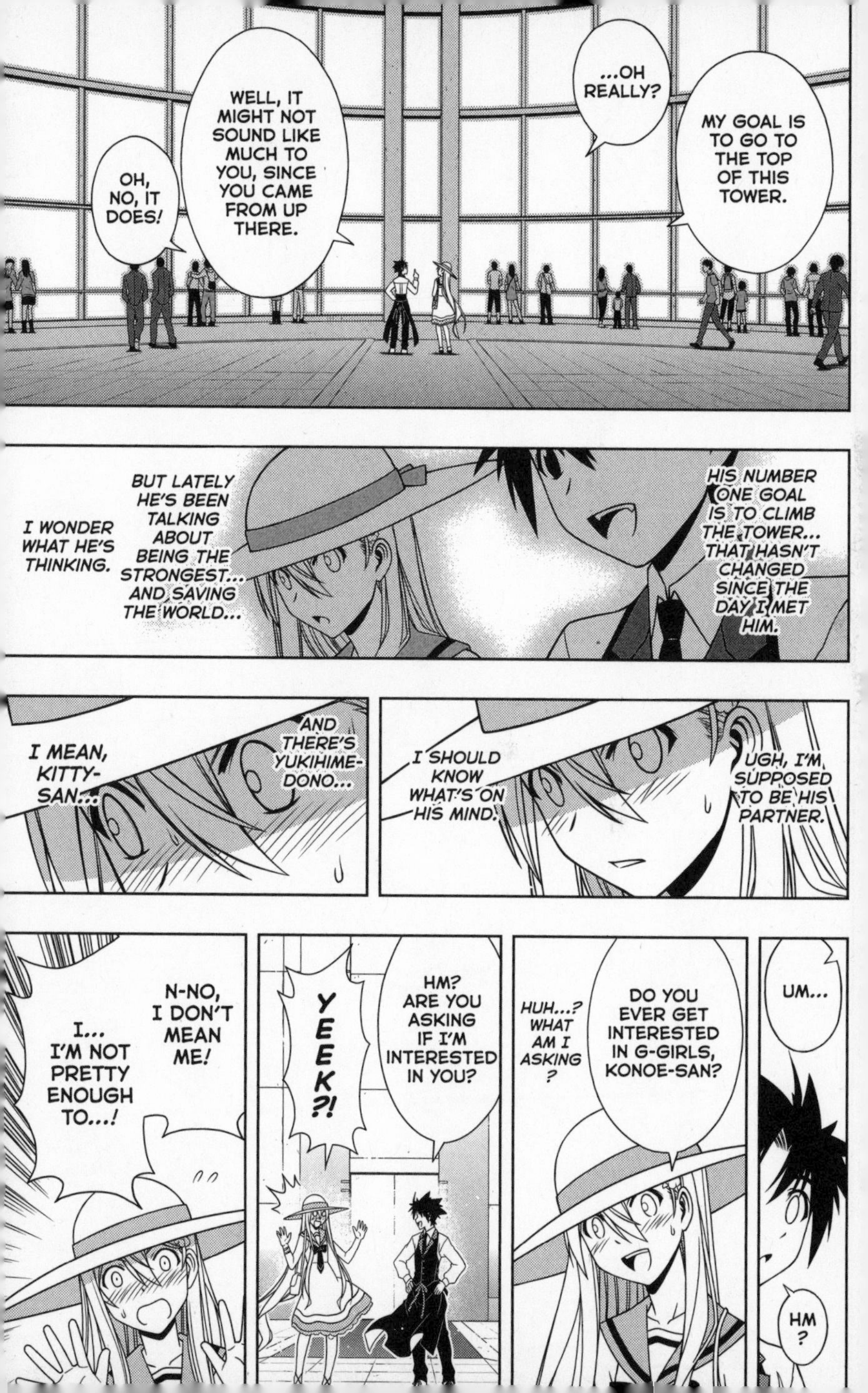
MY GOAL IS TO GO TO THE TOP OF THIS TOWER.
...OH REALLY?
WELL, IT MIGHT NOT SOUND LIKE MUCH TO YOU, SINCE YOU CAME FROM UP THERE.
OH, NO, IT DOES!
HIS NUMBER ONE GOAL IS TO CLIMB THE TOWER... THAT HASN'T CHANGED SINCE THE DAY I MET HIM.
BUT LATELY HE'S BEEN TALKING ABOUT BEING THE STRONGEST... AND SAVING THE WORLD...
I WONDER WHAT HE'S THINKING.
UGH, I'M SUPPOSED TO BE HIS PARTNER.
I SHOULD KNOW WHAT'S ON HIS MIND.
AND THERE'S YUKIHIME-DONO...
I MEAN, KITTY-SAN...
UM...
HM?
DO YOU EVER GET INTERESTED IN G-GIRLS, KONOE-SAN?
HUH...? WHAT AM I ASKING?
HM? ARE YOU ASKING IF I'M INTERESTED IN YOU?
YEEK?!
N-NO, I DON'T MEAN ME!
I... I'M NOT PRETTY ENOUGH TO...!

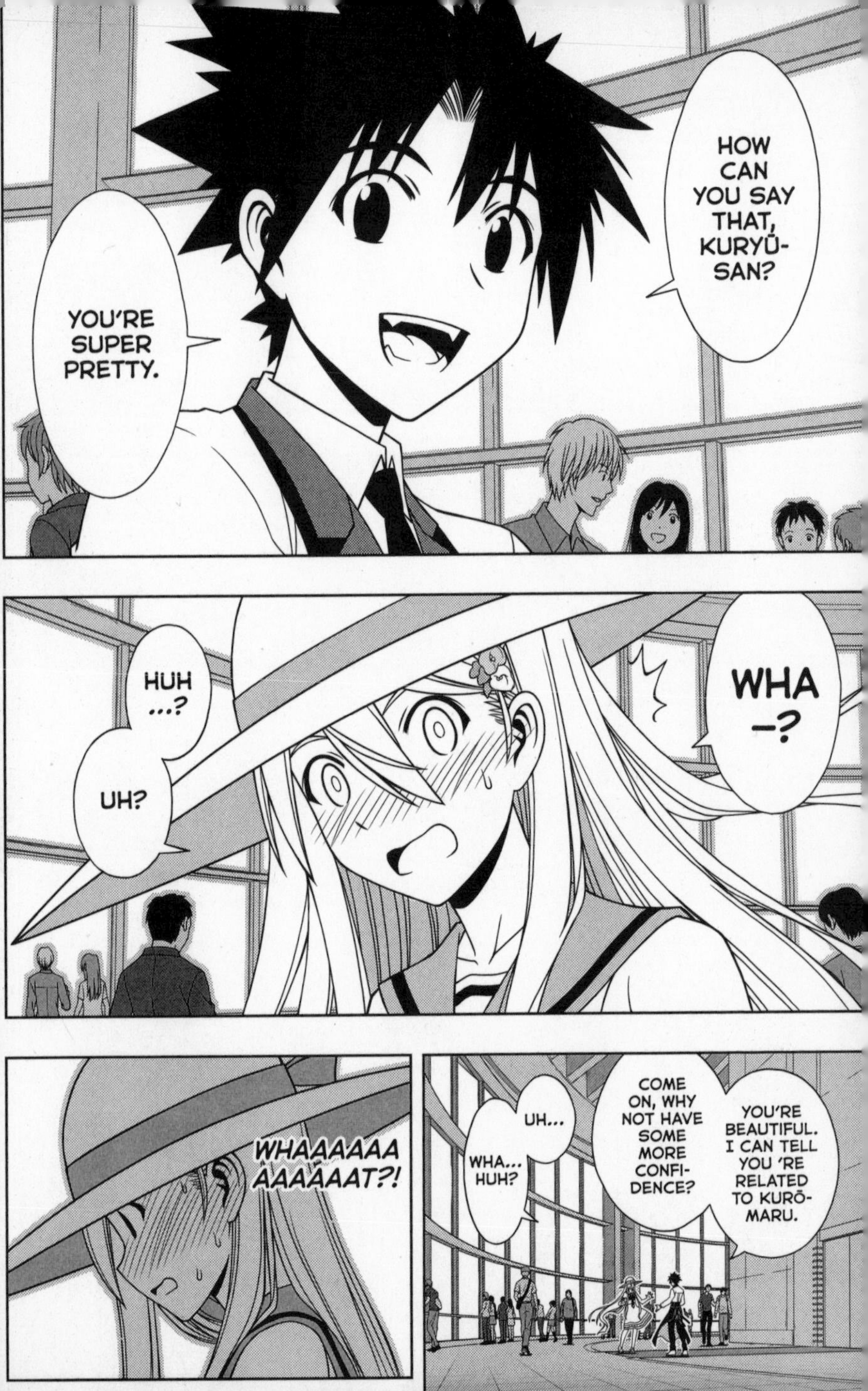
HOW CAN YOU SAY THAT, KURYŪ-SAN?
YOU'RE SUPER PRETTY.
WHA—?
HUH...?
UH?
YOU'RE BEAUTIFUL. I CAN TELL YOU 'RE RELATED TO KURŌMARU.
COME ON, WHY NOT HAVE SOME MORE CONFIDENCE?
UH...
WHA... HUH?
WHAAAAAAAAAAAAT?!

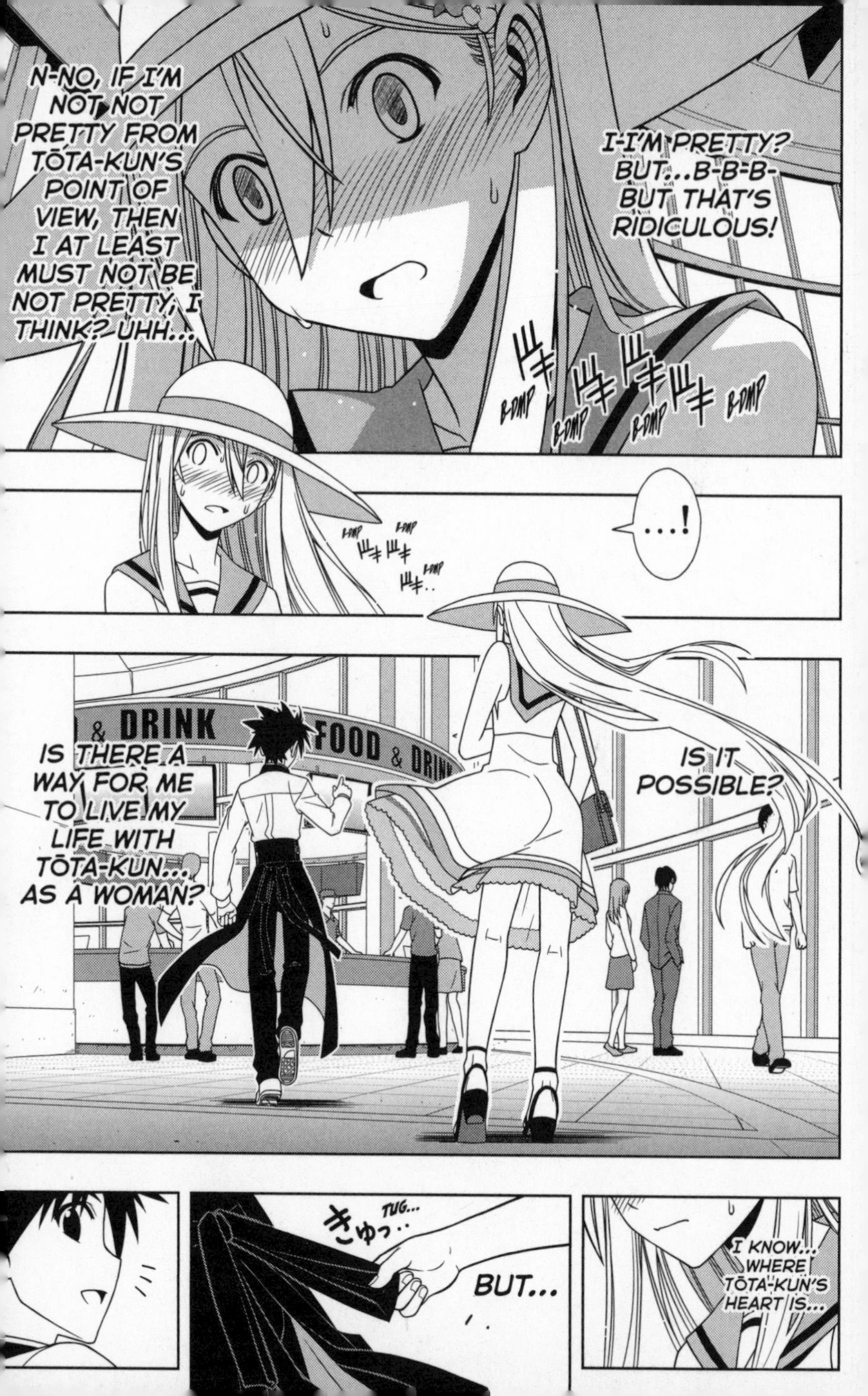
I-I'M PRETTY? BUT...B-B-B-BUT THAT'S RIDICULOUS!
N-NO, IF I'M NOT NOT PRETTY FROM TŌTA-KUN'S POINT OF VIEW, THEN I AT LEAST MUST NOT BE NOT PRETTY, I THINK? UHH...
B-DMP
B-DMP
B-DMP
B-DMP
...!
B-DMP
B-DMP
B-DMP
IS IT POSSIBLE?
FOOD & DRINK
& DRINK
IS THERE A WAY FOR ME TO LIVE MY LIFE WITH TŌTA-KUN... AS A WOMAN?
I KNOW... WHERE TŌTA-KUN'S HEART IS...
きゅっ..
TUG...
BUT...

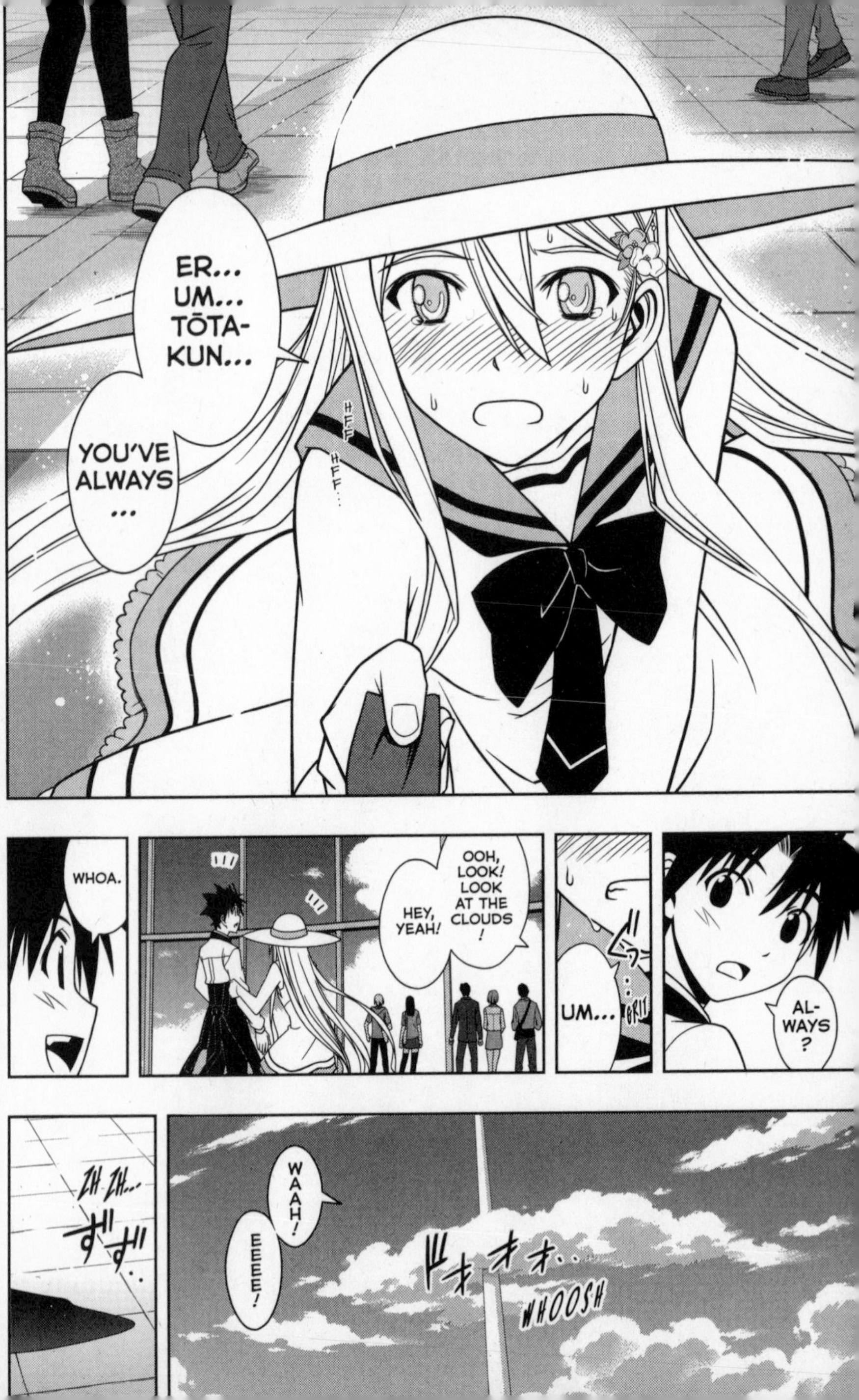
ER... UM... TŌTA-KUN...
YOU'VE ALWAYS ...
HFF HFF...
AL-WAYS?
UM...
OOH, LOOK! LOOK AT THE CLOUDS!
HEY, YEAH!
WHOA.
WAAH!
EEEE!
WHOOSH
ZH-ZH...

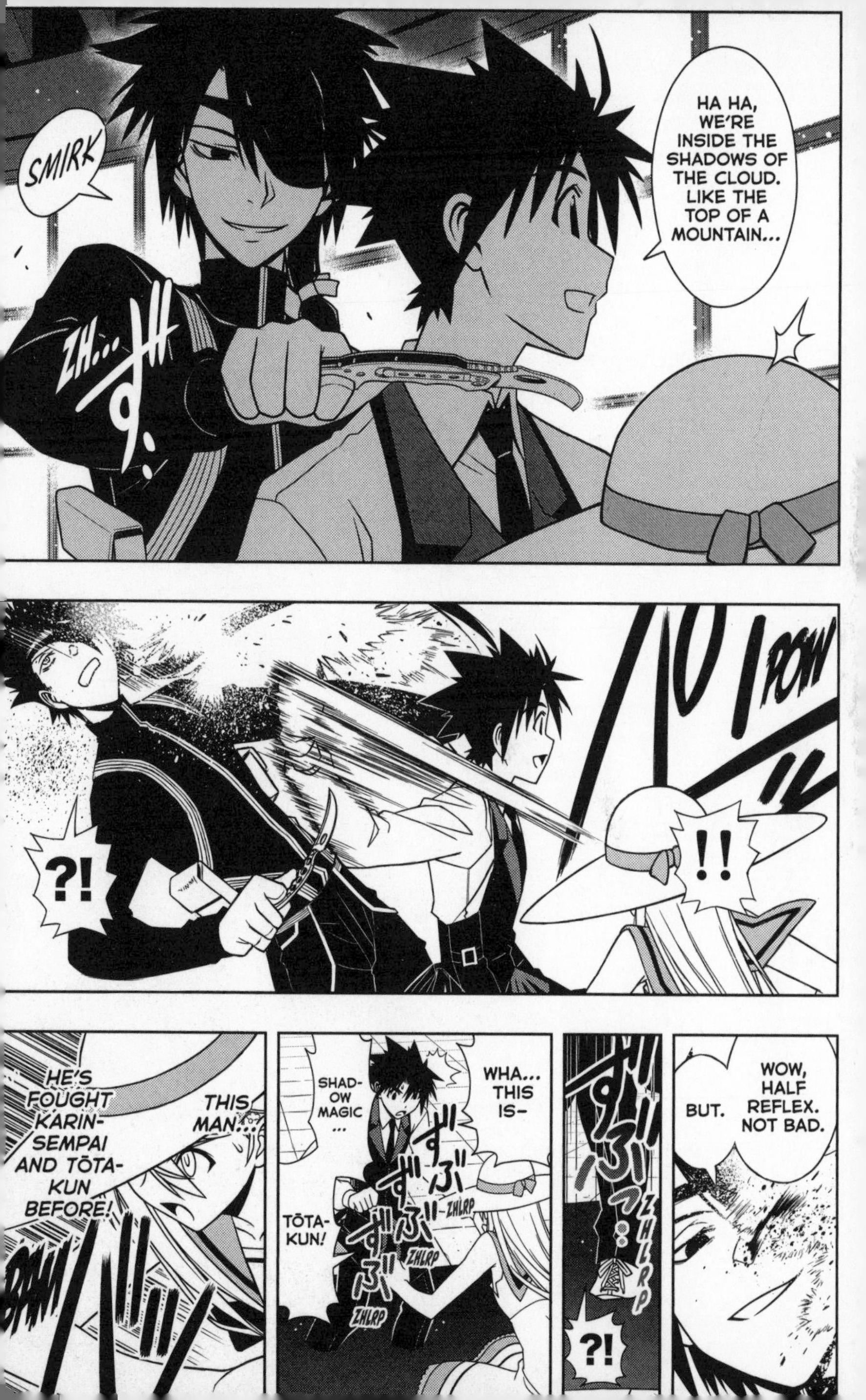

HA HA, WE'RE INSIDE THE SHADOWS OF THE CLOUD. LIKE THE TOP OF A MOUNTAIN...
SMIRK
ZH...
POW
!!
?!
WOW, HALF REFLEX. NOT BAD.
BUT.
ZHLRP
?!
WHA... THIS IS-
SHAD-OW MAGIC ...
ZHLRP
TŌTA-KUN!
ZHLRP
ZHLRP
THIS MAN...
HE'S FOUGHT KARIN-SEMPAI AND TŌTA-KUN BEFORE!

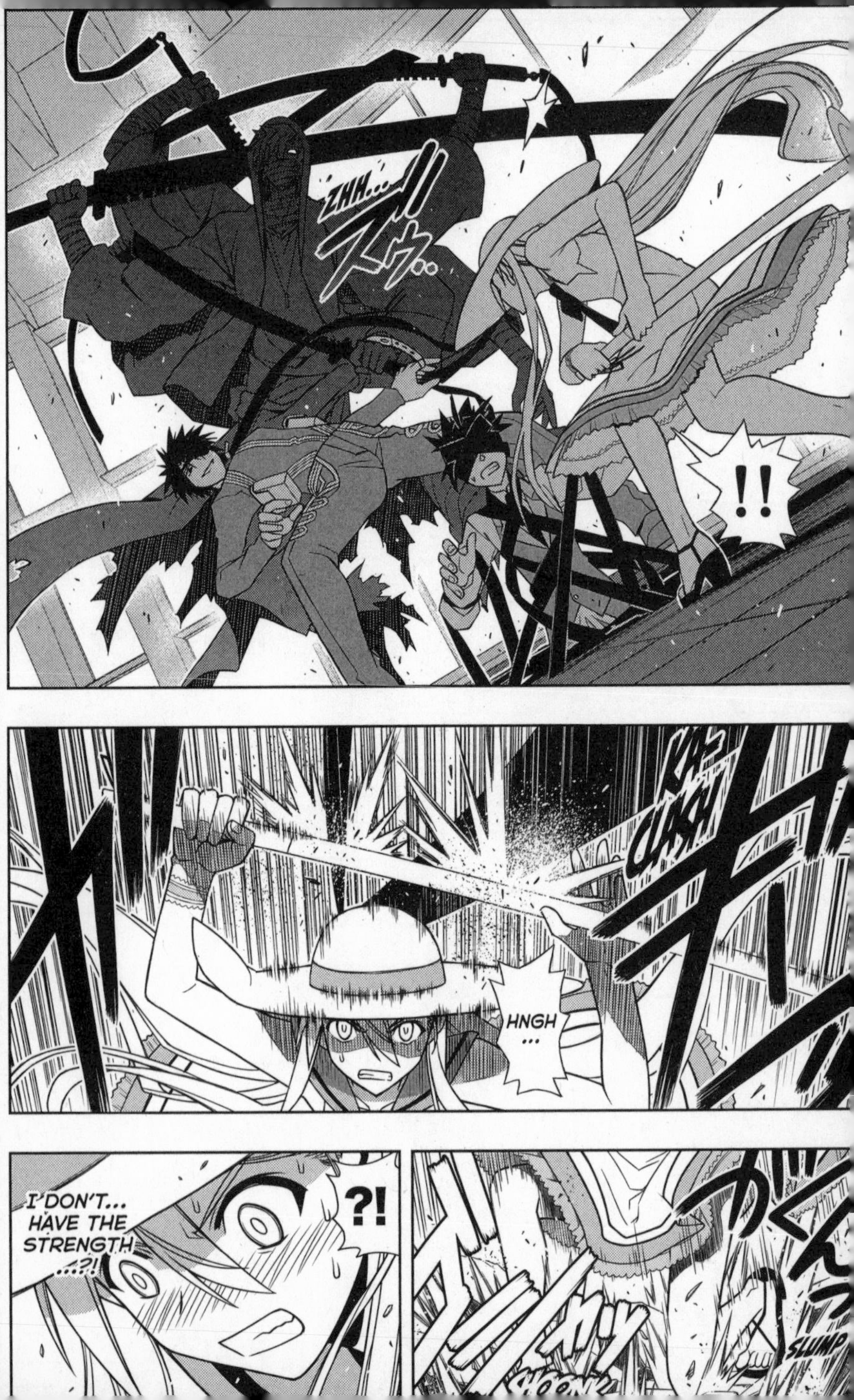

ZHH...
!!
KRA-CLASH
HNGH ...
SLUMP
?!
I DON'T... HAVE THE STRENGTH ...?!

STAGE 103: DO I WANT TO PROTECT? OR BE PROTECTED?

I CAN'T... WORK UP MY CHI!

WHY ?!

I DON'T... HAVE THE STRENGTH ...?!

SPLAT

HNGH!

NGH!!

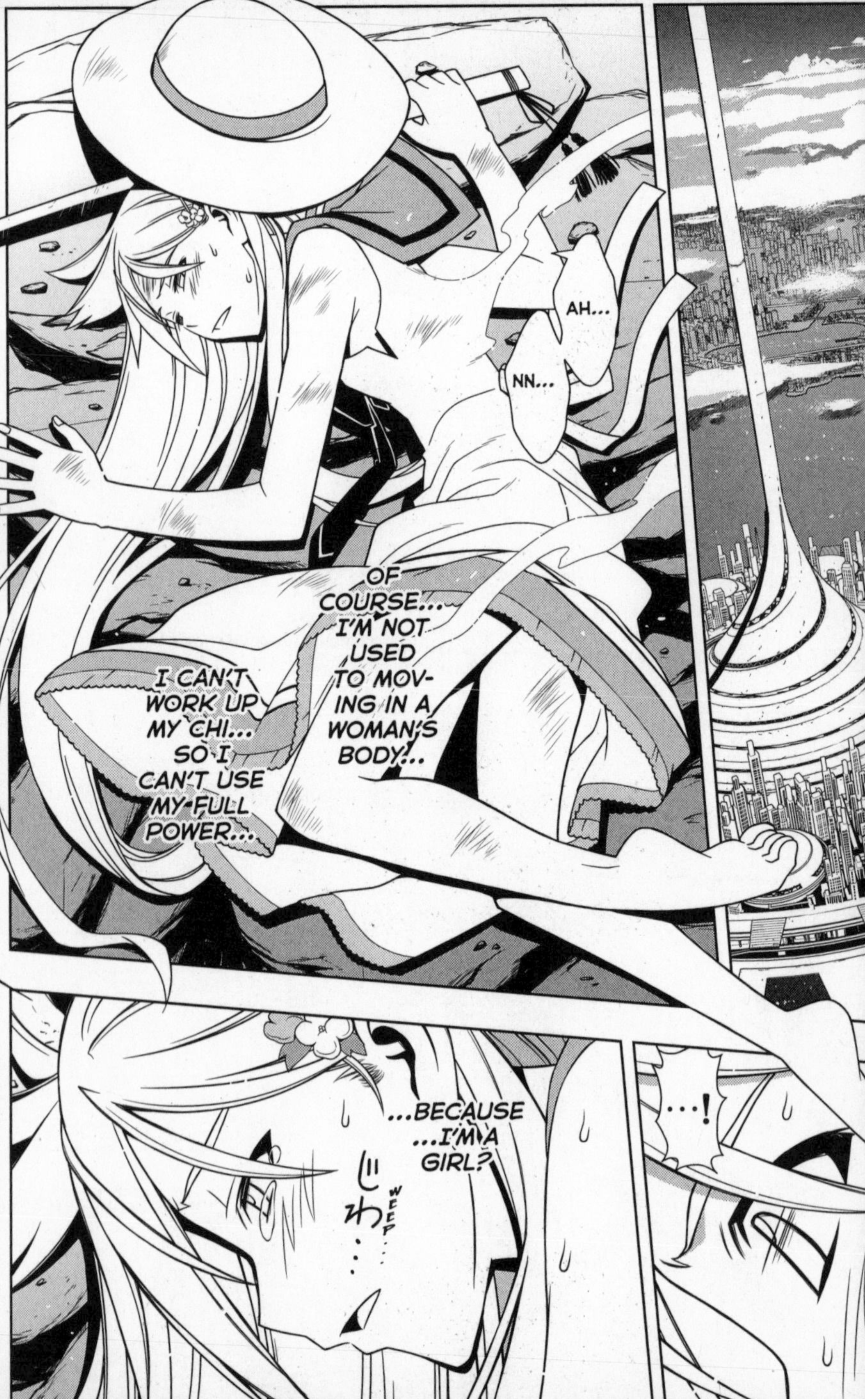
AH...
NN...
OF COURSE... I'M NOT USED TO MOVING IN A WOMAN'S BODY...
I CAN'T WORK UP MY CHI... SO I CAN'T USE MY FULL POWER...
...!
...BECAUSE ...I'M A GIRL?
じわ...
WEEP...

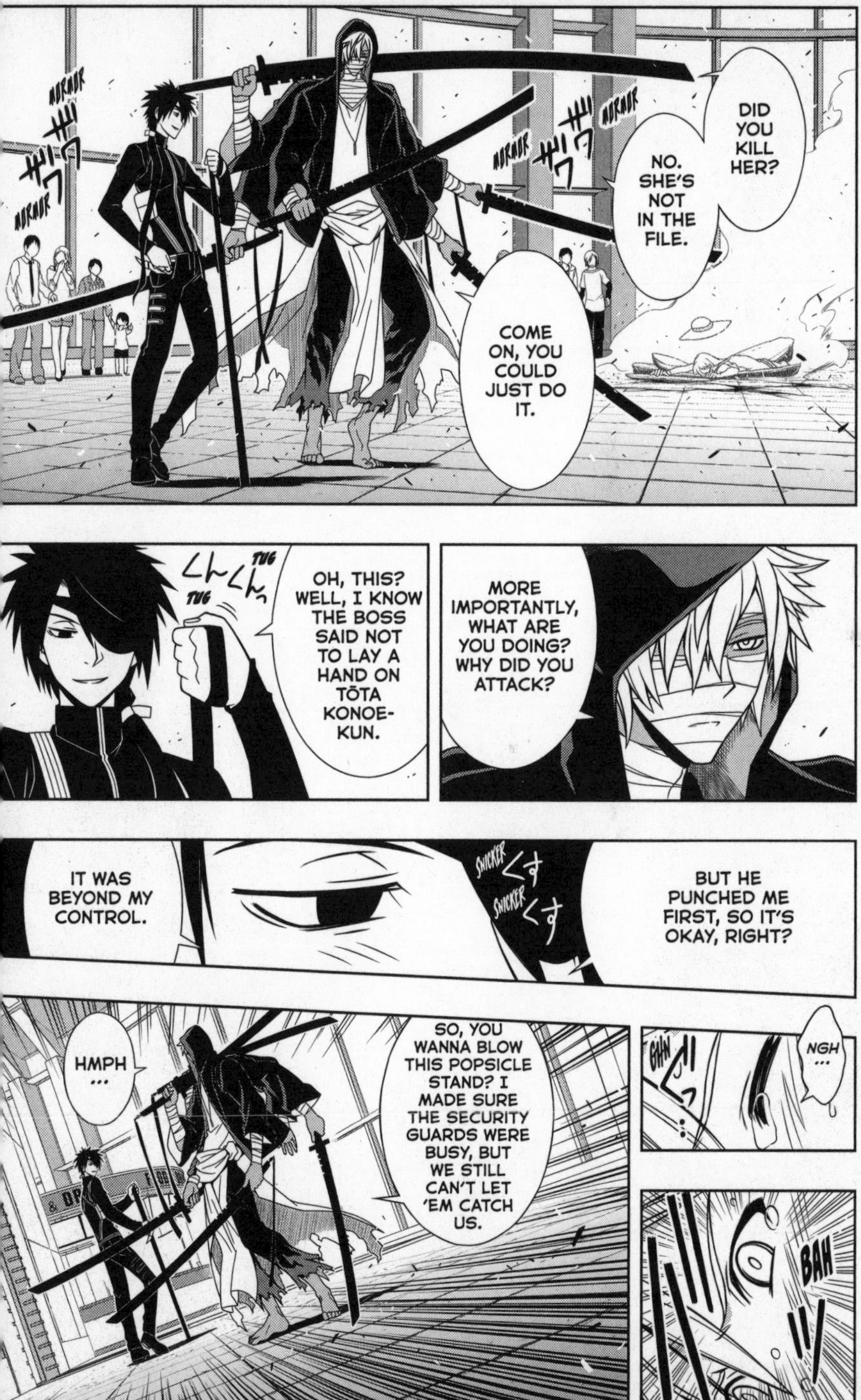
DID YOU KILL HER?
NO. SHE'S NOT IN THE FILE.
COME ON, YOU COULD JUST DO IT.
MORE IMPORTANTLY, WHAT ARE YOU DOING? WHY DID YOU ATTACK?
TUG くいくいっ TUG
OH, THIS? WELL, I KNOW THE BOSS SAID NOT TO LAY A HAND ON TŌTA KONOE-KUN.
BUT HE PUNCHED ME FIRST, SO IT'S OKAY, RIGHT?
SNICKER くす SNICKER くす
IT WAS BEYOND MY CONTROL.
NGH ...
BAH
SO, YOU WANNA BLOW THIS POPSICLE STAND? I MADE SURE THE SECURITY GUARDS WERE BUSY, BUT WE STILL CAN'T LET 'EM CATCH US.
HMPH ...

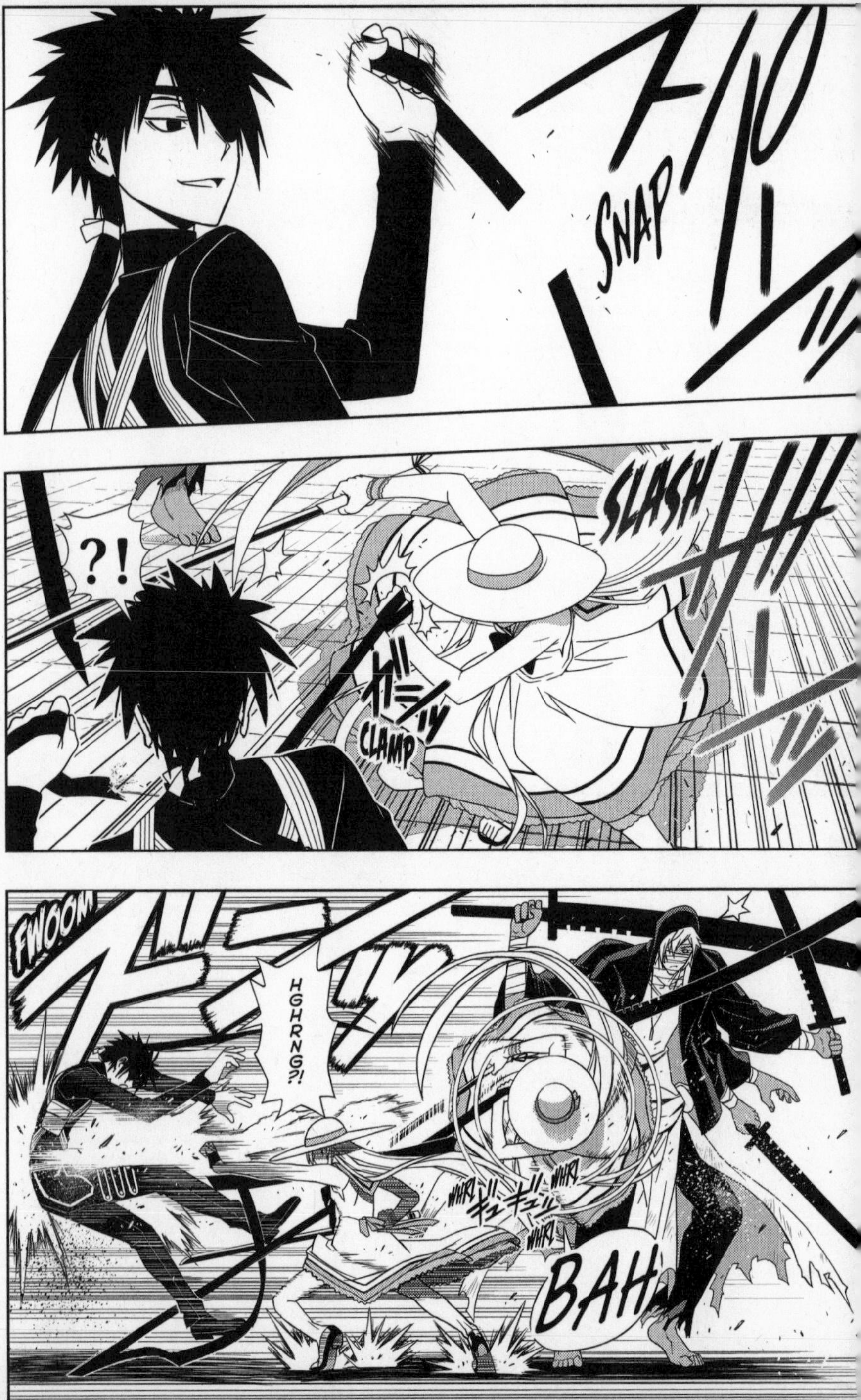
SNAP
SLASH
?!
CLAMP
FWOOM
HGHRNG?!
WHRL
WHRL
WHRL
BAH

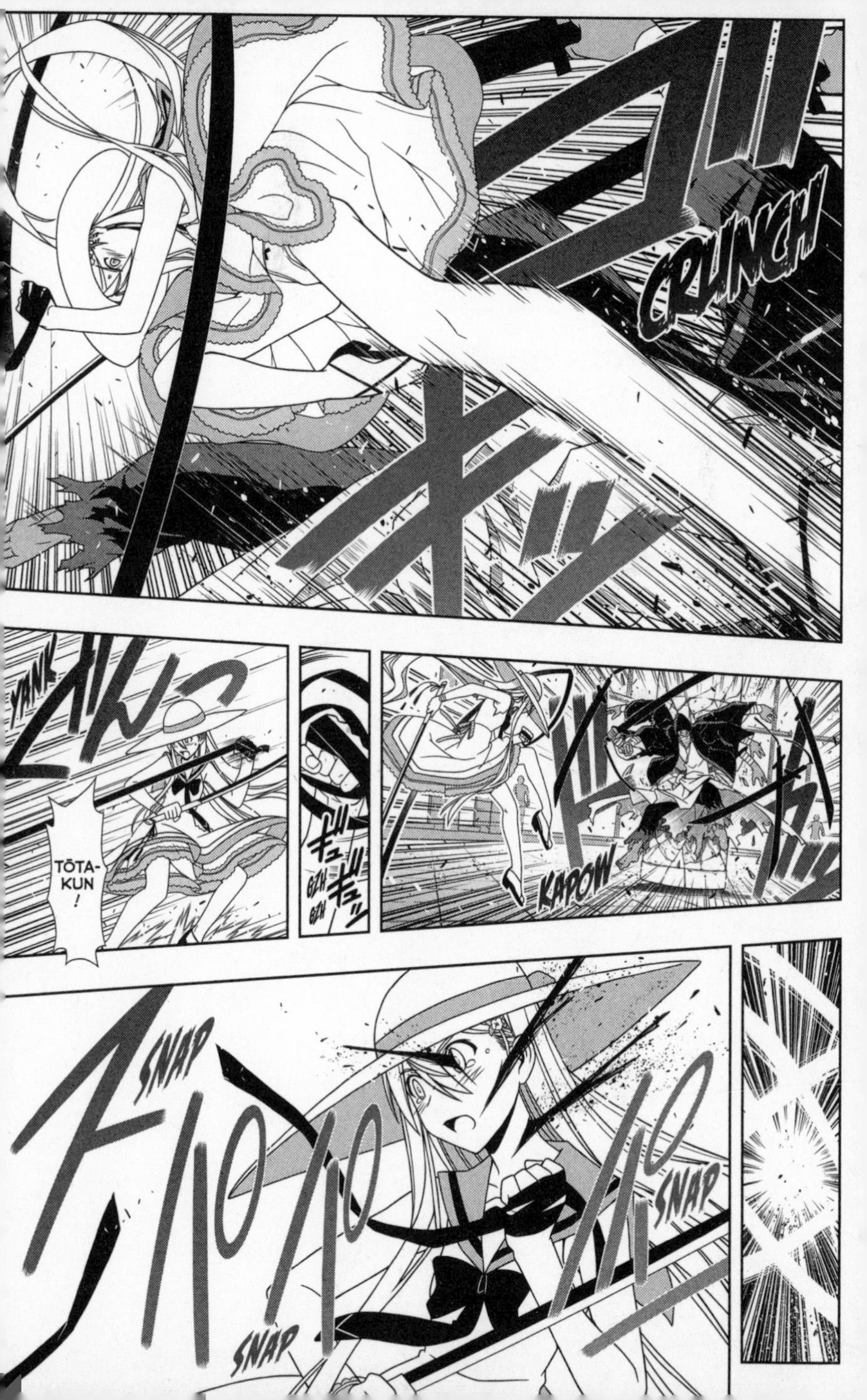
CRUNCH
KAPOW
GZH
GZH
YANK
TŌTA-KUN!
SNAP
SNAP
SNAP

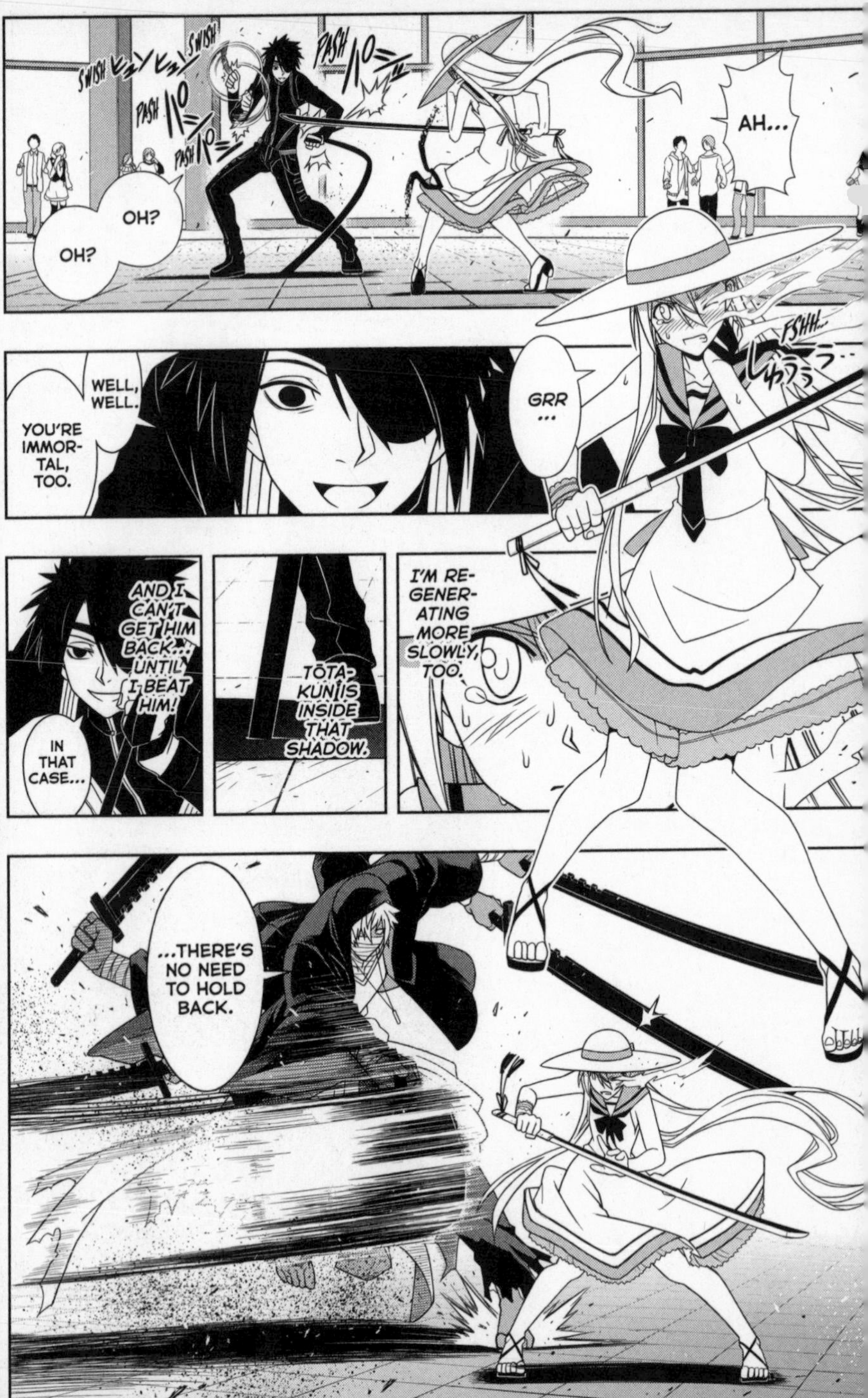
AH...
PASH
SWISH SWISH
PASH
PASH
OH?
OH?
FSHH...
GRR...
WELL, WELL.
YOU'RE IMMORTAL, TOO.
I'M REGENERATING MORE SLOWLY, TOO.
TŌTA-KUN IS INSIDE THAT SHADOW.
AND I CAN'T GET HIM BACK... UNTIL I BEAT HIM!
IN THAT CASE...
...THERE'S NO NEED TO HOLD BACK.

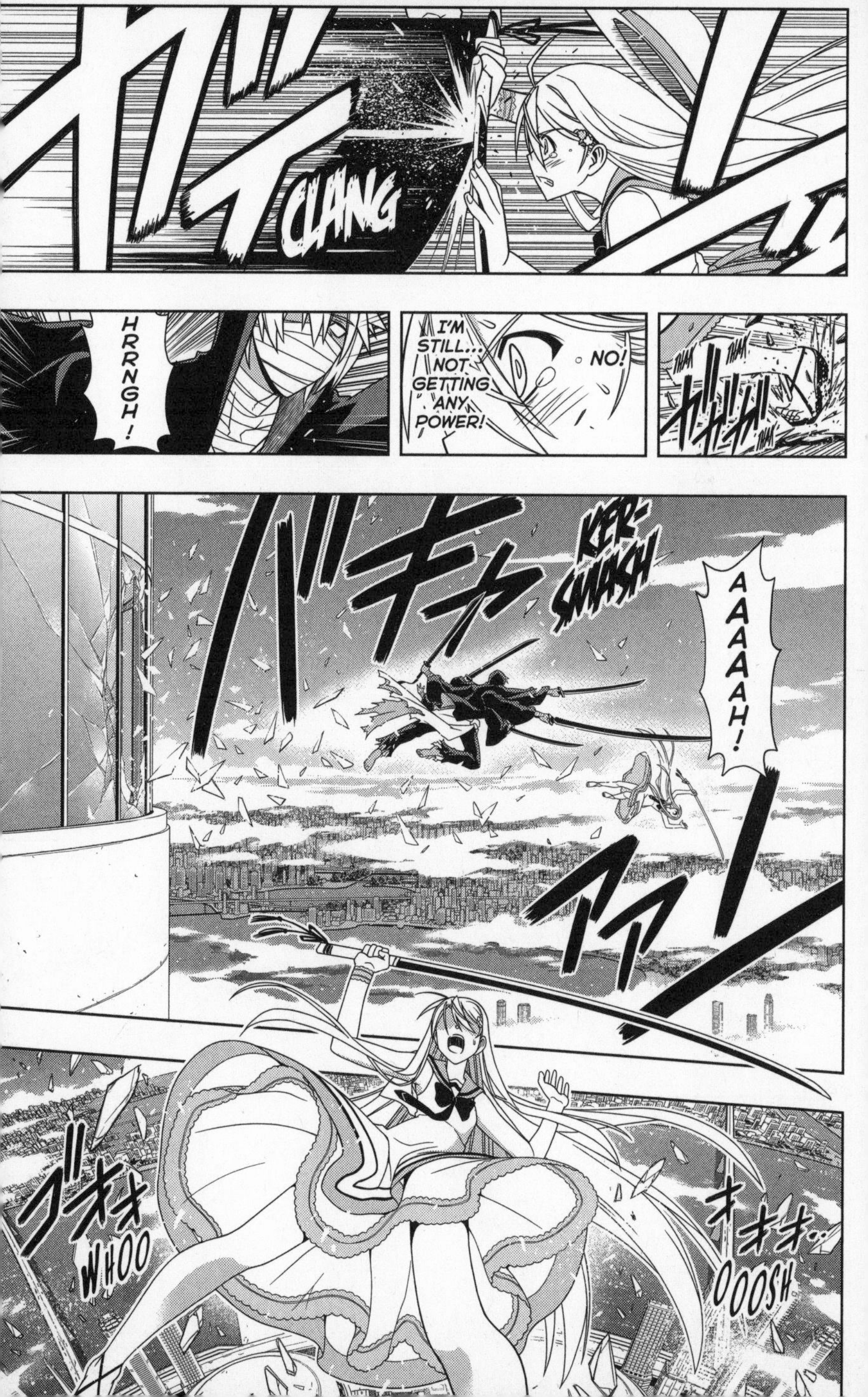
CLANG
THAK THAK THAK
I'M STILL... NOT GETTING ANY POWER!
NO!
HRRNGH!
KER-SMASH
AAAAAAH!
OOOSH
WHOO

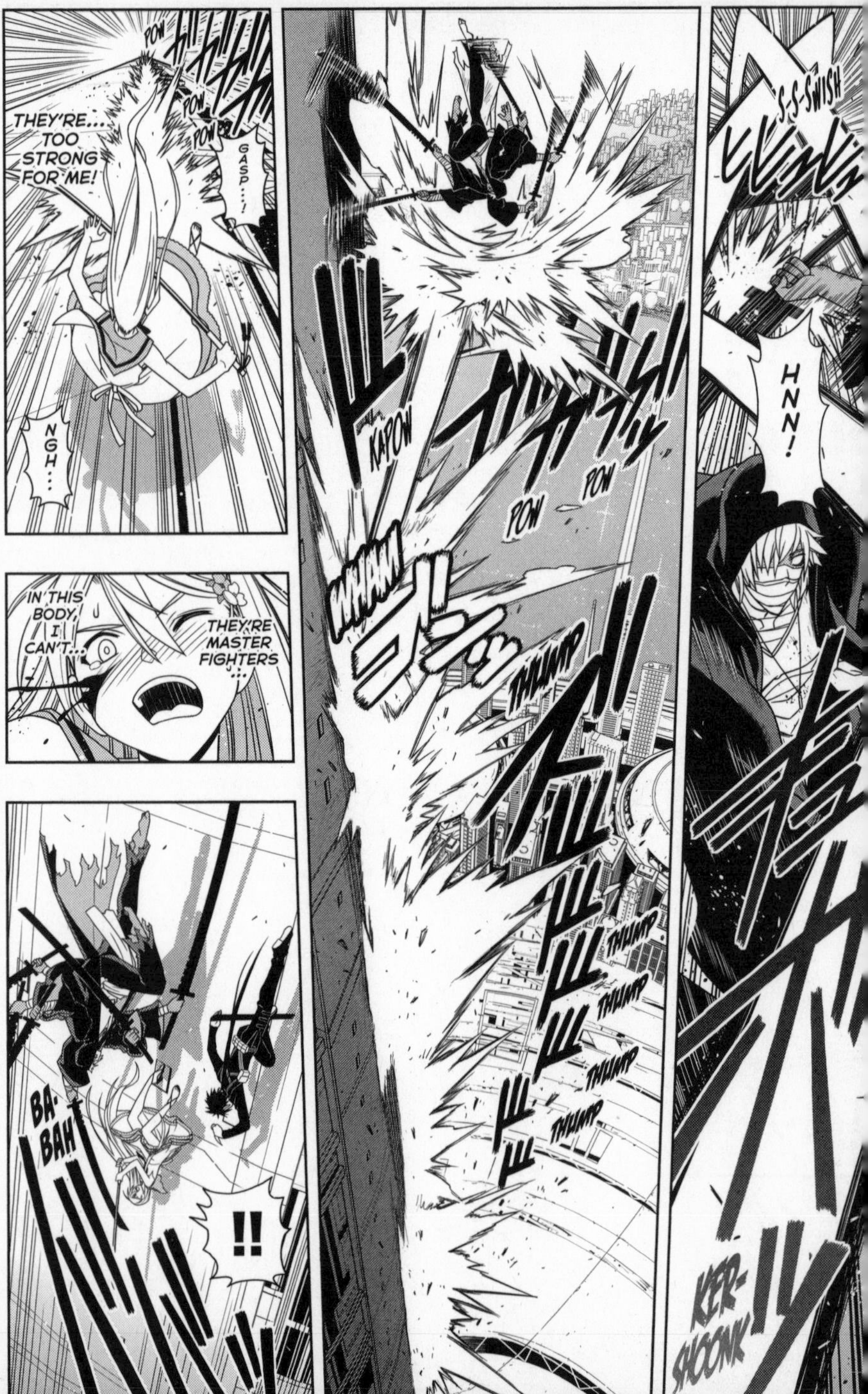
S-S-SWISH
HNN!
KER-SHOONK
KAPOW
POW
POW
WHAM
THUMP
THUMP
THUMP
THUMP
THUMP
POW
POW
POW
GASP...!
THEY'RE... TOO STRONG FOR ME!
NGH...
THEY'RE MASTER FIGHTERS...
IN THIS BODY, I CAN'T...
!!
BA-BAH

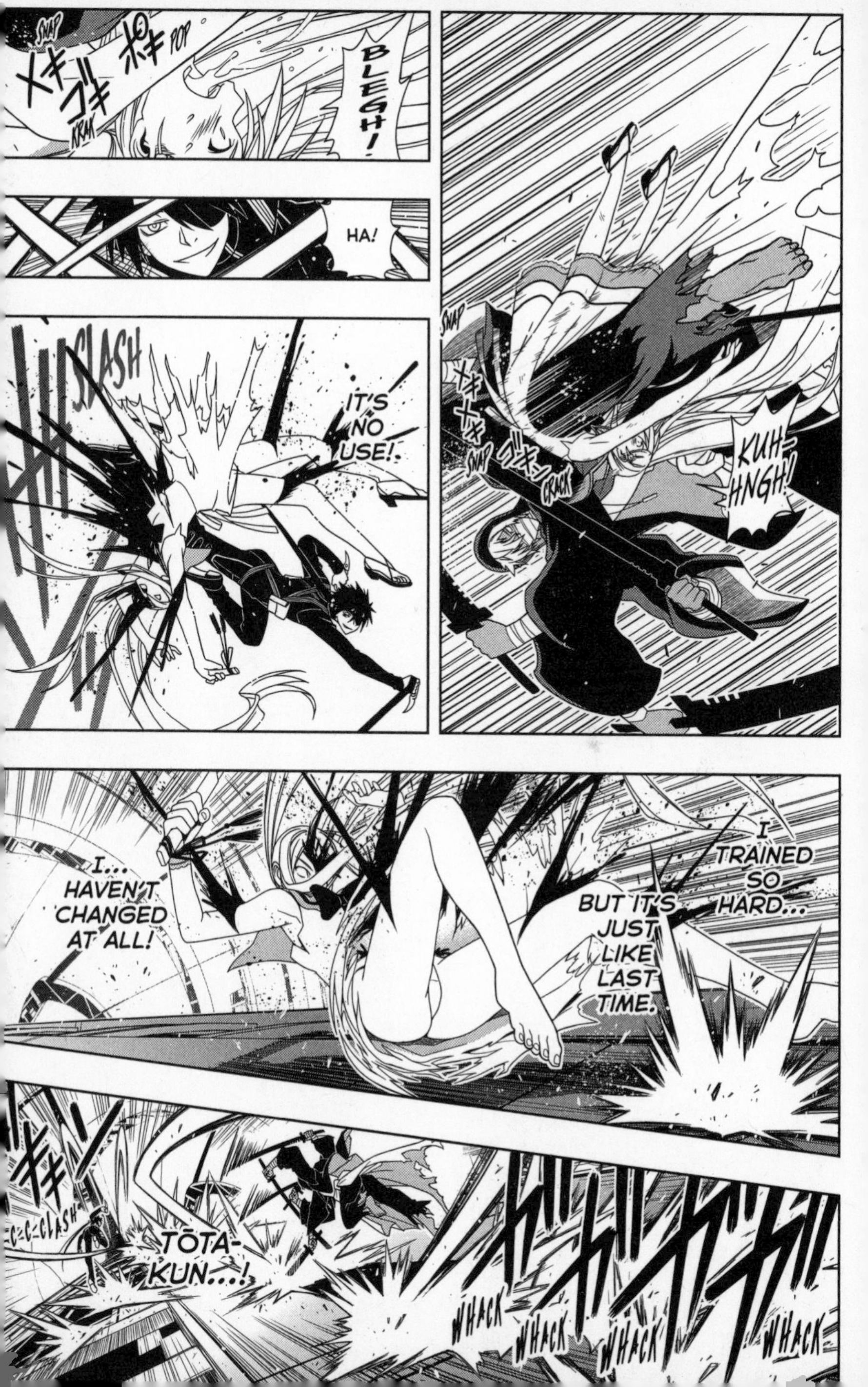
SNAP
SNAP
CRACK
KUH-HNGH!
SNAP
POP
KRAK
BLEGH!
HA!
SLASH
IT'S NO USE!
I TRAINED SO HARD...
BUT IT'S JUST LIKE LAST TIME.
I... HAVEN'T CHANGED AT ALL!
WHACK
WHACK
WHACK
WHACK
TŌTA-KUN...!
C-C-CLASH

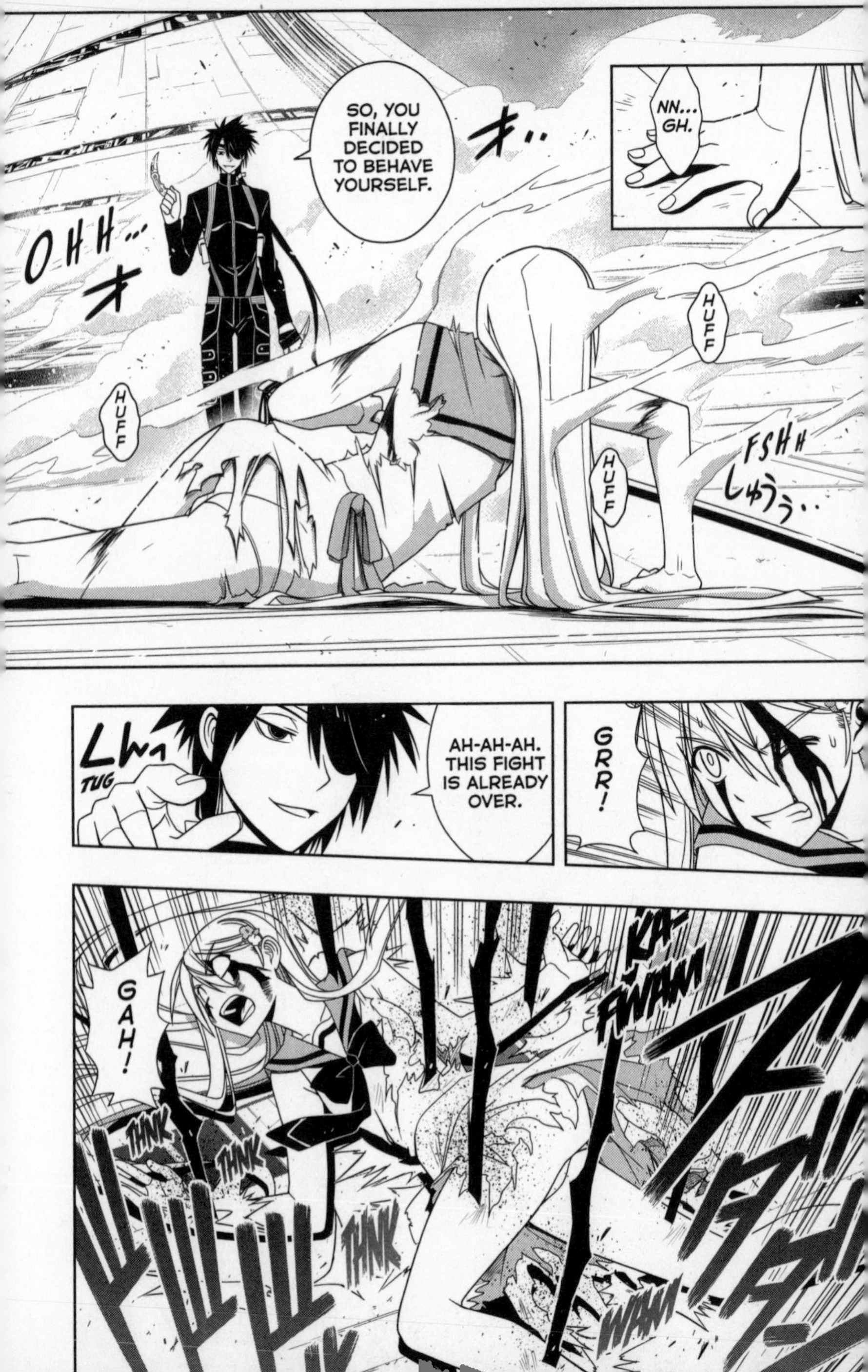

NN... GH.
SO, YOU FINALLY DECIDED TO BEHAVE YOURSELF.
OHH...
HUFF
HUFF
FSHH
しゅうぅ..
HUFF
GRR!
AH-AH-AH. THIS FIGHT IS ALREADY OVER.
TUG
KA-FWAM
GAH!
THNK
THNK
THNK
WHAM

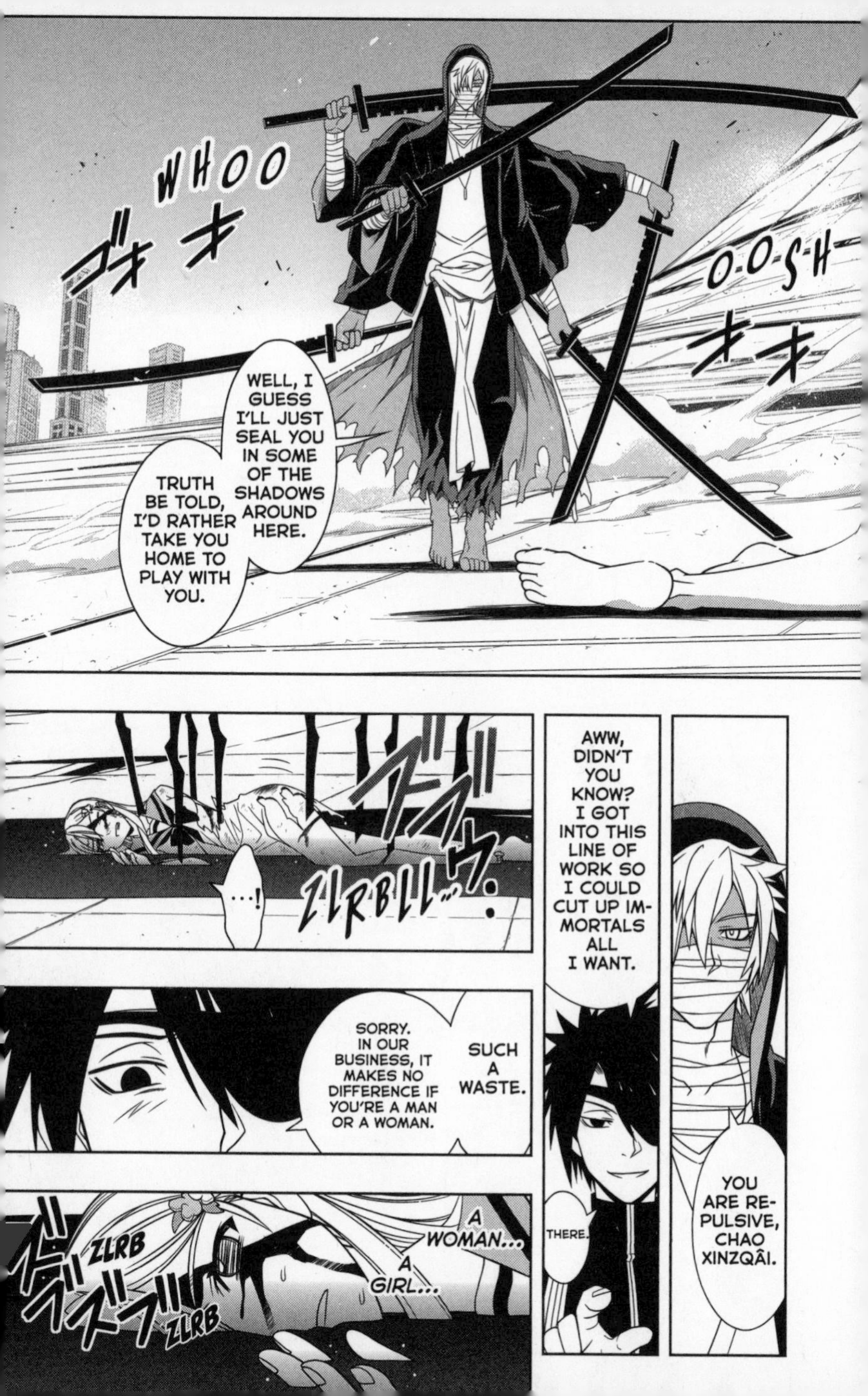
WHOO
O-O-SH
WELL, I GUESS I'LL JUST SEAL YOU IN SOME OF THE SHADOWS AROUND HERE.
TRUTH BE TOLD, I'D RATHER TAKE YOU HOME TO PLAY WITH YOU.
AWW, DIDN'T YOU KNOW? I GOT INTO THIS LINE OF WORK SO I COULD CUT UP IM-MORTALS ALL I WANT.
ZLRBLL...
...!
YOU ARE RE-PULSIVE, CHAO XINZQÂI.
THERE.
SUCH A WASTE.
SORRY. IN OUR BUSINESS, IT MAKES NO DIFFERENCE IF YOU'RE A MAN OR A WOMAN.
A WOMAN...
A GIRL...
ZLRB
ZLRB

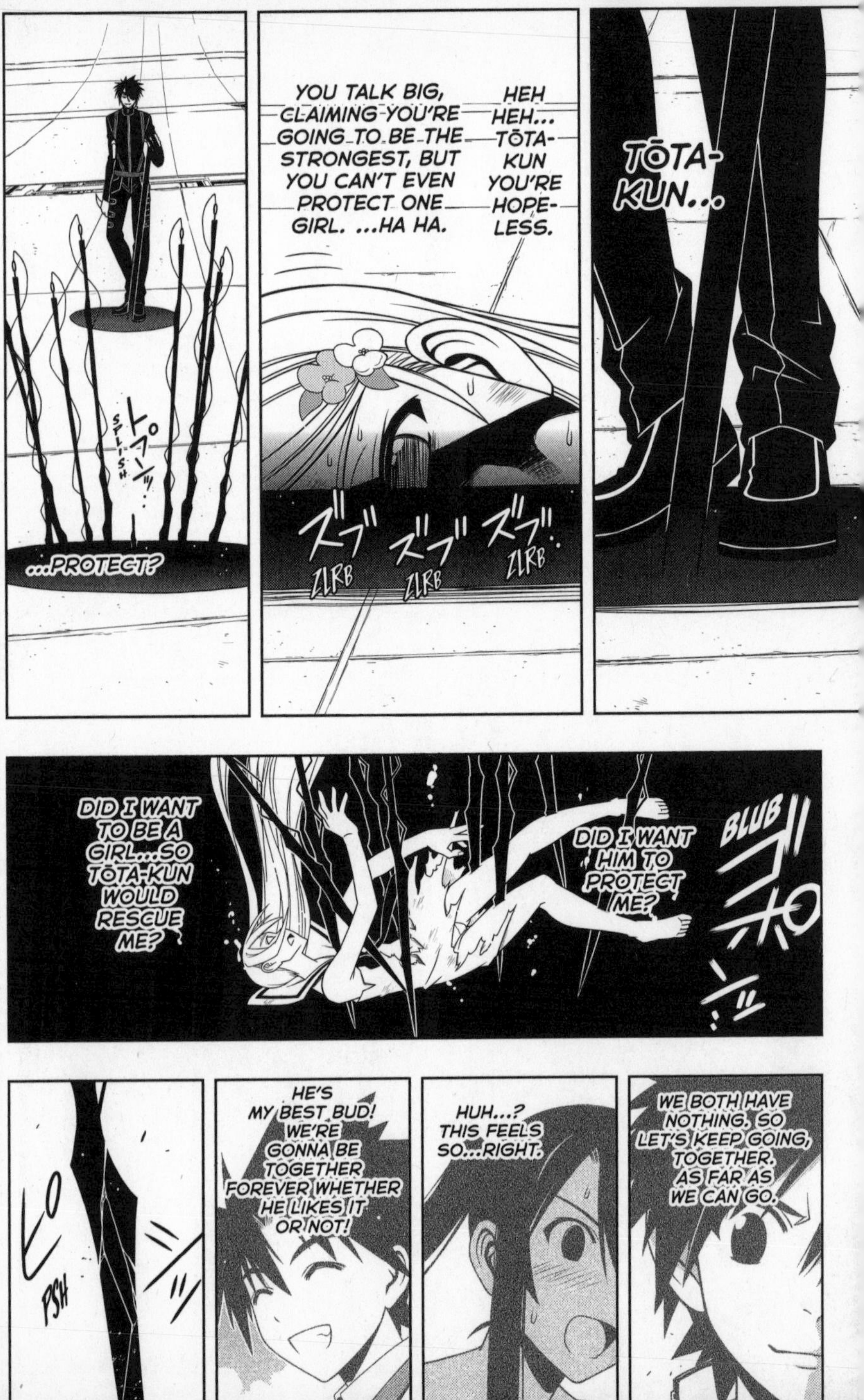
TŌTA-KUN...
HEH HEH... TŌTA-KUN YOU'RE HOPELESS.
YOU TALK BIG, CLAIMING YOU'RE GOING TO BE THE STRONGEST, BUT YOU CAN'T EVEN PROTECT ONE GIRL. ...HA HA.
ZLRB
ZLRB
ZLRB
SPLISH
...PROTECT?
BLUB
DID I WANT HIM TO PROTECT ME?
DID I WANT TO BE A GIRL...SO TŌTA-KUN WOULD RESCUE ME?
WE BOTH HAVE NOTHING. SO LET'S KEEP GOING, TOGETHER. AS FAR AS WE CAN GO.
HUH...? THIS FEELS SO...RIGHT.
HE'S MY BEST BUD! WE'RE GONNA BE TOGETHER FOREVER WHETHER HE LIKES IT OR NOT!
PSH

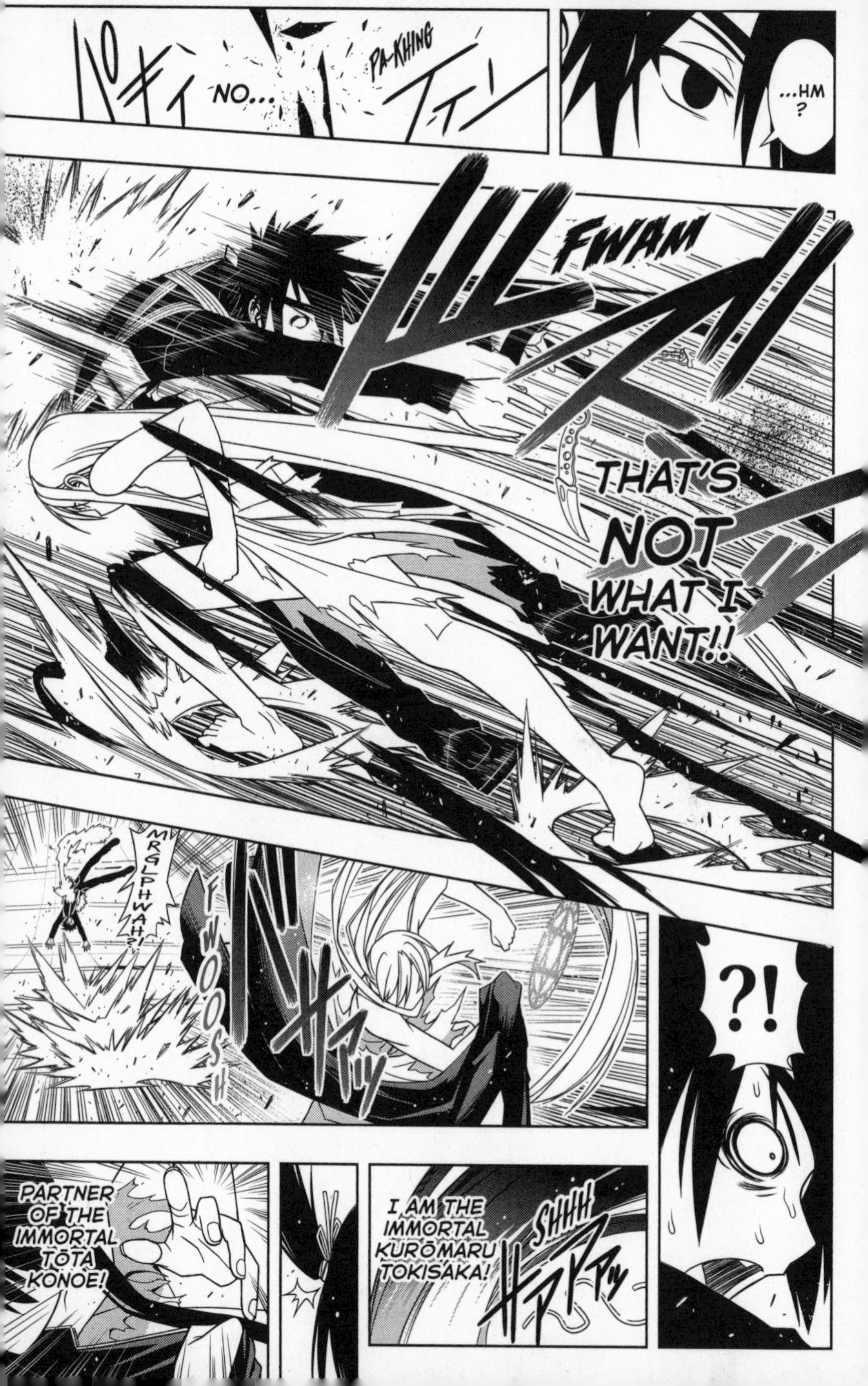
...HM ?
PA-KHING
NO...
FWAM
THAT'S NOT WHAT I WANT!!
?!
FWOOOSH
MRGLPHWAH?!
SHHH
I AM THE IMMORTAL KURŌMARU TOKISAKA!
PARTNER OF THE IMMORTAL TŌTA KONOE!

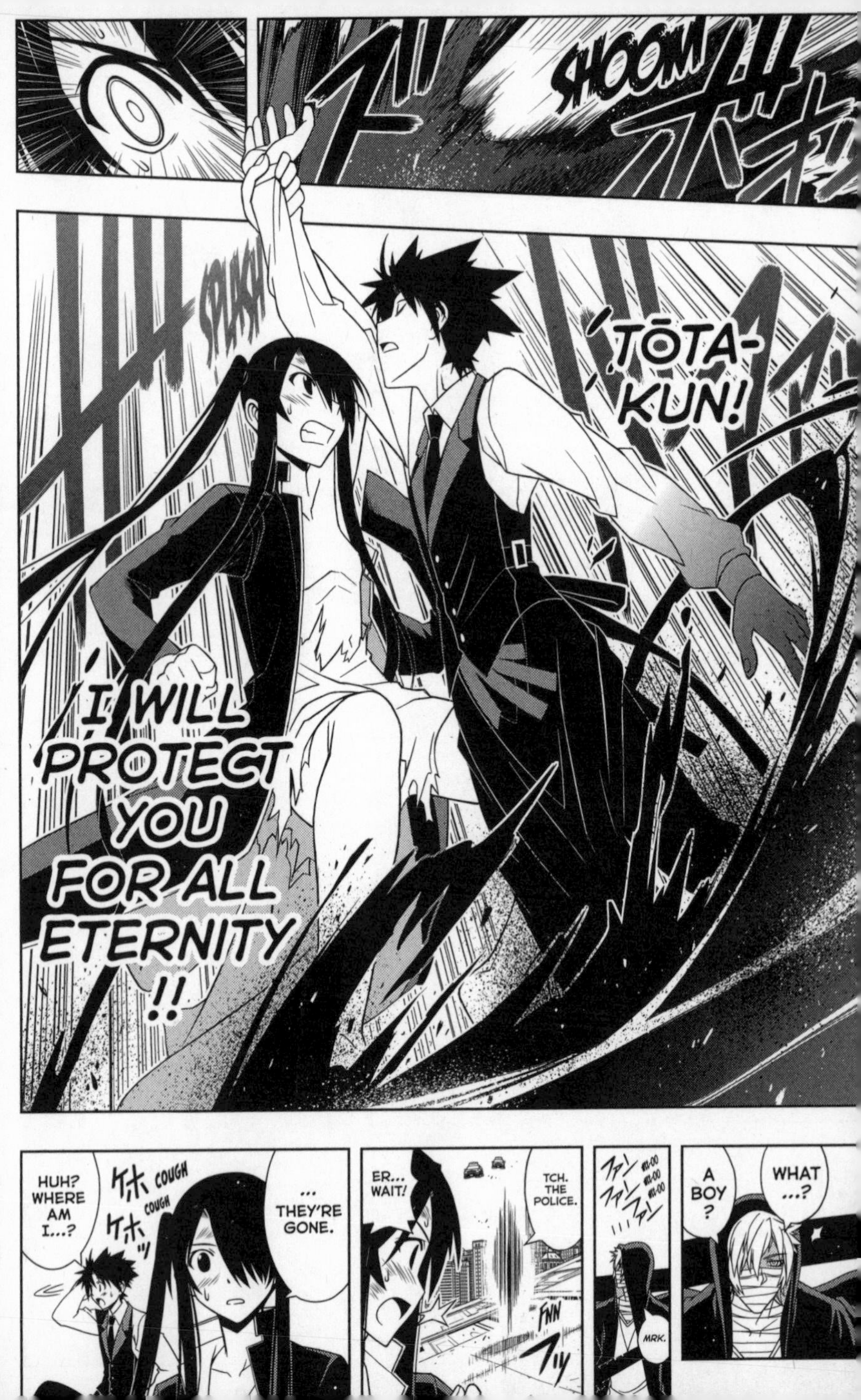
SHOOM!!
TŌTA-KUN!
I WILL PROTECT YOU FOR ALL ETERNITY!!
SPLASH
WHAT ...?
A BOY?
MRK.
ファン ファン ファン
TCH. THE POLICE.
FNN
フッ
ER... WAIT!
... THEY'RE GONE.
HUH? WHERE AM I...?
ケホ COUGH
ケホッ COUGH

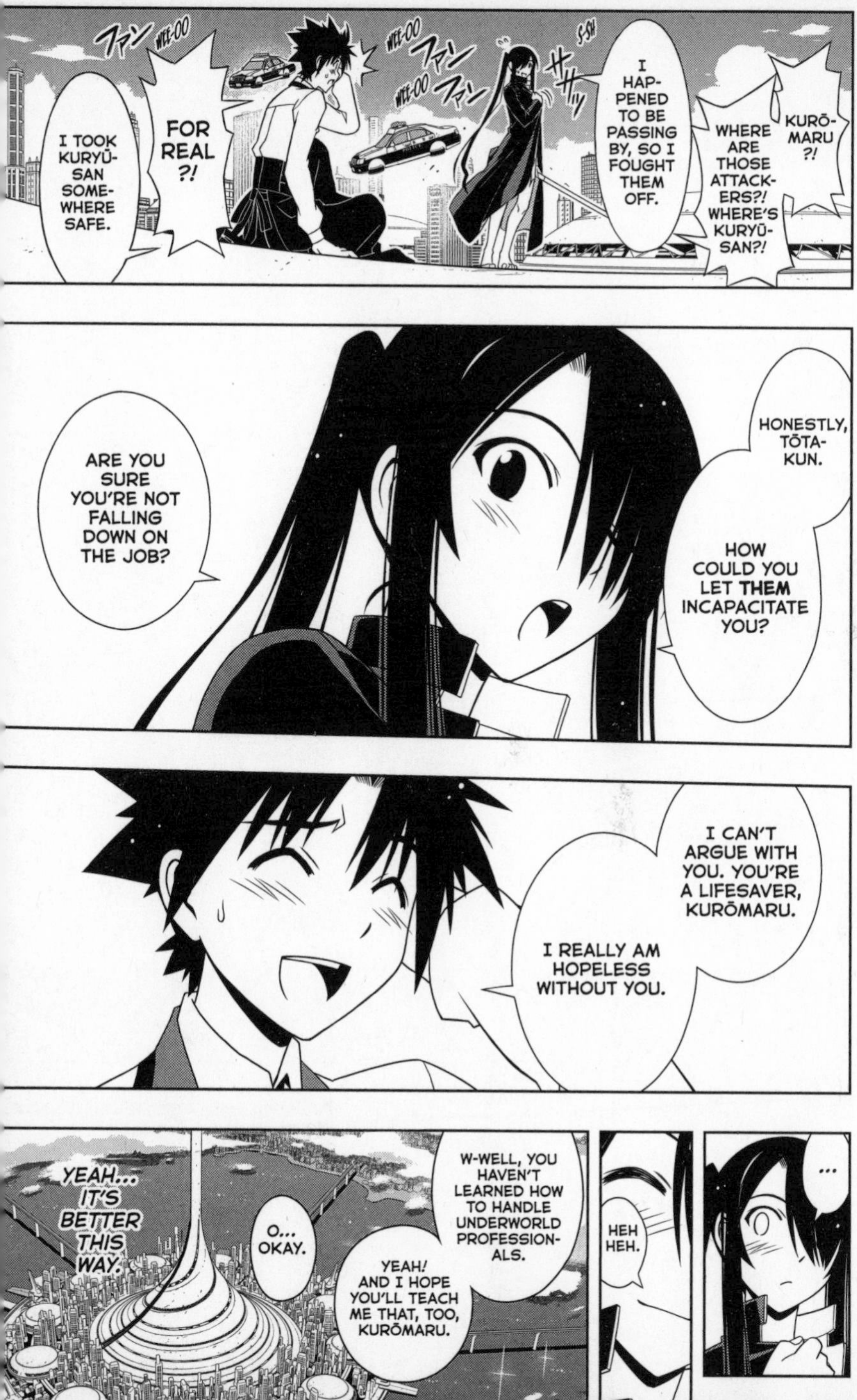
KURŌMARU?!
WHERE ARE THOSE ATTACKERS?! WHERE'S KURYŪ-SAN?!
S-SH
ササッ
I HAPPENED TO BE PASSING BY, SO I FOUGHT THEM OFF.
WEE-OO ファン
WEE-OO ファン
WEE-OO ファン
FOR REAL?!
I TOOK KURYŪ-SAN SOMEWHERE SAFE.
HONESTLY, TŌTA-KUN.
HOW COULD YOU LET **THEM** INCAPACITATE YOU?
ARE YOU SURE YOU'RE NOT FALLING DOWN ON THE JOB?
I CAN'T ARGUE WITH YOU. YOU'RE A LIFESAVER, KURŌMARU.
I REALLY AM HOPELESS WITHOUT YOU.
...
HEH HEH.
W-WELL, YOU HAVEN'T LEARNED HOW TO HANDLE UNDERWORLD PROFESSIONALS.
YEAH! AND I HOPE YOU'LL TEACH ME THAT, TOO, KURŌMARU.
O... OKAY.
YEAH... IT'S BETTER THIS WAY.

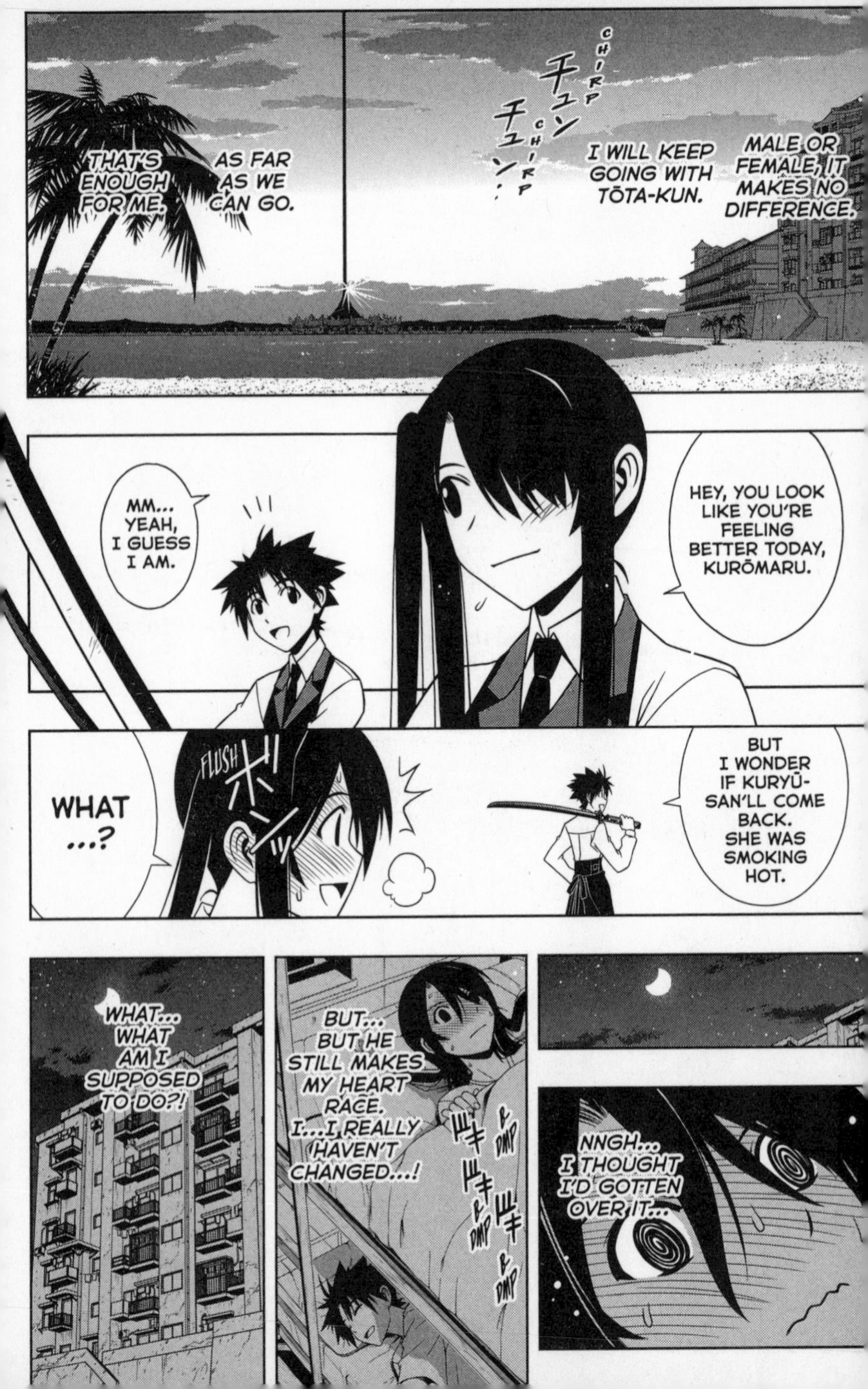
MALE OR FEMALE, IT MAKES NO DIFFERENCE.
I WILL KEEP GOING WITH TŌTA-KUN.
チュン CHIRP
チュン CHIRP
AS FAR AS WE CAN GO.
THAT'S ENOUGH FOR ME.
HEY, YOU LOOK LIKE YOU'RE FEELING BETTER TODAY, KURŌMARU.
MM... YEAH, I GUESS I AM.
BUT I WONDER IF KURYŪ-SAN'LL COME BACK. SHE WAS SMOKING HOT.
ボンッ FLUSH
WHAT ...?
NNGH... I THOUGHT I'D GOTTEN OVER IT...
BUT... BUT HE STILL MAKES MY HEART RACE. I... I REALLY HAVEN'T CHANGED...!
ドキ B-DMP
ドキ B-DMP
ドキ B-DMP
WHAT... WHAT AM I SUPPOSED TO DO?!

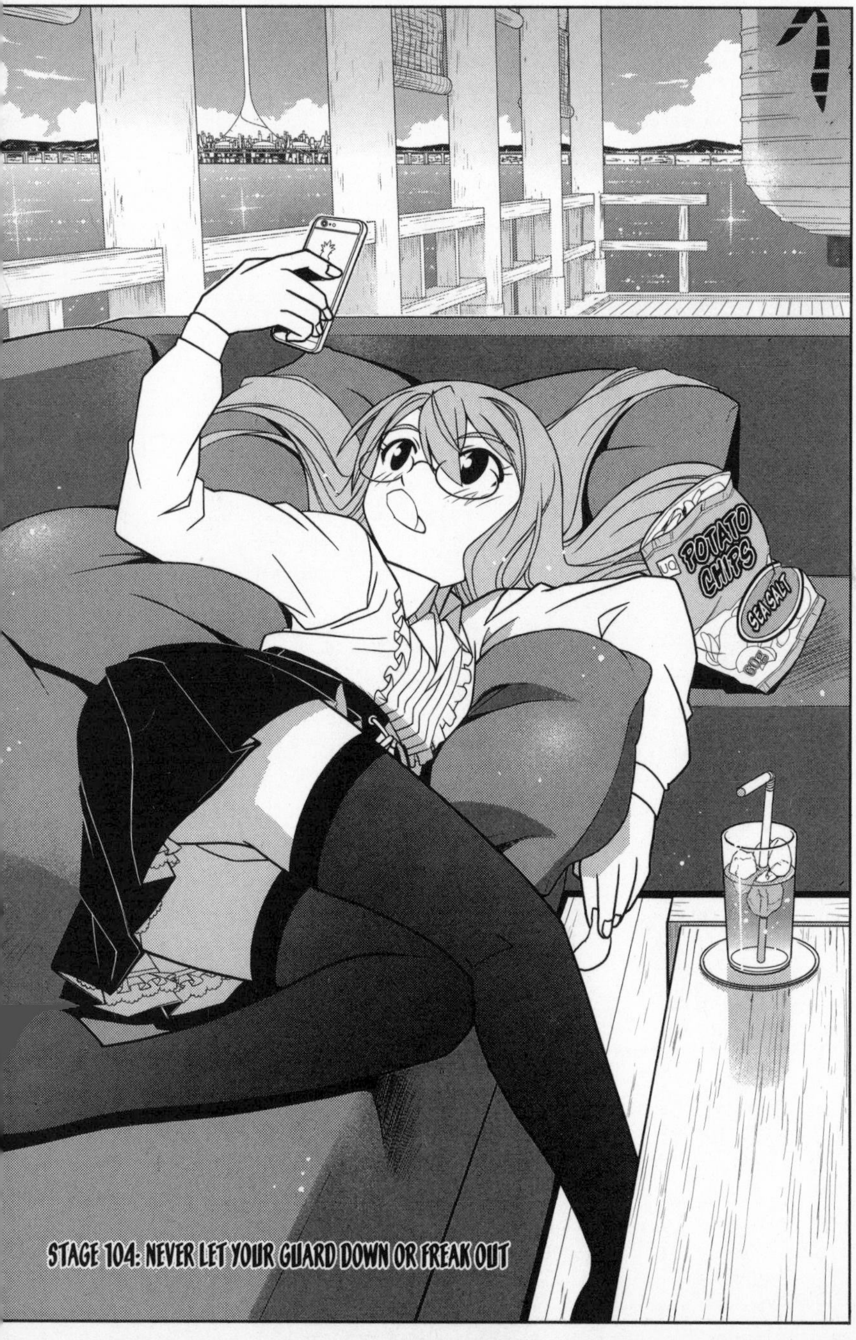
UQ
POTATO CHIPS
SEA SALT
60g
STAGE 104: NEVER LET YOUR GUARD DOWN OR FREAK OUT

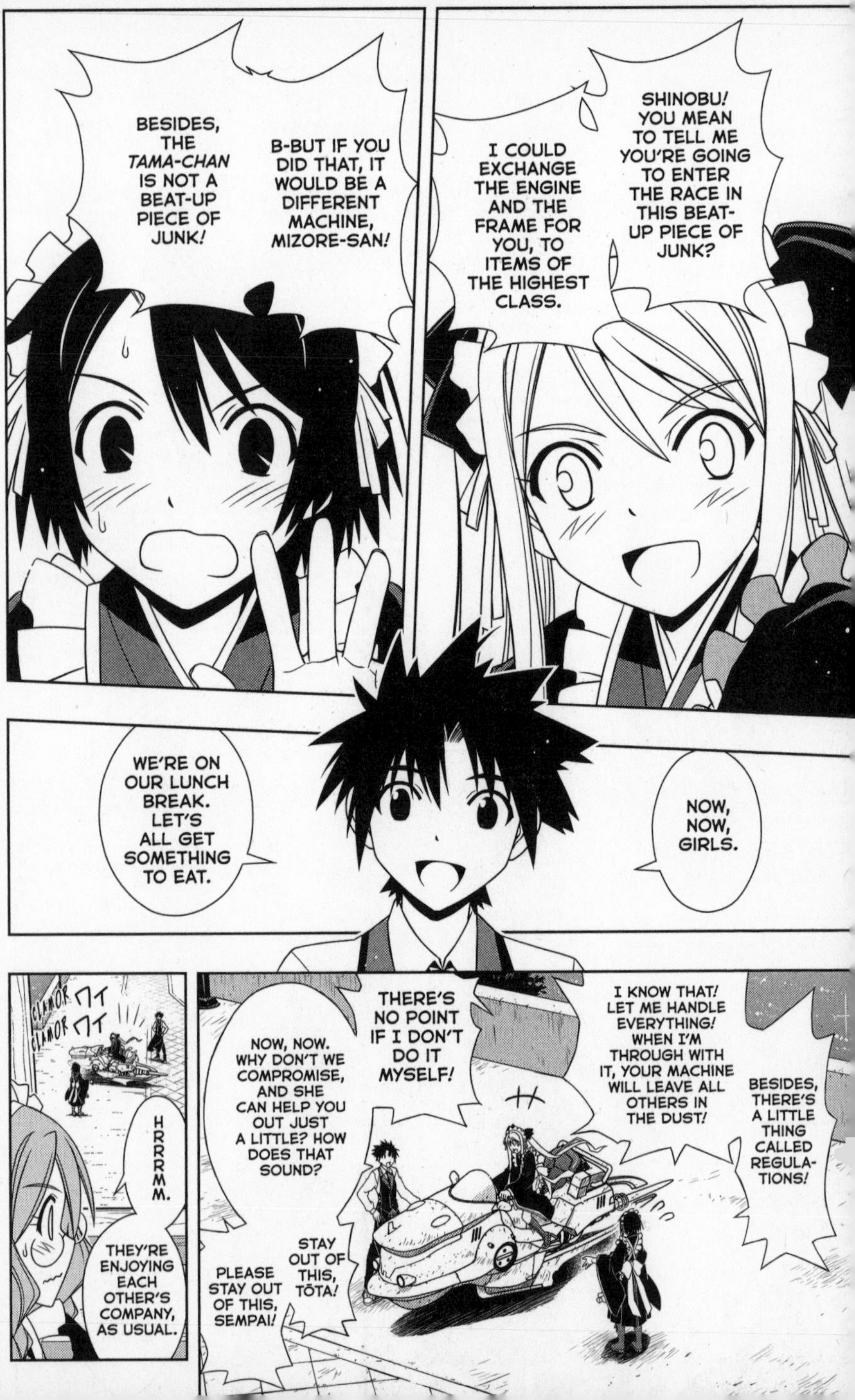
SHINOBU! YOU MEAN TO TELL ME YOU'RE GOING TO ENTER THE RACE IN THIS BEAT-UP PIECE OF JUNK?
I COULD EXCHANGE THE ENGINE AND THE FRAME FOR YOU, TO ITEMS OF THE HIGHEST CLASS.
B-BUT IF YOU DID THAT, IT WOULD BE A DIFFERENT MACHINE, MIZORE-SAN!
BESIDES, THE *TAMA-CHAN* IS NOT A BEAT-UP PIECE OF JUNK!
NOW, NOW, GIRLS.
WE'RE ON OUR LUNCH BREAK. LET'S ALL GET SOMETHING TO EAT.
BESIDES, THERE'S A LITTLE THING CALLED REGULATIONS!
I KNOW THAT! LET ME HANDLE EVERYTHING! WHEN I'M THROUGH WITH IT, YOUR MACHINE WILL LEAVE ALL OTHERS IN THE DUST!
THERE'S NO POINT IF I DON'T DO IT MYSELF!
NOW, NOW. WHY DON'T WE COMPROMISE, AND SHE CAN HELP YOU OUT JUST A LITTLE? HOW DOES THAT SOUND?
STAY OUT OF THIS, TŌTA!
PLEASE STAY OUT OF THIS, SEMPAI!
CLAMOR
CLAMOR
HRRRMM.
THEY'RE ENJOYING EACH OTHER'S COMPANY, AS USUAL.

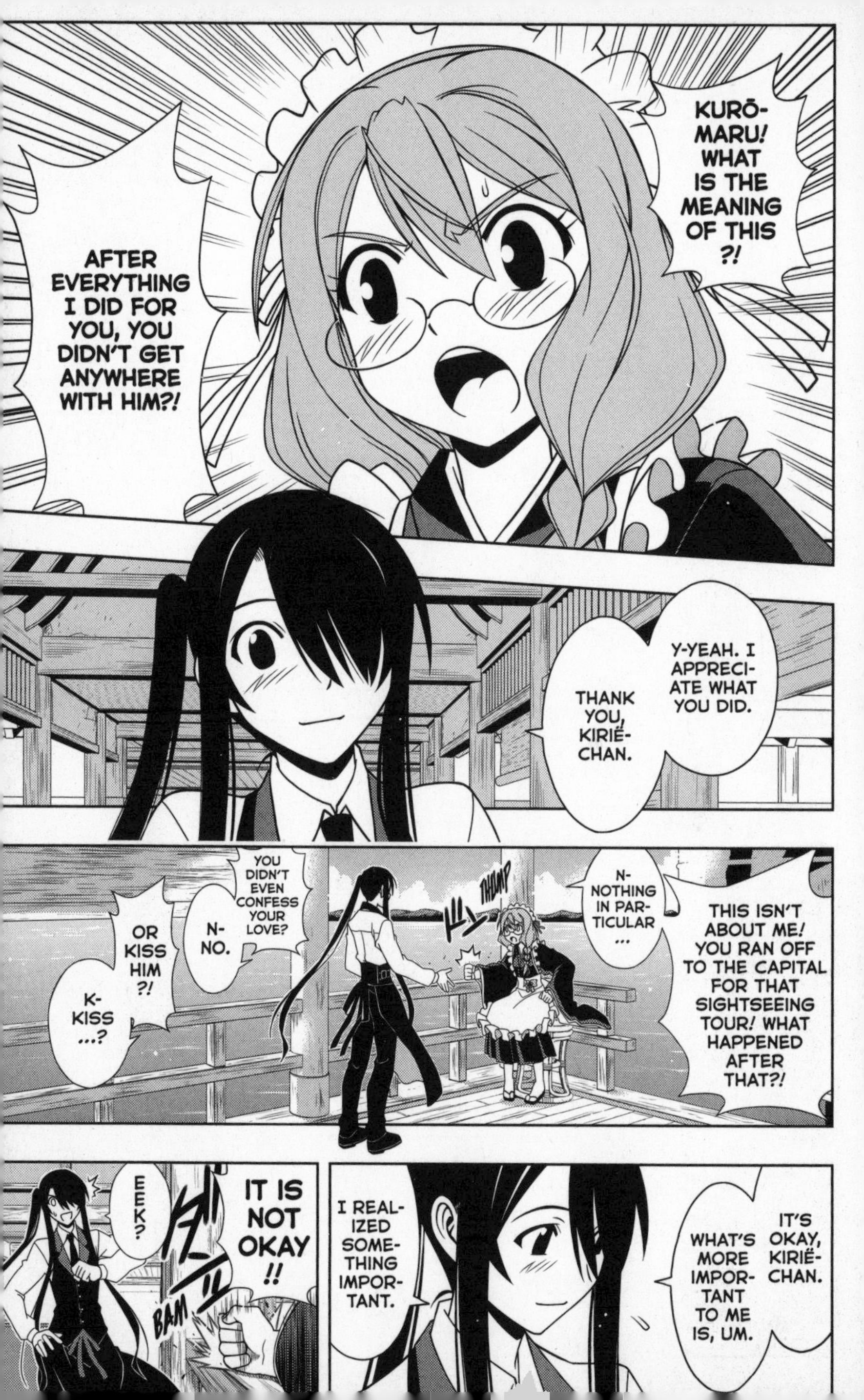
KURŌ-MARU! WHAT IS THE MEANING OF THIS ?!
AFTER EVERYTHING I DID FOR YOU, YOU DIDN'T GET ANYWHERE WITH HIM?!
Y-YEAH. I APPRECIATE WHAT YOU DID.
THANK YOU, KIRIË-CHAN.
THIS ISN'T ABOUT ME! YOU RAN OFF TO THE CAPITAL FOR THAT SIGHTSEEING TOUR! WHAT HAPPENED AFTER THAT?!
N-NOTHING IN PARTICULAR ...
THUMP
YOU DIDN'T EVEN CONFESS YOUR LOVE?
N-NO.
OR KISS HIM ?!
K-KISS ...?
IT'S OKAY, KIRIË-CHAN.
WHAT'S MORE IMPORTANT TO ME IS, UM.
I REALIZED SOMETHING IMPORTANT.
IT IS NOT OKAY !!
EEK?
BAM

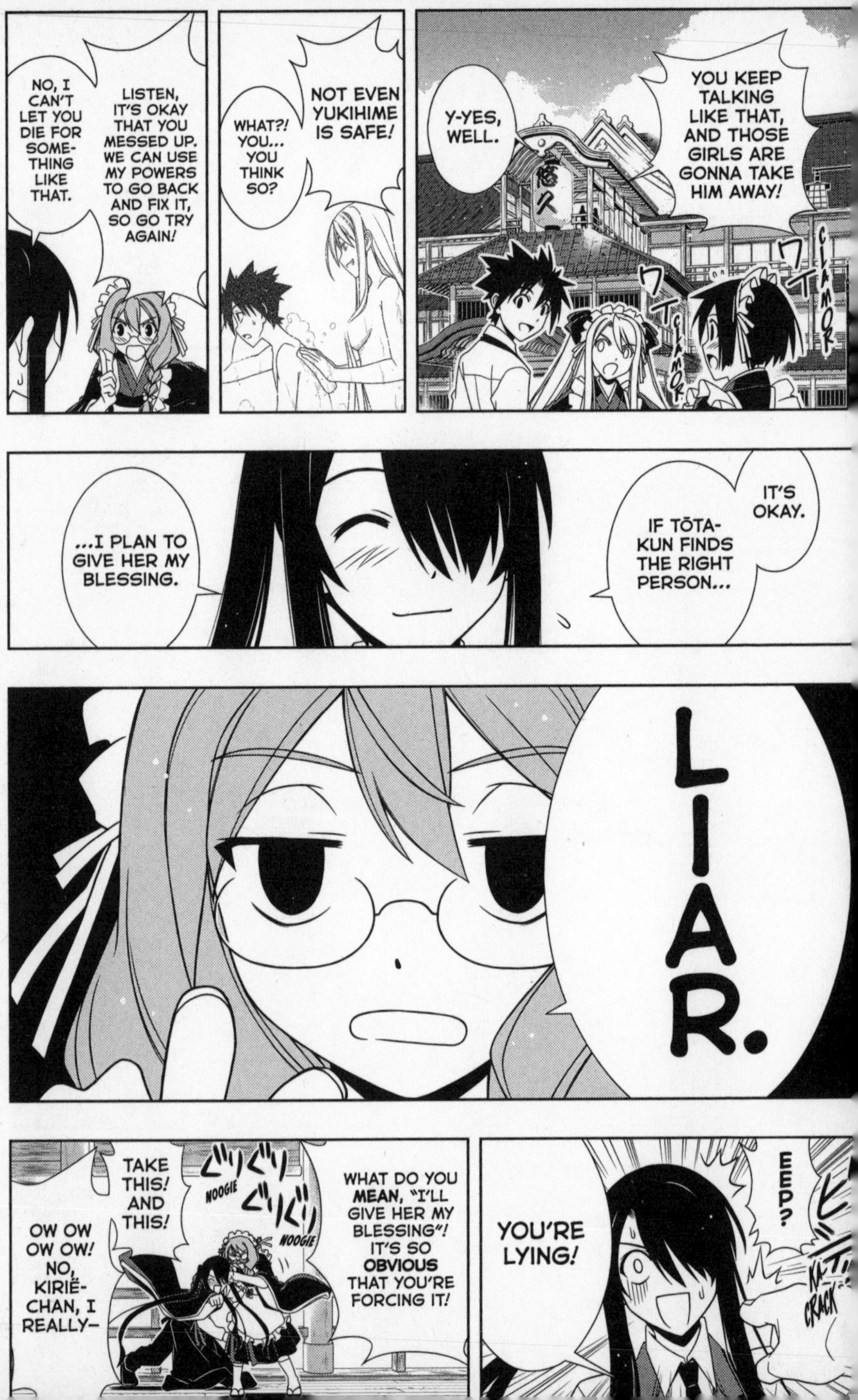
YOU KEEP TALKING LIKE THAT, AND THOSE GIRLS ARE GONNA TAKE HIM AWAY!
Y-YES, WELL.
CLAMOR
CLAMOR
NOT EVEN YUKIHIME IS SAFE!
WHAT?! YOU... YOU THINK SO?
LISTEN, IT'S OKAY THAT YOU MESSED UP. WE CAN USE MY POWERS TO GO BACK AND FIX IT, SO GO TRY AGAIN!
NO, I CAN'T LET YOU DIE FOR SOMETHING LIKE THAT.
IT'S OKAY.
IF TŌTA-KUN FINDS THE RIGHT PERSON...
...I PLAN TO GIVE HER MY BLESSING.
LIAR.
EEP?
KA-CRACK
YOU'RE LYING!
WHAT DO YOU **MEAN**, "I'LL GIVE HER MY BLESSING"! IT'S SO **OBVIOUS** THAT YOU'RE FORCING IT!
TAKE THIS! AND THIS!
NOOGIE
NOOGIE
OW OW OW OW! NO, KIRIË-CHAN, I REALLY—

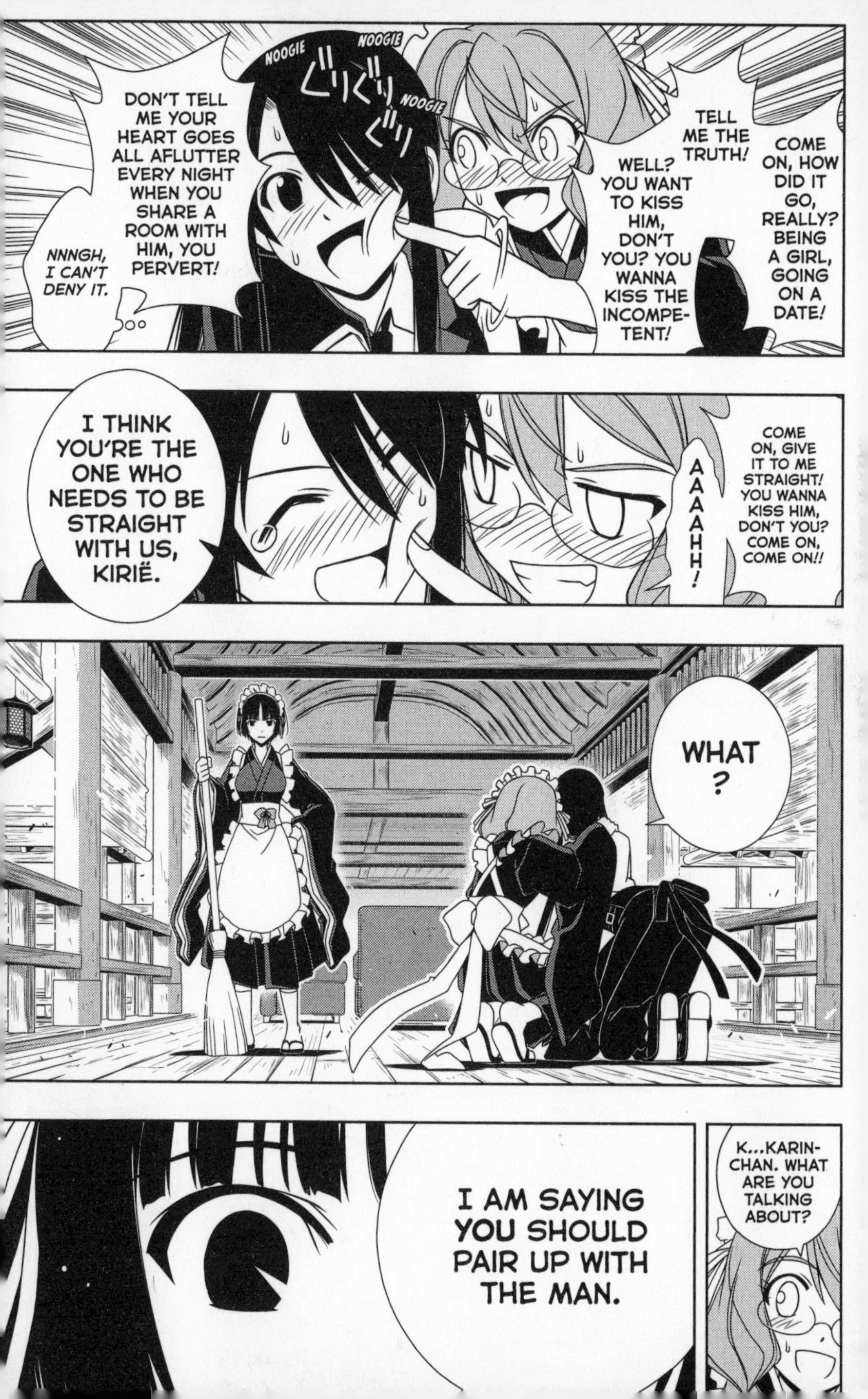
COME ON, HOW DID IT GO, REALLY? BEING A GIRL, GOING ON A DATE!
TELL ME THE TRUTH!
WELL? YOU WANT TO KISS HIM, DON'T YOU? YOU WANNA KISS THE INCOMPETENT!
NOOGIE
NOOGIE
NOOGIE
DON'T TELL ME YOUR HEART GOES ALL AFLUTTER EVERY NIGHT WHEN YOU SHARE A ROOM WITH HIM, YOU PERVERT!
NNNGH, I CAN'T DENY IT.
COME ON, GIVE IT TO ME STRAIGHT! YOU WANNA KISS HIM, DON'T YOU? COME ON, COME ON!!
AAAAHH!
I THINK YOU'RE THE ONE WHO NEEDS TO BE STRAIGHT WITH US, KIRIË.
WHAT?
K...KARIN-CHAN. WHAT ARE YOU TALKING ABOUT?
I AM SAYING YOU SHOULD PAIR UP WITH THE MAN.

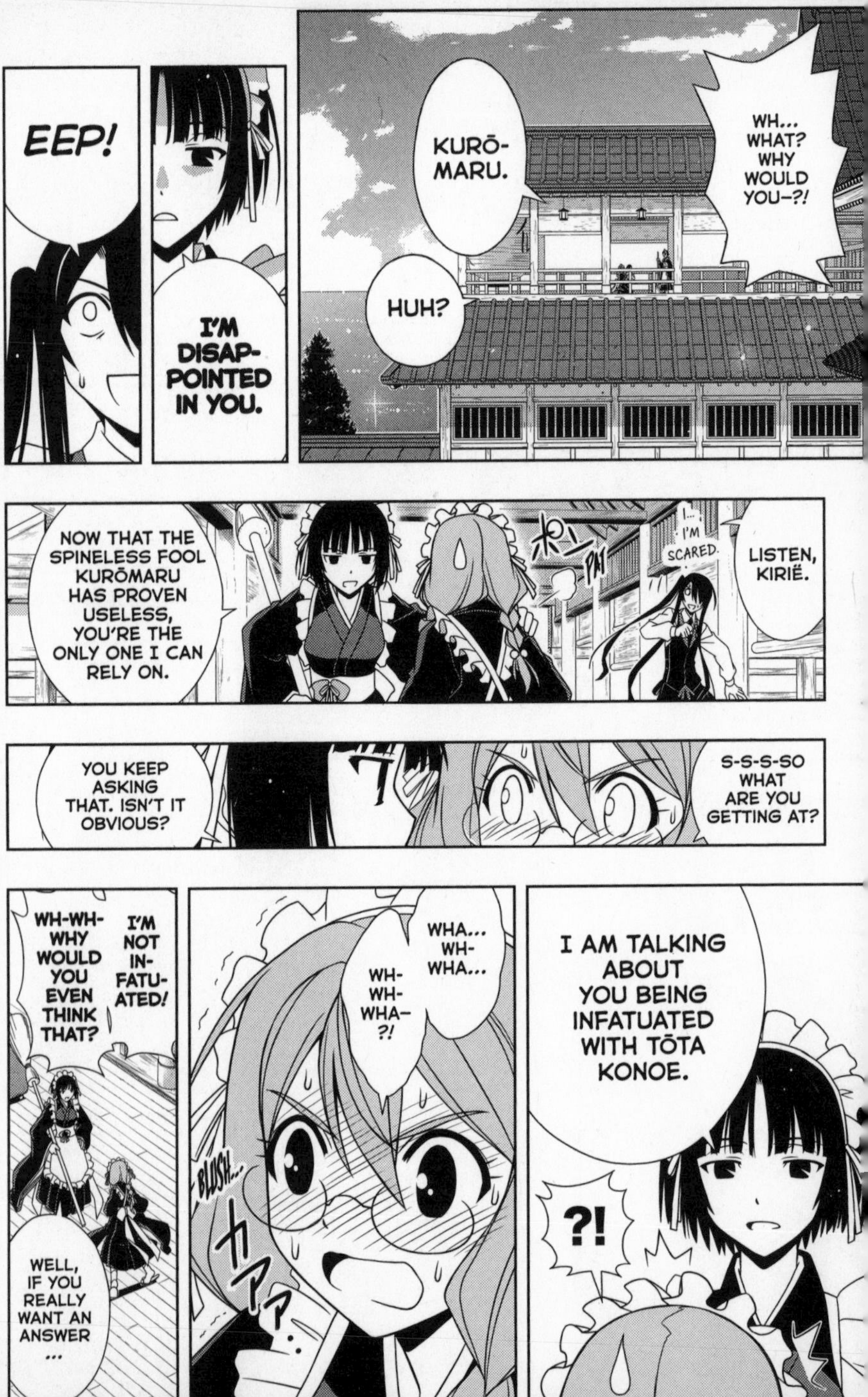
WH... WHAT? WHY WOULD YOU–?!
KURŌ-MARU.
HUH?
I'M DISAP-POINTED IN YOU.
EEP!
LISTEN, KIRIË.
I... I'M SCARED.
PA!
NOW THAT THE SPINELESS FOOL KURŌMARU HAS PROVEN USELESS, YOU'RE THE ONLY ONE I CAN RELY ON.
S-S-S-SO WHAT ARE YOU GETTING AT?
YOU KEEP ASKING THAT. ISN'T IT OBVIOUS?
I AM TALKING ABOUT YOU BEING INFATUATED WITH TŌTA KONOE.
?!
WHA... WH-WHA...
WH-WH-WHA-?!
BLUSH...
I'M NOT IN-FATU-ATED!
WH-WH-WHY WOULD YOU EVEN THINK THAT?
WELL, IF YOU REALLY WANT AN ANSWER...

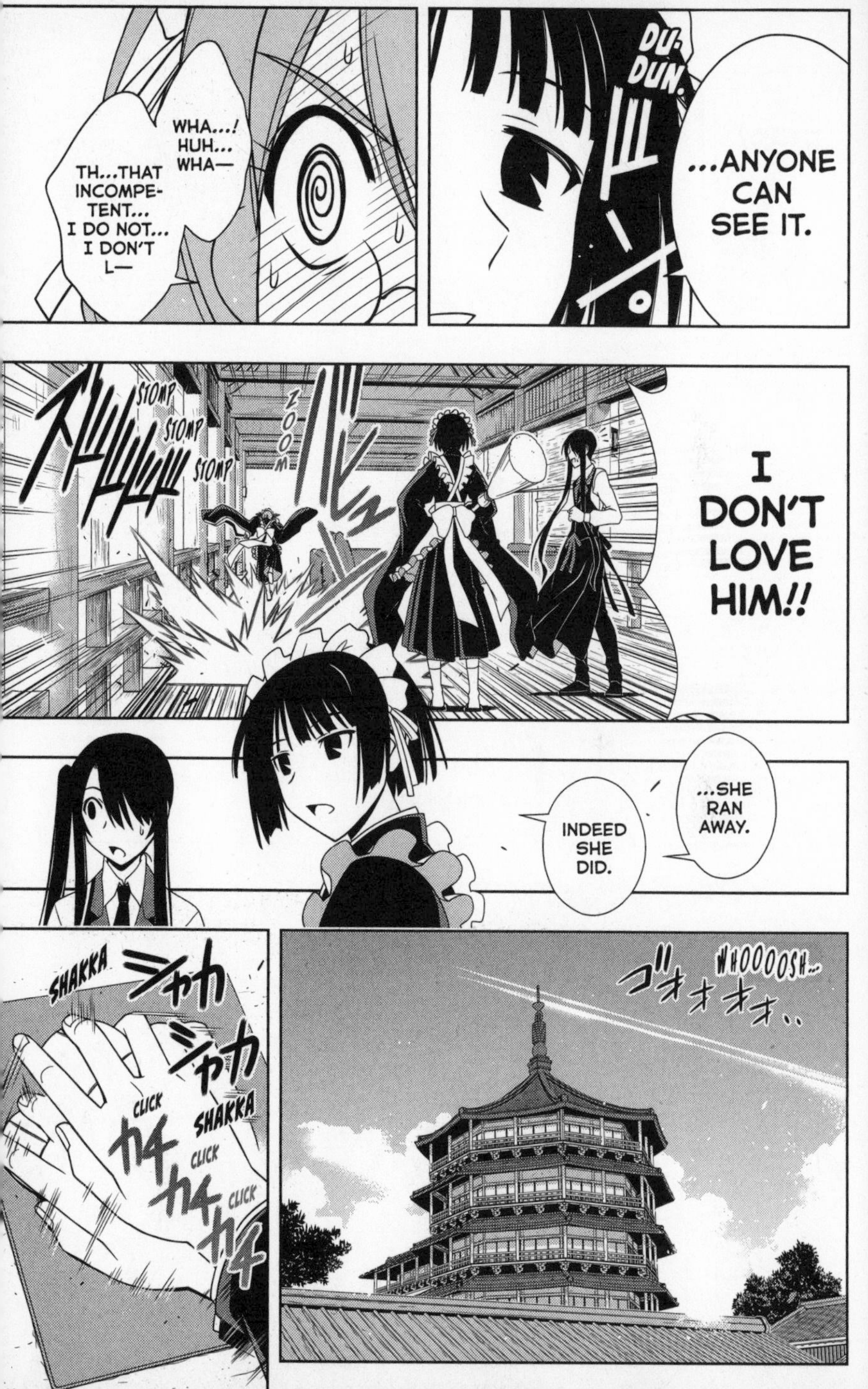
DU-DUN.
...ANYONE CAN SEE IT.
WHA...! HUH... WHA—
TH...THAT INCOMPETENT... I DO NOT... I DON'T L—
I DON'T LOVE HIM!!
ZOOOM
STOMP
STOMP
STOMP
...SHE RAN AWAY.
INDEED SHE DID.
WHOOOOSH...
SHAKKA
CLICK
SHAKKA
CLICK
CLICK

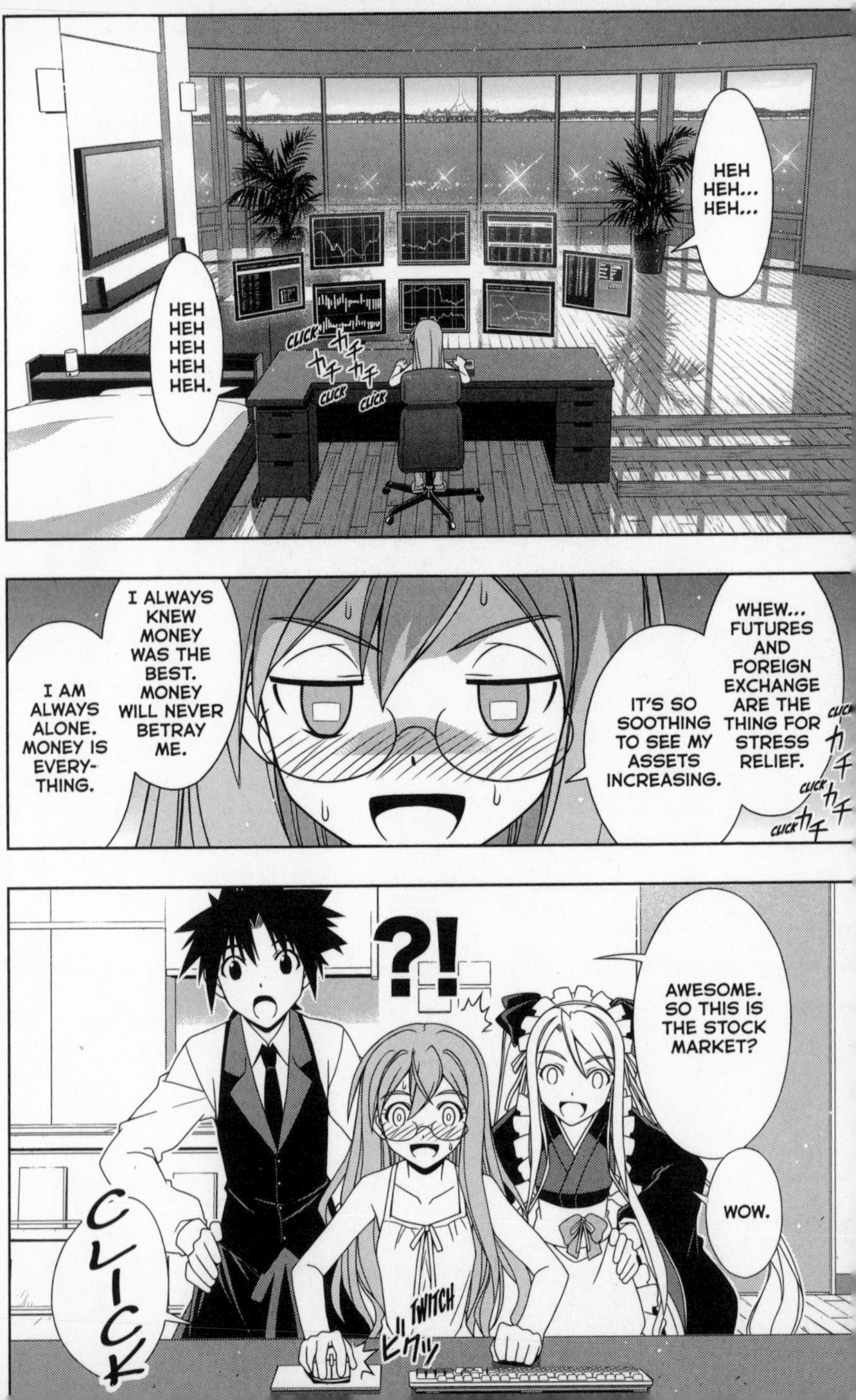
HEH HEH... HEH...
HEH HEH HEH HEH HEH.
CLICK カチ カチ カチ CLICK CLICK
WHEW... FUTURES AND FOREIGN EXCHANGE ARE THE THING FOR STRESS RELIEF.
IT'S SO SOOTHING TO SEE MY ASSETS INCREASING.
I ALWAYS KNEW MONEY WAS THE BEST. MONEY WILL NEVER BETRAY ME.
I AM ALWAYS ALONE. MONEY IS EVERY-THING.
CLICK カチ CLICK カチ CLICK カチ
AWESOME. SO THIS IS THE STOCK MARKET?
WOW.
?!
TWITCH ビクッ
CLICK

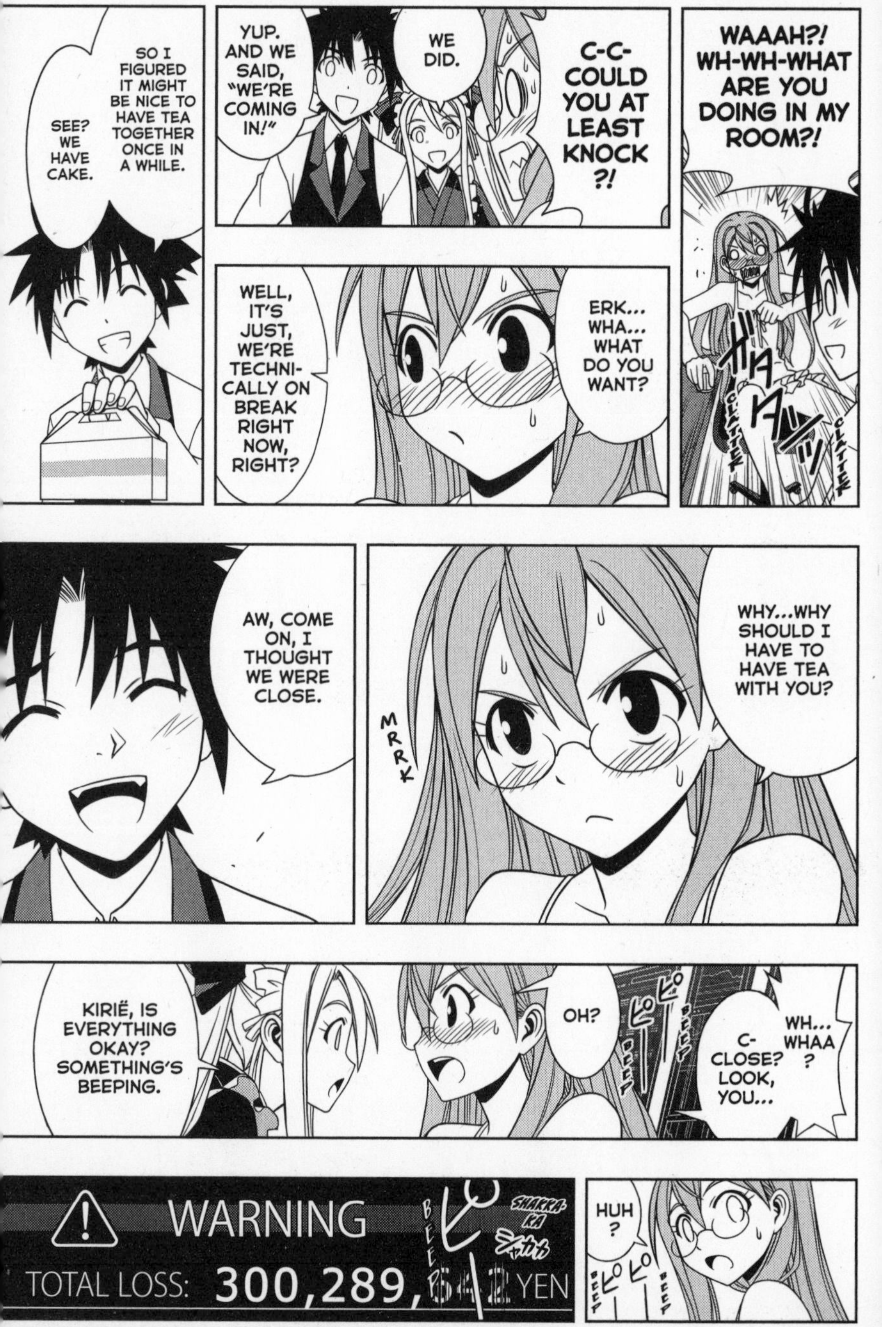
WAAAH?! WH-WH-WHAT ARE YOU DOING IN MY ROOM?!
CLATTER
CLATTER
C-C-COULD YOU AT LEAST KNOCK?!
WE DID.
YUP. AND WE SAID, "WE'RE COMING IN!"
ERK... WHA... WHAT DO YOU WANT?
WELL, IT'S JUST, WE'RE TECHNICALLY ON BREAK RIGHT NOW, RIGHT?
SO I FIGURED IT MIGHT BE NICE TO HAVE TEA TOGETHER ONCE IN A WHILE.
SEE? WE HAVE CAKE.
WHY...WHY SHOULD I HAVE TO HAVE TEA WITH YOU?
MRRK
AW, COME ON, I THOUGHT WE WERE CLOSE.
WH... WHAA?
C-CLOSE? LOOK, YOU...
BEEP
BEEP
OH?
KIRIË, IS EVERYTHING OKAY? SOMETHING'S BEEPING.
HUH?
BEEP
BEEP
SHAKKA-KA
BEEP
WARNING
TOTAL LOSS: 300,289,542 YEN

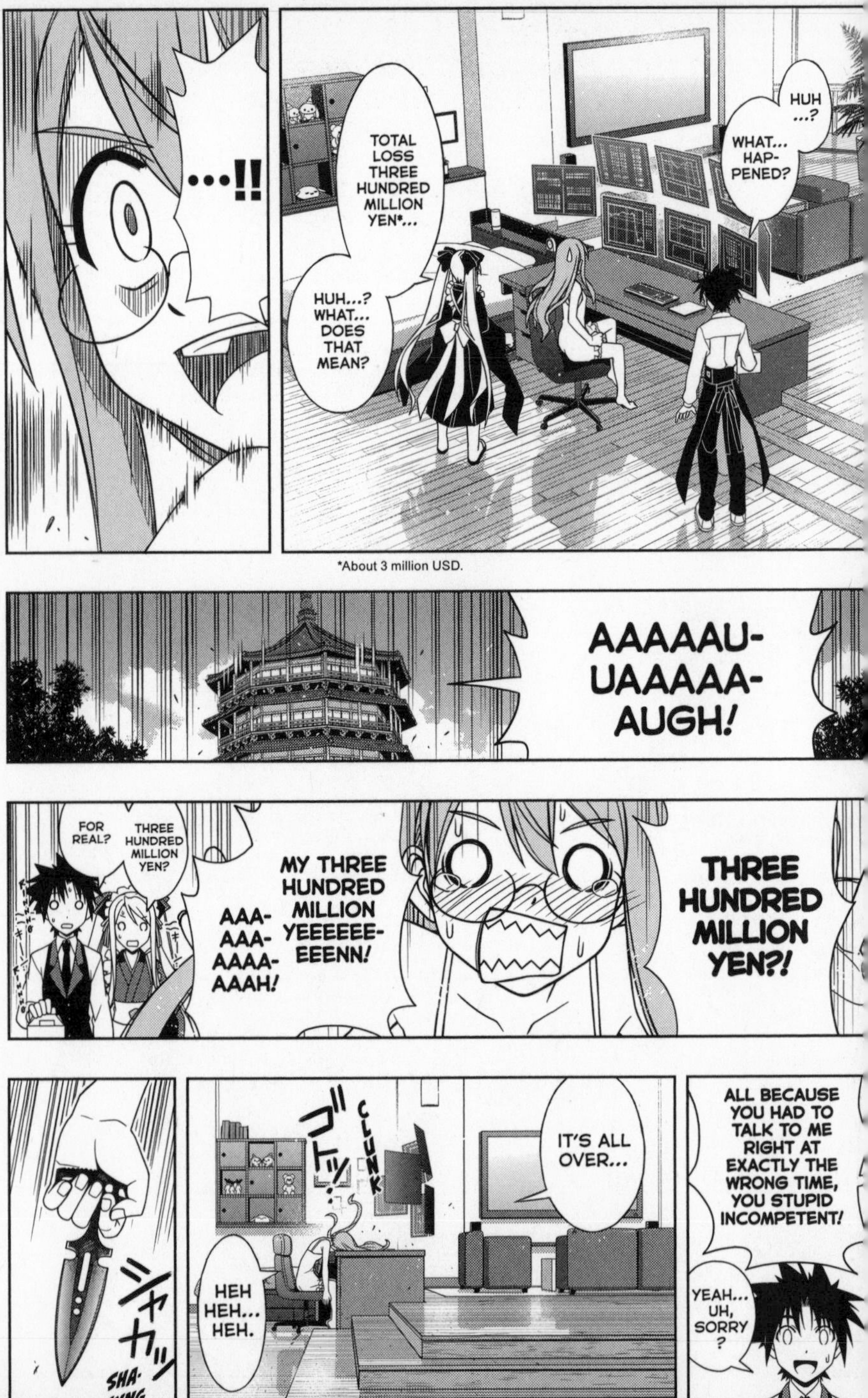
HUH ...?
WHAT... HAP-PENED?
TOTAL LOSS THREE HUNDRED MILLION YEN*...
HUH...? WHAT... DOES THAT MEAN?
...!!
AAAAAU-UAAAAA-AUGH!
THREE HUNDRED MILLION YEN?!
MY THREE HUNDRED MILLION YEEEEEE-EEENN!
AAA-AAA-AAAA-AAAH!
THREE HUNDRED MILLION YEN?
FOR REAL?
ALL BECAUSE YOU HAD TO TALK TO ME RIGHT AT EXACTLY THE WRONG TIME, YOU STUPID INCOMPETENT!
YEAH... UH, SORRY?
IT'S ALL OVER...
CLUNK
HEH HEH... HEH.
SHA-KING
*About 3 million USD.

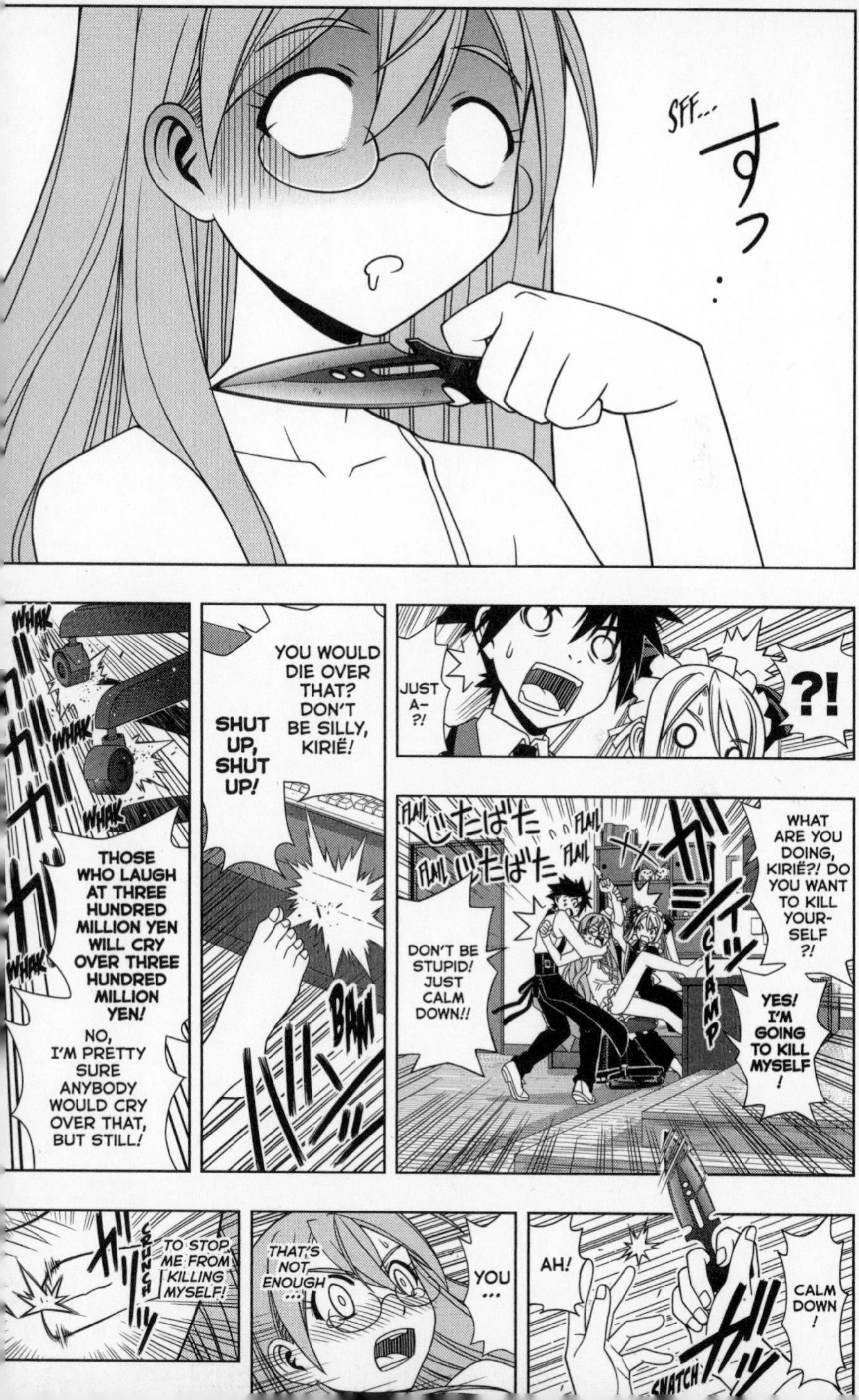
SFF...
すっ
?!
JUST A-?!
WHAT ARE YOU DOING, KIRIË?! DO YOU WANT TO KILL YOURSELF?!
FLAIL じたばた FLAIL
FLAIL じたばた FLAIL
CLAMP
YES! I'M GOING TO KILL MYSELF!
DON'T BE STUPID! JUST CALM DOWN!!
YOU WOULD DIE OVER THAT? DON'T BE SILLY, KIRIË!
SHUT UP, SHUT UP!
BAM
WHAK
WHAK
WHAK
WHAK
THOSE WHO LAUGH AT THREE HUNDRED MILLION YEN WILL CRY OVER THREE HUNDRED MILLION YEN!
NO, I'M PRETTY SURE ANYBODY WOULD CRY OVER THAT, BUT STILL!
CALM DOWN!
AH!
SNATCH
YOU...
THAT'S NOT ENOUGH...
TO STOP ME FROM KILLING MYSELF!
CRUNCH

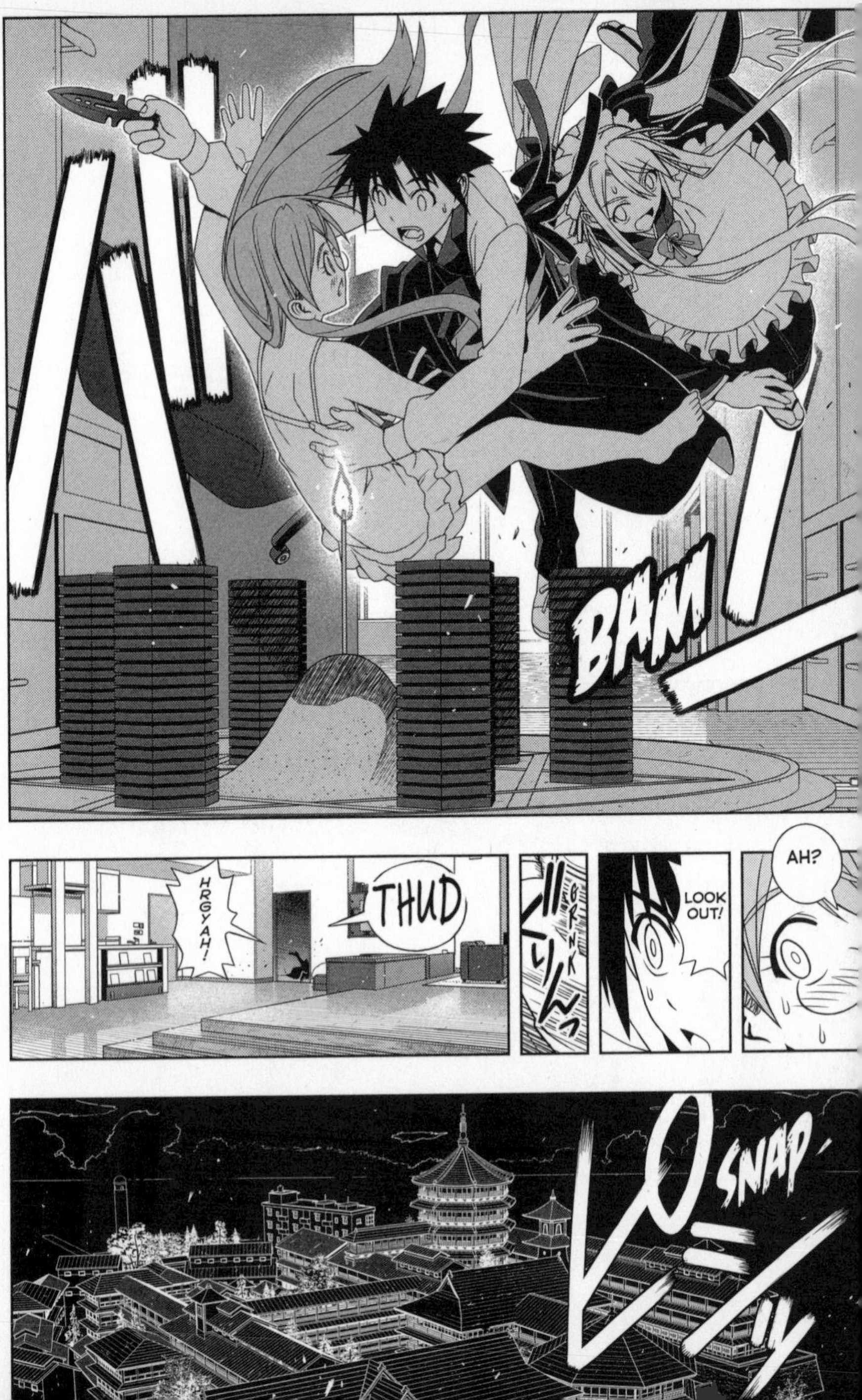
BAM
AH?
LOOK OUT!
GRNK
THUD
HRGYAH!
SNAP

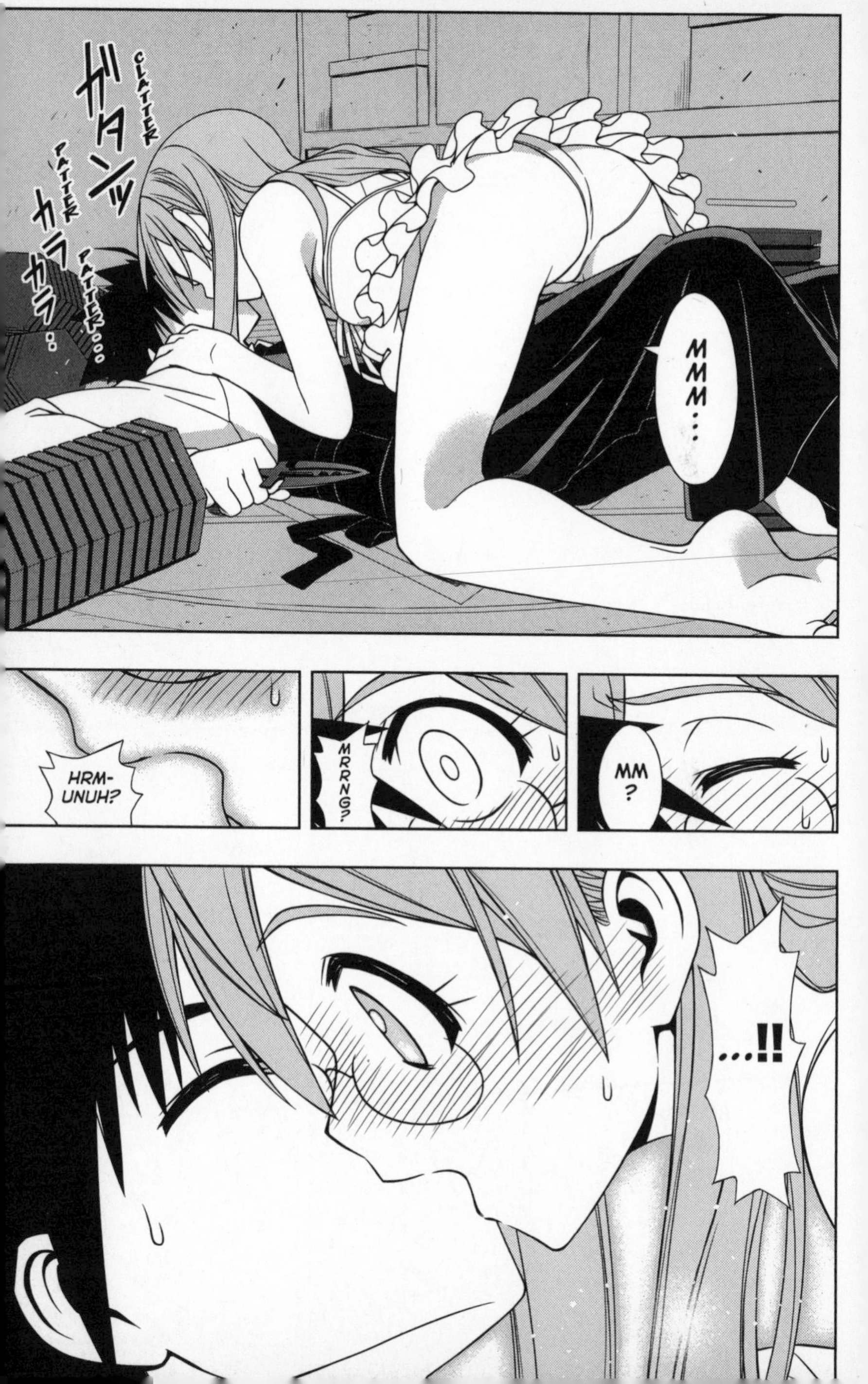

ガタンッ
CLATTER
カラカラ‥
PATTER PATTER...
MMM...
MM?
MRRNG?
HRM-UNUH?
...!!

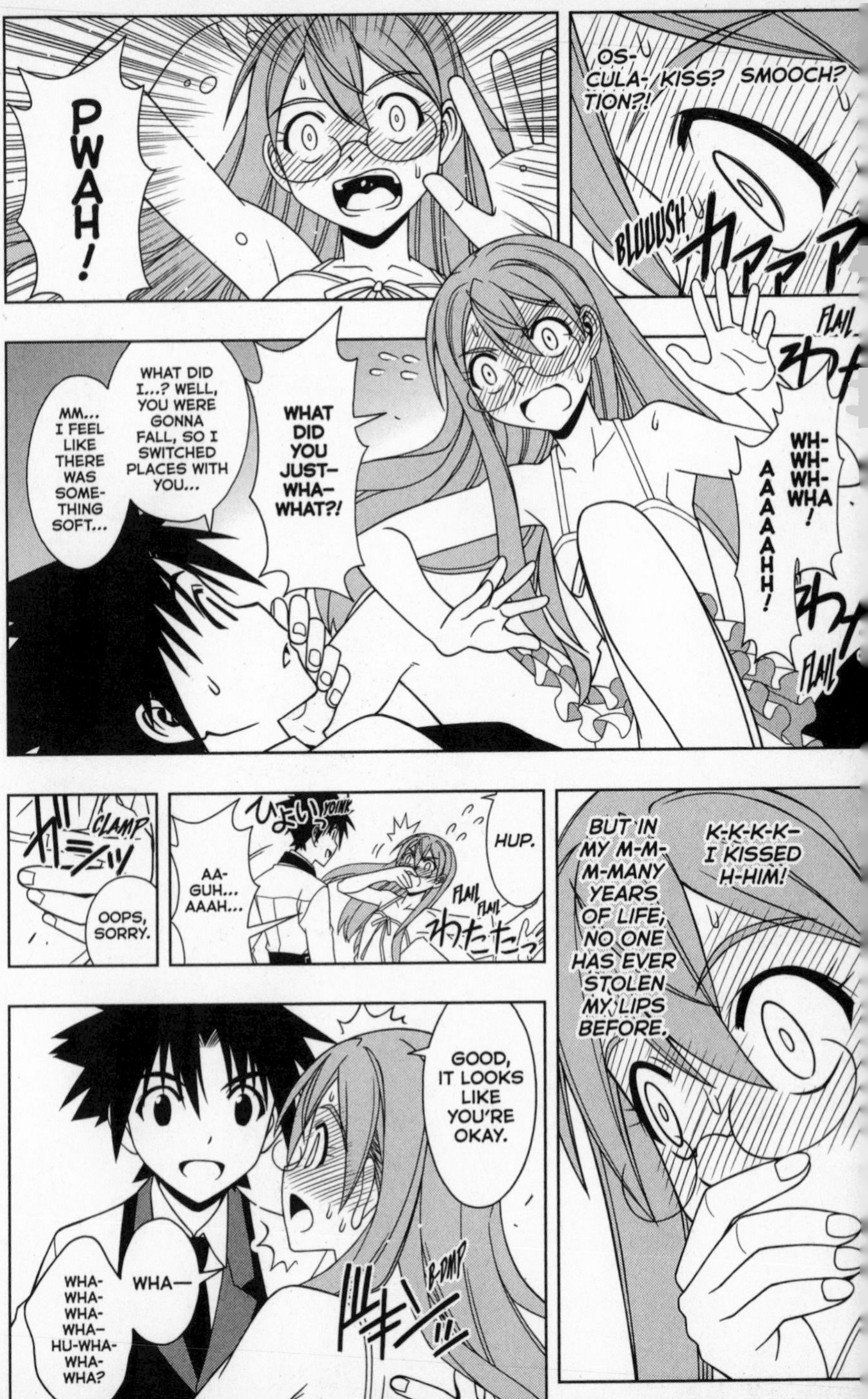
OS-CULA-TION?!
KISS?
SMOOCH?
BLUUUSH
PWAH!
FLAIL
WH-WH-WH-WHA!
AAAAAAHH!
FLAIL
WHAT DID YOU JUST—WHA-WHAT?!
WHAT DID I...? WELL, YOU WERE GONNA FALL, SO I SWITCHED PLACES WITH YOU...
MM... I FEEL LIKE THERE WAS SOME-THING SOFT...
K-K-K-K-I KISSED H-HIM!
BUT IN MY M-M-M-MANY YEARS OF LIFE, NO ONE HAS EVER STOLEN MY LIPS BEFORE.
HUP.
ひょいっ YOINK
FLAIL FLAIL わたたっ
AA-GUH... AAAH...
CLAMP
OOPS, SORRY.
GOOD, IT LOOKS LIKE YOU'RE OKAY.
B-DMP
WHA—
WHA-WHA-WHA-WHA-HU-WHA-WHA-WHA?

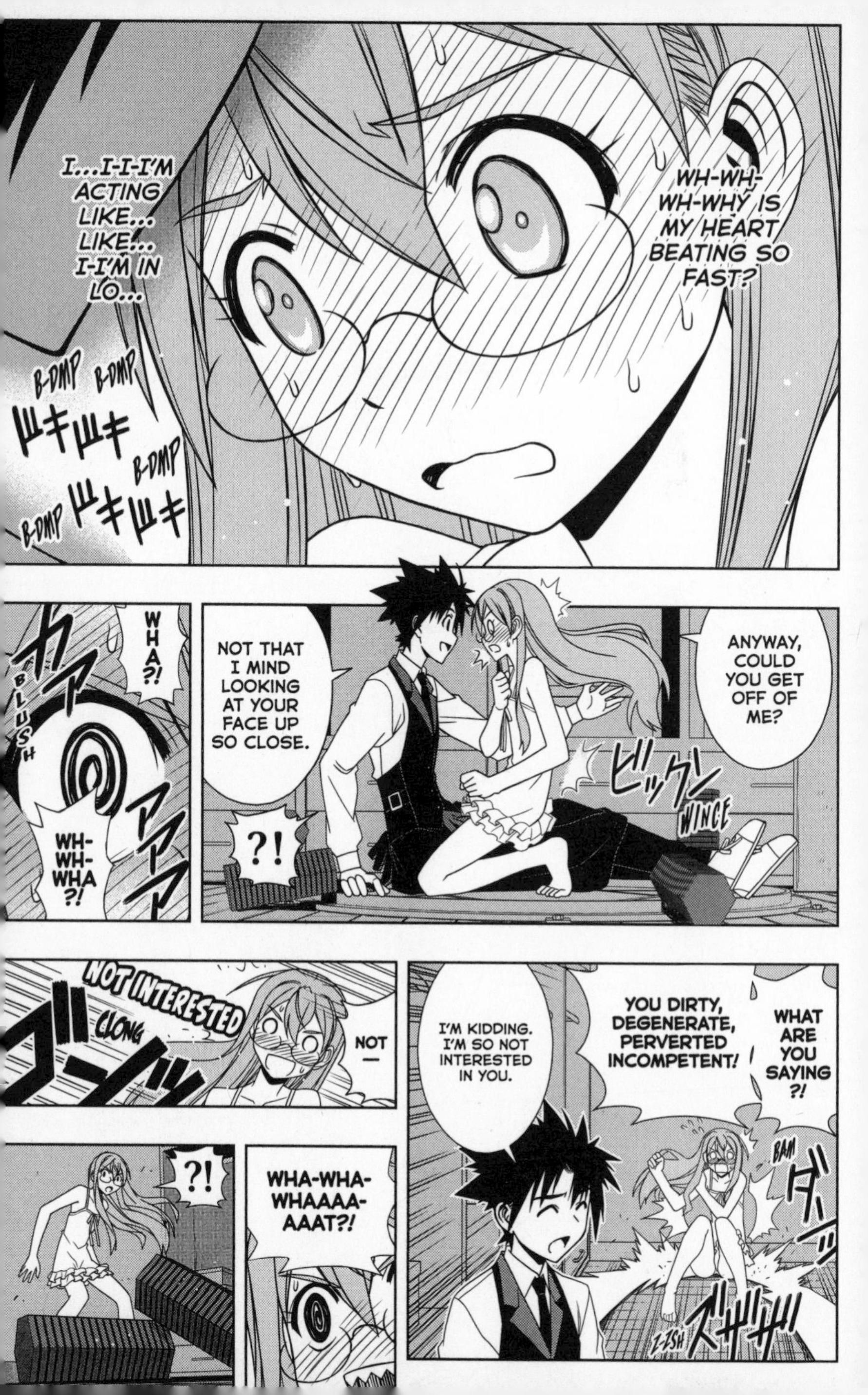
WH-WH-WH-WHY IS MY HEART BEATING SO FAST?
I...I-I-I'M ACTING LIKE... LIKE... I-I'M IN LO...
B-DMP B-DMP
B-DMP B-DMP
ANYWAY, COULD YOU GET OFF OF ME?
WINCE
NOT THAT I MIND LOOKING AT YOUR FACE UP SO CLOSE.
?!
WHA?!
BLUSH
WH-WH-WHA?!
WHAT ARE YOU SAYING?!
YOU DIRTY, DEGENERATE, PERVERTED INCOMPETENT!
I'M KIDDING. I'M SO NOT INTERESTED IN YOU.
BAM
Z-ZSH
NOT —
NOT INTERESTED
CLONG
WHA-WHA-WHAAAA-AAAT?!
?!

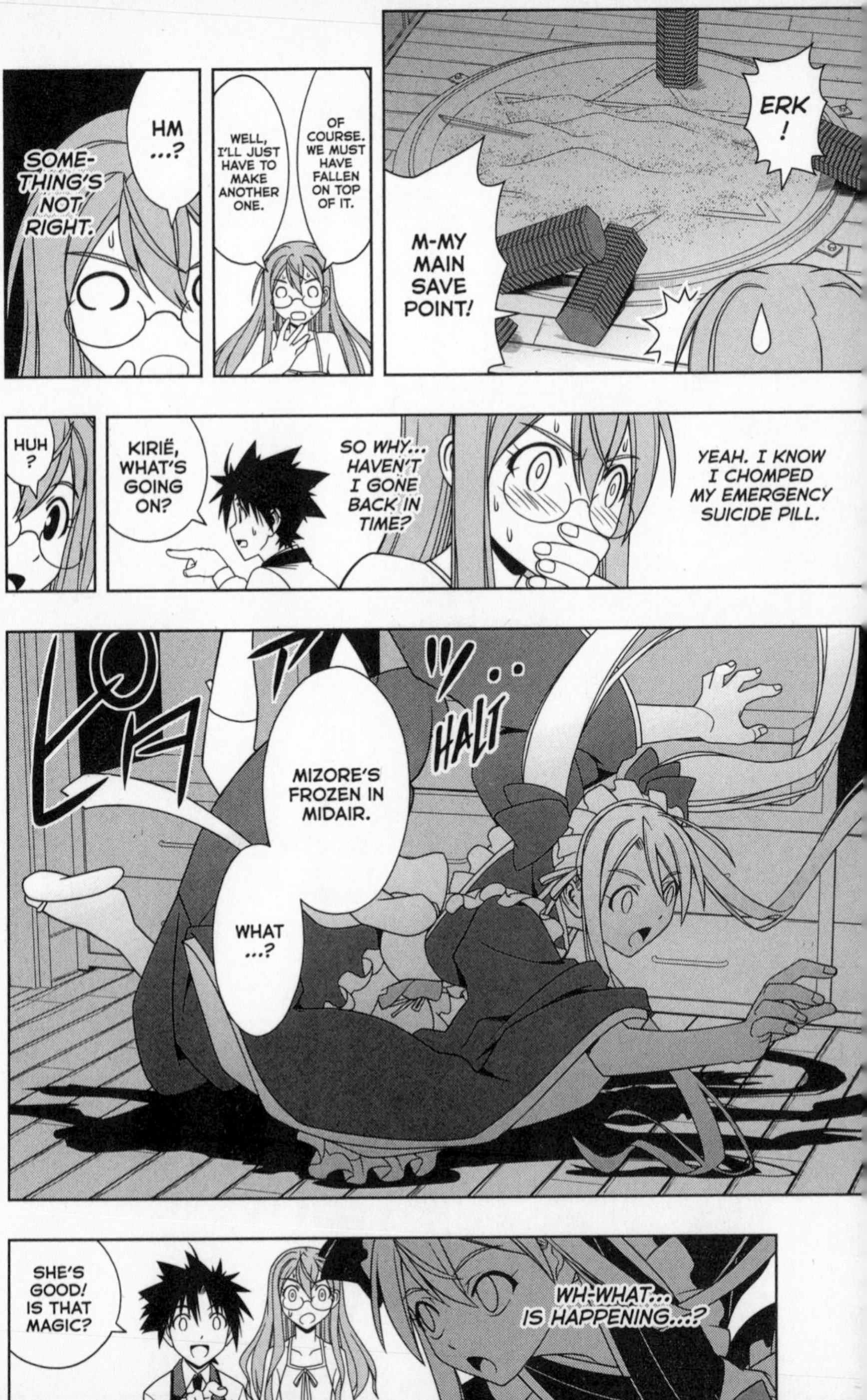
ERK!
M-MY MAIN SAVE POINT!
OF COURSE. WE MUST HAVE FALLEN ON TOP OF IT.
WELL, I'LL JUST HAVE TO MAKE ANOTHER ONE.
HM ...?
SOME-THING'S NOT RIGHT.
YEAH. I KNOW I CHOMPED MY EMERGENCY SUICIDE PILL.
SO WHY... HAVEN'T I GONE BACK IN TIME?
KIRIË, WHAT'S GOING ON?
HUH ?
HALT
MIZORE'S FROZEN IN MIDAIR.
WHAT ...?
WH-WHAT... IS HAPPENING...?
SHE'S GOOD! IS THAT MAGIC?

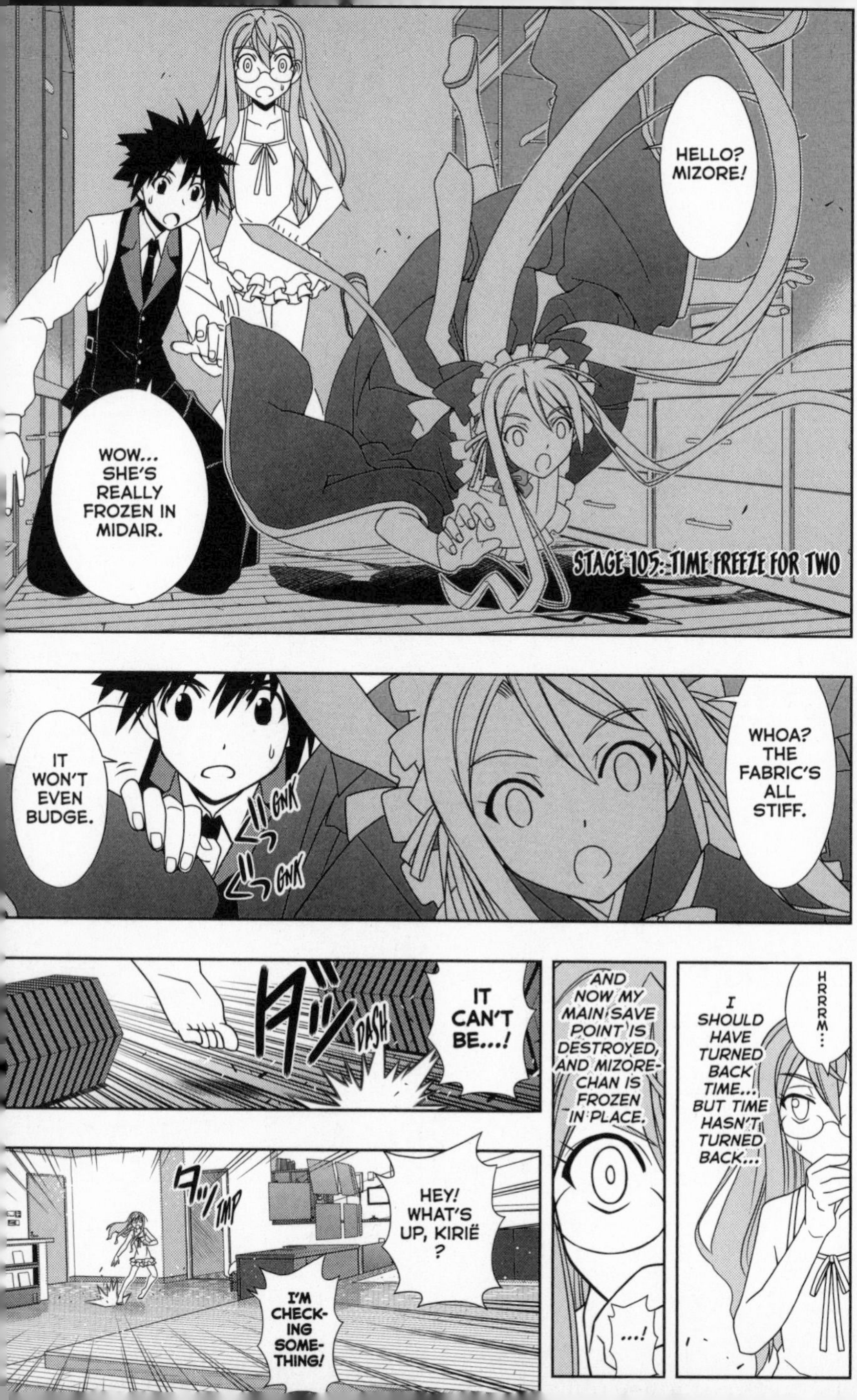
HELLO? MIZORE!
WOW... SHE'S REALLY FROZEN IN MIDAIR.
STAGE 105: TIME FREEZE FOR TWO
WHOA? THE FABRIC'S ALL STIFF.
GNK
GNK
IT WON'T EVEN BUDGE.
HRRRM...
I SHOULD HAVE TURNED BACK TIME... BUT TIME HASN'T TURNED BACK...
AND NOW MY MAIN SAVE POINT IS DESTROYED, AND MIZORE-CHAN IS FROZEN IN PLACE.
...!
IT CAN'T BE...!
DASH
HEY! WHAT'S UP, KIRIË?
TMP
I'M CHECKING SOMETHING!

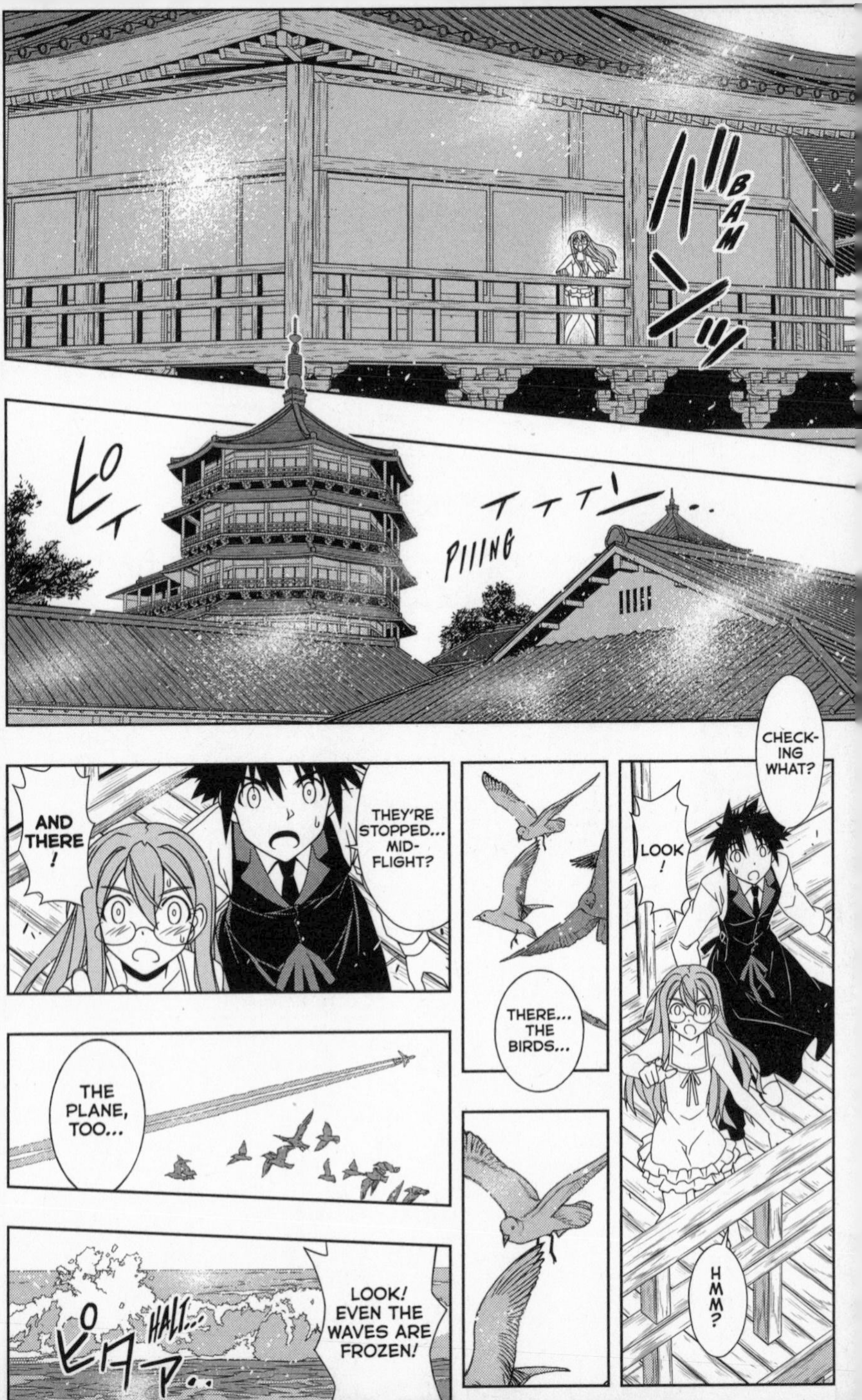
BAM
PIIING
CHECKING WHAT?
LOOK!
HMM?
THERE... THE BIRDS...
THEY'RE STOPPED... MID-FLIGHT?
AND THERE!
THE PLANE, TOO...
LOOK! EVEN THE WAVES ARE FROZEN!
HALT...

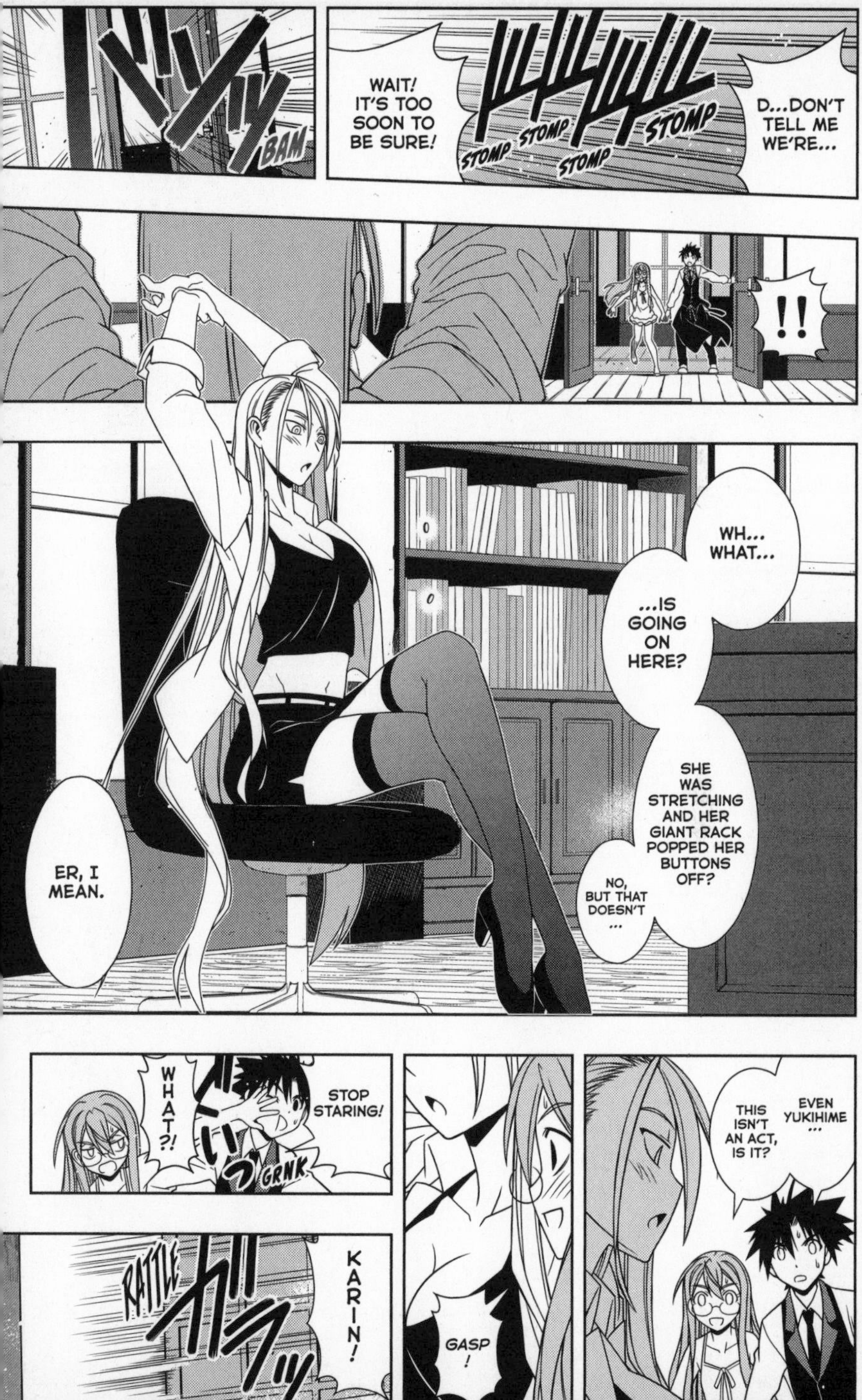
D...DON'T TELL ME WE'RE...
STOMP
STOMP
STOMP
STOMP
WAIT! IT'S TOO SOON TO BE SURE!
BAM
!!
WH... WHAT...
...IS GOING ON HERE?
SHE WAS STRETCHING AND HER GIANT RACK POPPED HER BUTTONS OFF?
NO, BUT THAT DOESN'T ...
ER, I MEAN.
EVEN YUKIHIME ...
THIS ISN'T AN ACT, IS IT?
GASP!
STOP STARING!
WHAT?!
GRNK
KARIN!
RATTLE

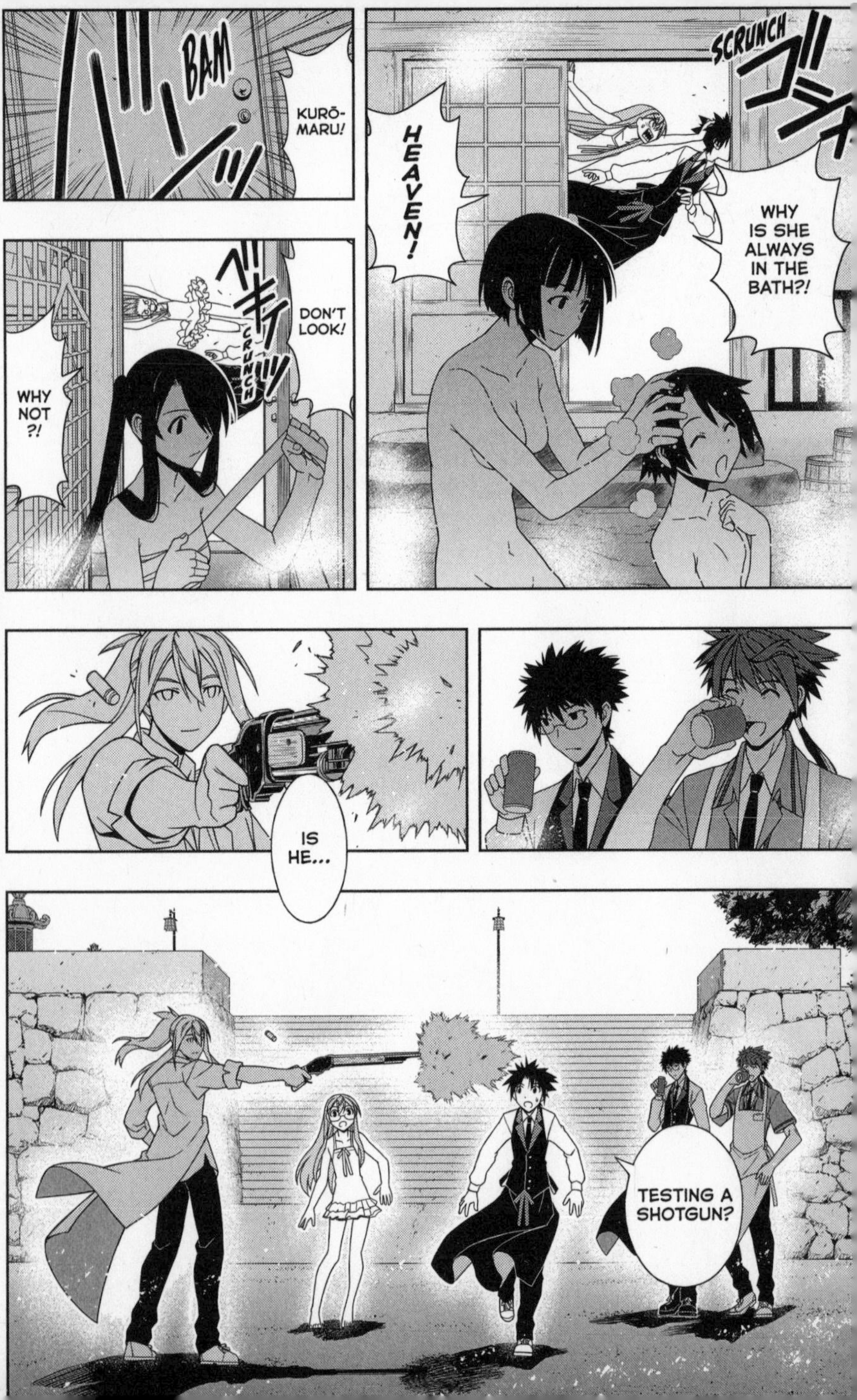
SCRUNCH
WHY IS SHE ALWAYS IN THE BATH?!
HEAVEN!
BAM
KURŌ-MARU!
CRUNCH
DON'T LOOK!
WHY NOT?!
IS HE...
TESTING A SHOTGUN?

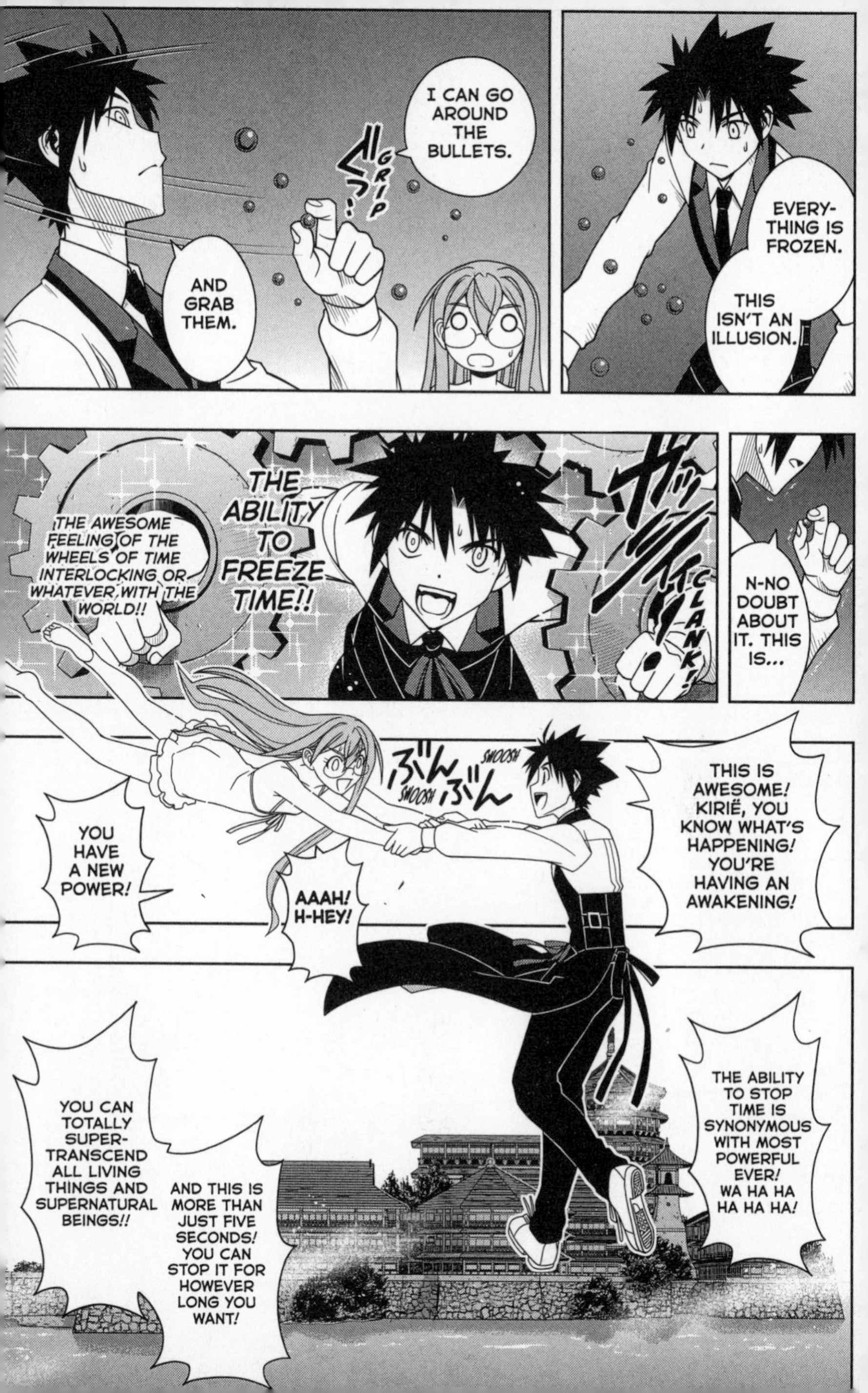
EVERY-THING IS FROZEN.
THIS ISN'T AN ILLUSION.
I CAN GO AROUND THE BULLETS.
GRIP
AND GRAB THEM.
N-NO DOUBT ABOUT IT. THIS IS...
CLANK!
THE ABILITY TO FREEZE TIME!!
THE AWESOME FEELING OF THE WHEELS OF TIME INTERLOCKING OR WHATEVER WITH THE WORLD!!
THIS IS AWESOME! KIRIË, YOU KNOW WHAT'S HAPPENING! YOU'RE HAVING AN AWAKENING!
SMOOSH
ぶんぶん
SMOOSH
AAAH! H-HEY!
YOU HAVE A NEW POWER!
THE ABILITY TO STOP TIME IS SYNONYMOUS WITH MOST POWERFUL EVER! WA HA HA HA HA HA!
AND THIS IS MORE THAN JUST FIVE SECONDS! YOU CAN STOP IT FOR HOWEVER LONG YOU WANT!
YOU CAN TOTALLY SUPER-TRANSCEND ALL LIVING THINGS AND SUPERNATURAL BEINGS!!

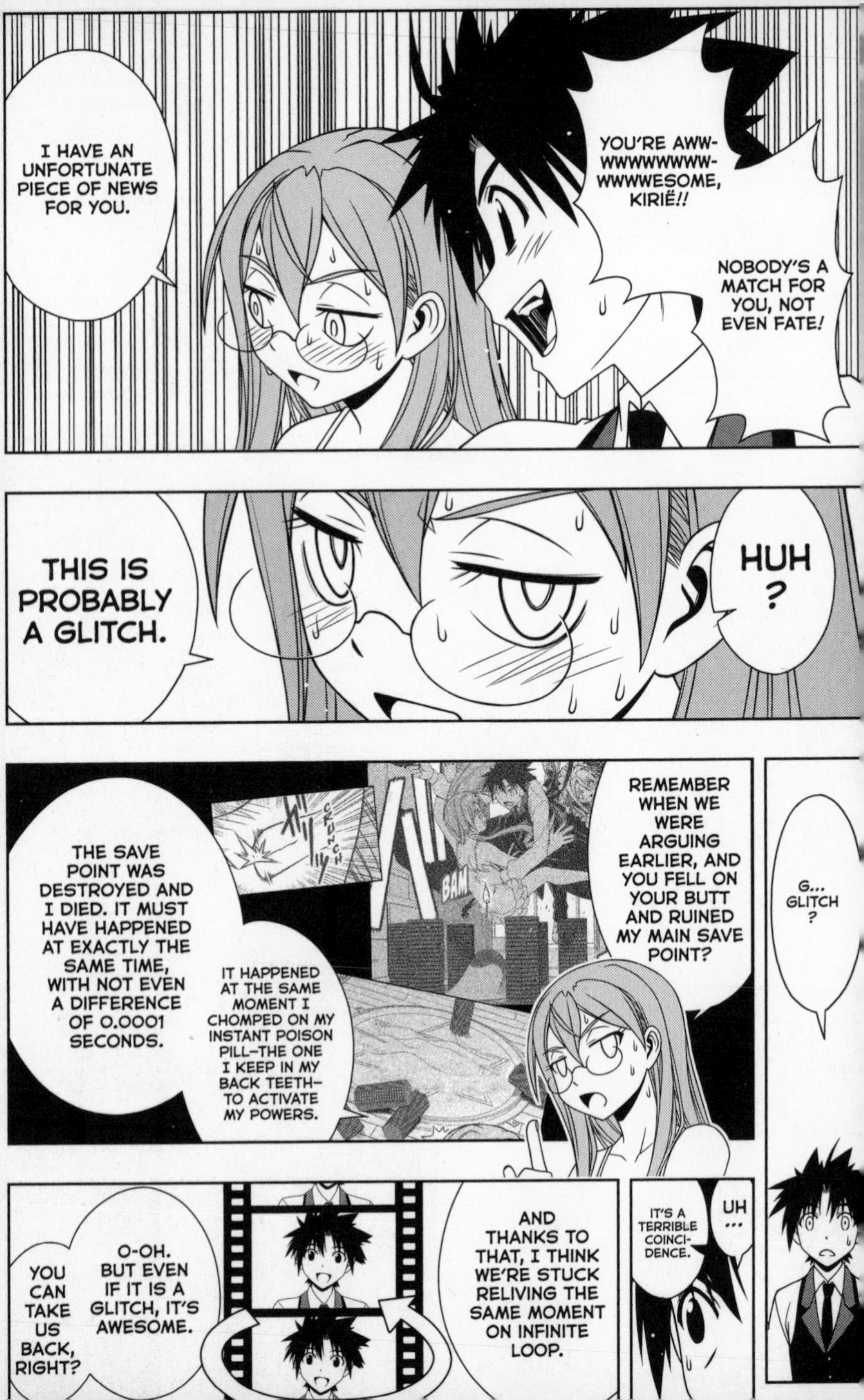
YOU'RE AWW-WWWWWWWWW-WWWWESOME, KIRIË!!
NOBODY'S A MATCH FOR YOU, NOT EVEN FATE!
I HAVE AN UNFORTUNATE PIECE OF NEWS FOR YOU.
HUH ?
THIS IS PROBABLY A GLITCH.
G... GLITCH ?
REMEMBER WHEN WE WERE ARGUING EARLIER, AND YOU FELL ON YOUR BUTT AND RUINED MY MAIN SAVE POINT?
BAM
CRUNCH
IT HAPPENED AT THE SAME MOMENT I CHOMPED ON MY INSTANT POISON PILL–THE ONE I KEEP IN MY BACK TEETH–TO ACTIVATE MY POWERS.
THE SAVE POINT WAS DESTROYED AND I DIED. IT MUST HAVE HAPPENED AT EXACTLY THE SAME TIME, WITH NOT EVEN A DIFFERENCE OF 0.0001 SECONDS.
UH ...
IT'S A TERRIBLE COINCI-DENCE.
AND THANKS TO THAT, I THINK WE'RE STUCK RELIVING THE SAME MOMENT ON INFINITE LOOP.
O-OH. BUT EVEN IF IT IS A GLITCH, IT'S AWESOME.
YOU CAN TAKE US BACK, RIGHT?

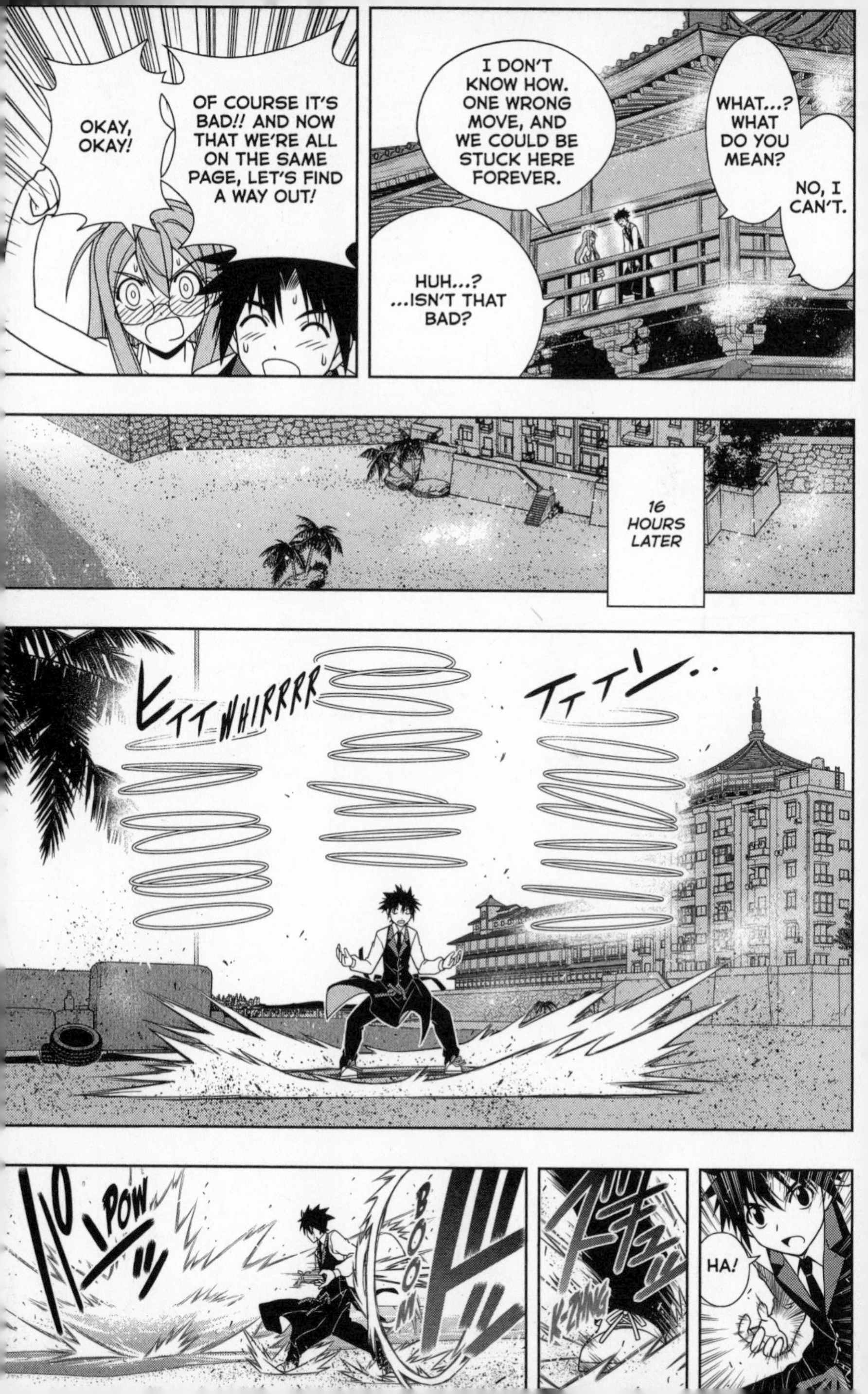

NO, I CAN'T.
WHAT...? WHAT DO YOU MEAN?
I DON'T KNOW HOW. ONE WRONG MOVE, AND WE COULD BE STUCK HERE FOREVER.
HUH...? ...ISN'T THAT BAD?
OF COURSE IT'S BAD!! AND NOW THAT WE'RE ALL ON THE SAME PAGE, LET'S FIND A WAY OUT!
OKAY, OKAY!
16 HOURS LATER
WHIRRRR
HA!
K-ZHING
BOOM
POW

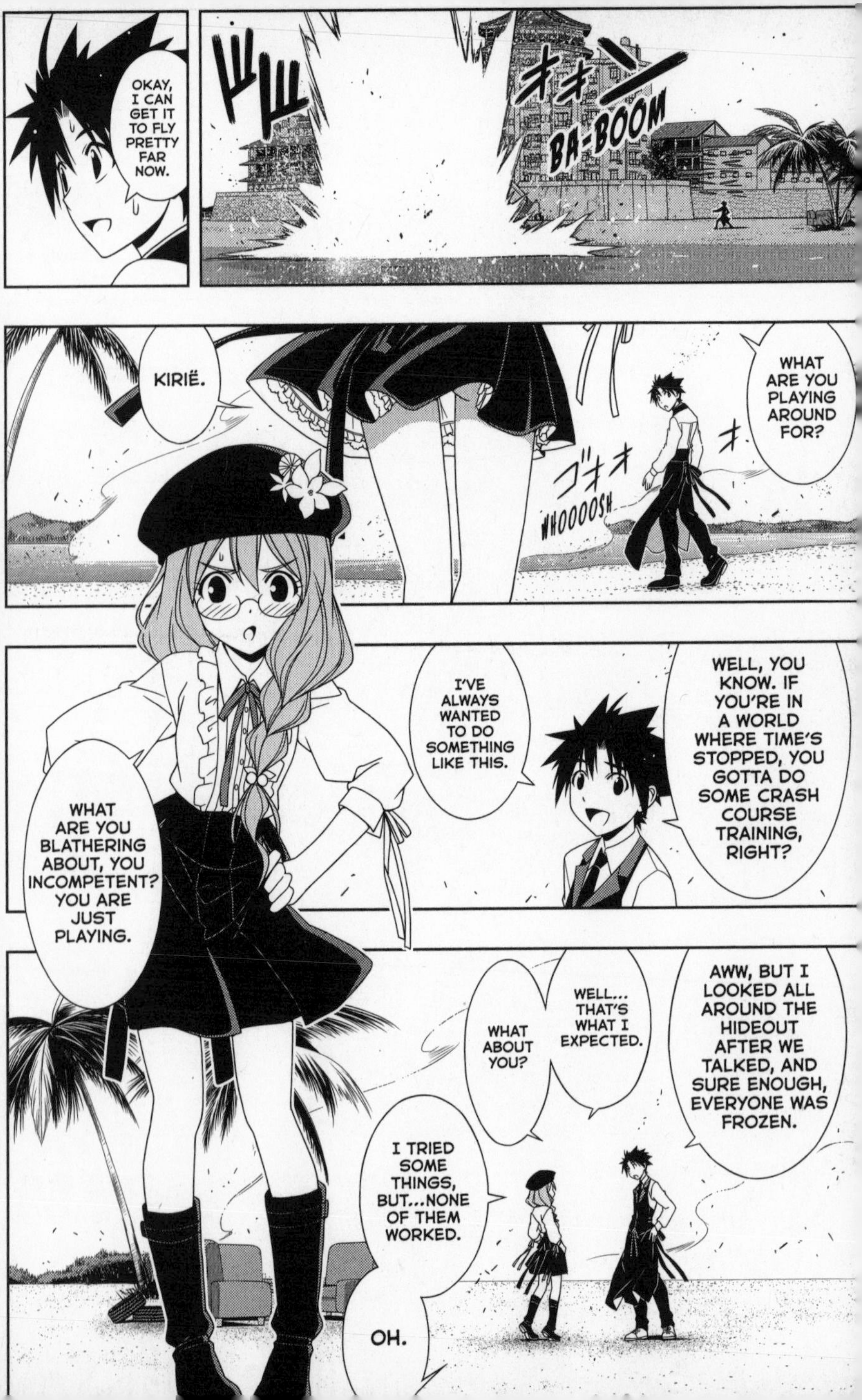
BA-BOOM
OKAY, I CAN GET IT TO FLY PRETTY FAR NOW.
WHAT ARE YOU PLAYING AROUND FOR?
WHOOOOSH
KIRIË.
WELL, YOU KNOW. IF YOU'RE IN A WORLD WHERE TIME'S STOPPED, YOU GOTTA DO SOME CRASH COURSE TRAINING, RIGHT?
I'VE ALWAYS WANTED TO DO SOMETHING LIKE THIS.
WHAT ARE YOU BLATHERING ABOUT, YOU INCOMPETENT? YOU ARE JUST PLAYING.
AWW, BUT I LOOKED ALL AROUND THE HIDEOUT AFTER WE TALKED, AND SURE ENOUGH, EVERYONE WAS FROZEN.
WELL... THAT'S WHAT I EXPECTED.
WHAT ABOUT YOU?
I TRIED SOME THINGS, BUT...NONE OF THEM WORKED.
OH.

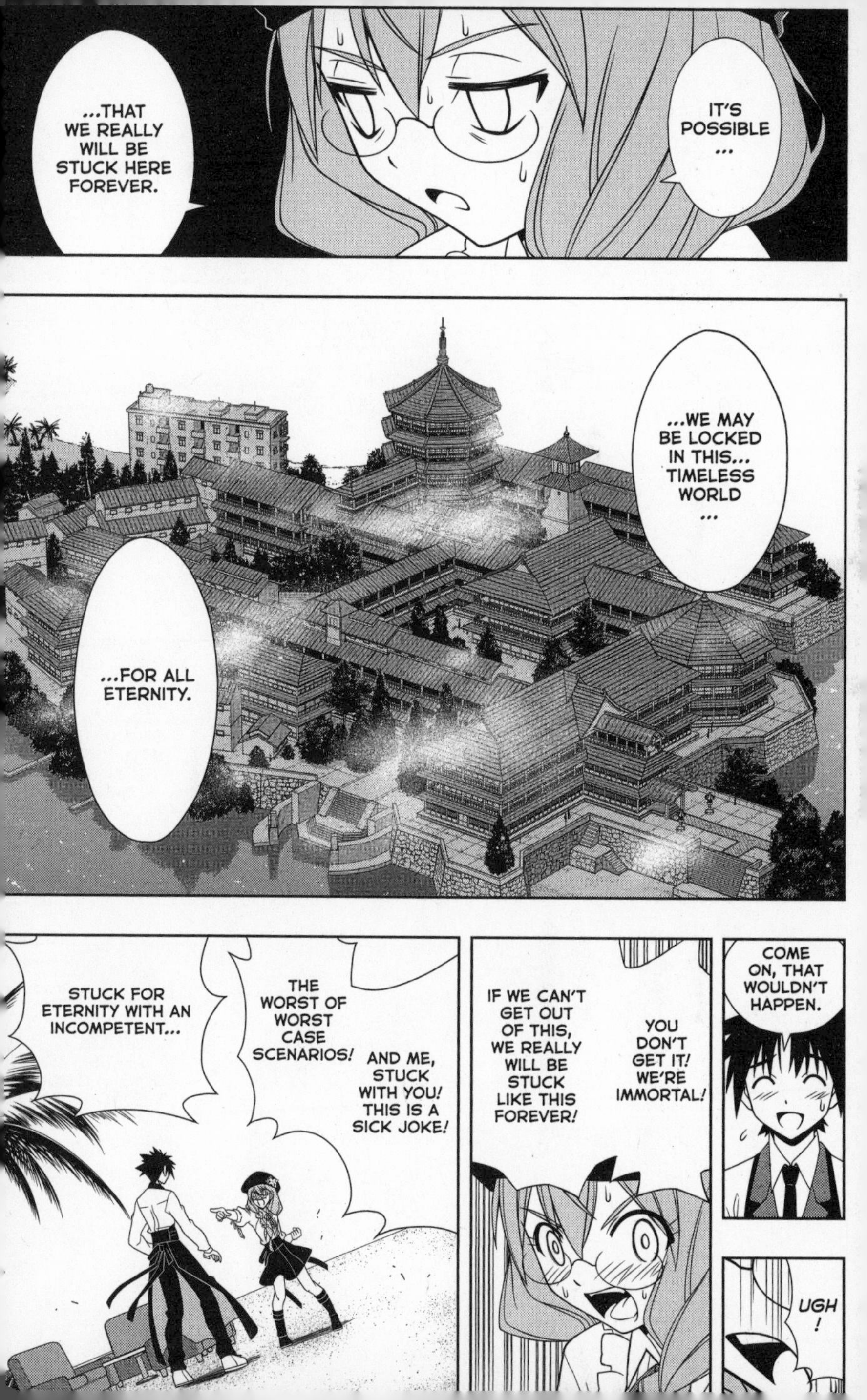
IT'S POSSIBLE ...
...THAT WE REALLY WILL BE STUCK HERE FOREVER.
...WE MAY BE LOCKED IN THIS... TIMELESS WORLD ...
...FOR ALL ETERNITY.
COME ON, THAT WOULDN'T HAPPEN.
UGH!
YOU DON'T GET IT! WE'RE IMMORTAL!
IF WE CAN'T GET OUT OF THIS, WE REALLY WILL BE STUCK LIKE THIS FOREVER!
STUCK FOR ETERNITY WITH AN INCOMPETENT...
THE WORST OF WORST CASE SCENARIOS!
AND ME, STUCK WITH YOU! THIS IS A SICK JOKE!

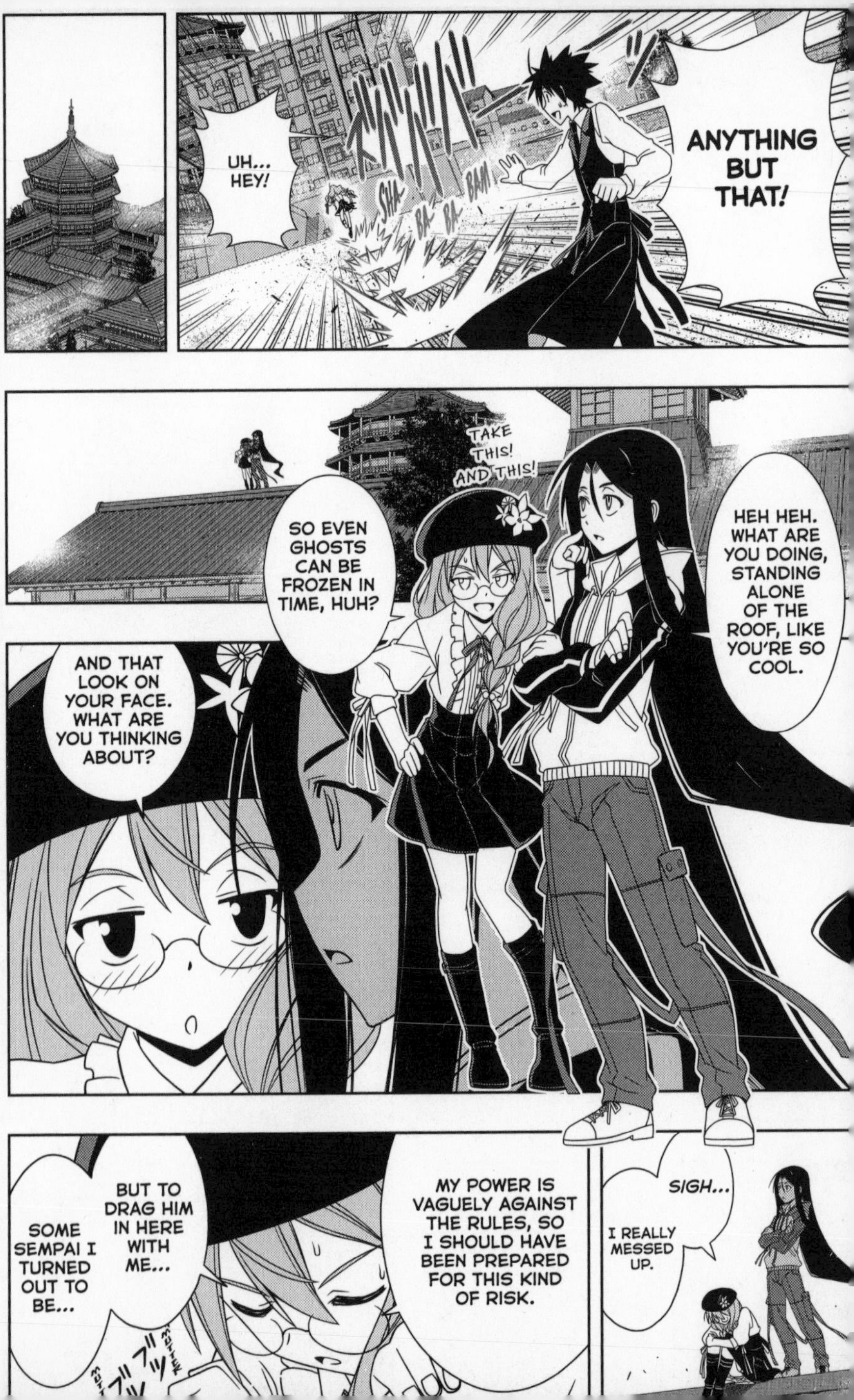
ANYTHING BUT THAT!
SHA BA BA BAM
UH... HEY!
TAKE THIS! AND THIS!
HEH HEH. WHAT ARE YOU DOING, STANDING ALONE OF THE ROOF, LIKE YOU'RE SO COOL.
SO EVEN GHOSTS CAN BE FROZEN IN TIME, HUH?
AND THAT LOOK ON YOUR FACE. WHAT ARE YOU THINKING ABOUT?
SIGH...
I REALLY MESSED UP.
MY POWER IS VAGUELY AGAINST THE RULES, SO I SHOULD HAVE BEEN PREPARED FOR THIS KIND OF RISK.
BUT TO DRAG HIM IN HERE WITH ME...
SOME SEMPAI I TURNED OUT TO BE...
MUTTER

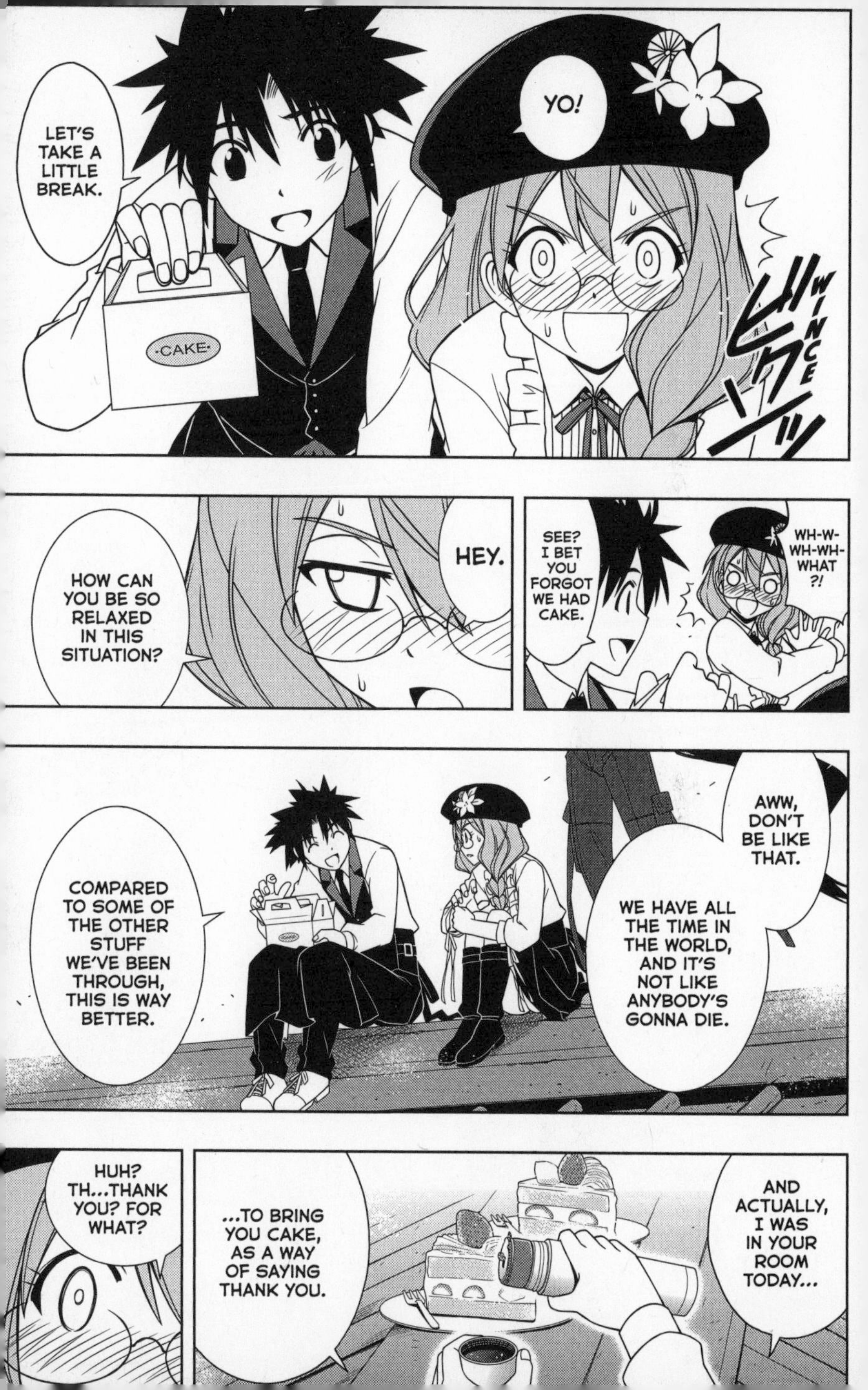
YO!
WINCE
LET'S TAKE A LITTLE BREAK.
CAKE
WH-W-WH-WH-WHAT?!
SEE? I BET YOU FORGOT WE HAD CAKE.
HEY.
HOW CAN YOU BE SO RELAXED IN THIS SITUATION?
AWW, DON'T BE LIKE THAT.
WE HAVE ALL THE TIME IN THE WORLD, AND IT'S NOT LIKE ANYBODY'S GONNA DIE.
COMPARED TO SOME OF THE OTHER STUFF WE'VE BEEN THROUGH, THIS IS WAY BETTER.
AND ACTUALLY, I WAS IN YOUR ROOM TODAY...
...TO BRING YOU CAKE, AS A WAY OF SAYING THANK YOU.
HUH? TH...THANK YOU? FOR WHAT?

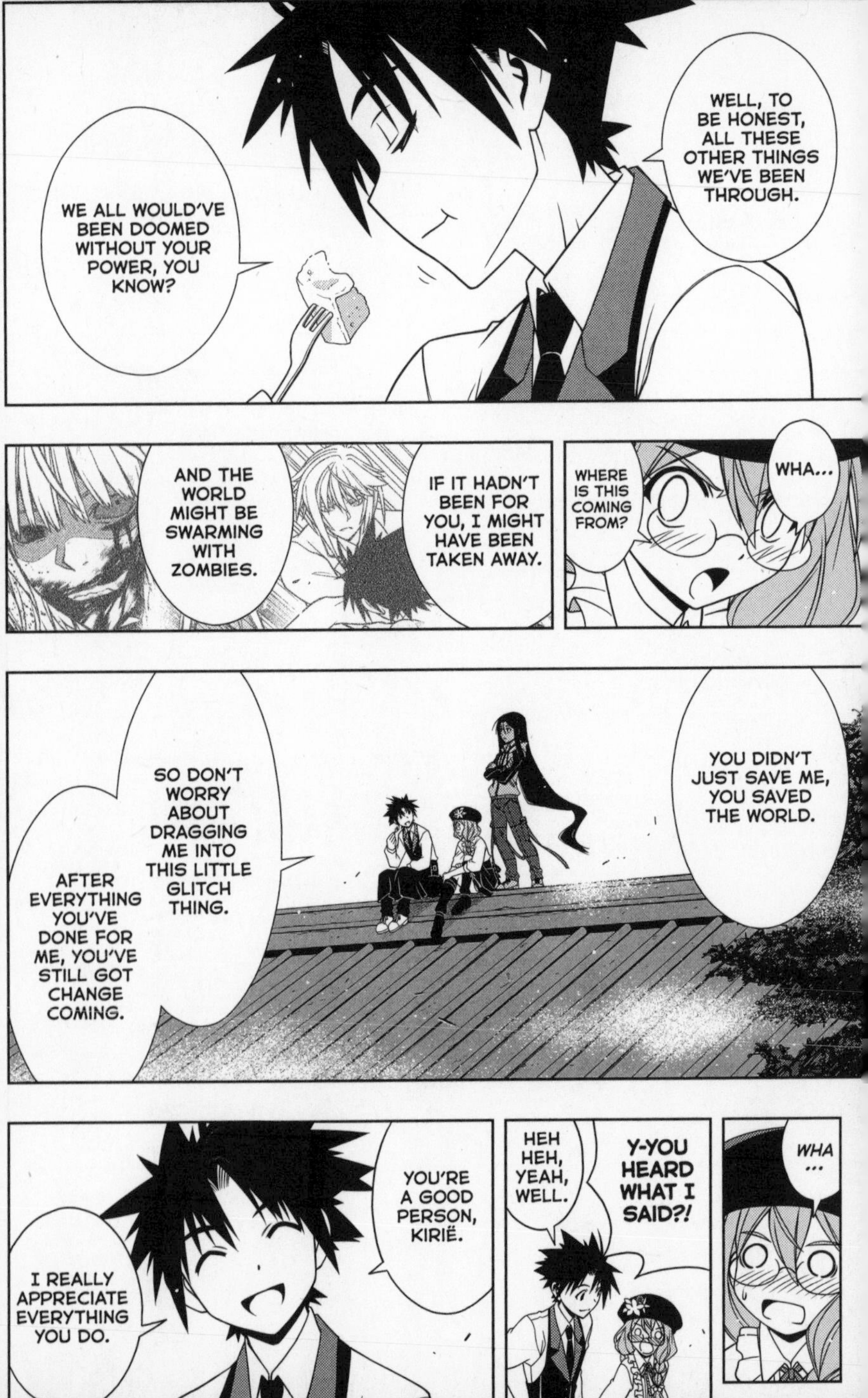
WELL, TO BE HONEST, ALL THESE OTHER THINGS WE'VE BEEN THROUGH.
WE ALL WOULD'VE BEEN DOOMED WITHOUT YOUR POWER, YOU KNOW?
WHA...
WHERE IS THIS COMING FROM?
IF IT HADN'T BEEN FOR YOU, I MIGHT HAVE BEEN TAKEN AWAY.
AND THE WORLD MIGHT BE SWARMING WITH ZOMBIES.
YOU DIDN'T JUST SAVE ME, YOU SAVED THE WORLD.
SO DON'T WORRY ABOUT DRAGGING ME INTO THIS LITTLE GLITCH THING.
AFTER EVERYTHING YOU'VE DONE FOR ME, YOU'VE STILL GOT CHANGE COMING.
WHA...
Y-YOU HEARD WHAT I SAID?!
HEH HEH, YEAH, WELL.
YOU'RE A GOOD PERSON, KIRIË.
I REALLY APPRECIATE EVERYTHING YOU DO.

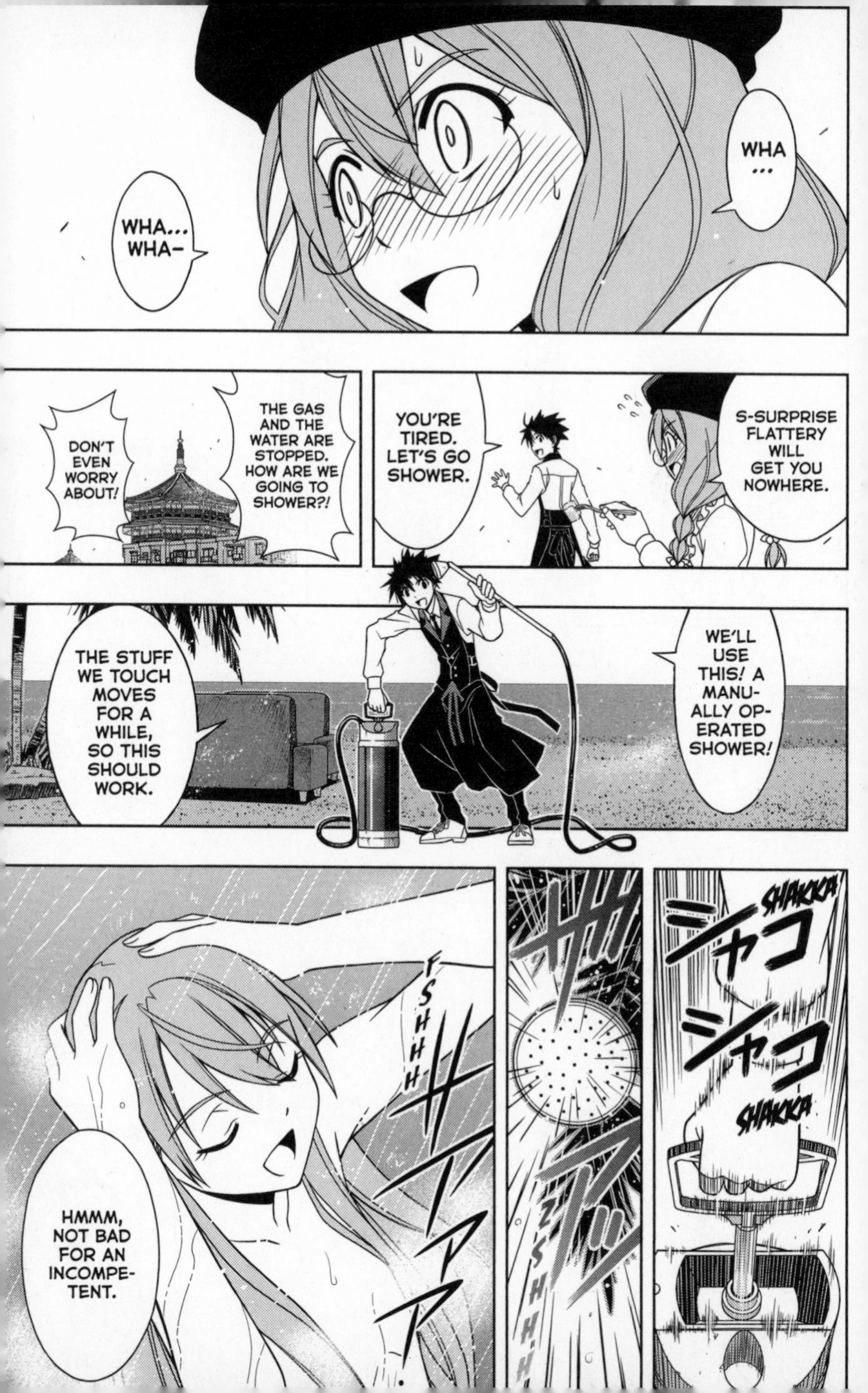
WHA...
WHA... WHA–
S-SURPRISE FLATTERY WILL GET YOU NOWHERE.
YOU'RE TIRED. LET'S GO SHOWER.
THE GAS AND THE WATER ARE STOPPED. HOW ARE WE GOING TO SHOWER?!
DON'T EVEN WORRY ABOUT!
WE'LL USE THIS! A MANU-ALLY OP-ERATED SHOWER!
THE STUFF WE TOUCH MOVES FOR A WHILE, SO THIS SHOULD WORK.
シャコ
SHAKKA
シャコ
SHAKKA
ZSHHHH
FSHHHH
HMMM, NOT BAD FOR AN INCOMPE-TENT.

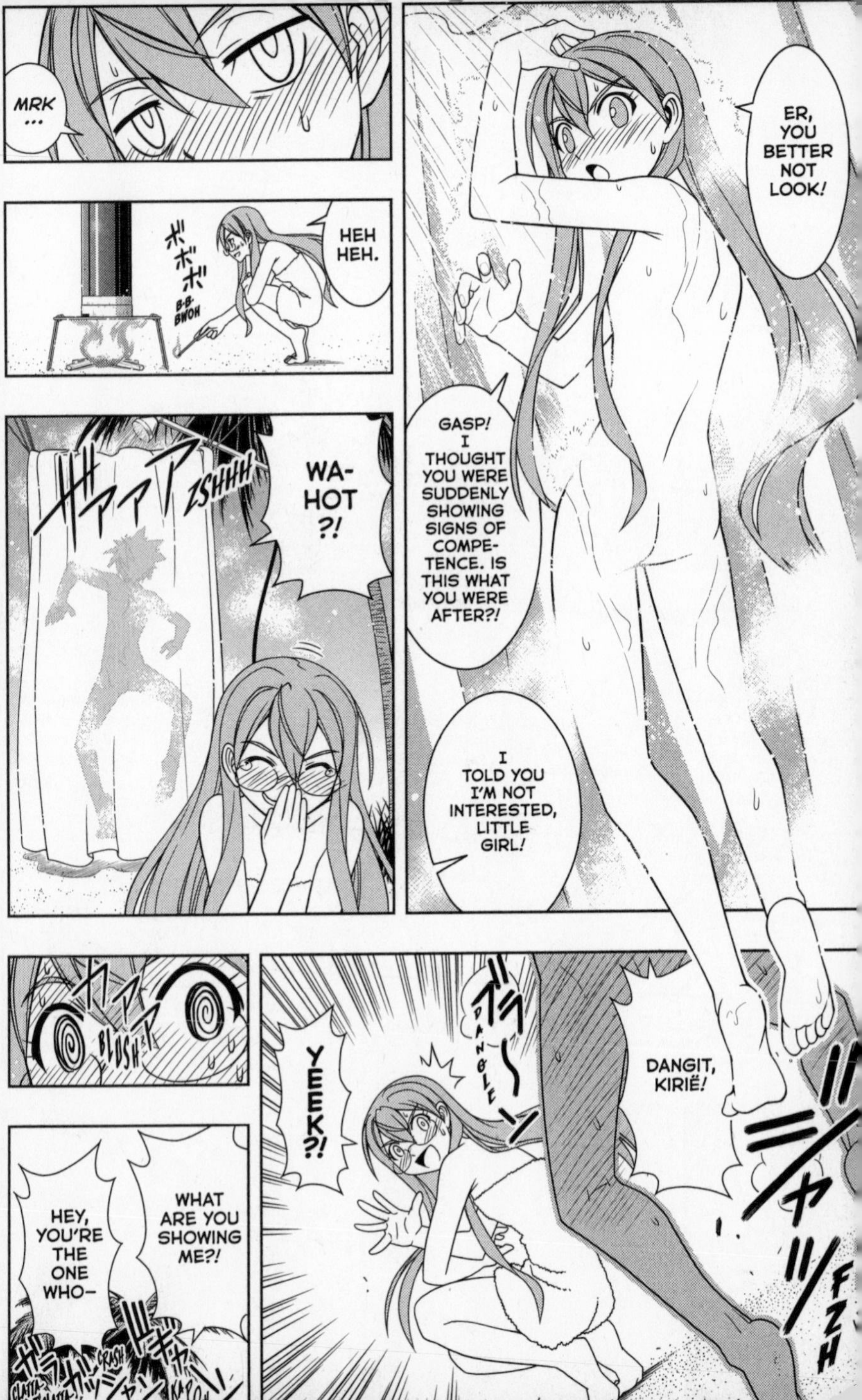
ER, YOU BETTER NOT LOOK!
GASP! I THOUGHT YOU WERE SUDDENLY SHOWING SIGNS OF COMPETENCE. IS THIS WHAT YOU WERE AFTER?!
I TOLD YOU I'M NOT INTERESTED, LITTLE GIRL!
MRK ...
ボボボ
B-B-BWOH
HEH HEH.
WA-HOT?!
ザァァァ
ZSHHH
DANGIT, KIRIË!
FZH
YEEK?!
DANGLE
BLUSH
WHAT ARE YOU SHOWING ME?!
HEY, YOU'RE THE ONE WHO–
CRASH

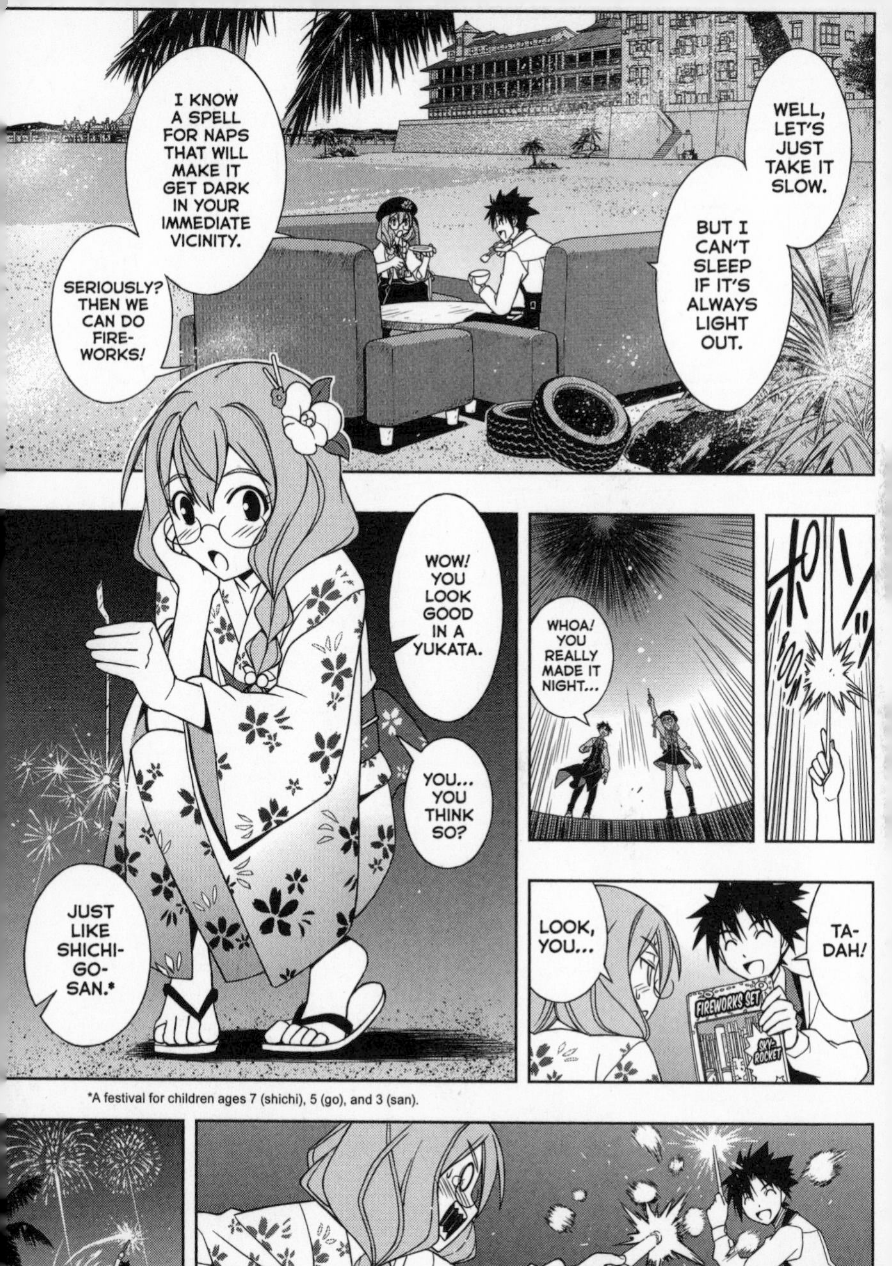
WELL, LET'S JUST TAKE IT SLOW.
BUT I CAN'T SLEEP IF IT'S ALWAYS LIGHT OUT.
I KNOW A SPELL FOR NAPS THAT WILL MAKE IT GET DARK IN YOUR IMMEDIATE VICINITY.
SERIOUSLY? THEN WE CAN DO FIRE-WORKS!
WHOA! YOU REALLY MADE IT NIGHT...
TA-DAH!
FIREWORKS SET
SKY-ROCKET
LOOK, YOU...
WOW! YOU LOOK GOOD IN A YUKATA.
YOU... YOU THINK SO?
JUST LIKE SHICHI-GO-SAN.*

*A festival for children ages 7 (shichi), 5 (go), and 3 (san).

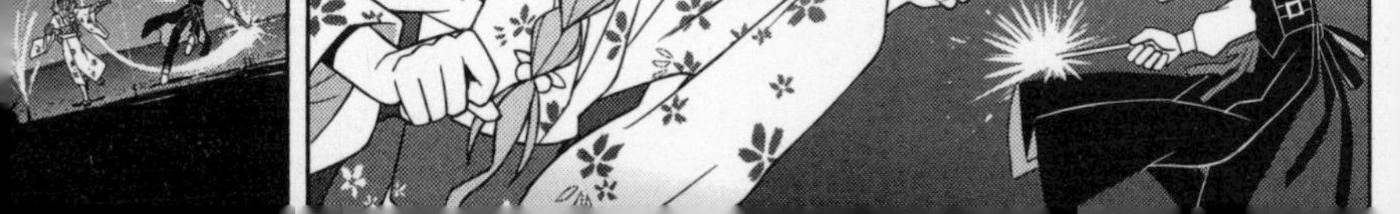

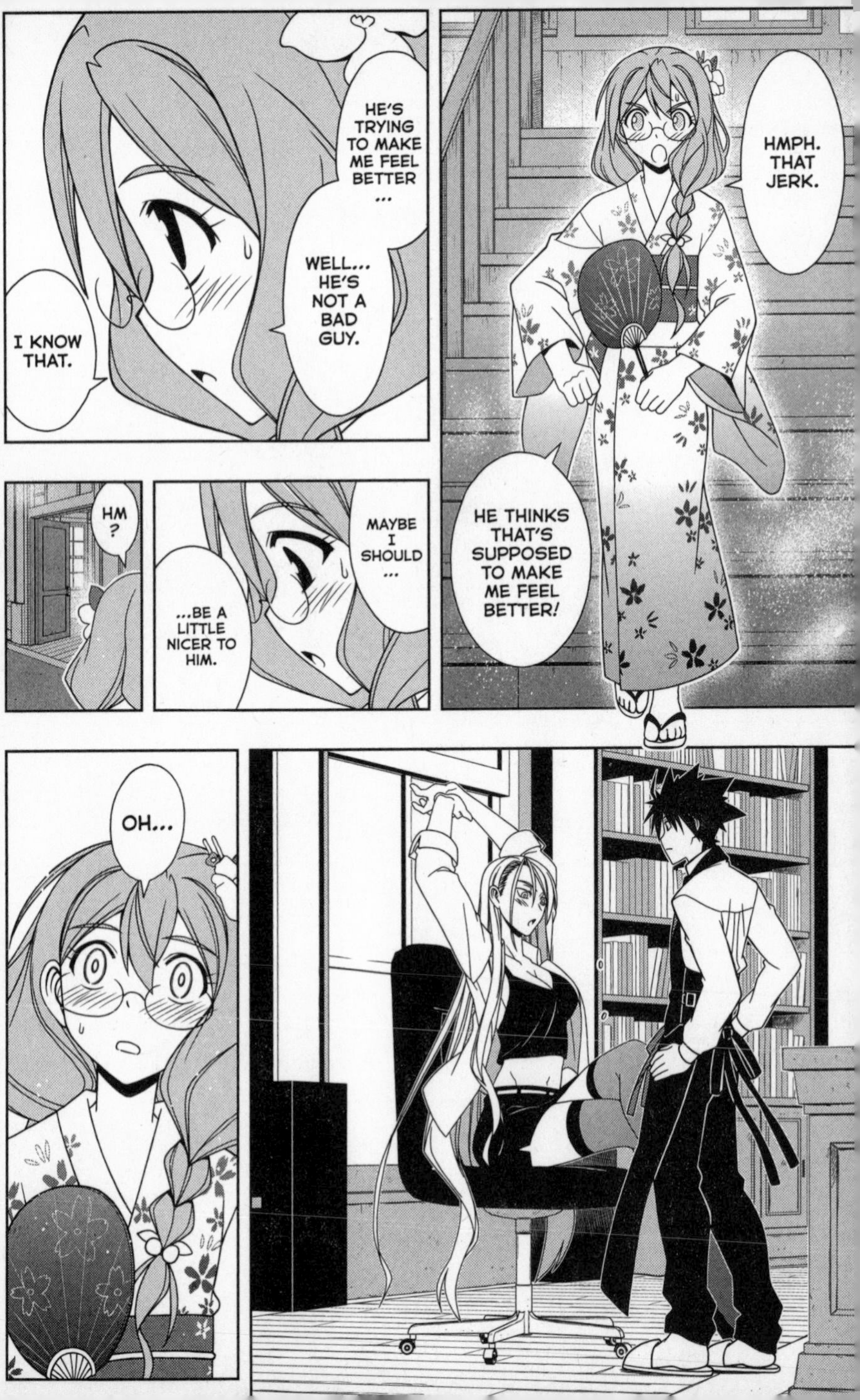
HMPH. THAT JERK.
HE THINKS THAT'S SUPPOSED TO MAKE ME FEEL BETTER!
HE'S TRYING TO MAKE ME FEEL BETTER...
WELL... HE'S NOT A BAD GUY.
I KNOW THAT.
MAYBE I SHOULD...
...BE A LITTLE NICER TO HIM.
HM?
OH...

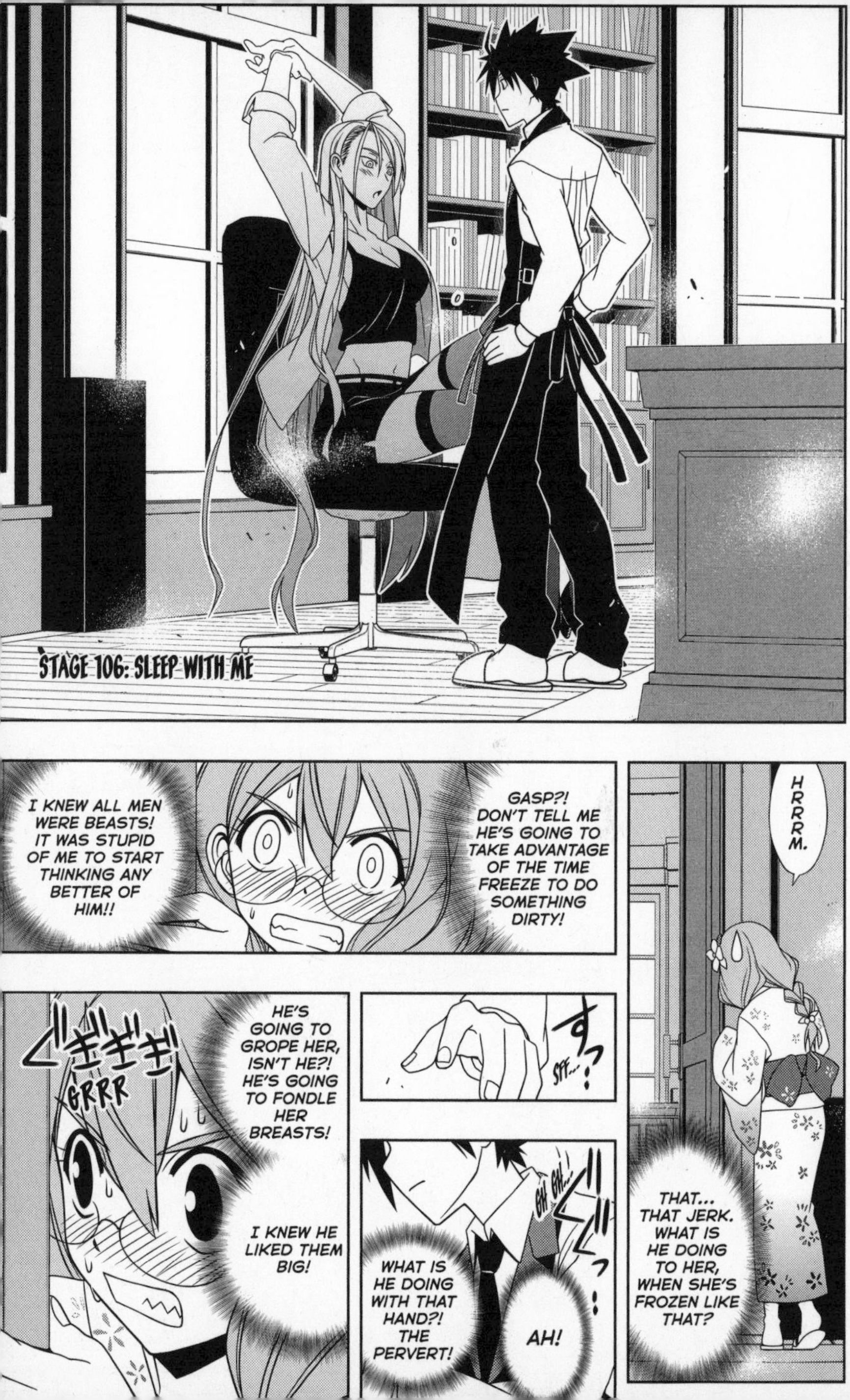
STAGE 106: SLEEP WITH ME
HRRRM.
THAT... THAT JERK. WHAT IS HE DOING TO HER, WHEN SHE'S FROZEN LIKE THAT?
GASP?! DON'T TELL ME HE'S GOING TO TAKE ADVANTAGE OF THE TIME FREEZE TO DO SOMETHING DIRTY!
I KNEW ALL MEN WERE BEASTS! IT WAS STUPID OF ME TO START THINKING ANY BETTER OF HIM!!
すっ
SFF...
ぐぐっ
GH GH...
AH!
WHAT IS HE DOING WITH THAT HAND?! THE PERVERT!
ぐぎぎぎ
GRRR
HE'S GOING TO GROPE HER, ISN'T HE?! HE'S GOING TO FONDLE HER BREASTS!
I KNEW HE LIKED THEM BIG!

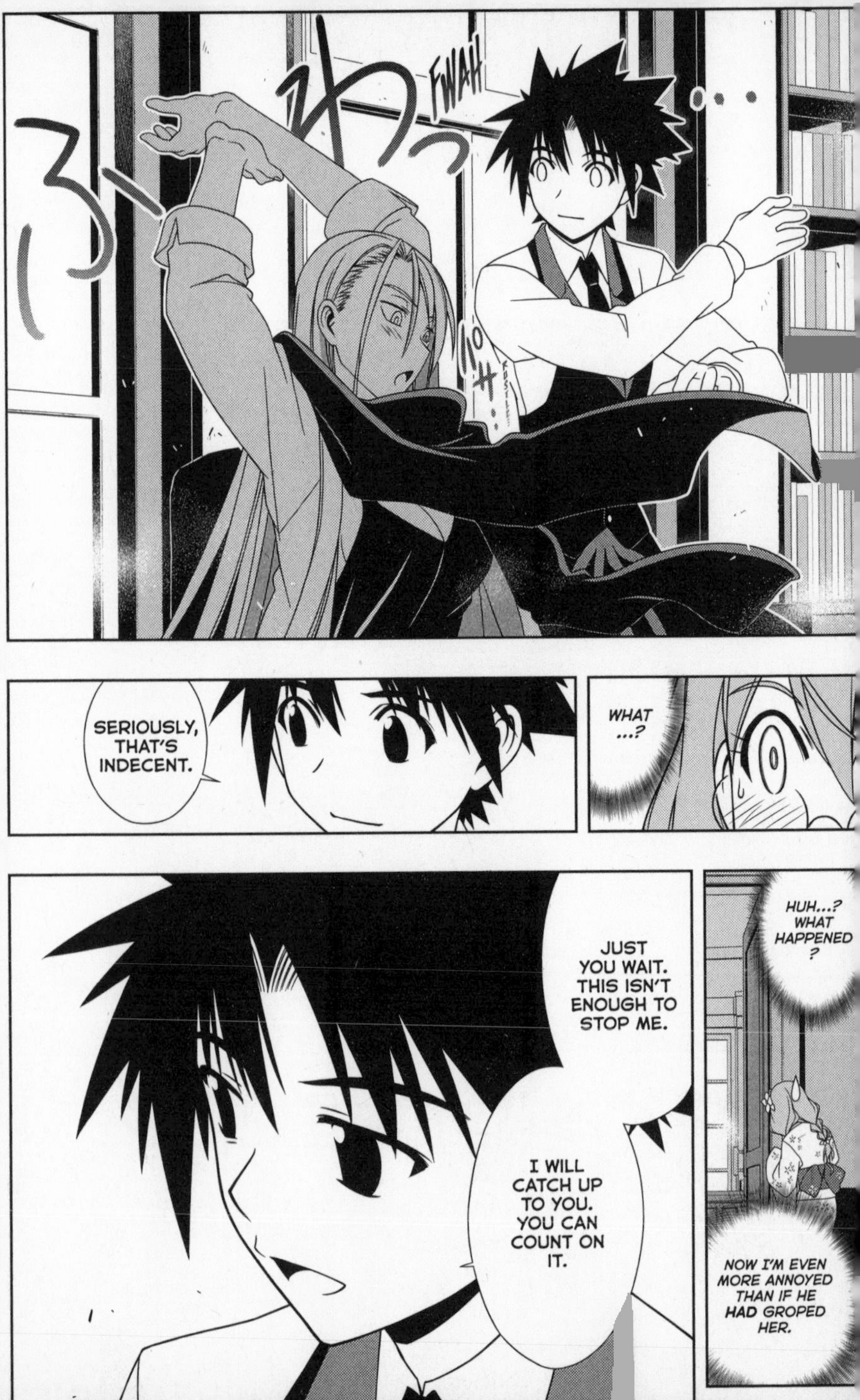

FWAH
...
WHAT ...?
SERIOUSLY, THAT'S INDECENT.
HUH...? WHAT HAPPENED?
NOW I'M EVEN MORE ANNOYED THAN IF HE **HAD** GROPED HER.
JUST YOU WAIT. THIS ISN'T ENOUGH TO STOP ME.
I WILL CATCH UP TO YOU. YOU CAN COUNT ON IT.

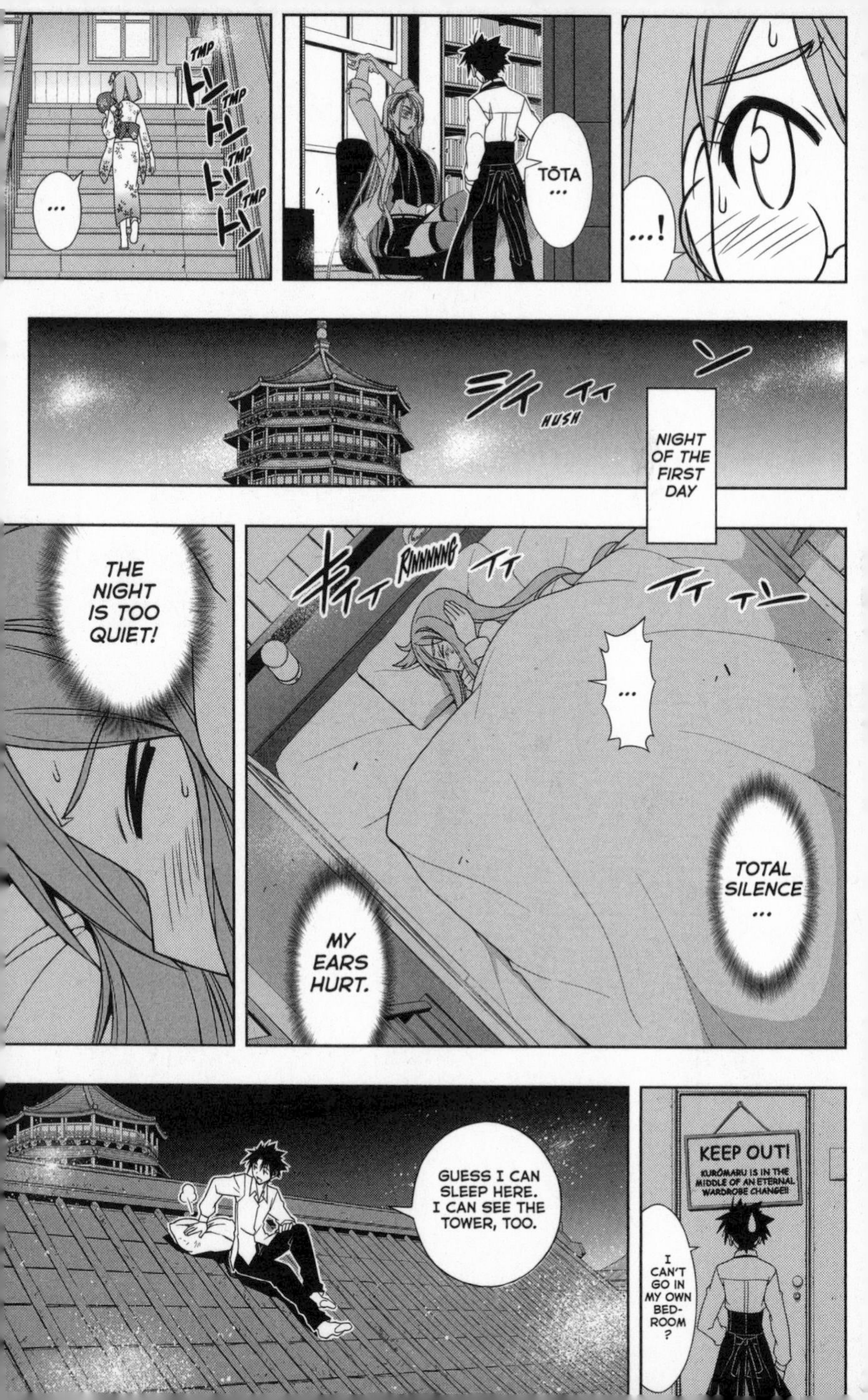
...!
TŌTA ...
TMP TMP TMP TMP
...
HUSH
NIGHT OF THE FIRST DAY
RINNNNNG
...
TOTAL SILENCE ...
MY EARS HURT.
THE NIGHT IS TOO QUIET!
KEEP OUT!
KURŌMARU IS IN THE MIDDLE OF AN ETERNAL WARDROBE CHANGE!!
I CAN'T GO IN MY OWN BED-ROOM?
GUESS I CAN SLEEP HERE. I CAN SEE THE TOWER, TOO.

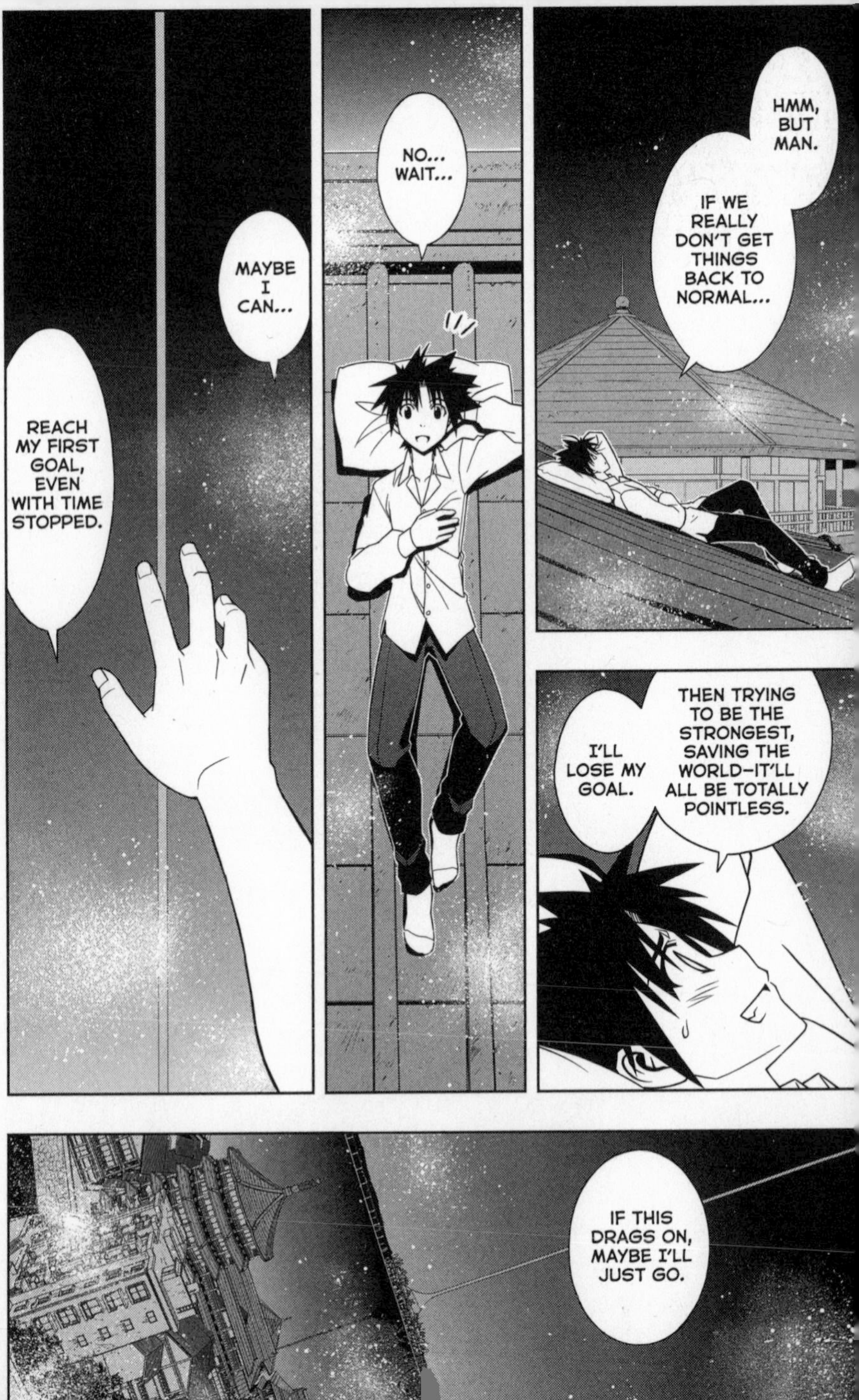
HMM, BUT MAN.
IF WE REALLY DON'T GET THINGS BACK TO NORMAL...
THEN TRYING TO BE THE STRONGEST, SAVING THE WORLD—IT'LL ALL BE TOTALLY POINTLESS.
I'LL LOSE MY GOAL.
NO... WAIT...
MAYBE I CAN...
REACH MY FIRST GOAL, EVEN WITH TIME STOPPED.
IF THIS DRAGS ON, MAYBE I'LL JUST GO.

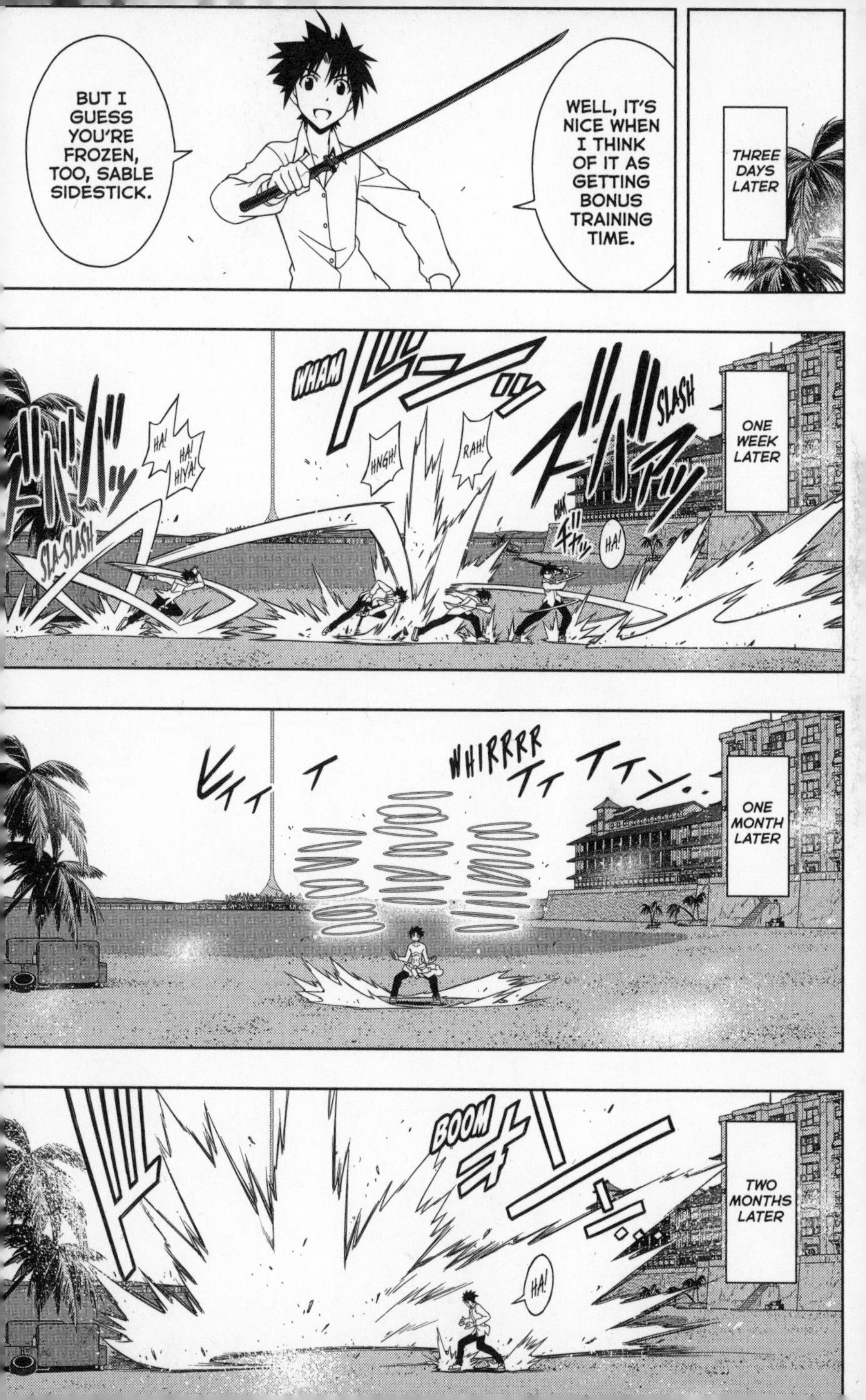
THREE DAYS LATER
WELL, IT'S NICE WHEN I THINK OF IT AS GETTING BONUS TRAINING TIME.
BUT I GUESS YOU'RE FROZEN, TOO, SABLE SIDESTICK.
ONE WEEK LATER
SLASH
WHAM
RAH!
HNGH!
HA! HA! HIYA!
HA!
SLA-SLASH
ONE MONTH LATER
WHIRRRR
TWO MONTHS LATER
BOOM
HA!

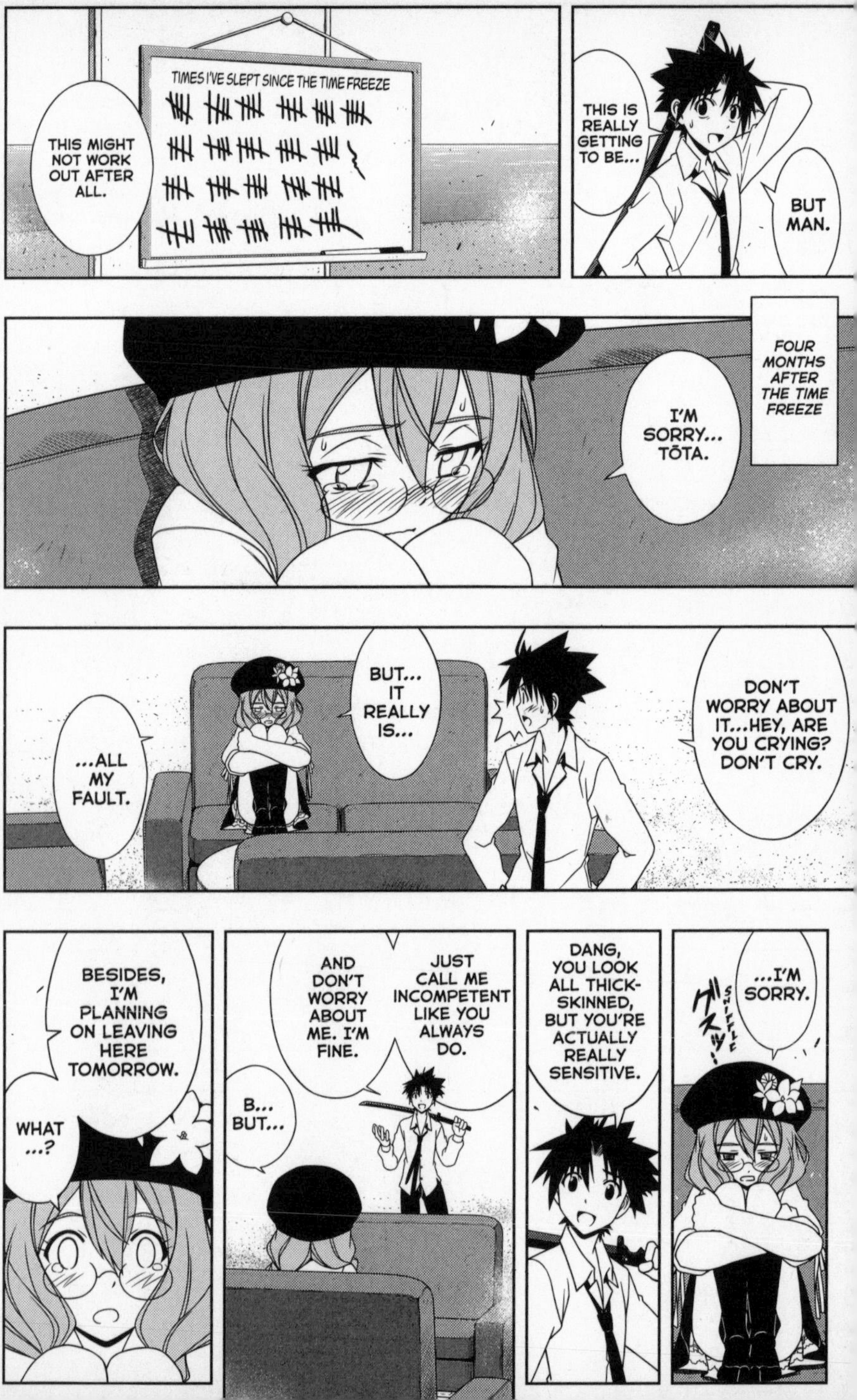
BUT MAN.
THIS IS REALLY GETTING TO BE...
TIMES I'VE SLEPT SINCE THE TIME FREEZE
THIS MIGHT NOT WORK OUT AFTER ALL.
FOUR MONTHS AFTER THE TIME FREEZE
I'M SORRY... TŌTA.
DON'T WORRY ABOUT IT...HEY, ARE YOU CRYING? DON'T CRY.
BUT... IT REALLY IS...
...ALL MY FAULT.
...I'M SORRY.
SNIFFLE
DANG, YOU LOOK ALL THICK-SKINNED, BUT YOU'RE ACTUALLY REALLY SENSITIVE.
JUST CALL ME INCOMPETENT LIKE YOU ALWAYS DO.
AND DON'T WORRY ABOUT ME. I'M FINE.
B... BUT...
BESIDES, I'M PLANNING ON LEAVING HERE TOMORROW.
WHAT ...?

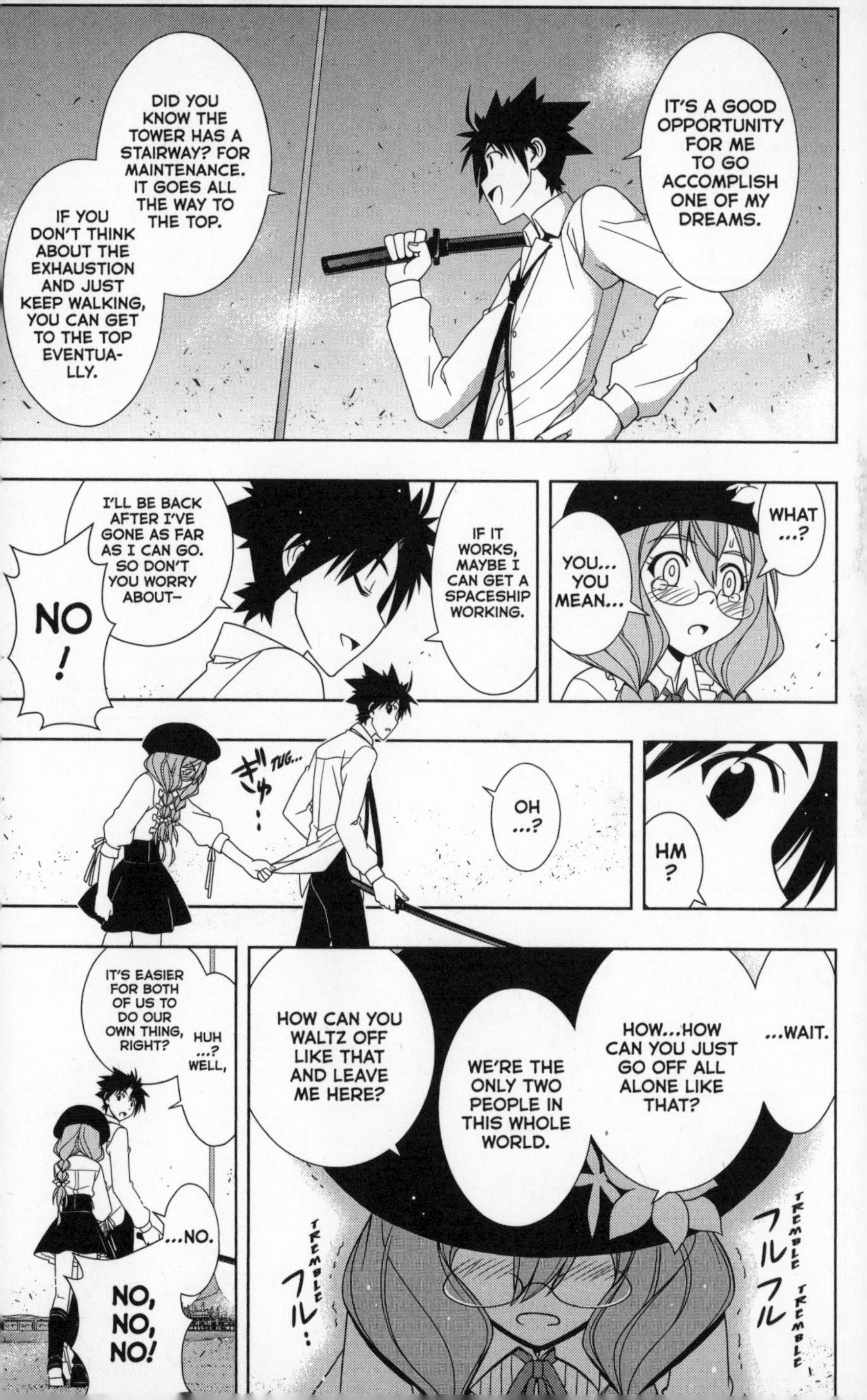
IT'S A GOOD OPPORTUNITY FOR ME TO GO ACCOMPLISH ONE OF MY DREAMS.
DID YOU KNOW THE TOWER HAS A STAIRWAY? FOR MAINTENANCE. IT GOES ALL THE WAY TO THE TOP.
IF YOU DON'T THINK ABOUT THE EXHAUSTION AND JUST KEEP WALKING, YOU CAN GET TO THE TOP EVENTUA-LLY.
WHAT ...?
YOU... YOU MEAN...
IF IT WORKS, MAYBE I CAN GET A SPACESHIP WORKING.
I'LL BE BACK AFTER I'VE GONE AS FAR AS I CAN GO. SO DON'T YOU WORRY ABOUT–
NO !
HM ?
OH ...?
ぎゅ・・
TUG...
...WAIT.
HOW...HOW CAN YOU JUST GO OFF ALL ALONE LIKE THAT?
WE'RE THE ONLY TWO PEOPLE IN THIS WHOLE WORLD.
HOW CAN YOU WALTZ OFF LIKE THAT AND LEAVE ME HERE?
フルフル
TREMBLE TREMBLE
フル・
TREMBLE
IT'S EASIER FOR BOTH OF US TO DO OUR OWN THING, RIGHT?
HUH ...? WELL,
...NO.
NO, NO, NO!

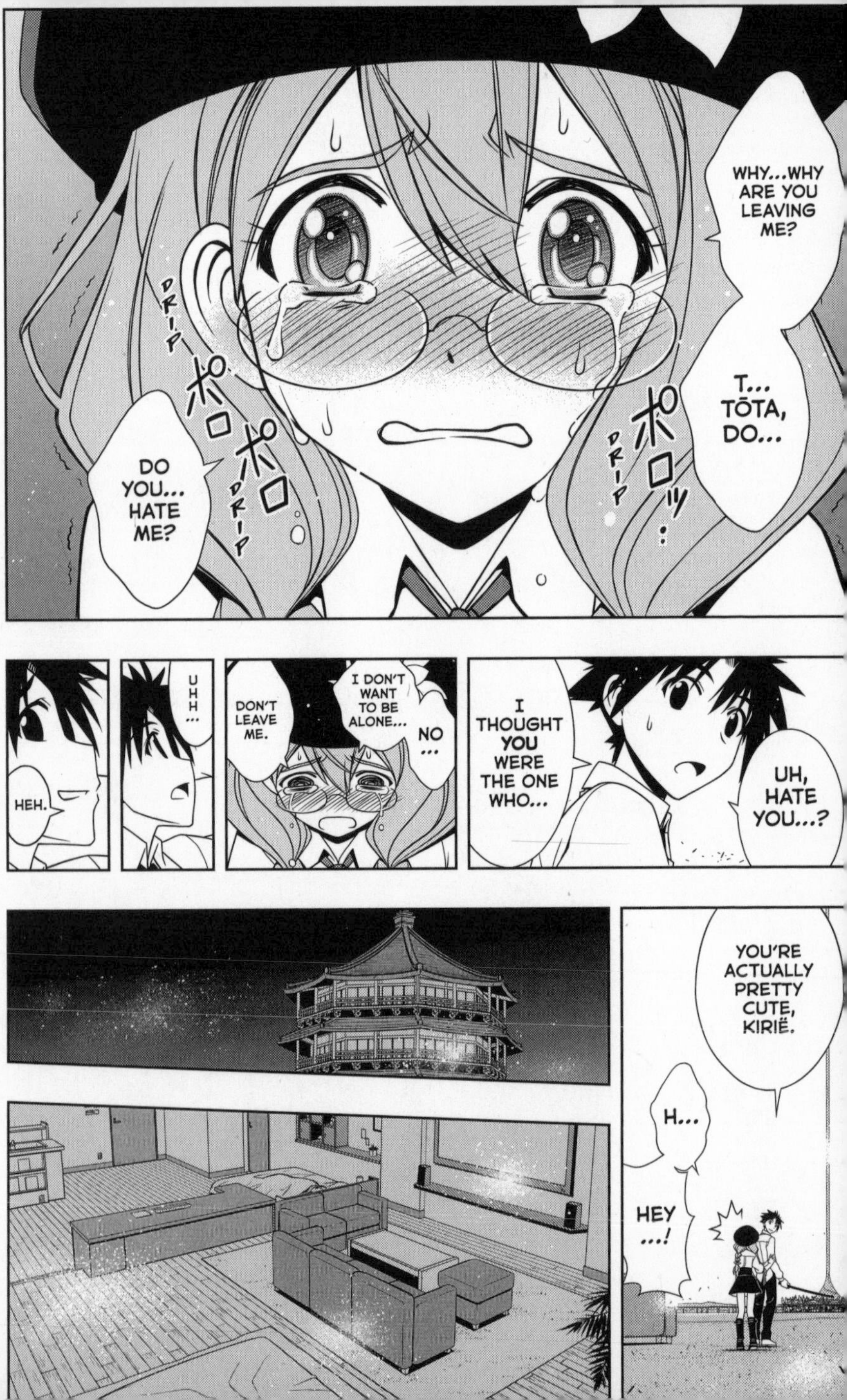
WHY...WHY ARE YOU LEAVING ME?
T... TŌTA, DO...
ポロッ
DRIP
ポロポロ
DRIP
DRIP
DO YOU... HATE ME?
UH, HATE YOU...?
I THOUGHT YOU WERE THE ONE WHO...
NO...
I DON'T WANT TO BE ALONE...
DON'T LEAVE ME.
UHH...
HEH.
YOU'RE ACTUALLY PRETTY CUTE, KIRIË.
H...
HEY...!

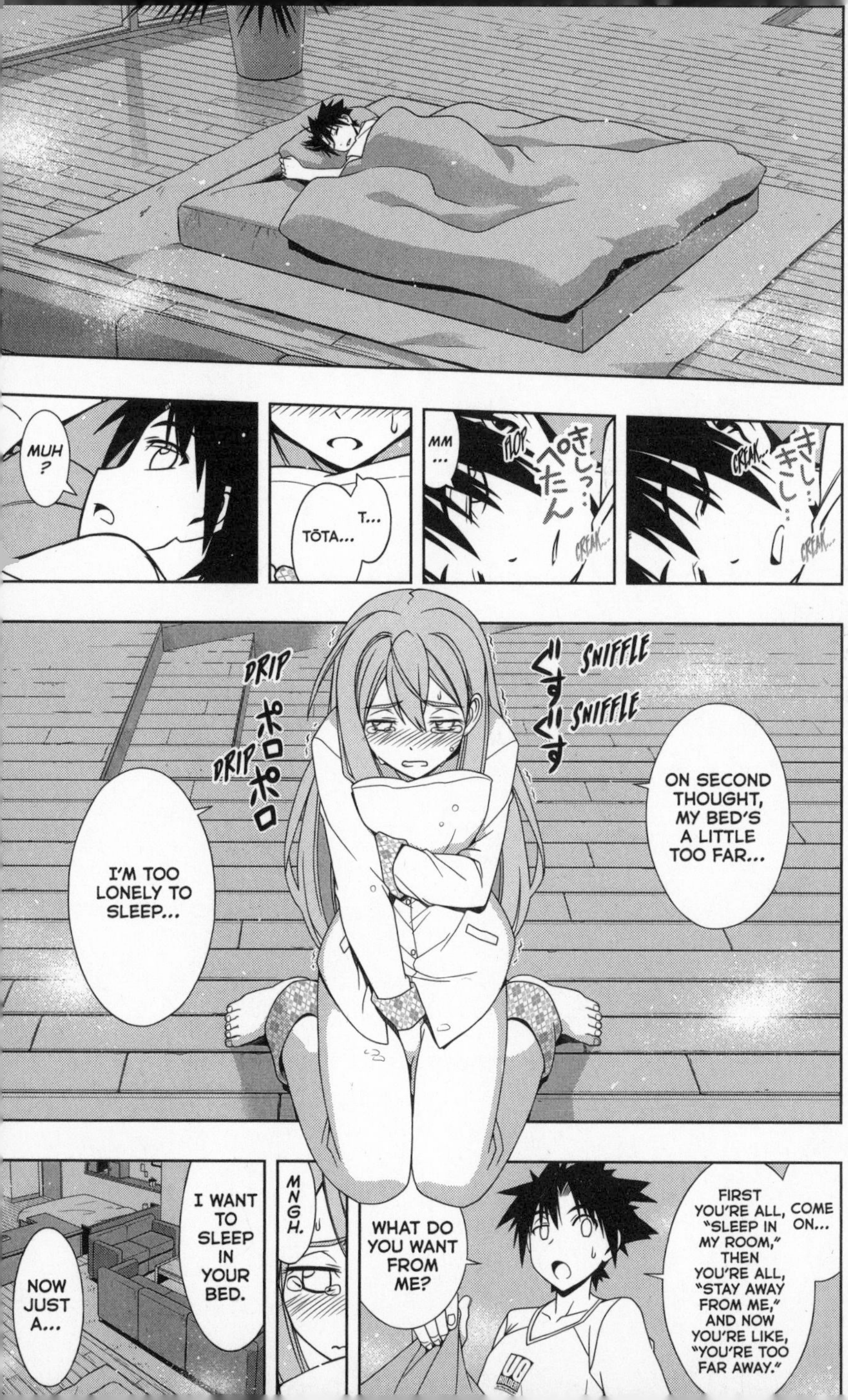

CREAK...
きし…
きし…
CREAK...
MM...
FLOP
きしっ…
ぺたん
CREAK...
T...
TŌTA...
MUH?
ON SECOND THOUGHT, MY BED'S A LITTLE TOO FAR...
SNIFFLE
ぐすぐす
SNIFFLE
DRIP
ポロポロ
DRIP
I'M TOO LONELY TO SLEEP...
COME ON...
FIRST YOU'RE ALL, "SLEEP IN MY ROOM," THEN YOU'RE ALL, "STAY AWAY FROM ME," AND NOW YOU'RE LIKE, "YOU'RE TOO FAR AWAY."
WHAT DO YOU WANT FROM ME?
MNGH.
I WANT TO SLEEP IN YOUR BED.
NOW JUST A...

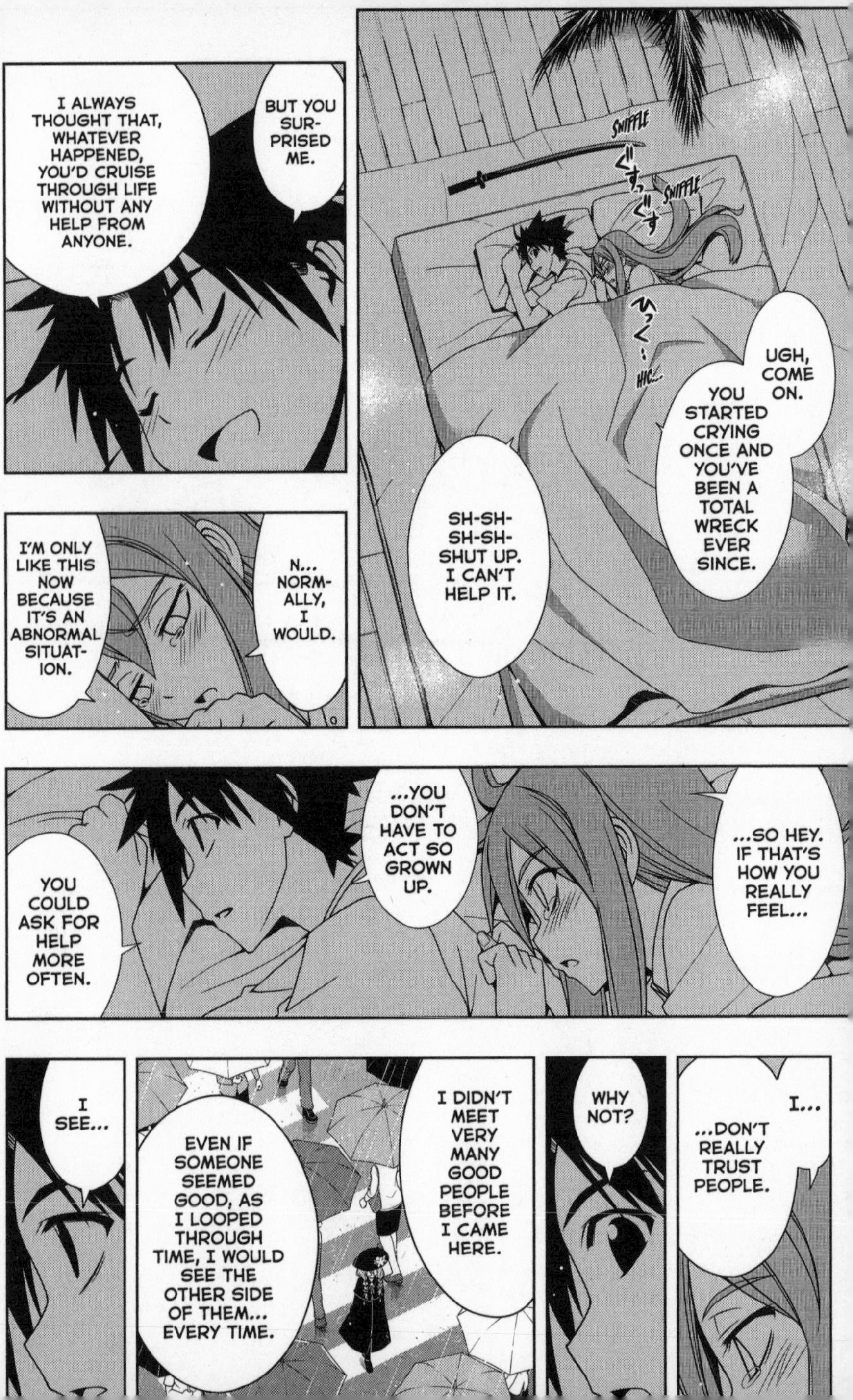
SNIFFLE
SNIFFLE
HIC...
UGH, COME ON. YOU STARTED CRYING ONCE AND YOU'VE BEEN A TOTAL WRECK EVER SINCE.
SH-SH-SH-SH-SHUT UP. I CAN'T HELP IT.
BUT YOU SUR-PRISED ME.
I ALWAYS THOUGHT THAT, WHATEVER HAPPENED, YOU'D CRUISE THROUGH LIFE WITHOUT ANY HELP FROM ANYONE.
N... NORM-ALLY, I WOULD.
I'M ONLY LIKE THIS NOW BECAUSE IT'S AN ABNORMAL SITUAT-ION.
...SO HEY. IF THAT'S HOW YOU REALLY FEEL...
...YOU DON'T HAVE TO ACT SO GROWN UP.
YOU COULD ASK FOR HELP MORE OFTEN.
I...
...DON'T REALLY TRUST PEOPLE.
WHY NOT?
I DIDN'T MEET VERY MANY GOOD PEOPLE BEFORE I CAME HERE.
EVEN IF SOMEONE SEEMED GOOD, AS I LOOPED THROUGH TIME, I WOULD SEE THE OTHER SIDE OF THEM... EVERY TIME.
I SEE...

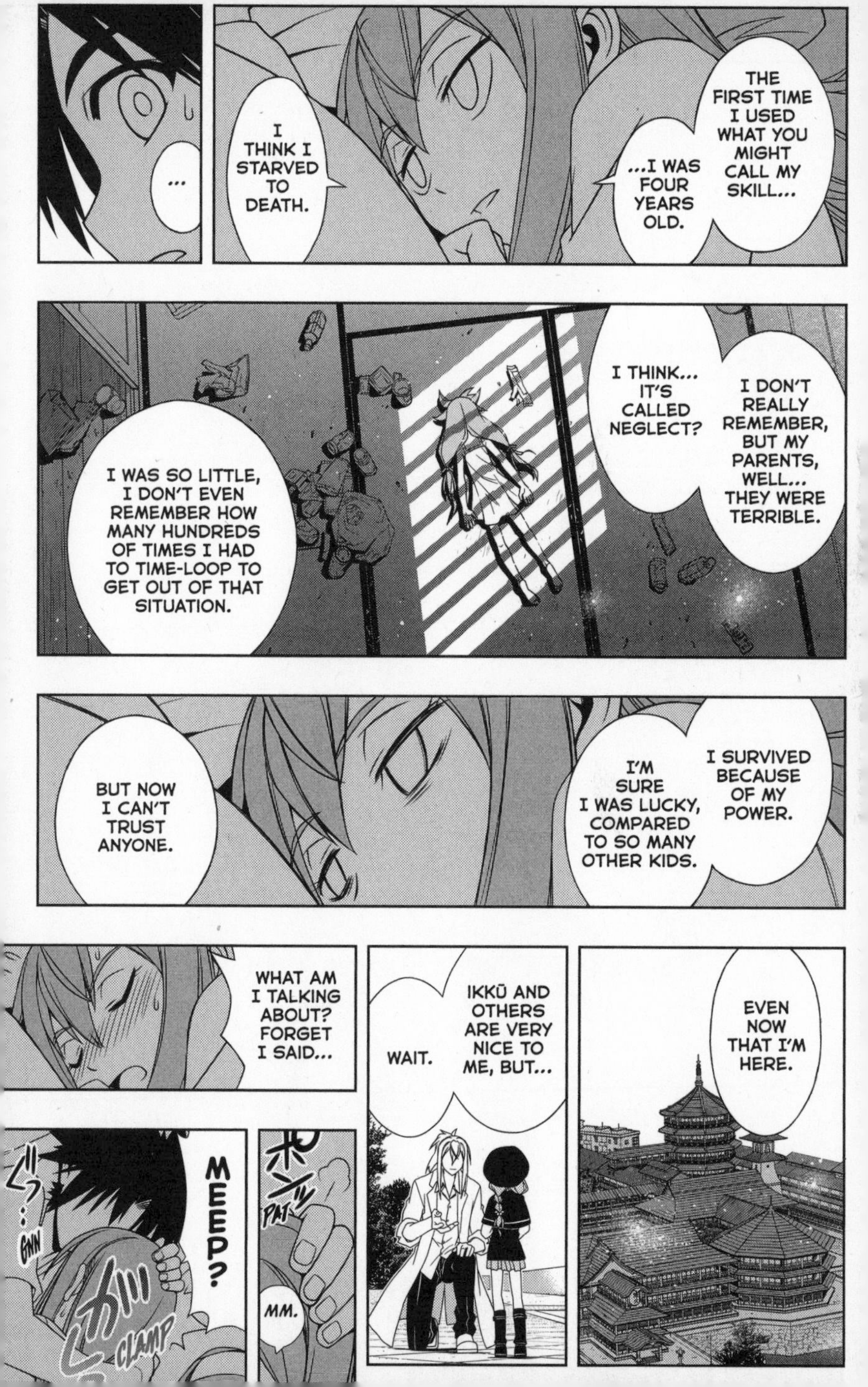
THE FIRST TIME I USED WHAT YOU MIGHT CALL MY SKILL...
...I WAS FOUR YEARS OLD.
I THINK I STARVED TO DEATH.
...
I DON'T REALLY REMEMBER, BUT MY PARENTS, WELL... THEY WERE TERRIBLE.
I THINK... IT'S CALLED NEGLECT?
I WAS SO LITTLE, I DON'T EVEN REMEMBER HOW MANY HUNDREDS OF TIMES I HAD TO TIME-LOOP TO GET OUT OF THAT SITUATION.
I SURVIVED BECAUSE OF MY POWER.
I'M SURE I WAS LUCKY, COMPARED TO SO MANY OTHER KIDS.
BUT NOW I CAN'T TRUST ANYONE.
EVEN NOW THAT I'M HERE.
IKKŪ AND OTHERS ARE VERY NICE TO ME, BUT...
WAIT.
WHAT AM I TALKING ABOUT? FORGET I SAID...
PAT
MM.
MEEP?
GNN
CLAMP

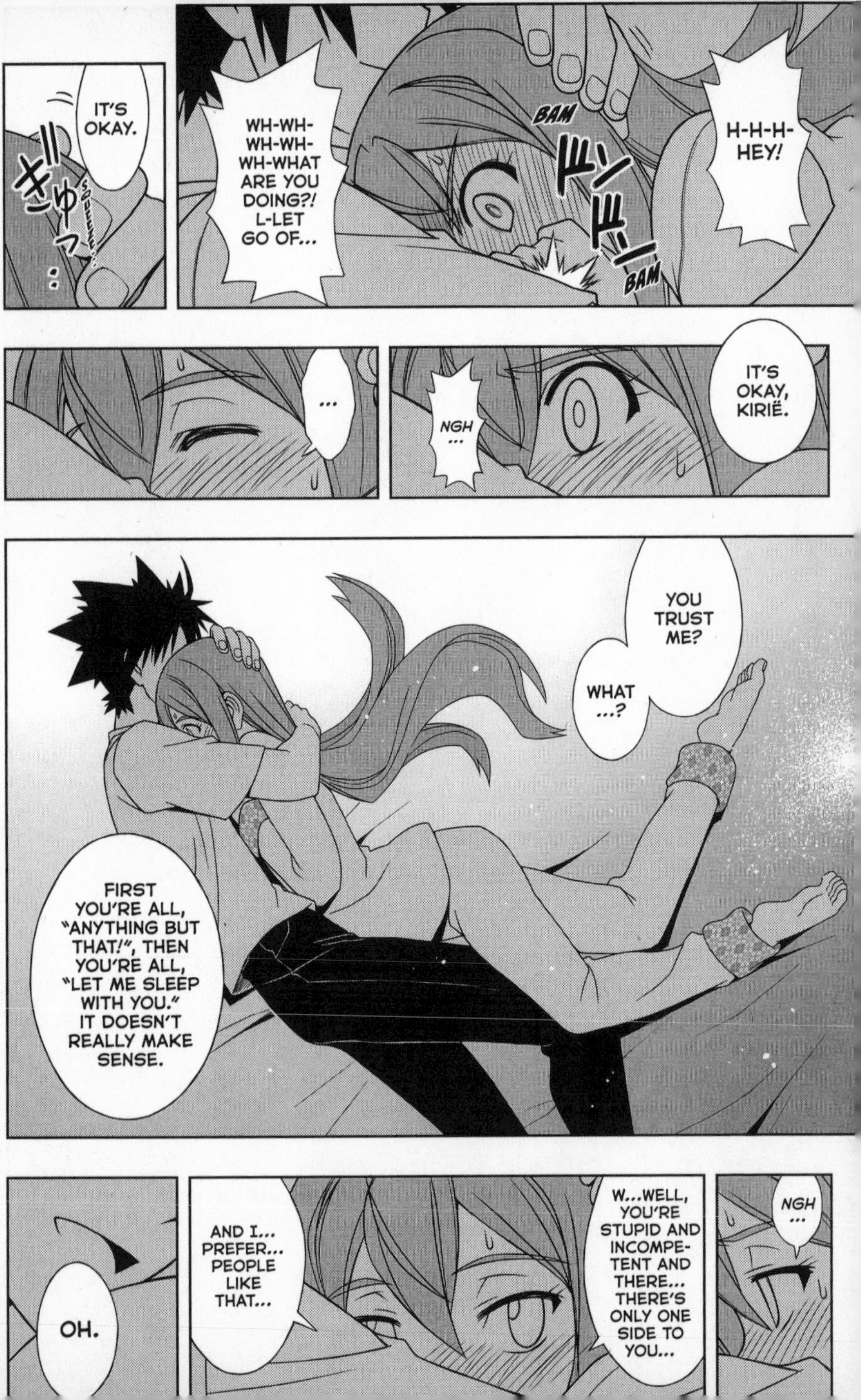
H-H-H-HEY!
BAM
BAM
WH-WH-WH-WH-WH-WHAT ARE YOU DOING?! L-LET GO OF...
IT'S OKAY.
SQUEEZE...
IT'S OKAY, KIRIË.
NGH ...
...
YOU TRUST ME?
WHAT ...?
FIRST YOU'RE ALL, "ANYTHING BUT THAT!", THEN YOU'RE ALL, "LET ME SLEEP WITH YOU." IT DOESN'T REALLY MAKE SENSE.
NGH ...
W...WELL, YOU'RE STUPID AND INCOMPETENT AND THERE... THERE'S ONLY ONE SIDE TO YOU...
AND I... PREFER... PEOPLE LIKE THAT...
OH.

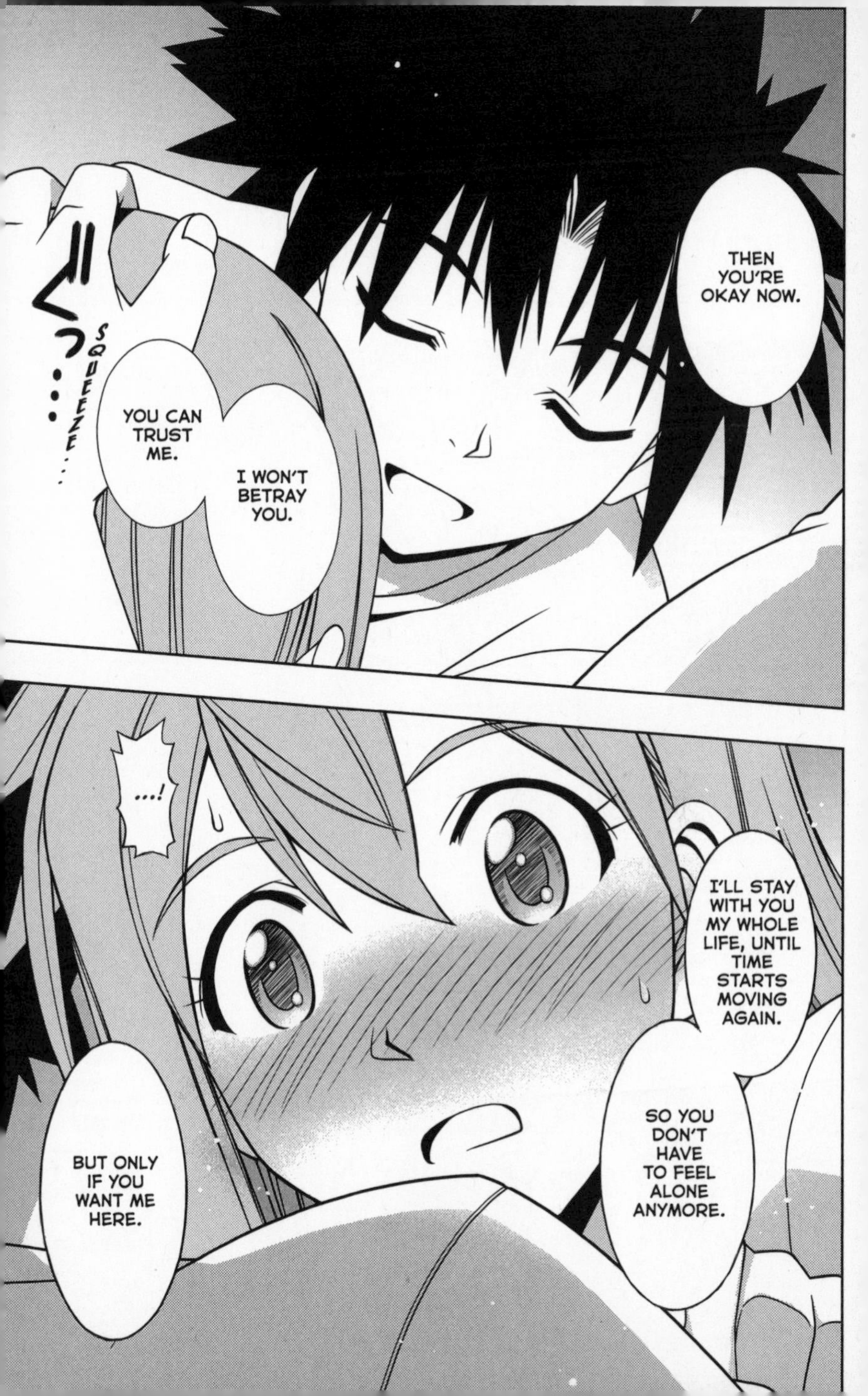
THEN YOU'RE OKAY NOW.
YOU CAN TRUST ME.
I WON'T BETRAY YOU.
ぎゅっ…
SQUEEZE...
...!
I'LL STAY WITH YOU MY WHOLE LIFE, UNTIL TIME STARTS MOVING AGAIN.
SO YOU DON'T HAVE TO FEEL ALONE ANYMORE.
BUT ONLY IF YOU WANT ME HERE.

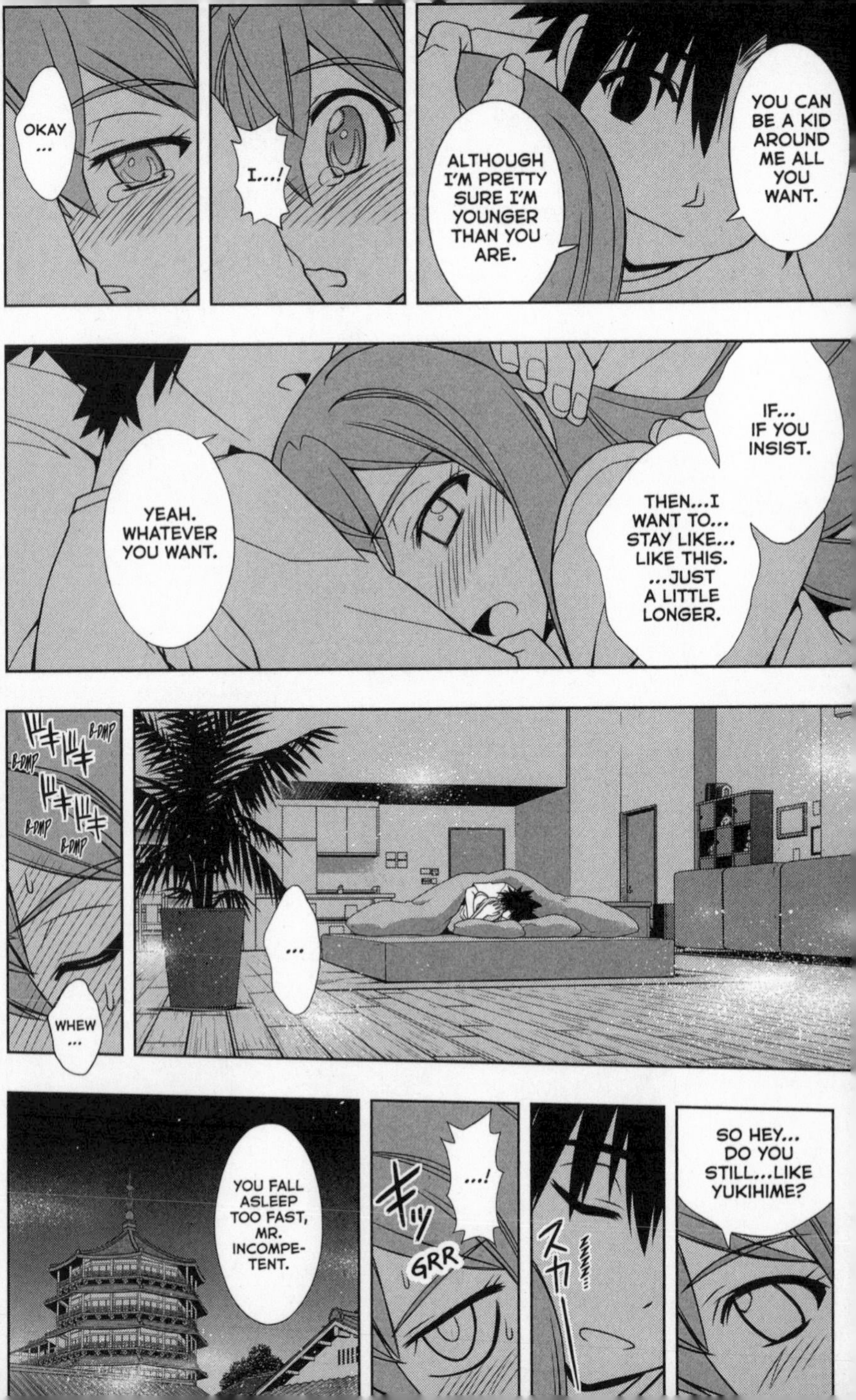
YOU CAN BE A KID AROUND ME ALL YOU WANT.
ALTHOUGH I'M PRETTY SURE I'M YOUNGER THAN YOU ARE.
I...!
OKAY ...
IF... IF YOU INSIST.
THEN...I WANT TO... STAY LIKE... LIKE THIS. ...JUST A LITTLE LONGER.
YEAH. WHATEVER YOU WANT.
...
ドキドキ
B-DMP
B-DMP
ドキドキ
B-DMP
B-DMP
WHEW ...
SO HEY... DO YOU STILL...LIKE YUKIHIME?
スカー
ZZZ...
...!
ギッ
GRR
YOU FALL ASLEEP TOO FAST, MR. INCOMPETENT.

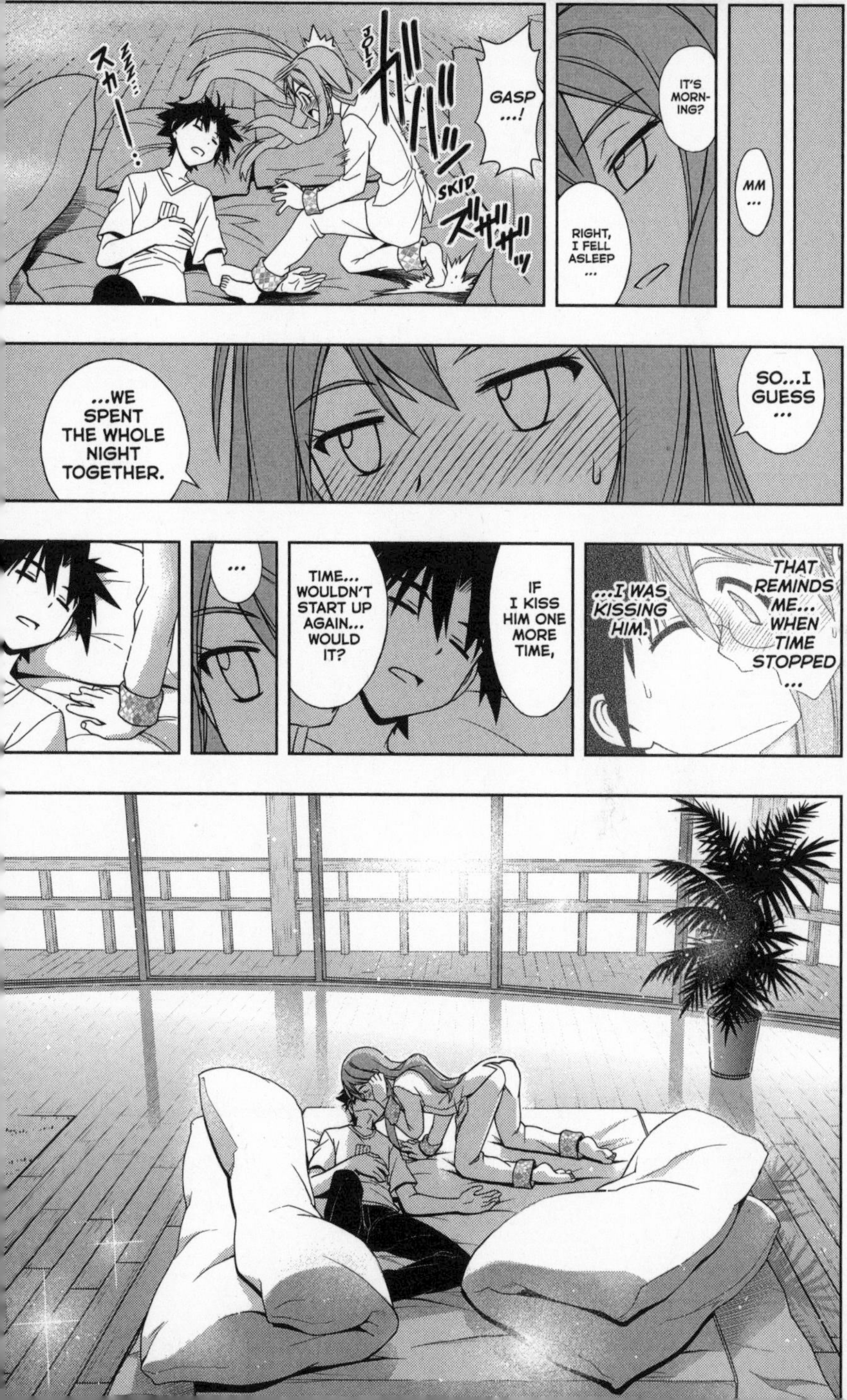
MM...
IT'S MORNING?
RIGHT, I FELL ASLEEP...
GASP...!
JOLT
ガバッ
SKID
ズザザッ
ZZZ...
スカー…
SO...I GUESS...
...WE SPENT THE WHOLE NIGHT TOGETHER.
THAT REMINDS ME... WHEN TIME STOPPED...
...I WAS KISSING HIM.
IF I KISS HIM ONE MORE TIME,
TIME... WOULDN'T START UP AGAIN... WOULD IT?
...

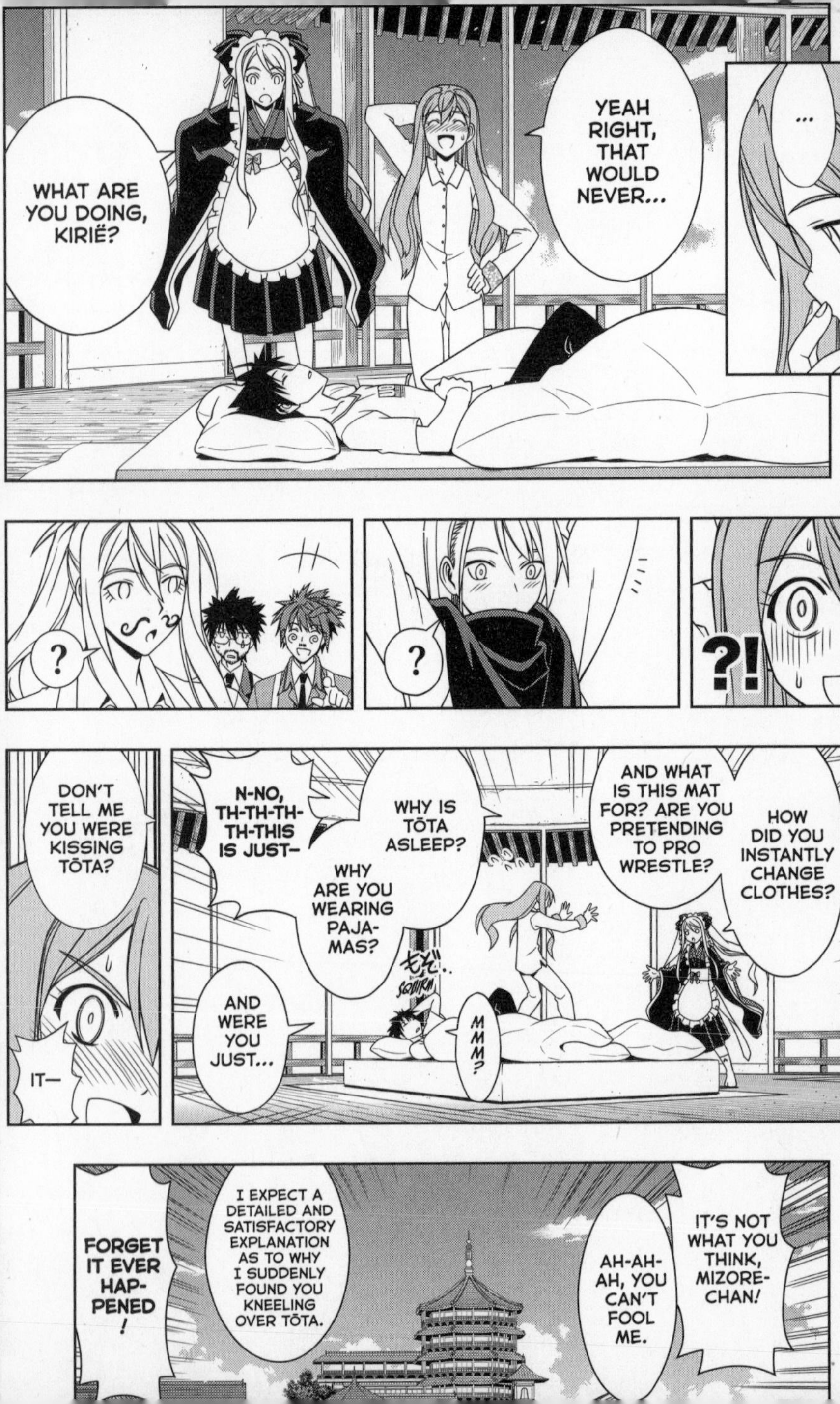
...
YEAH RIGHT, THAT WOULD NEVER...
WHAT ARE YOU DOING, KIRIË?
?!
?
?
HOW DID YOU INSTANTLY CHANGE CLOTHES?
AND WHAT IS THIS MAT FOR? ARE YOU PRETENDING TO PRO WRESTLE?
WHY IS TŌTA ASLEEP?
N-NO, TH-TH-TH-TH-THIS IS JUST–
WHY ARE YOU WEARING PAJAMAS?
SQUIRM
MMM?
AND WERE YOU JUST...
DON'T TELL ME YOU WERE KISSING TŌTA?
IT—
IT'S NOT WHAT YOU THINK, MIZORE-CHAN!
AH-AH-AH, YOU CAN'T FOOL ME.
I EXPECT A DETAILED AND SATISFACTORY EXPLANATION AS TO WHY I SUDDENLY FOUND YOU KNEELING OVER TŌTA.
FORGET IT EVER HAPPENED!

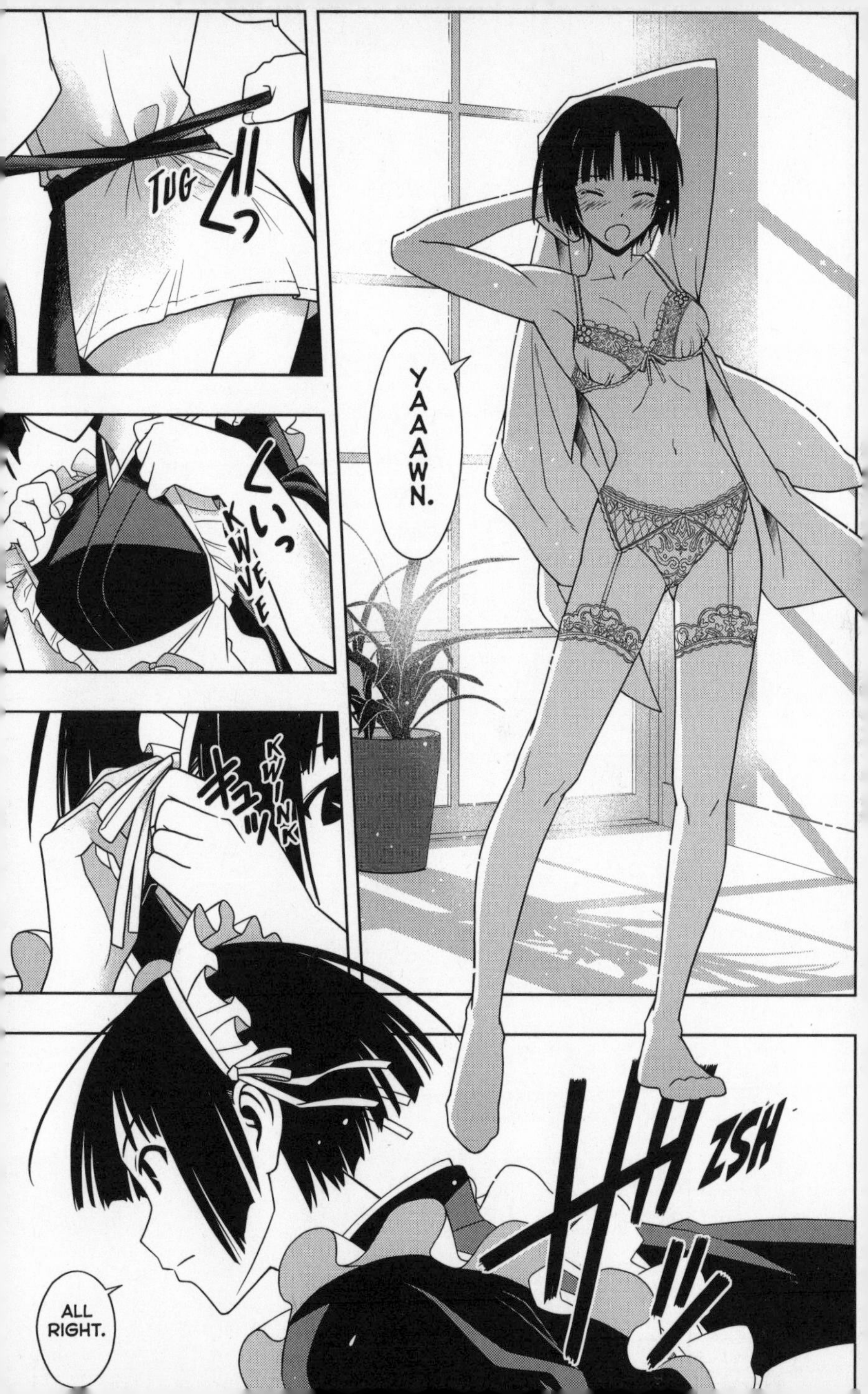
YAAAWN.
TUG
くっ
くいっ
KWVEE
キュッ
KWINK
ZSH
ALL RIGHT.

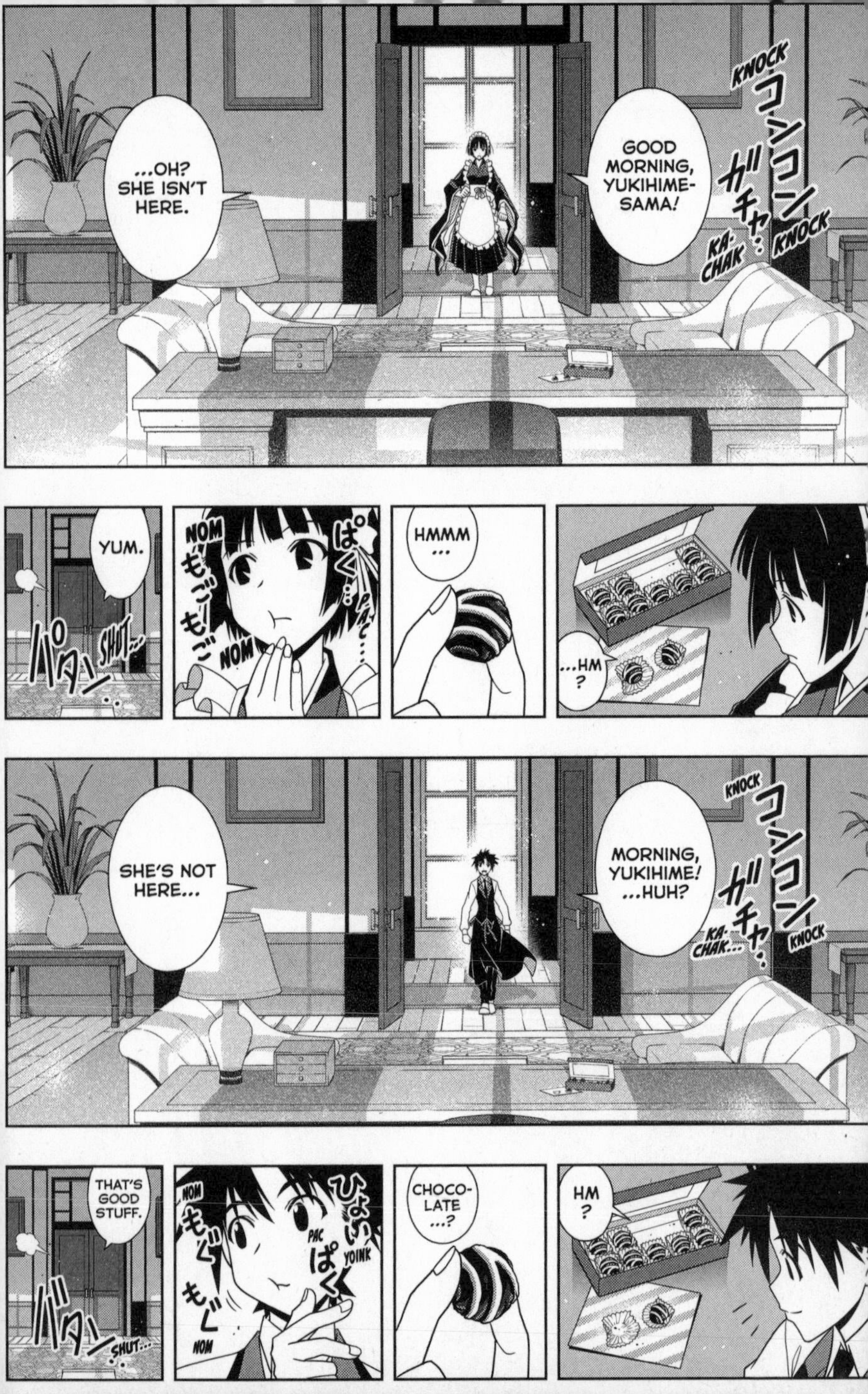
KNOCK
コンコン
KNOCK
ガチャ
KA-CHAK
GOOD MORNING, YUKIHIME-SAMA!
...OH? SHE ISN'T HERE.
...HM ?
HMMM ...
ぱく…
PAC...
NOM
もごもご
NOM
YUM.
パタン
SHUT...
KNOCK
コンコン
KNOCK
ガチャ
KA-CHAK...
MORNING, YUKIHIME! ...HUH?
SHE'S NOT HERE...
HM ?
CHOCO-LATE ...?
ひょい
YOINK
ぱく
PAC
NOM
もぐもぐ
NOM
THAT'S GOOD STUFF.
バタン
SHUT...

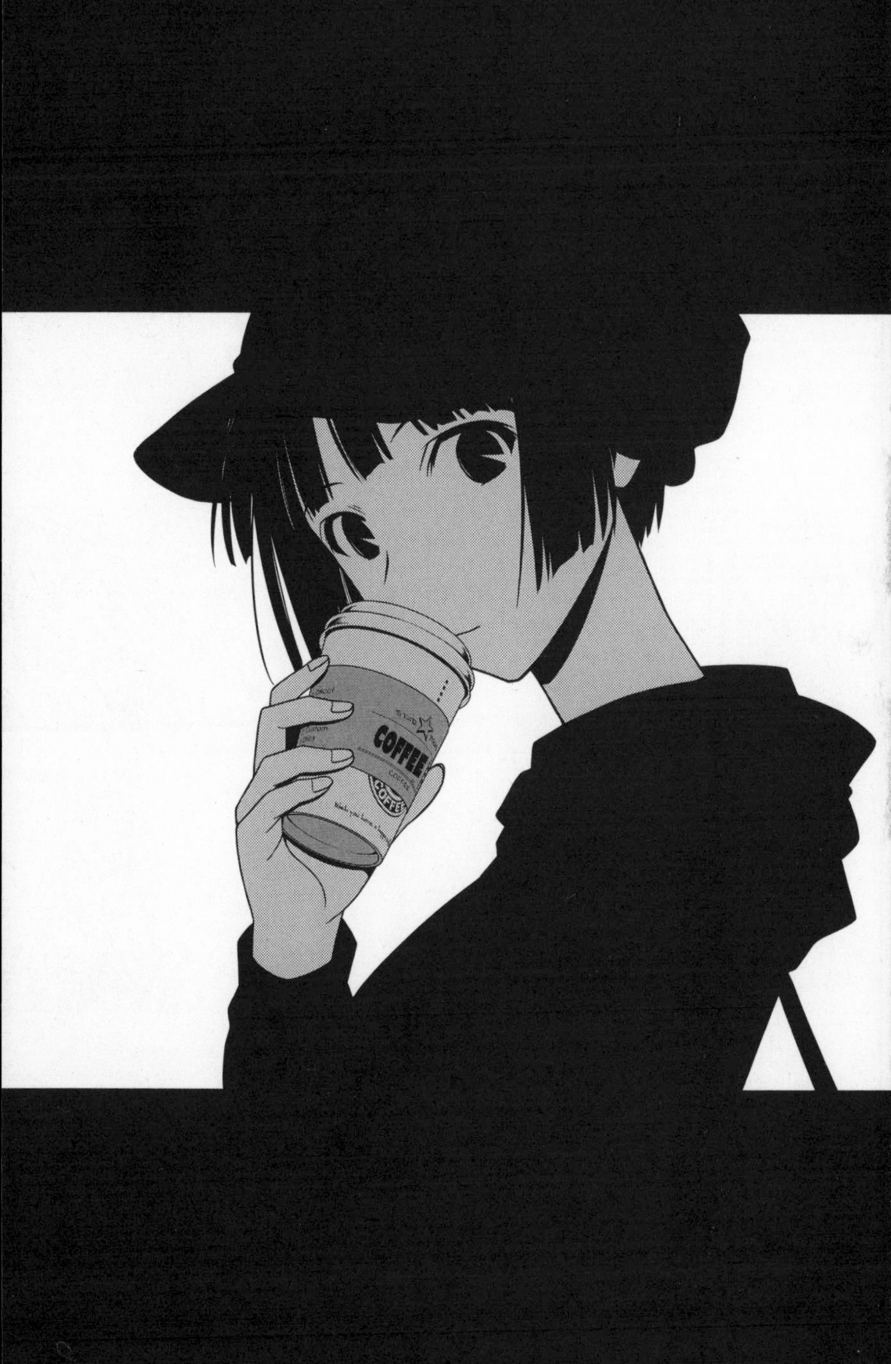
COFFEE

## STAGE 107: ALLOW ME TO SAY ONE THING

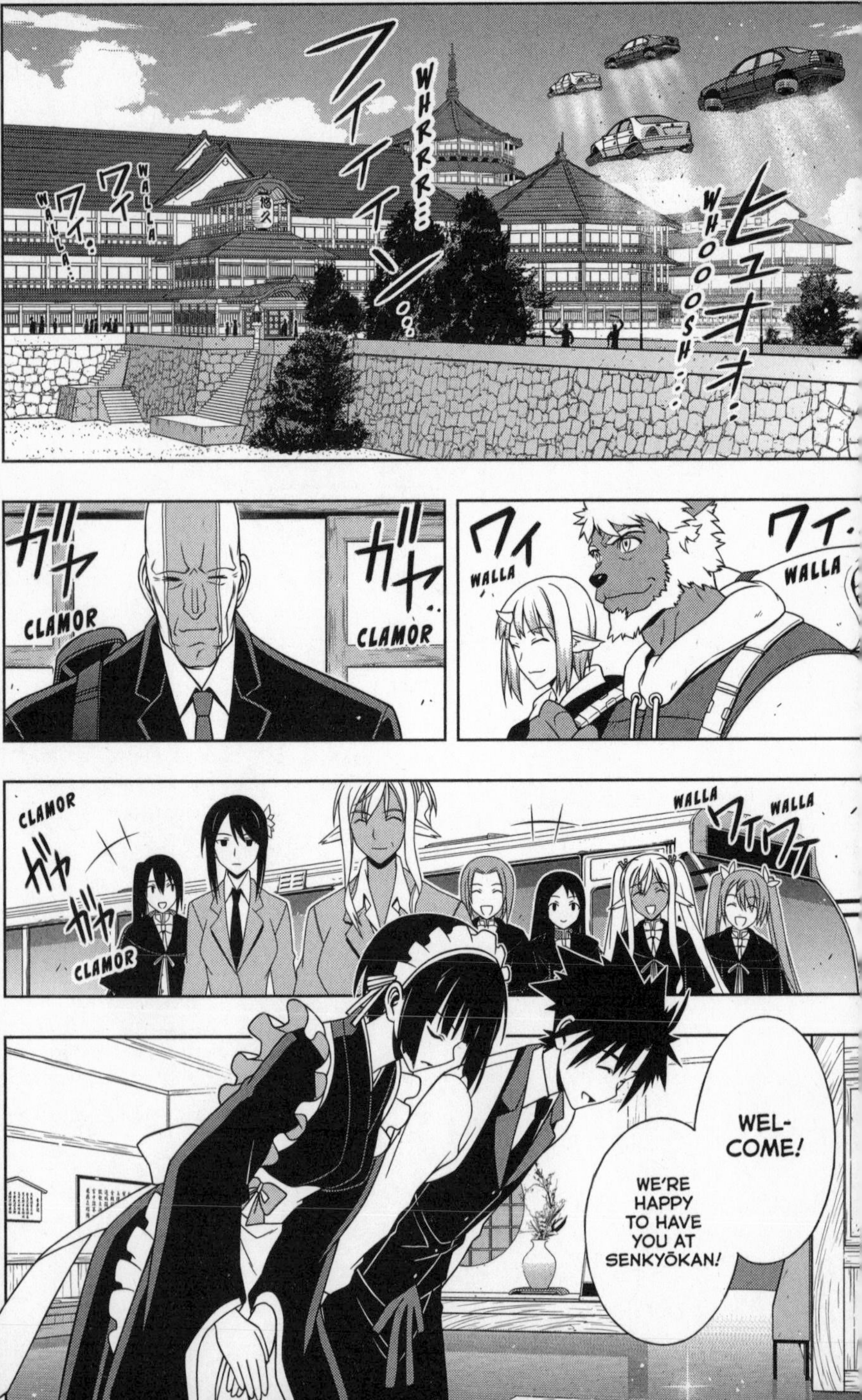
ヒュオオ…
WHOOOOSH...
フイイン…
WHRRR...
ワイ ワイ
WALLA WALLA...
ワイ
WALLA
ワイ
WALLA
ガヤ
CLAMOR
ガヤ
CLAMOR
ワイワイ
WALLA WALLA
ガヤガヤ
CLAMOR CLAMOR
WEL-COME!
WE'RE HAPPY TO HAVE YOU AT SENKYŌKAN!

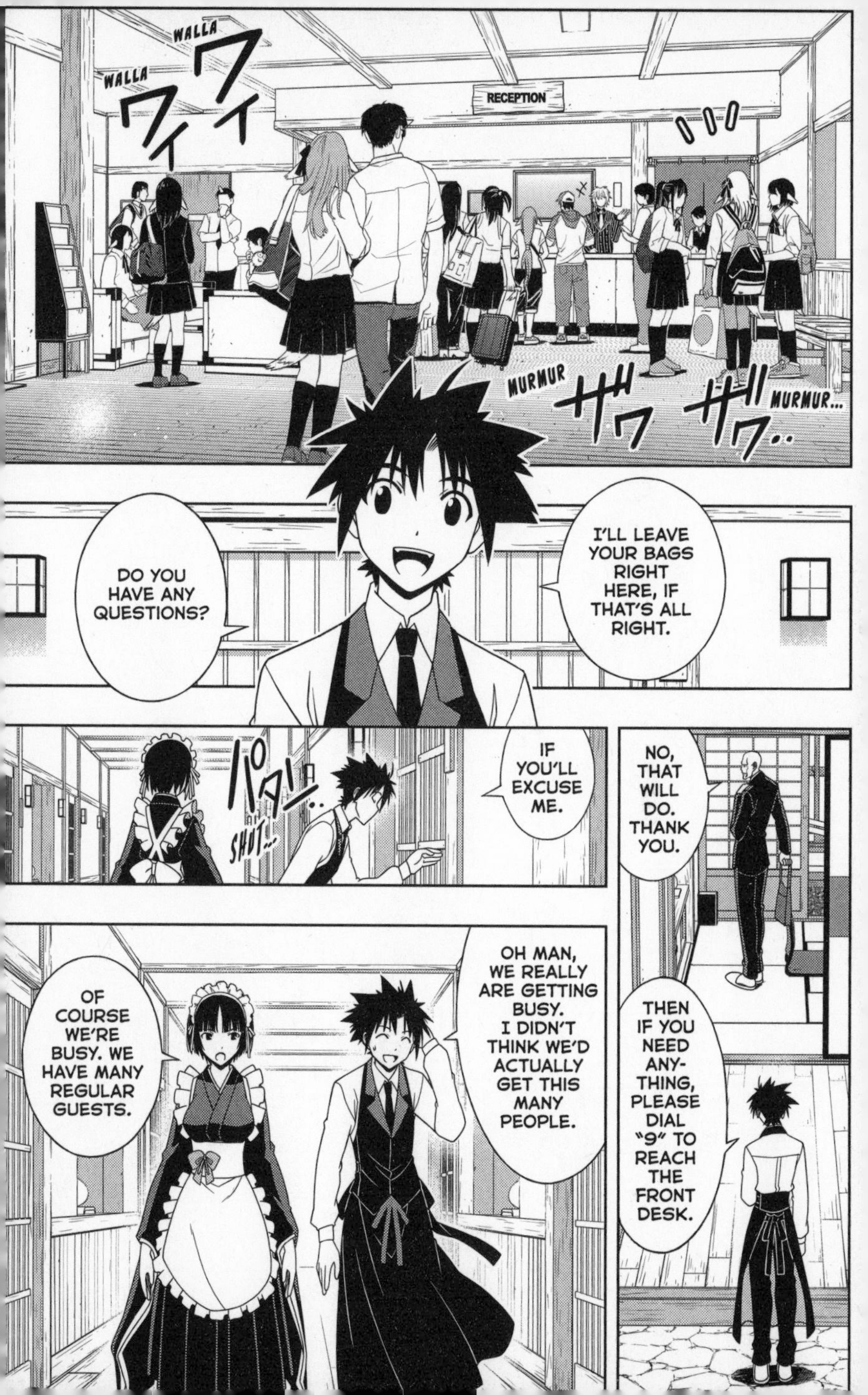

RECEPTION
WALLA
WALLA
ワイワイ
MURMUR...
ザワ ザワ
MURMUR
I'LL LEAVE YOUR BAGS RIGHT HERE, IF THAT'S ALL RIGHT.
DO YOU HAVE ANY QUESTIONS?
NO, THAT WILL DO. THANK YOU.
THEN IF YOU NEED ANY-THING, PLEASE DIAL "9" TO REACH THE FRONT DESK.
IF YOU'LL EXCUSE ME.
パタン
SHUT!..
OH MAN, WE REALLY ARE GETTING BUSY. I DIDN'T THINK WE'D ACTUALLY GET THIS MANY PEOPLE.
OF COURSE WE'RE BUSY. WE HAVE MANY REGULAR GUESTS.

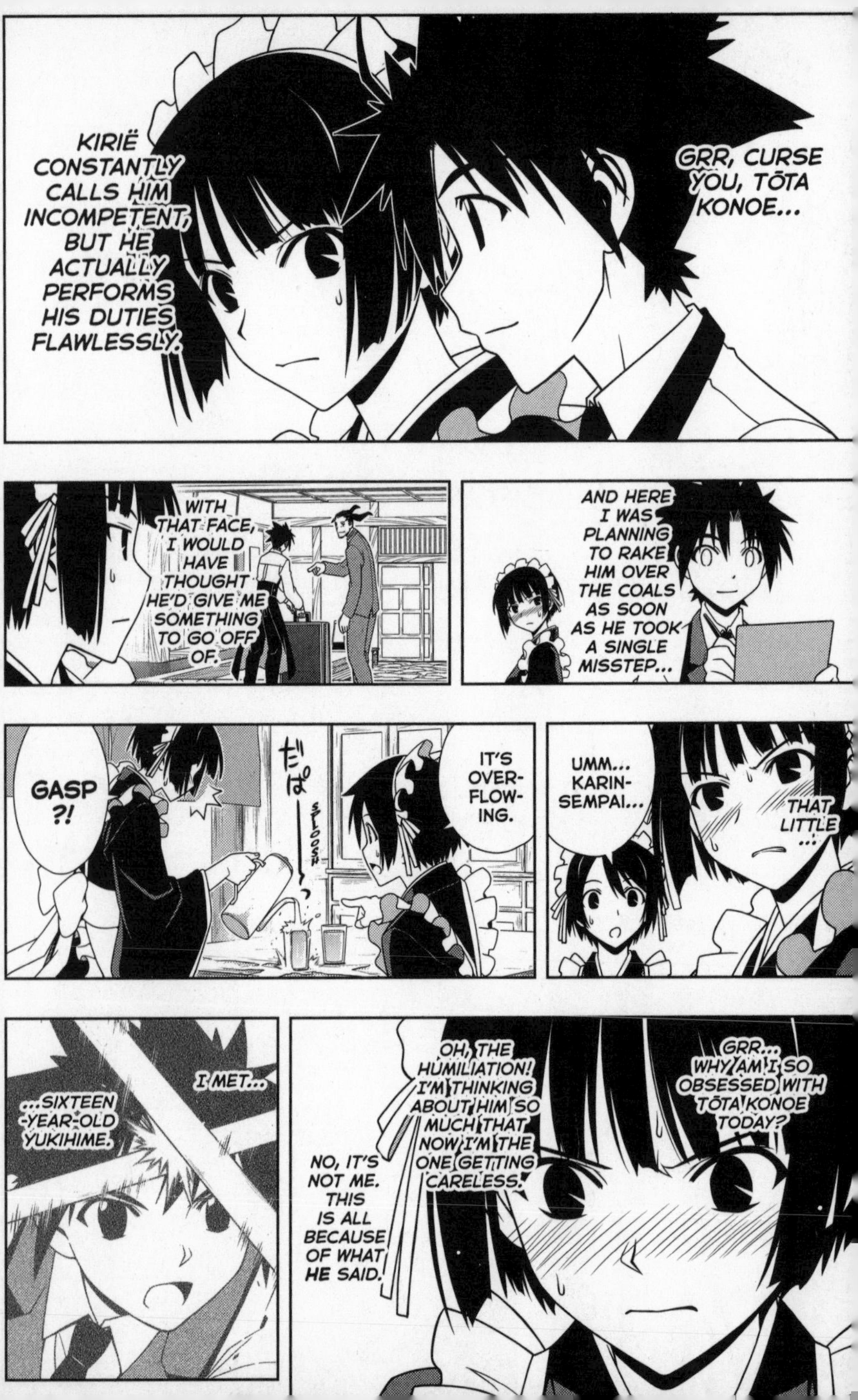
GRR, CURSE YOU, TŌTA KONOE...
KIRIË CONSTANTLY CALLS HIM INCOMPETENT, BUT HE ACTUALLY PERFORMS HIS DUTIES FLAWLESSLY.
AND HERE I WAS PLANNING TO RAKE HIM OVER THE COALS AS SOON AS HE TOOK A SINGLE MISSTEP...
WITH THAT FACE, I WOULD HAVE THOUGHT HE'D GIVE ME SOMETHING TO GO OFF OF.
THAT LITTLE ...!
UMM... KARIN-SEMPAI...
IT'S OVER-FLOWING.
だぱ
SPLOOSH
GASP ?!
GRR... WHY AM I SO OBSESSED WITH TŌTA KONOE TODAY?
OH, THE HUMILIATION! I'M THINKING ABOUT HIM SO MUCH THAT NOW I'M THE ONE GETTING CARELESS.
NO, IT'S NOT ME. THIS IS ALL BECAUSE OF WHAT HE SAID.
I MET...
...SIXTEEN-YEAR-OLD YUKIHIME.

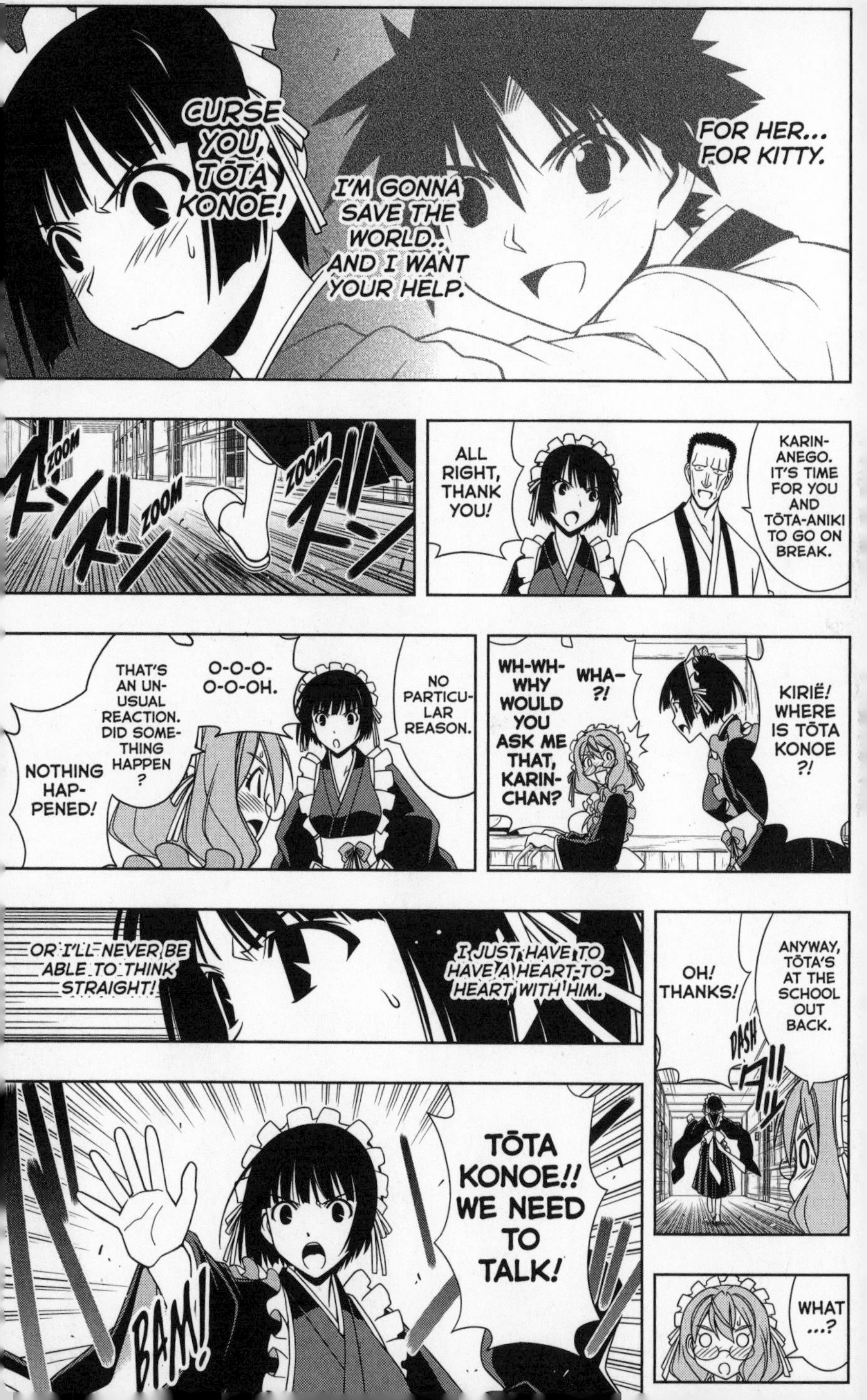
I'M GONNA SAVE THE WORLD.. AND I WANT YOUR HELP.
FOR HER... FOR KITTY.
CURSE YOU, TŌTA KONOE!
KARIN-ANEGO. IT'S TIME FOR YOU AND TŌTA-ANIKI TO GO ON BREAK.
ALL RIGHT, THANK YOU!
ZOOM
ZOOM
ZOOM
ZOOM
KIRIË! WHERE IS TŌTA KONOE?!
WHA-?!
WH-WH-WHY WOULD YOU ASK ME THAT, KARIN-CHAN?
NO PARTICULAR REASON.
O-O-O-O-O-OH.
THAT'S AN UNUSUAL REACTION. DID SOMETHING HAPPEN?
NOTHING HAPPENED!
ANYWAY, TŌTA'S AT THE SCHOOL OUT BACK.
OH! THANKS!
DASH
WHAT...?
I JUST HAVE TO HAVE A HEART-TO-HEART WITH HIM.
OR I'LL NEVER BE ABLE TO THINK STRAIGHT!
TŌTA KONOE!! WE NEED TO TALK!
BAM!

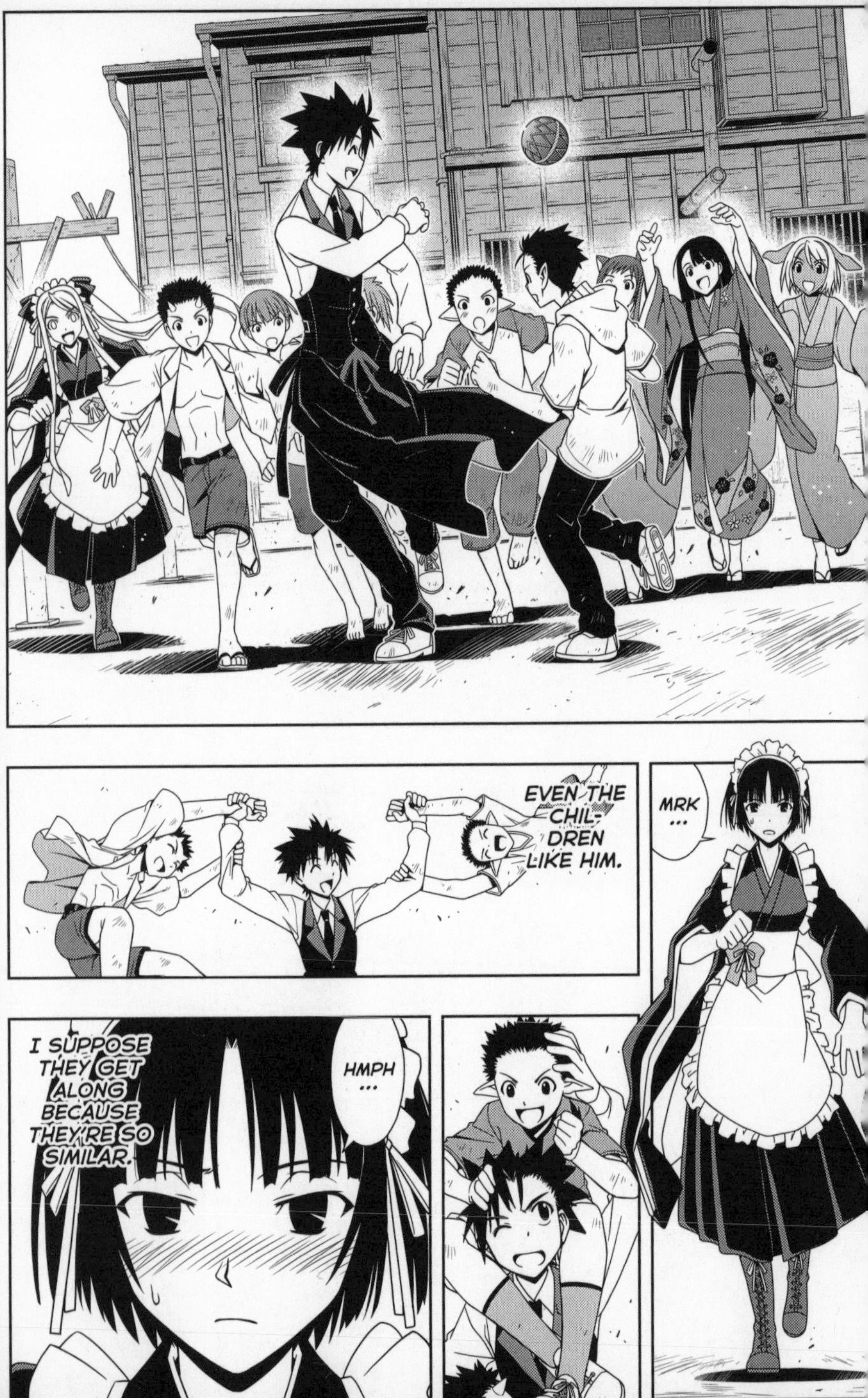
MRK...
EVEN THE CHIL-DREN LIKE HIM.
HMPH...
I SUPPOSE THEY GET ALONG BECAUSE THEY'RE SO SIMILAR.

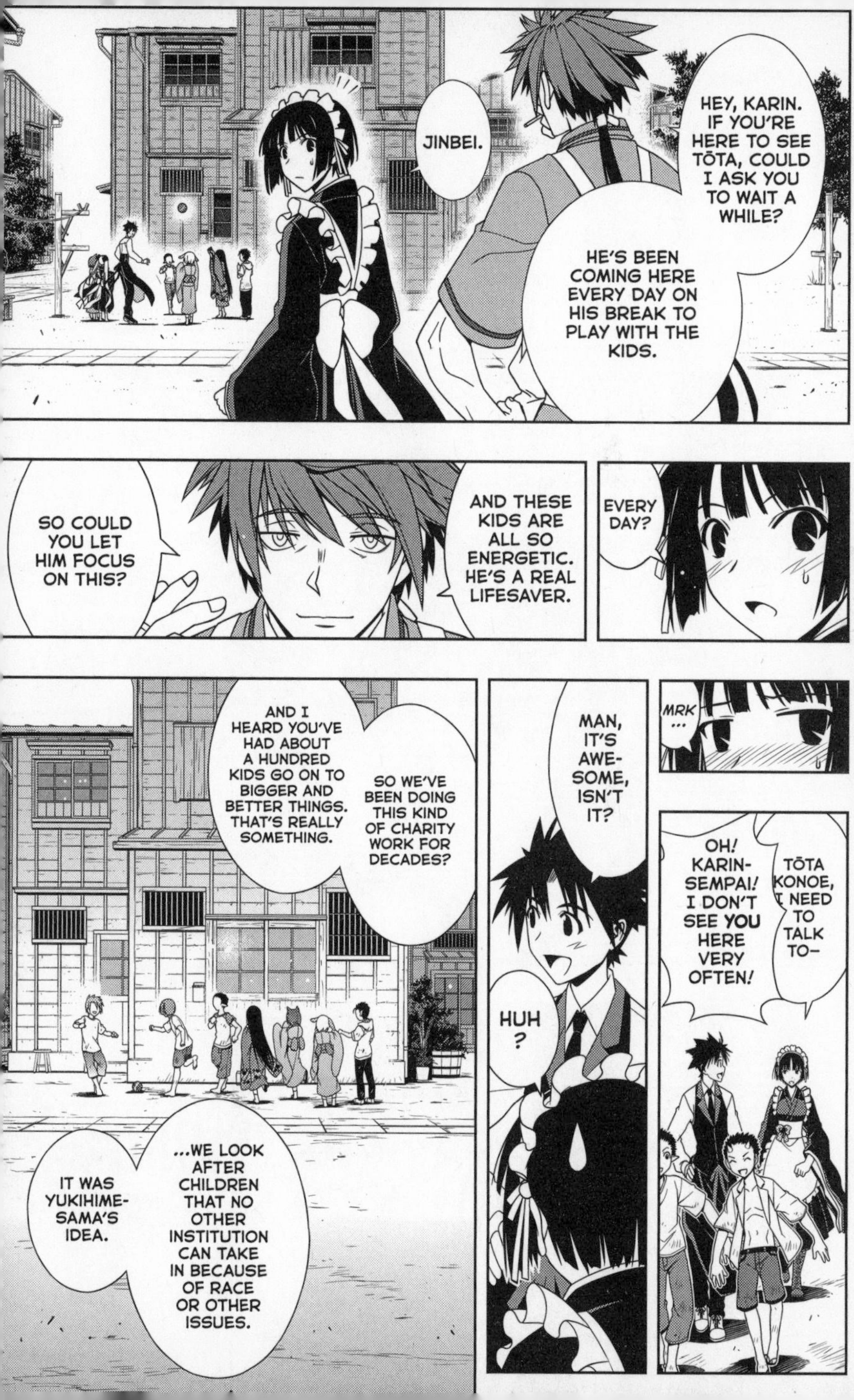
HEY, KARIN. IF YOU'RE HERE TO SEE TŌTA, COULD I ASK YOU TO WAIT A WHILE?
JINBEI.
HE'S BEEN COMING HERE EVERY DAY ON HIS BREAK TO PLAY WITH THE KIDS.
EVERY DAY?
AND THESE KIDS ARE ALL SO ENERGETIC. HE'S A REAL LIFESAVER.
SO COULD YOU LET HIM FOCUS ON THIS?
MRK...
TŌTA KONOE, I NEED TO TALK TO—
OH! KARIN-SEMPAI! I DON'T SEE YOU HERE VERY OFTEN!
MAN, IT'S AWE-SOME, ISN'T IT?
HUH?
SO WE'VE BEEN DOING THIS KIND OF CHARITY WORK FOR DECADES?
AND I HEARD YOU'VE HAD ABOUT A HUNDRED KIDS GO ON TO BIGGER AND BETTER THINGS. THAT'S REALLY SOMETHING.
...WE LOOK AFTER CHILDREN THAT NO OTHER INSTITUTION CAN TAKE IN BECAUSE OF RACE OR OTHER ISSUES.
IT WAS YUKIHIME-SAMA'S IDEA.

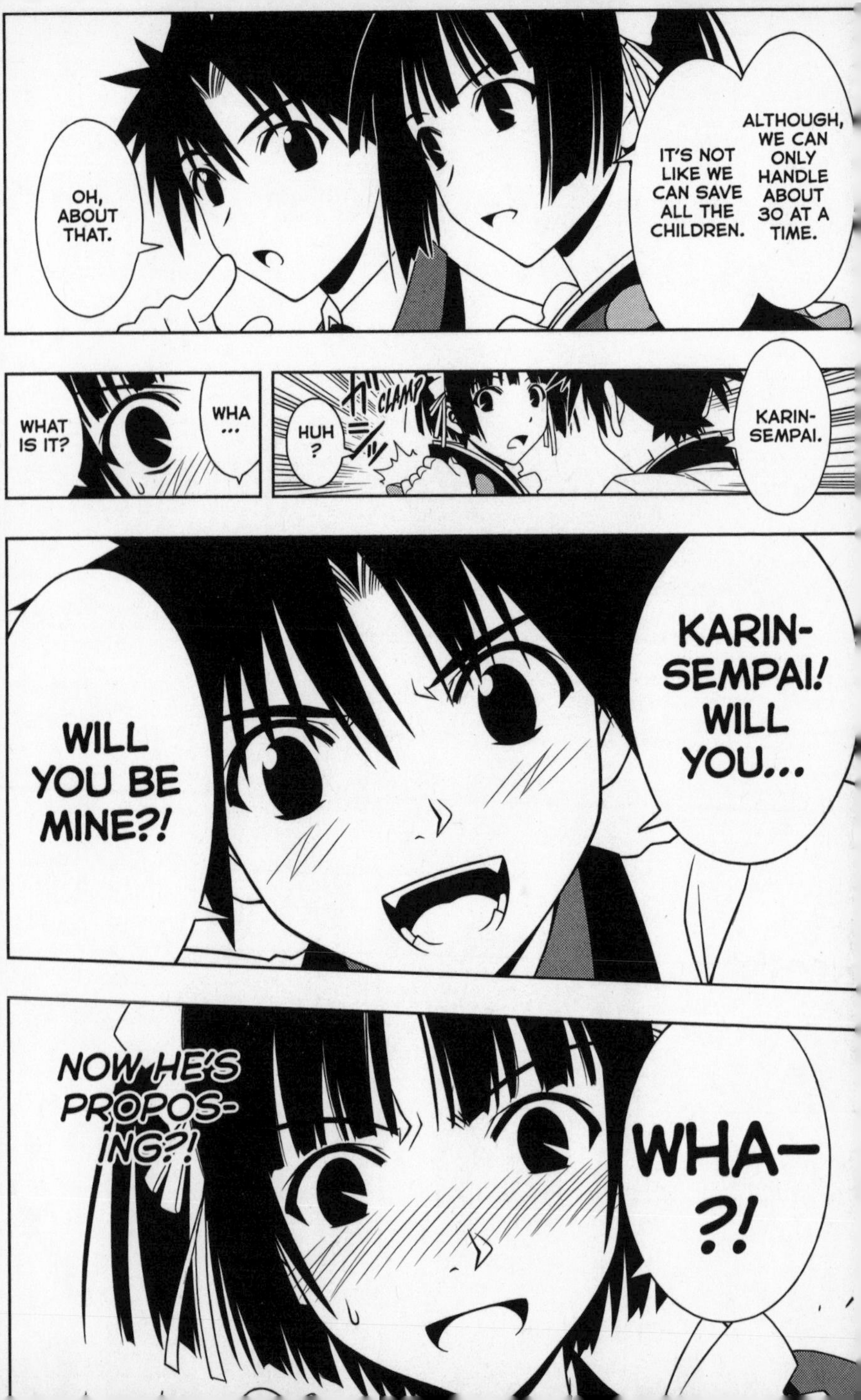
ALTHOUGH, WE CAN ONLY HANDLE ABOUT 30 AT A TIME.
IT'S NOT LIKE WE CAN SAVE ALL THE CHILDREN.
OH, ABOUT THAT.
KARIN-SEMPAI.
CLAMP
HUH?
WHA...
WHAT IS IT?
KARIN-SEMPAI! WILL YOU...
WILL YOU BE MINE?!
WHA-?!
NOW HE'S PROPOS-ING?!

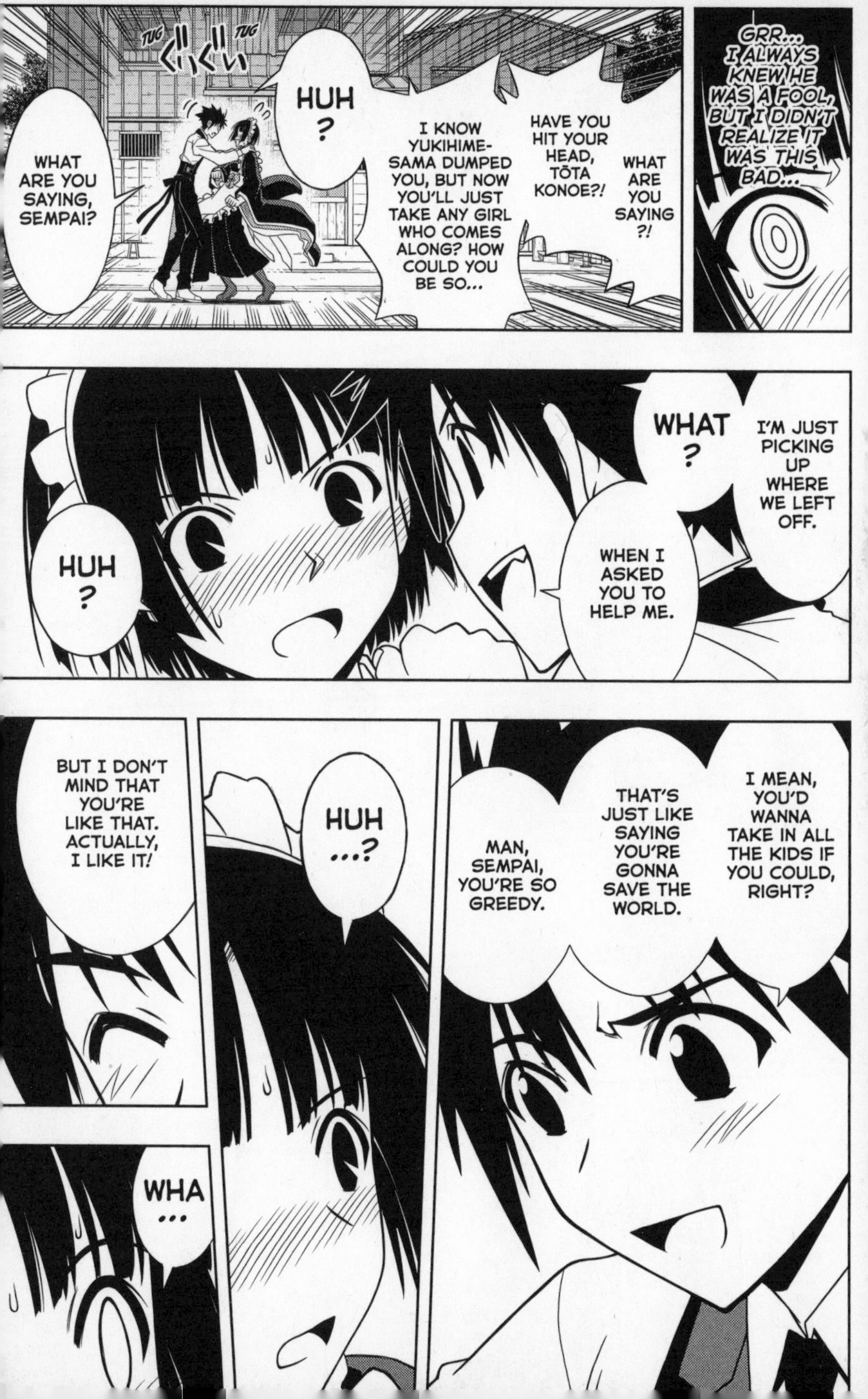
GRR... I ALWAYS KNEW HE WAS A FOOL, BUT I DIDN'T REALIZE IT WAS THIS BAD...
WHAT ARE YOU SAYING ?!
HAVE YOU HIT YOUR HEAD, TŌTA KONOE?!
I KNOW YUKIHIME-SAMA DUMPED YOU, BUT NOW YOU'LL JUST TAKE ANY GIRL WHO COMES ALONG? HOW COULD YOU BE SO...
HUH ?
TUG TUG
WHAT ARE YOU SAYING, SEMPAI?
I'M JUST PICKING UP WHERE WE LEFT OFF.
WHAT ?
WHEN I ASKED YOU TO HELP ME.
HUH ?
I MEAN, YOU'D WANNA TAKE IN ALL THE KIDS IF YOU COULD, RIGHT?
THAT'S JUST LIKE SAYING YOU'RE GONNA SAVE THE WORLD.
MAN, SEMPAI, YOU'RE SO GREEDY.
HUH ...?
BUT I DON'T MIND THAT YOU'RE LIKE THAT. ACTUALLY, I LIKE IT!
WHA ...

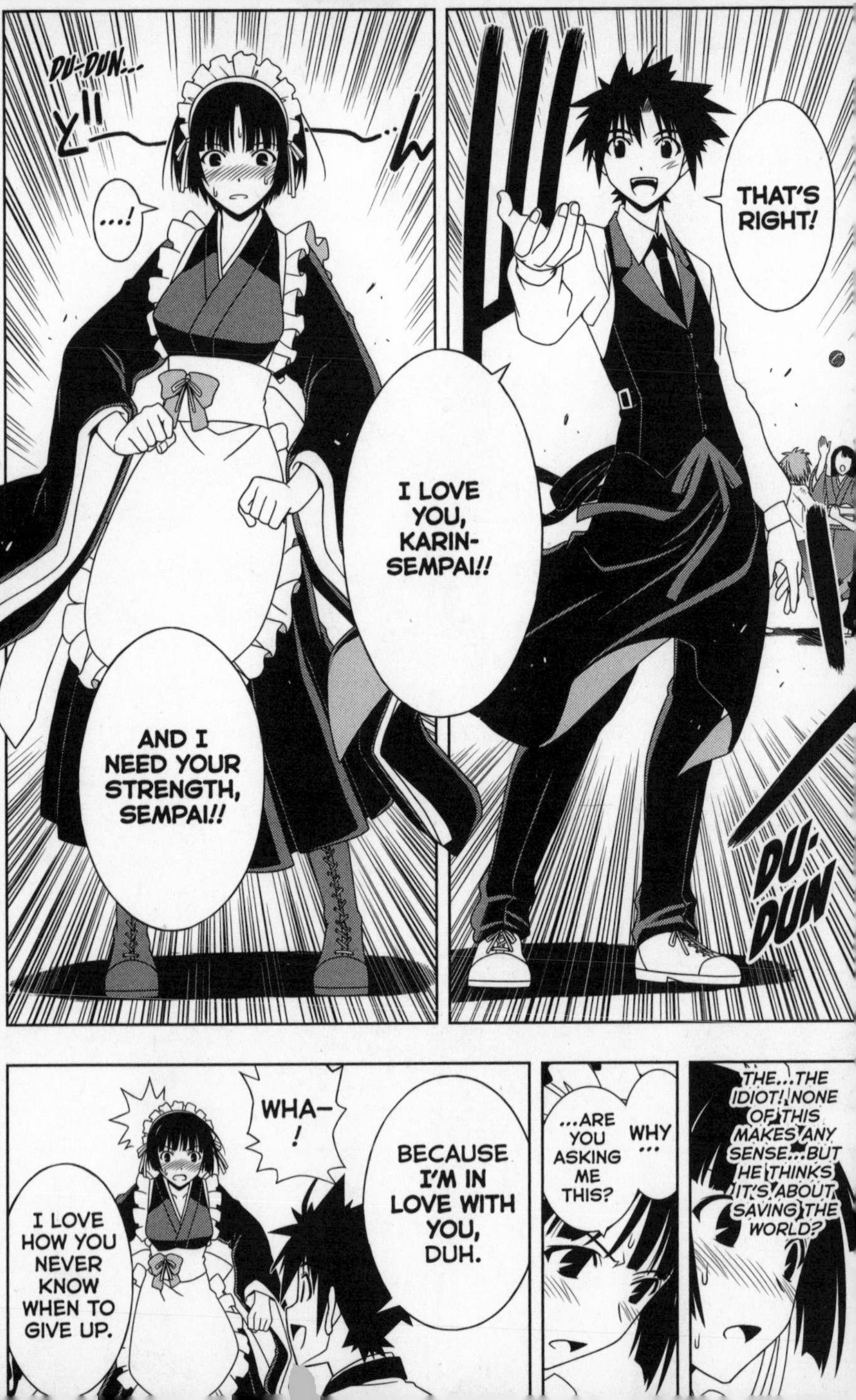
THAT'S RIGHT!
I LOVE YOU, KARIN-SEMPAI!!
DU-DUN
DU-DUN...
...!
AND I NEED YOUR STRENGTH, SEMPAI!!
THE... THE IDIOT! NONE OF THIS MAKES ANY SENSE... BUT HE THINKS IT'S ABOUT SAVING THE WORLD?
WHY...
...ARE YOU ASKING ME THIS?
BECAUSE I'M IN LOVE WITH YOU, DUH.
WHA-!
I LOVE HOW YOU NEVER KNOW WHEN TO GIVE UP.

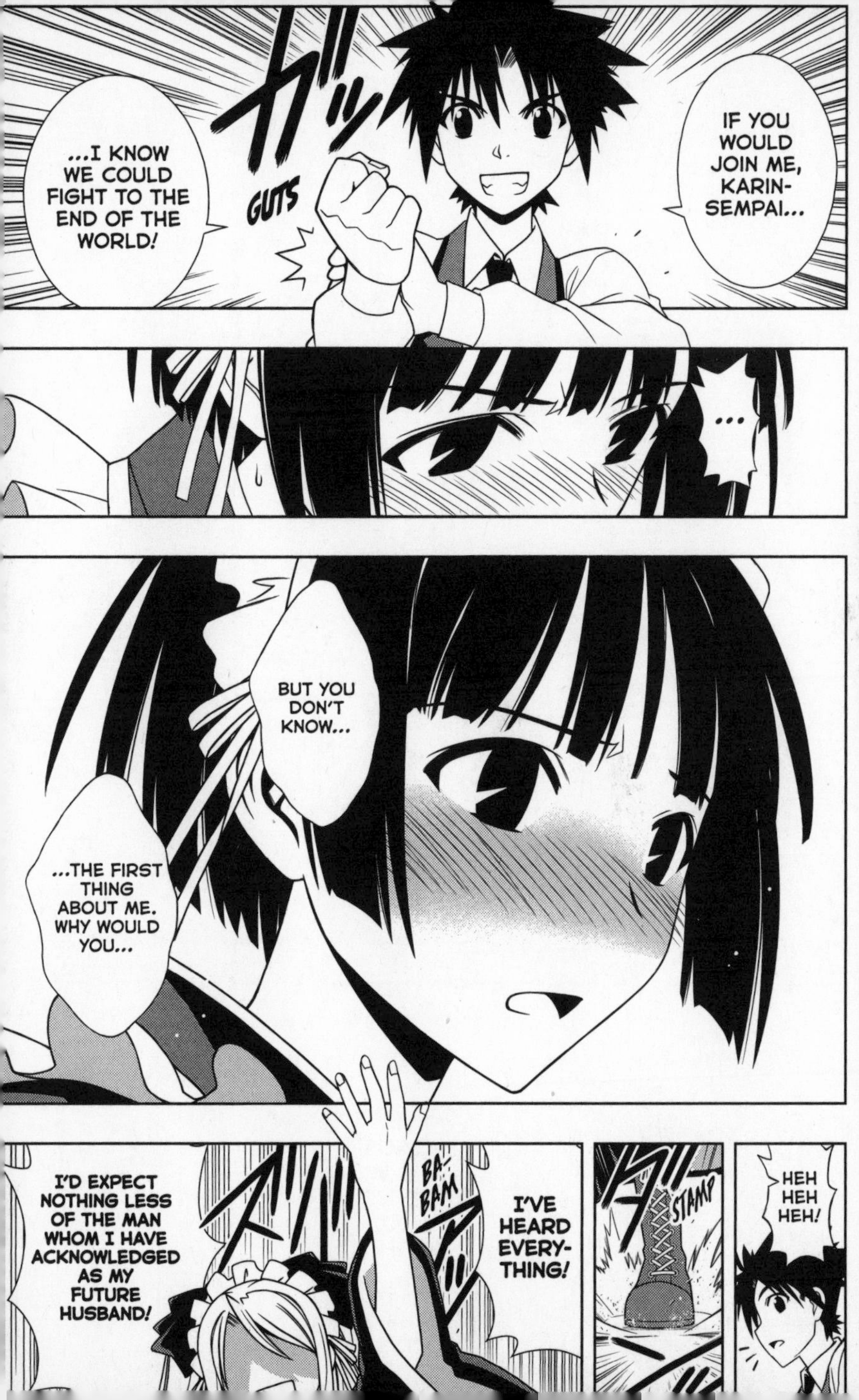
IF YOU WOULD JOIN ME, KARIN-SEMPAI...
GUTS
...I KNOW WE COULD FIGHT TO THE END OF THE WORLD!
...
BUT YOU DON'T KNOW...
...THE FIRST THING ABOUT ME. WHY WOULD YOU...
HEH HEH HEH!
STAMP
I'VE HEARD EVERYTHING!
BA-BAM
I'D EXPECT NOTHING LESS OF THE MAN WHOM I HAVE ACKNOWLEDGED AS MY FUTURE HUSBAND!

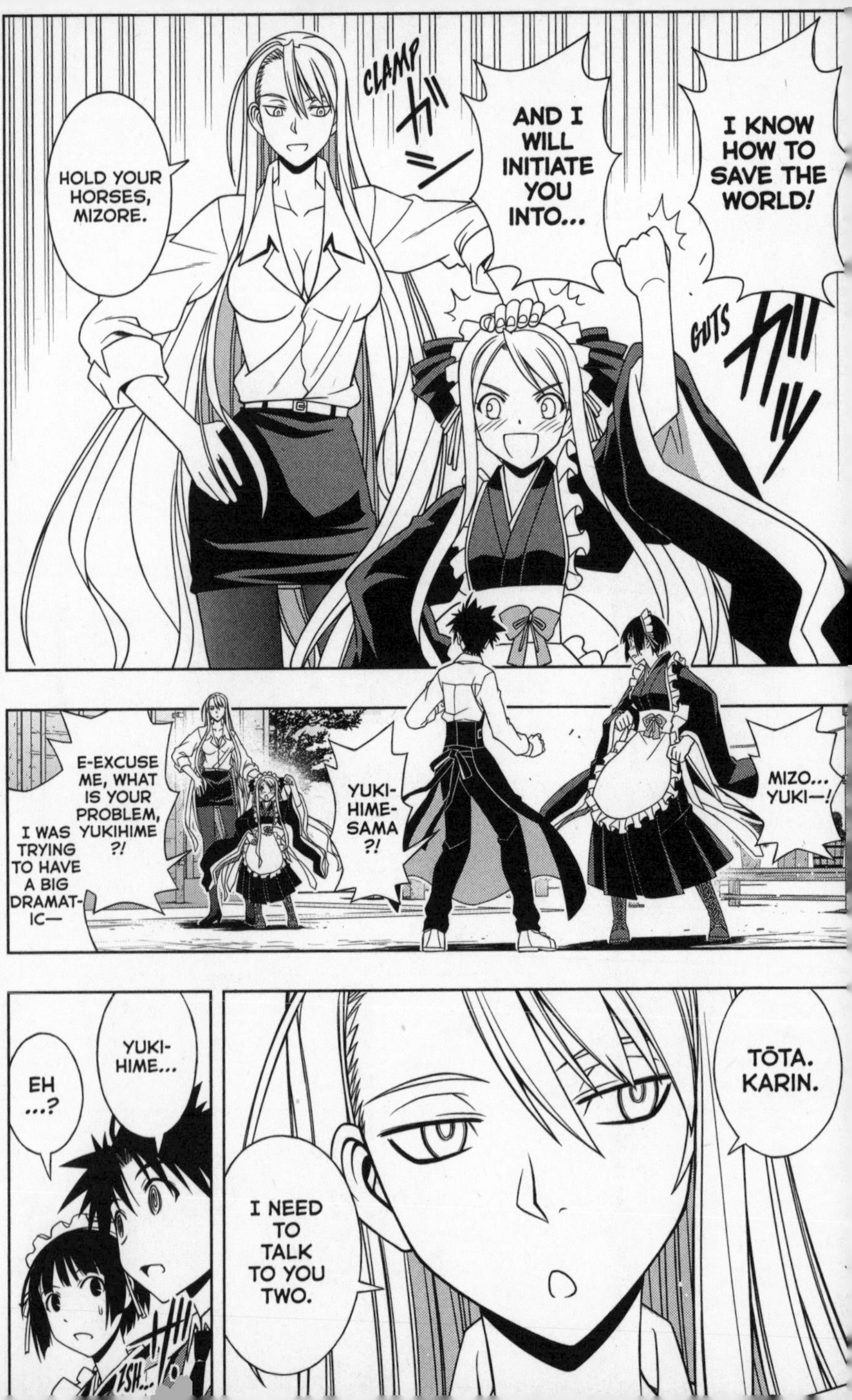
I KNOW HOW TO SAVE THE WORLD!
AND I WILL INITIATE YOU INTO...
CLAMP
HOLD YOUR HORSES, MIZORE.
GUTS
MIZO... YUKI—!
YUKI-HIME-SAMA ?!
E-EXCUSE ME, WHAT IS YOUR PROBLEM, YUKIHIME ?!
I WAS TRYING TO HAVE A BIG DRAMAT-IC—
TŌTA. KARIN.
I NEED TO TALK TO YOU TWO.
YUKI-HIME...
EH ...?

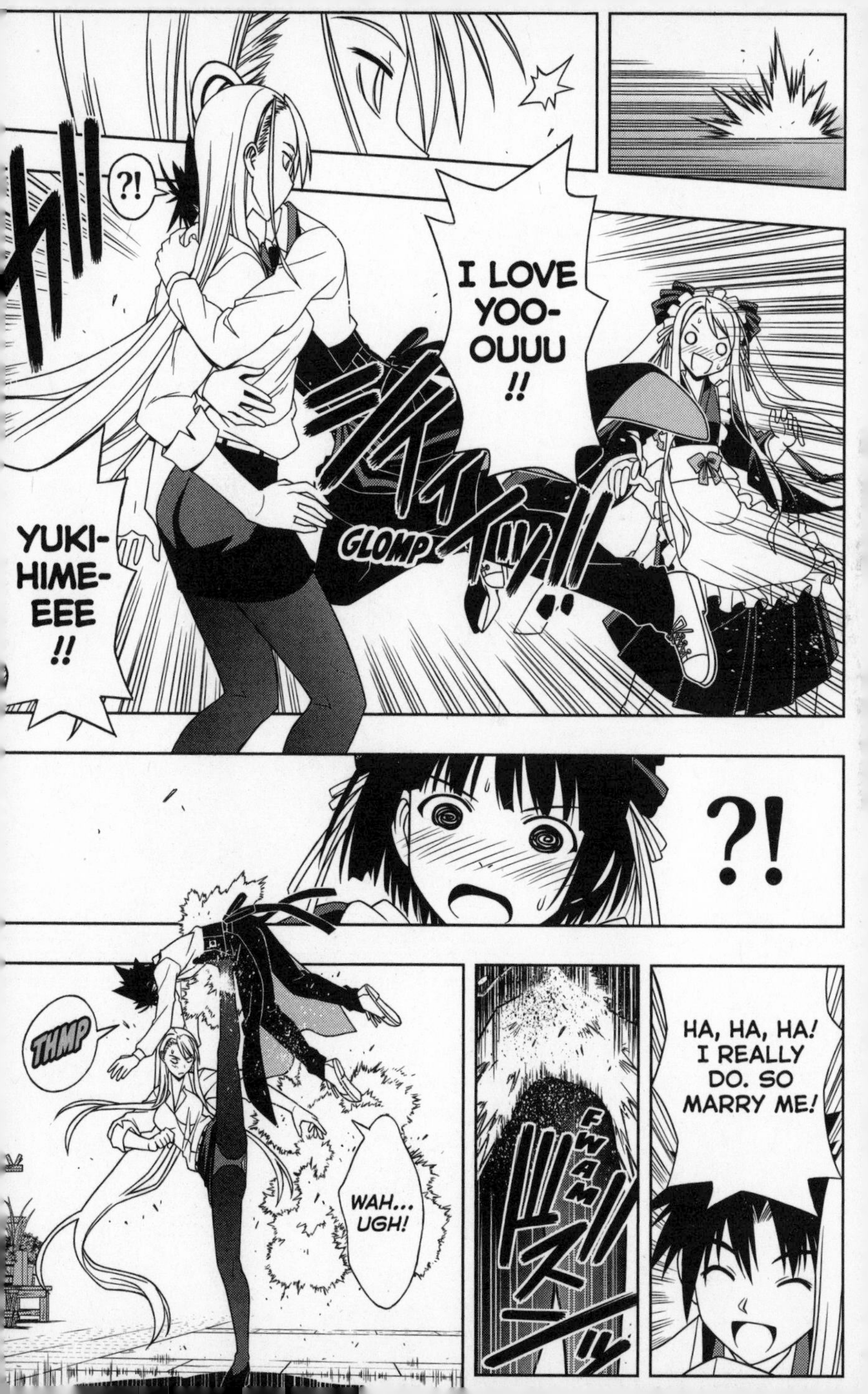
I LOVE YOO-OUUU!!
?!
GLOMP
YUKI-HIME-EEE!!
?!
HA, HA, HA! I REALLY DO. SO MARRY ME!
FWAM
THMP
WAH... UGH!

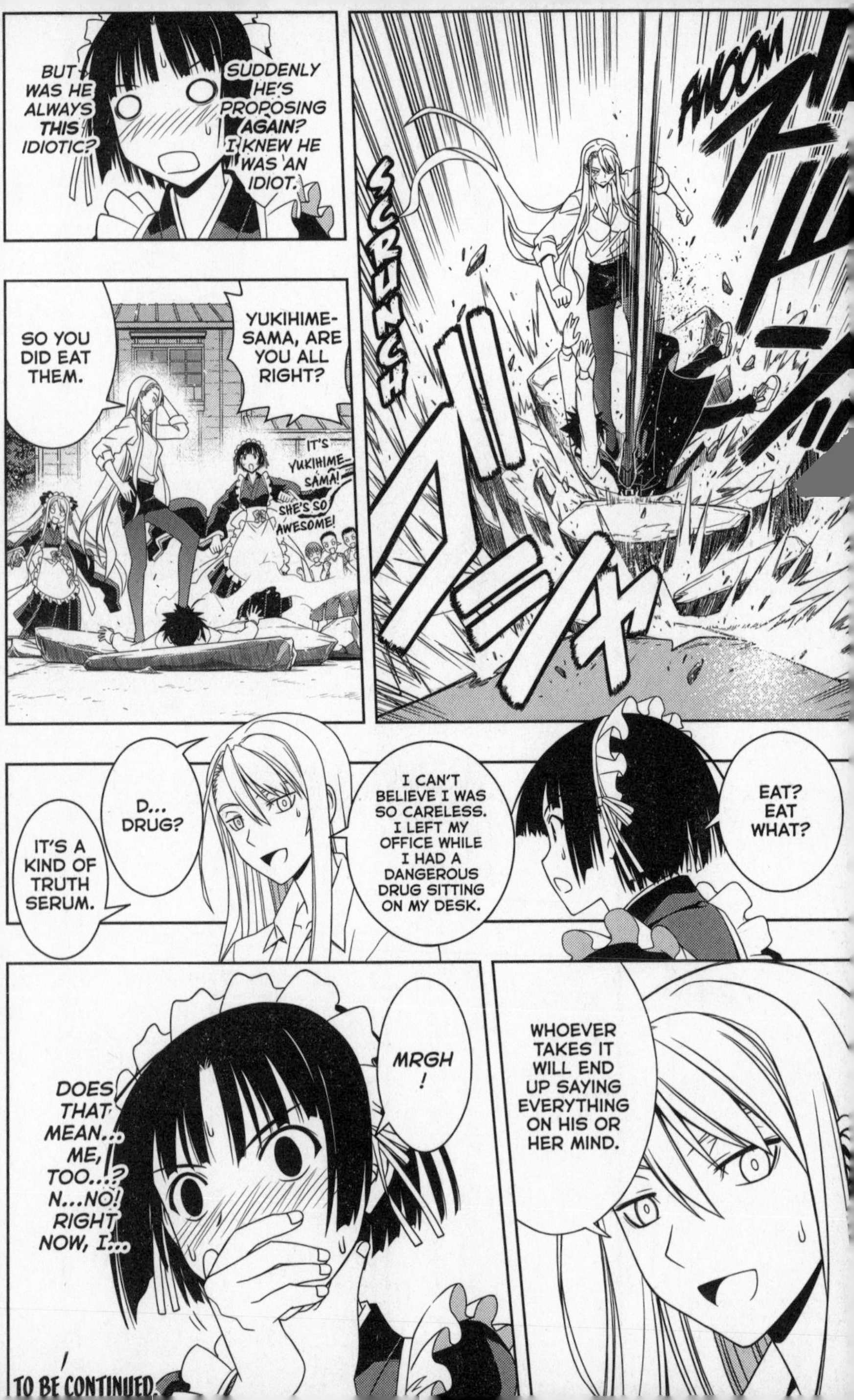
FWOOM
SCRUNCH
SUDDENLY HE'S PROPOSING AGAIN? I KNEW HE WAS AN IDIOT.
BUT WAS HE ALWAYS THIS IDIOTIC?
YUKIHIME-SAMA, ARE YOU ALL RIGHT?
SO YOU DID EAT THEM.
IT'S YUKIHIME-SAMA!
SHE'S SO AWESOME!
EAT? EAT WHAT?
I CAN'T BELIEVE I WAS SO CARELESS. I LEFT MY OFFICE WHILE I HAD A DANGEROUS DRUG SITTING ON MY DESK.
D... DRUG?
IT'S A KIND OF TRUTH SERUM.
WHOEVER TAKES IT WILL END UP SAYING EVERYTHING ON HIS OR HER MIND.
MRGH!
DOES THAT MEAN... ME, TOO...? N...NO! RIGHT NOW, I...
TO BE CONTINUED.

# UQ HOLDER!

STAFF

Ken Akamatsu
Takashi Takemoto
Kenichi Nakamura
Keiichi Yamashita
Tohru Mitsuhashi
Susumu Kuwabara
Yuri Sasaki

Thanks to Ran Ayanaga

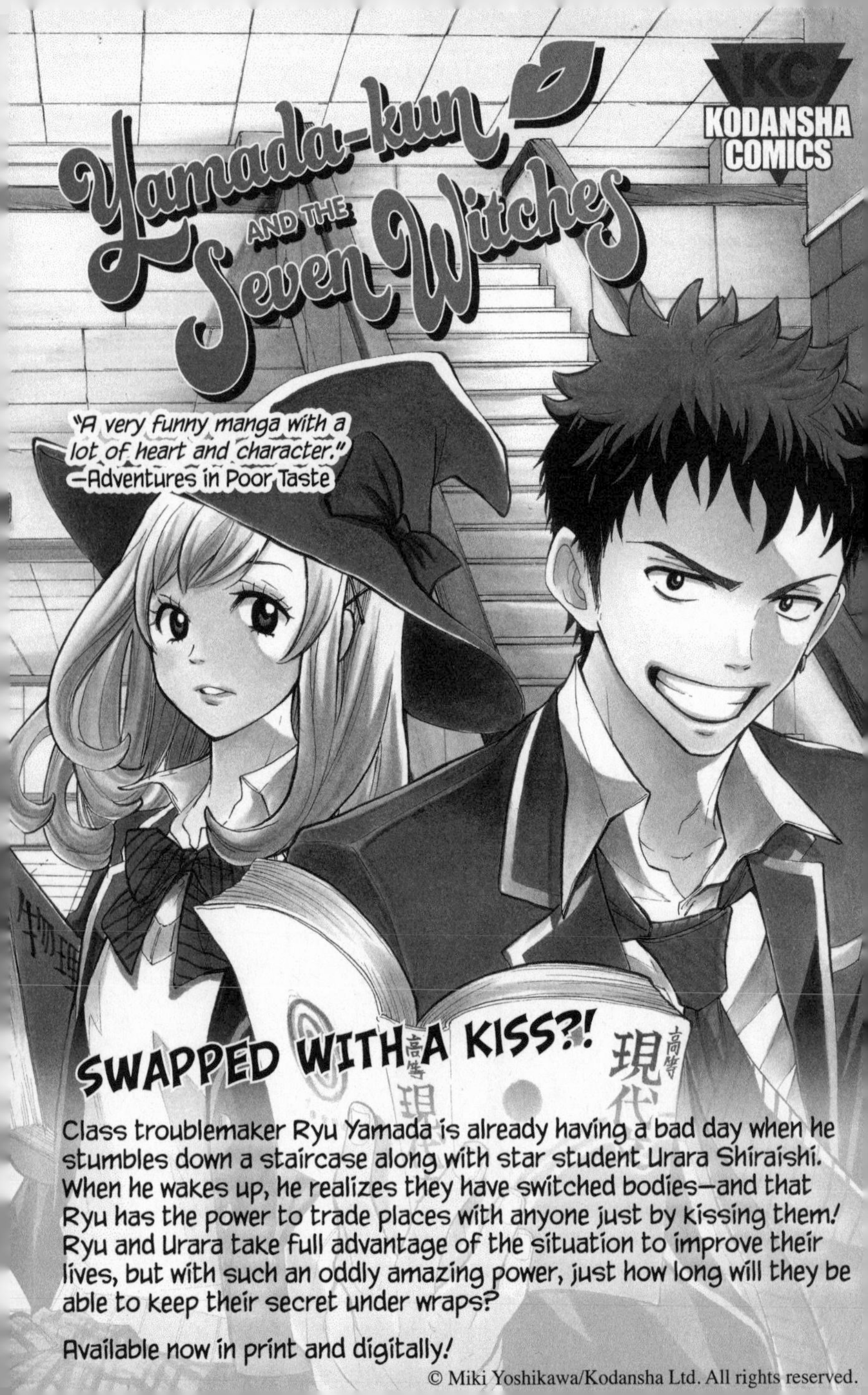
KC
KODANSHA COMICS
Yamada-kun AND THE Seven Witches
"A very funny manga with a lot of heart and character."
—Adventures in Poor Taste
SWAPPED WITH A KISS?!
Class troublemaker Ryu Yamada is already having a bad day when he stumbles down a staircase along with star student Urara Shiraishi. When he wakes up, he realizes they have switched bodies—and that Ryu has the power to trade places with anyone just by kissing them! Ryu and Urara take full advantage of the situation to improve their lives, but with such an oddly amazing power, just how long will they be able to keep their secret under wraps?
Available now in print and digitally!
© Miki Yoshikawa/Kodansha Ltd. All rights reserved.

# DEVIL SURVIVOR

AFTER DEMONS BREAK THROUGH INTO THE HUMAN WORLD, TOKYO MUST BE QUARANTINED. WITHOUT POWER AND STUCK IN A SUPERNATURAL WARZONE, 17-YEAR-OLD KAZUYA HAS ONLY ONE HOPE: HE MUST USE THE "COMP," A DEVICE CREATED BY HIS COUSIN NAOYA CAPABLE OF SUMMONING AND SUBDUING DEMONS, TO DEFEAT THE INVADERS AND TAKE BACK THE CITY.

BASED ON THE POPULAR VIDEO GAME FRANCHISE BY ATLUS!

A KODANSHA COMICS TRADE PAPERBACK ORIGINAL

*UQ HOLDER!* VOLUME 10 COPYRIGHT © 2016 KEN AKAMATSU
ENGLISH TRANSLATION COPYRIGHT © 2017 KEN AKAMATSU

PUBLISHED IN THE UNITED STATES BY KODANSHA COMICS, AN IMPRINT OF KODANSHA USA PUBLISHING, LLC, NEW YORK.

PUBLICATION RIGHTS FOR THIS ENGLISH EDITION ARRANGED THROUGH KODANSHA LTD., TOKYO.

FIRST PUBLISHED IN JAPAN IN 2016 BY KODANSHA LTD., TOKYO.

ISBN 978-1-63236-353-4

PRINTED IN THE UNITED STATES OF AMERICA.

WWW.KODANSHACOMICS.COM

9 8 7 6 5 4 3 2 1

TRANSLATION: ALETHEA NIBLEY AND ATHENA NIBLEY
LETTERING: JAMES DASHIELL
EDITING: MEGAN MCPHERSON
KODANSHA COMICS EDITION COVER DESIGN: PHIL BALSMAN